CUBA

BUSINESS AND INVESTMENT OPPORTUNITIES YEARBOOK

VOLUME 1

STRATEGIC, PRACTICAL INFORMATION AND OPPORTUNITIES

International Business Publications, USA
Washington DC, USA

CUBA

BUSINESS AND INVESTMENT OPPORTUNITIES YEARBOOK

VOLUME 1 STRATEGIC, PRACTICAL INFORMATION AND OPPORTUNITIES

UPDATED ANNUALLY

We express our sincere appreciation to all government agencies and international organizations which provided information and other materials for this yearbook

Cover Design: **International Business Publications, USA**

2016 Edition Updated Reprint International Business Publications, USA
ISBN 1-4387-7195-9

For customer service and information, please contact:

in the USA: **International Business Publications, USA**
P.O.Box 15343, Washington, DC 20003
Phone: (202) 546-2103, Fax: (202) 546-3275.
E-mail: rusric@erols.com

Printed in the USA

CUBA

BUSINESS AND INVESTMENT OPPORTUNITIES YEARBOOK

VOLUME 1

STRATEGIC, PRACTICAL INFORMATION AND OPPORTUNITIES

TABLE OF CONTENTS

BUSINESS AND DEVELOPMENT PROFILES

STRATEGIC INFORMATION

Capital and largest city	Havana 23°8′N 82°23′W23.133°N 82.383°W
Official languages	Spanish
Ethnic groups	64.1% White 26.6% Mulatto / Mestizo 9.3% Black
Demonym	Cuban
Government	Single-party Marxist-Leninist state
- President	Raúl Castro
- First Vice President	Miguel Díaz-Canel
- President of the National Assembly	Esteban Lazo Hernández
Legislature	National Assembly
	Independence from Spain
- Ten Years' War	October 10, 1868 – 1878
- Republic declared	May 20, 1902
- Cuban Revolution	July 26, 1953 - January 1, 1959
- Current constitution	February 24, 1976
	Area
- Total	109,884 km^2 (106th) 42,426 sq mi
- Water (%)	negligible
	Population
- 2012 census	11,167,325
- Density	102/km^2 (106th) 264.0/sq mi
GDP (PPP)	2011 estimate
- Total	$212 billion (58th)
- Per capita	$18,796 (60th)
GDP (nominal)	2011 estimate
- Total	$68.233 billion (68th)
- Per capita	$6,051 (90th)
Gini	38.0 medium
HDI	0.815 very high · 44th
Currency	Peso (CUP) Convertible peso[a] (CUC)
Time zone	CST (UTC−5)
- Summer (DST)	CDT (UTC−4)
Drives on the	right
Calling code	+53
ISO 3166 code	CU
Internet TLD	.cu

Cuba, officially the **Republic of Cuba** is an island country in the Caribbean. The nation of Cuba comprises the main island of Cuba, the Isla de la Juventud, and several archipelagos. Havana is the capital of Cuba and its largest city. The second largest city is Santiago de Cuba. To the north of Cuba lies the United States (150 km or 93 mi away), the Bahamas and the Turks and Caicos Islands are to the northeast, Mexico is to the west (210 km or 130 mi away), the Cayman Islands and Jamaica are to the south, and Haiti and the Dominican Republic are to the southeast.

The island of Cuba was inhabited by numerous Mesoamerican tribes prior to the landing of explorer Christopher Columbus in 1492, who claimed it for the Kingdom of Spain. Cuba remained a colony of Spain until the Spanish–American War of 1898, after which it was briefly administered by the United States until gaining nominal independence in 1902. The fragile republic endured increasingly radical politics and social strife, and despite efforts to strengthen its democratic system, Cuba came under the dictatorship of former president Fulgencio Batista in 1952.

Growing unrest and instability led to Batista's ousting in January 1959 by the July 26 movement, which afterwards established a socialist government under the leadership of Fidel Castro. Since 1965, the country has been governed as a single-party state by the Communist Party.

Cuba is the largest island in the Caribbean, and with over 11 million inhabitants, is the second-most populous after Hispaniola, albeit with a much lower population density than most nations in the region. A multiethnic country, its people, culture, and customs derive from diverse origins, including the aboriginal Taíno and Ciboney peoples, the long period of Spanish colonialism, the introduction of African slaves, a close relationship with the Soviet Union during the Cold War, and proximity to the United States.

Cuba ranks high in metrics of health and education, with a very high Human Development Index of 0.815 as of 2014. According to data it presents to the United Nations, Cuba was the only nation in the world in 2006 that met the World Wide Fund for Nature's definition of sustainable development, with an ecological footprint of less than 1.8 hectares per capita, 1.5 hectares, and a Human Development Index of over 0.855

Background: Fidel CASTRO led a rebel army to victory in 1959, and his guiding vision has defined Cuba's Communist revolution while his iron will has held the country together for more than four decades. CASTRO brought Cuba onto the world stage by inviting Soviet support in the 1960s, inciting revolutionary movements throughout Latin America and Africa in the 1970s, and sending his army to fight in Angola in the 1980s. At home, Havana provided Cubans with high levels of healthcare, education, and social security while suppressing the Roman Catholic Church and arresting political dissidents. Cuba is slowly recovering from severe economic recession following the withdrawal of former-Soviet subsidies, worth $4billion-$6 billion per year, in 1990.

GEOGRAPHY

Location: Caribbean, island between the Caribbean Sea and the North Atlantic Ocean, south of Florida
Geographic coordinates: 21 30 N, 80 00 W
Map references: Central America and the Caribbean

Area:
total: 110,860 sq km
land: 110,860 sq km
water: 0 sq km

Area—comparative: slightly smaller than Pennsylvania

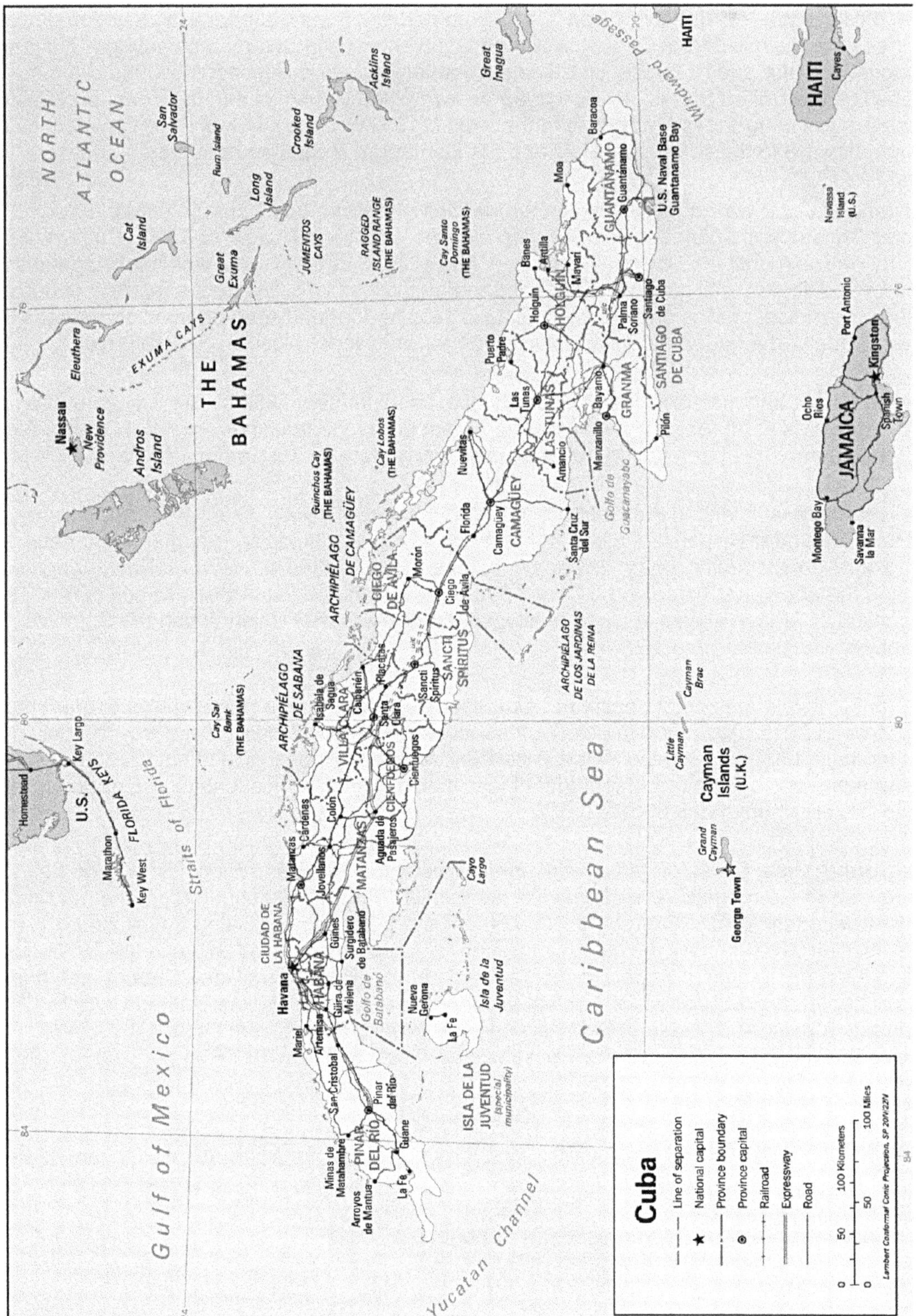

Land boundaries:
total: 29 km

border countries: US Naval Base at Guantanamo Bay 29 km
note: Guantanamo Naval Base is leased by the US and thus remains part of Cuba

Coastline: 3,735 km

Maritime claims:
exclusive economic zone: 200 nm
territorial sea: 12 nm

Climate: tropical; moderated by trade winds; dry season (November to April); rainy season (May to October)

Terrain: mostly flat to rolling plains, with rugged hills and mountains in the southeast

Elevation extremes:
lowest point: Caribbean Sea 0 m *highest point:* Pico Turquino 2,005 m

Natural resources: cobalt, nickel, iron ore, copper, manganese, salt, timber, silica, petroleum

Land use:
arable land: 24% *permanent crops:* 7% *permanent pastures:* 27%
forests and woodland: 24% *other:* 18%

Irrigated land: 9,100 sq km

Natural hazards: the east coast is subject to hurricanes from August to October (in general, the country averages about one hurricane every other year); droughts are common

Environment—current issues: pollution of Havana Bay; overhunting threatens wildlife populations; deforestation

Environment—international agreements:
party to: Antarctic Treaty, Biodiversity, Climate Change, Desertification, Endangered Species, Environmental Modification, Hazardous Wastes, Law of the Sea, Marine Dumping, Ozone Layer Protection, Ship Pollution
signed, but not ratified: Antarctic-Environmental Protocol, Marine Life Conservation

Geography—note: largest country in Caribbean

PEOPLE

Population: 11,096,395

Age structure:
0-14 years: 22% (male 1,236,899; female 1,172,560)
15-64 years: 69% (male 3,820,255; female 3,801,768)
65 years and over: 9% (male 496,772; female 568,141)

Population growth rate: 0.4%
Birth rate: 12.9 births/1,000 population
Death rate: 7.38 deaths/1,000 population

Net migration rate: -1.52 migrant(s)/1,000 population

Sex ratio:
at birth: 1.06 male(s)/female
under 15 years: 1.05 male(s)/female
15-64 years: 1 male(s)/female
65 years and over: 0.87 male(s)/female
total population: 1 male(s)/female

Infant mortality rate: 7.81 deaths/1,000 live births

Life expectancy at birth:
total population: 75.78 years
male: 73.41 years
female: 78.3 years

Total fertility rate: 1.58 children born/woman

Nationality:
noun: Cuban(s)
adjective: Cuban

Ethnic groups: mulatto 51%, white 37%, black 11%, Chinese 1%
Religions: nominally 85% Roman Catholic prior to CASTRO assuming power; Protestants, Jehovah's Witnesses, Jews, and Santeria are also represented

Languages: Spanish

Literacy:
definition: age 15 and over can read and write
total population: 95.7%
male: 96.2%
female: 95.3%

GOVERNMENT

Country name:
conventional long form:
Republic of Cuba
conventional short form:
Cuba
local long form:
Republica de Cuba
local short form:
Cuba

Government type:
Communist state

Capital:
name:
Havana
geographic coordinates:
23 07 N, 82 21 W
time difference:
UTC-5 (same time as Washington, DC, during Standard Time)
daylight saving time:
+1hr, begins second Sunday in March; ends first Sunday in November; note - Cuba has been known to alter the schedule of DST on short notice in an attempt to conserve electricity for lighting

Administrative divisions:
15 provinces (provincias, singular - provincia) and 1 special municipality* (municipio especial); Artemisa, Camaguey, Ciego de Avila, Cienfuegos, Granma, Guantanamo, Holguin, Isla de la Juventud*, La Habana, Las Tunas, Matanzas, Mayabeque, Pinar del Rio, Sancti Spiritus, Santiago de Cuba, Villa Clara

Independence:
20 May 1902 (from Spain 10 December 1898; administered by the US from 1898 to 1902); noacknowledged by the Cuban Government as a day of independence

National holiday:
Triumph of the Revolution, 1 January (1959)

Constitution:
several previous; latest adopted by referendum 15 February 1976, effective 24 February 1976; amended 1978, 1992, 2002 (2010)

Legal system:
civil law system based on Spanish civil code

International law organization participation:
has not submitted an ICJ jurisdiction declaration; non-party state to the ICCt

Suffrage:
16 years of age; universal

Executive branch:
chief of state:
President of the Council of State and President of the Council of Ministers Gen. Raul CASTRO Ruz (president since 24 February 2008); First Vice President of the Council of State and First Vice President of the Council of Ministers Miguel DIAZ-CANEL Bermudez (since 24 February 2013); note - the president is both chief of state and head of government
head of government:
President of the Council of State and President of the Council of Ministers Gen. Raul CASTRO Ruz (president since 24 February 2008); First Vice President of the Council of State and First Vice President of the Council of Ministers Miguel DIAZ-CANEL Bermudez (since 24 February 2013)
cabinet:
Council of Ministers proposed by the president of the Council of State, appointed by the National

Assembly or the 28-member Council of State, and elected by the assembly to act on its behalf when it is not in session

elections:

president and vice presidents elected by the National Assembly for a five-year term; election last held on 24 February 2013 (next to be held in 2018)

election results:

Gen. Raul CASTRO Ruz reelected president; percent of legislative vote - 100%; Miguel DIAZ-CANEL Bermudez elected vice president; percent of legislative vote - 100%

Legislative branch:

unicameral National Assembly of People's Power or Asamblea Nacional del Poder Popular (number of seats in the National Assembly is based on population and currently exceeds 600; members elected directly from slates approved by special candidacy commissions to serve five-year terms)

elections:

last held on 3 February 2013 (next to be held in 2018)

election results:

Cuba's Communist Party is the only legal party, and officially sanctioned candidates run unopposed

Judicial branch:

highest court(s):

People's Supreme Court (consists of court president, vice president, 41 professional justices, and NA lay judges; organized into the "Whole," State Council, and criminal, civil, administrative, labor, crimes against the state, and military courts)

judge selection and term of office:

professional judges elected by the National Assembly to serve 2.5-year terms; lay judges nominated by workplace collectives and neighborhood associations and elected by municipal or provincial assemblies; lay judges appointed for 5-year terms and serve up to 30 days per year

subordinate courts:

People's Provincial Courts; People's Regional Courts; People's Courts

Political parties and leaders:

Cuban Communist Party or PCC [Raul CASTRO Ruz, first secretary]

Political pressure groups and leaders:

Damas de Blanco
National Association of Small Farmers
Patriotic Union of Cuba
political dissidents and bloggers
The Cuban Commission for Human Rights and National Reconciliation

International organization participation:

ACP, ALBA, AOSIS, CELAC, FAO, G-77, IAEA, ICAO, ICC (national committees), ICRM, IFAD, IFRCS, IHO, ILO, IMO, IMSO, Interpol, IOC, IOM (observer), IPU, ISO, ITSO, ITU, LAES, LAIA, NAM, OAS (excluded from formal participation since 1962), OPANAL, OPCW, PCA, Petrocaribe, UN, UNCTAD, UNESCO, UNIDO, Union Latina, UNWTO, UPU, WCO, WFTU (NGOs), WHO, WIPO, WMO, WTO

Diplomatic representation in the US:

none; note - the Cuban Interests Section of the Embassy of Switzerland is headed by Jose R. CABANAS Rodriguez (since October 2012); address: Cuban Interests Section, Swiss

Embassy, 2630 16th Street NW, Washington, DC 20009; telephone: (202) 797-8518; FAX: (202) 986-7283

Diplomatic representation from the US:
none; note - the United States Interests Section of the Embassy of Switzerland is headed by John P. CAULFIELD (since September 2011); address: USINT, Swiss Embassy, Calzada between L and M Streets, Vedado, Havana; telephone: [53] (7) 839-4100; FAX: [53] (7) 839-4247; protecting power in Cuba is Switzerland

Flag description:
five equal horizontal bands of blue (top, center, and bottom) alternating with white; a red equilateral triangle based on the hoist side bears a white, five-pointed star in the center; the blue bands refer to the three old divisions of the island: central, occidental, and oriental; the white bands describe the purity of the independence ideal; the triangle symbolizes liberty, equality, and fraternity, while the red color stands for the blood shed in the independence struggle; the white star, called La Estrella Solitaria (the Lone Star) lights the way to freedom and was taken from the flag of Texas
note:design similar to the Puerto Rican flag, with the colors of the bands and triangle reversed

National anthem:
name:
"La Bayamesa" (The Bayamo Song)

ECONOMY

The government continues to balance the need for loosening its socialist economic system against a desire for firm political control. The government in April 2011 held the first Cuban Communist Party Congress in almost 13 years, during which leaders approved a plan for wide-ranging economic changes. Since then, the Cuban government has slowly and incrementally implemented limited economic reforms, including allowing Cubans to buy electronic appliances and cell phones, stay in hotels, and buy and sell used cars.

The Cuban government also opened up some retail services to "self-employment," leading to the rise of so-called "cuentapropistas" or entrepreneurs. Recent moves include permitting the private ownership and sale of real estate and new vehicles, allowing private farmers to sell agricultural goods directly to hotels, and expanding categories of self-employment. Despite these reforms, the average Cuban's standard of living remains at a lower level than before the collapse of the Soviet Union and the resulting downturn of the 1990s. Since late 2000, Venezuela has been providing oil on preferential terms, and it currently supplies over 100,000 barrels per day of petroleum products. Cuba has been paying for the oil, in part, with the services of Cuban personnel in Venezuela, including some 30,000 medical professionals.

GDP (purchasing power parity):
$121 billion (2012 est.)
country comparison to the world: 68
$117.3 billion (2011 est.)
$114.1 billion (2010 est.)
note:data are in 2012 US dollars

GDP (official exchange rate):
$72.3 billion (2012 est.)

GDP - real growth rate:
3.1% (2012 est.)
country comparison to the world: 112
2.8% (2011 est.)
2.4% (2010 est.)

GDP - per capita (PPP):
$10,200 (2010 est.)
country comparison to the world: 118
$10,000 (2009 est.)
$10,000 (2008 est.)
note:data are in 2010 US dollars

Gross national saving:
13.4% of GDP (2013 est.)
country comparison to the world: 118
11.1% of GDP (2012 est.)
11.7% of GDP (2011 est.)

GDP - composition, by end use:
household consumption:
52.1%
government consumption:
34.4%
investment in fixed capital:
10%
investment in inventories:
-3.4%
exports of goods and services:
26%
imports of goods and services:
-19.2%
(2013 est.)

GDP - composition, by sector of origin:
agriculture:
3.8%
industry:
22.3%
services:
73.9% (2013 est.)

Agriculture - products:
sugar, tobacco, citrus, coffee, rice, potatoes, beans; livestock

Industries:
petroleum, nickel, cobalt, pharmaceuticals, tobacco, construction, steel, cement, agricultural machinery, sugar

Industrial production growth rate:

2.6% (2013 est.)
country comparison to the world: 114

Labor force:
5.233 million
country comparison to the world: 72
note:state sector 72.3%, non-state sector 27.7% (2013 est.)

Labor force - by occupation:
agriculture:
19.7%
industry:
17.1%
services:
63.2% (2011)

Unemployment rate:
4.3% (2013 est.)
country comparison to the world: 39
3.8% (2012 est.)
note:these are official rates; unofficial estimates are about double the official figures

Population below poverty line:
NA%

Household income or consumption by percentage share:
lowest 10%:
NA%
highest 10%:
NA%

Budget:
revenues:
$47.62 billion
expenditures:
$50.29 billion (2013 est.)

Taxes and other revenues:
65.9% of GDP (2013 est.)
country comparison to the world: 2

Budget surplus (+) or deficit (-):
-3.7% of GDP (2013 est.)
country comparison to the world: 140

Public debt:
35.9% of GDP (2013 est.)
country comparison to the world: 105
35.8% of GDP (2012 est.)

Fiscal year:
calendar year

Inflation rate (consumer prices):
6% (2013 est.)
country comparison to the world: 172
5.5% (2012 est.)

Central bank discount rate:
NA%

Commercial bank prime lending rate:
NA%

Stock of narrow money:
$11.21 billion (31 December 2013 est.)
country comparison to the world: 74
$10.97 billion (31 December 2012 est.)

Stock of broad money:
$24.63 billion (31 December 2013 est.)
country comparison to the world: 78
$24.08 billion (31 December 2012 est.)

Stock of domestic credit:
$NA

Current account balance:
$289.8 million (2013 est.)
country comparison to the world: 55
-$134.4 million (2012 est.)

Exports:
$6.252 billion (2013 est.)
country comparison to the world: 107
$5.972 billion (2012 est.)

Exports - commodities:
petroleum, nickel, medical products, sugar, tobacco, fish, citrus, coffee

Exports - partners:
Canada 17.7%, China 16.9%, Venezuela 12.5%, Netherlands 9%, Spain 5.9% (2012)

Imports:
$13.6 billion (2013 est.)
country comparison to the world: 89
$13.72 billion (2012 est.)

Imports - commodities:

petroleum, food, machinery and equipment, chemicals

Imports - partners:
Venezuela 38.3%, China 10.8%, Spain 8.9%, Brazil 5.2%, US 4.3% (2012)

Reserves of foreign exchange and gold:
$4.993 billion (31 December 2013 est.)
country comparison to the world: 96
$4.693 billion (31 December 2012 est.)

Debt - external:
$23.44 billion (31 December 2013 est.)
country comparison to the world: 78
$22.51 billion (31 December 2012 est.)

Stock of direct foreign investment - at home:
$NA

Stock of direct foreign investment - abroad:
$4.138 billion (2006 est.)
country comparison to the world: 63

Exchange rates:
Cuban pesos (CUP) per US dollar -
1 (2013 est.)
1 (2012 est.)
0.9259 (2010 est.)
0.9259 (2009)
0.9259 (2008)

ENERGY

Electricity - production:
17.8 billion kWh
country comparison to the world: 77

Electricity - consumption:
13.64 billion kWh
country comparison to the world: 80

Electricity - exports:
0 kWh
country comparison to the world: 124

Electricity - imports:
0 kWh
country comparison to the world: 132

Electricity - installed generating capacity:

5.914 million kW
country comparison to the world: 72

Electricity - from fossil fuels:
99.3% of total installed capacity
country comparison to the world: 51

Electricity - from nuclear fuels:
0% of total installed capacity
country comparison to the world: 71

Electricity - from hydroelectric plants:
0.6% of total installed capacity
country comparison to the world: 143

Electricity - from other renewable sources:
0.1% of total installed capacity
country comparison to the world: 103

Crude oil - production:
50,800 bbl/day
country comparison to the world: 61

Crude oil - exports:
83,000 bbl/day
country comparison to the world: 41

Crude oil - imports:
165,000 bbl/day
country comparison to the world: 36

Crude oil - proved reserves:
124 million bbl
country comparison to the world: 69

Refined petroleum products - production:
100,600 bbl/day
country comparison to the world: 73

Refined petroleum products - consumption:
150,200 bbl/day
country comparison to the world: 66

Refined petroleum products - exports:
11,320 bbl/day

country comparison to the world: 83

Refined petroleum products - imports:
4,877 bbl/day
country comparison to the world: 151

Natural gas - production:
1.03 billion cu m
country comparison to the world: 64

Natural gas - consumption:
1.03 billion cu m
country comparison to the world: 88

Natural gas - exports:
0 cu m
country comparison to the world: 85

Natural gas - imports:
0 cu m
country comparison to the world: 180

Natural gas - proved reserves:
70.79 billion cu m
country comparison to the world: 59

Carbon dioxide emissions from consumption of energy:
28.41 million Mt

COMMUNICATIONS

Telephones - main lines in use:
1.217 million
country comparison to the world: 68

Telephones - mobile cellular:
1.682 million
country comparison to the world: 149

Telephone system:
general assessment:
greater investment beginning in 1994 and the establishment of a new Ministry of Information Technology and Communications in 2000 has resulted in improvements in the system; national fiber-optic system under development; 95% of switches digitized by end of 2006; mobile-cellular telephone service is expensive and must be paid in convertible pesos; cell phones in Cuba number around 2 million; state communications started service of email to cell phones through nauta.cu accounts; Cuban Government has opened Internet cafes around the island, which are expensive and offer slow-speed connections
domestic:

fixed-line density remains low at 10 per 100 inhabitants; mobile-cellular service expanding but remains only about 10 per 100 persons
international:
country code - 53; the ALBA-1 fiber-optic submarine cable links Cuba, Jamaica, and Venezuela; fiber-optic cable laid to but not linked to US network; satellite earth station - 1 Intersputnik (Atlantic Ocean region)

Broadcast media:
government owns and controls all broadcast media with private ownership of electronic media prohibited; government operates 4 national TV networks and many local TV stations; government operates 6 national radio networks, an international station, and many local radio stations; Radio-TV Marti is beamed from the US

Internet country code:
.cu

Internet hosts:
3,244
country comparison to the world: 154

Internet users:
1.606 million
country comparison to the world: 79
note:private citizens are prohibited from buying computers or accessing the Internet without special authorization; foreigners may access the Internet in large hotels but are subject to firewalls; some Cubans buy illegal passwords on the black market or take advantage of public outlets to access limited email and the government-controlled "intranet"

TRANSPORTATION

Airports:
133
country comparison to the world: 42

Airports - with paved runways:
total:
64
over 3,047 m:
7
2,438 to 3,047 m:
10
1,524 to 2,437 m:
16
914 to 1,523 m:
4
under 914 m:
27

Airports - with unpaved runways:
total:
69
914 to 1,523 m:

11
under 914 m:
58

Pipelines:
gas 41 km; oil 230 km

Railways:
total:
8,203 km
country comparison to the world: 25
standard gauge:
8,134 km 1.435-m gauge (124 km electrified)
narrow gauge:
69 km 1.000-m gauge
note:48 km of standard gauge track is not for public use

Roadways:
total:
60,858 km
country comparison to the world: 69
paved:
29,820 km (includes 639 km of expressways)
unpaved:
31,038 km

Waterways:
240 km (almost all navigable inland waterways are near the mouths of rivers) (2011)
country comparison to the world: 95

Merchant marine:
total:
3
country comparison to the world: 136
by type:
cargo 1, passenger 1, refrigerated cargo 1
registered in other countries:
5 (Curacao 1, Panama 2, unknown 2) (2010)

Ports and terminals:
major seaport(s):
Antilla, Cienfuegos, Guantanamo, Havana, Matanzas, Mariel, Nuevitas Bay, Santiago de Cuba

MILITARY

Military branches:
Revolutionary Armed Forces (Fuerzas Armadas Revolucionarias, FAR): Revolutionary Army (Ejercito Revolucionario, ER, includes Territorial Militia Troops (Milicia de Tropas de Territoriales, MTT)); Revolutionary Navy (Marina de Guerra Revolucionaria, MGR, includes Marine Corps); Revolutionary Air and Air Defense Forces (Defensas Anti-Aereas y Fuerza Aerea Revolucionaria, DAAFAR), Youth Labor Army (Ejercito Juvenil del Trabajo, EJT)

Military service age and obligation:
17-28 years of age for compulsory military service; 2-year service obligation; both sexes subject to military service

Manpower available for military service:
males age 16-49: 2,998,201
females age 16-49: 2,919,107

Manpower fit for military service:
males age 16-49: 2,446,131
females age 16-49: 2,375,590

Manpower reaching militarily significant age annually:
male: 72,823
female: 69,108

Military - note:
the collapse of the Soviet Union deprived the Cuban military of its major economic and logistic support and had a significant impact on the state of Cuban equipment; the army remains well trained and professional in nature; the lack of replacement parts for its existing equipment has increasingly affected operational capabilities

TRANSNATIONAL ISSUES

Disputes - international:
US Naval Base at Guantanamo Bay is leased to US and only mutual agreement or US abandonment of the facility can terminate the lease

Trafficking in persons:
current situation: Cuba is a source country for adults and children subjected to forced labor and sex trafficking; child prostitution and child sex tourism reportedly occurs in Cuba, and laws do not appear to penalize the prostitution of children between the ages of 16 and 18; allegations have been made of Cubans being subjected to forced labor, particularly with Cuban work missions abroad; the scope of trafficking within Cuba is particularly difficult to gauge due to the closed nature of the government and sparse non-governmental or independent reporting
tier rating: Tier 3 - Cuba does not fully comply with the minimum standards for the elimination of trafficking and is not making significant efforts to do so; the government has not publicized information about government measures to address human trafficking through prosecution, protection, or prevention efforts but did share information about its general approach to protection for children and youth; the government has a network of shelters for victims of domestic violence and child abuse but has not verified if trafficking victims receive care in those centers

Illicit drugs:
territorial waters and air space serve as transshipment zone for US- and European-bound drugs; established the death penalty for certain drug-related crimes in 1999 (2008)

IMPORTANT INFORMATION FOR UNDERSTANDING CUBA

PROFILE

OFFICIAL NAME: Republic of Cuba

Geography
Area: 110,860 sq. km. (44,200 sq. mi.); about the size of Pennsylvania.
Cities: *Capital*--Havana (pop. 2 million). *Other major cities*--Santiago de Cuba, Camaguey, Santa Clara, Holguin, Guantanamo, Matanzas, Cienfuegos, Pinar del Rio.
Terrain: Flat or gently rolling plains, hills; mountains up to 2,000 meters (6,000 ft.) in the southeast.
Climate: Tropical, moderated by trade winds; dry season (November-April); rainy season (May-October).

People
Population: 11 million; 70% urban, 30% rural.
Ethnic groups: 51% mulatto, 37% white, 11% black, 1% Chinese (according to Cuban census data).
Language: Spanish. *Literacy*--97% (according to Cuban government sources).
Work force (4.6 million): *Government and services*--30%; *industry*--22%; *agriculture*--24%; *commerce*--11%; *construction*--11%; *transportation and communications*--6%.

Government
Type: Totalitarian Communist state; current government assumed power by force January 1, 1959.
Independence: May 20, 1902.
Political party: Cuban Communist Party (PCC); only one party allowed.
Administrative subdivisions: 14 provinces, including the city of Havana, and one special municipality (Isle of Youth).

Economy
Natural resources: Nickel, cobalt, iron ore, copper, manganese, salt, timber, oil, natural gas.
Agriculture: *Products*--sugar, citrus and tropical fruits, tobacco, coffee, rice, beans, meat, vegetables.
Industry: *Types*--sugar and food processing, oil refining, cement, electric power, light consumer and industrial products, pharmaceutical and biotech products.
Trade: *Exports*--$1.999 billion f.o.b. (2005): nickel/cobalt, pharmaceutical and biotech products, sugar and its byproducts, tobacco, seafood, citrus, tropical fruits, coffee. *Major markets* (2005)--Netherlands $599.7 million (30%); Canada $437.9 (22%); Venezuela $241 million (12%); Spain $161.2 million (8%); China $99.6 million (5%); Russia $57.6 million (3%); France $49.3 million (2%); others $352.5 million (18%). *Imports* --$7.528 billion f.o.b. (2005): petroleum, food, machinery, chemicals. *Major suppliers* (2005)--Venezuela $1.859 billion (25%); China $885.4 million (12%); Spain $653.3 (9%); United States $470.3 (9%); Canada $327.9 million (4%); Brazil $312.4 million (4%); Germany $309.3 million (4%); Italy $292 million (4%); Mexico (4%); Vietnam $251.8 (3%); others (25%).
Official exchange rate: Convertible pesos per U.S.$1 = 0.93.
Cuba has two currencies in circulation: the Cuban peso (CUP), and the convertible peso (CUC). In April 2005, the official exchange rate changed from $1 per CUC to $1.08 per CUC (0.93 CUC per $1), both for individuals and enterprises. Individuals can buy 24 Cuban pesos (CUP) for each

CUC sold, or sell 25 Cuban pesos for each CUC bought; enterprises, however, must exchange CUP and CUC at a 1:1 ratio. It is also important to note that the Cuban regime taxes and receives approximately 10% of each conversion of U.S. dollars into CUCs.

PEOPLE AND RELIGION

Cuba is a multiracial society with a population of mainly Spanish and African origins. The largest organized religion is the Roman Catholic Church, but evangelical protestant denominations continue to grow rapidly. Afro-Cuban religions, a blend of native African religions and Roman Catholicism, are widely practiced in Cuba. Officially, Cuba has been an atheist state for most of the Castro era. In 1962, the government of Fidel Castro seized and shut down more than 400 Catholic schools, charging that they spread dangerous beliefs among the people. In 1991, however, the Communist Party lifted its prohibition against religious believers seeking membership, and a year later the constitution was amended to characterize the state as secular instead of atheist.

While the Cuban constitution recognizes the right of citizens to freedom of religion, the government de facto restricts that freedom. Twenty-two denominations, including Presbyterians, Episcopalians, and Methodists, are members of the Cuban Council of Churches (CCC). Most CCC members are officially recognized by the State, though several, including the Evangelical Lutheran Church, are not registered and are recognized only through their membership in the CCC. Another 31 officially recognized denominations, including Jehovah's Witnesses and the small Jewish community, do not belong to the CCC. The government does not favor any one particular religion or church; however, the government appears to be most tolerant of those churches that maintain close relations to the State through the CCC. Unregistered religious groups experience various degrees of official interference, harassment, and repression. The Ministry of Interior engages in active efforts to control and monitor the country's religious institutions, including through surveillance, infiltration and harassment of religious professionals and practitioners. The most independent religious organizations--including the Catholic Church, the largest independent institution in Cuba today--continue to operate under significant restrictions and pressure imposed on them by the Cuban regime. The Cuban Government continues to refuse to allow the church to have independent printing press capabilities; full access to the media; to train enough priests for its needs or allow adequate numbers of foreign priests to work in the country; or to establish socially useful institutions, including schools and universities, hospitals and clinics, and nursing homes. All registered denominations must report to the Ministry of Interior's Office of Religious Affairs.

The visit of Pope John Paul II in January 1998 was seen as an important, positive event for bringing a message of hope and the need for respect of human rights. Unfortunately, these improvements did not continue once the Pope left the island. While some visas were issued for additional priests to enter Cuba around the time of the visit, the regime has again sharply restricted issuance of visas. Moreover, despite explicit regime guarantees and repeated follow-up requests, the regime has refused to permit the Catholic Church to establish Internet connections or an intranet among dioceses on the Island. In a pastoral letter entitled "There is No Country Without Virtue" ("No Hay Patria Sin Virtud"), the Cuban Conference of Catholic Bishops in February 2003 openly criticized the government's strict control over the activities of the Catholic Church, especially state restrictions on religious education and Church access to mass media, as well as the increasingly amoral and irreligious character of Cuban society under Communist rule.

Other Cuban religious groups--including evangelical Christians, whose numbers continue to grow rapidly--also have benefited from the relative relaxation of official restrictions on religious organizations and activities. Although particularly hard hit by emigration, Cuba's small Jewish community continues to hold services in Havana and has members in Santiago, Camaguey, and other parts of the island. See also the Department's report on international religious freedom for further information.

HISTORY

Spanish settlers established the raising of cattle, sugarcane, and tobacco as Cuba's primary economic pursuits. As the native Indian population died out, African slaves were imported to work the ranches and plantations. Slavery was abolished in 1886.

Cuba was the last major Spanish colony to gain independence, following a lengthy struggle begun in 1868. Jose Marti, Cuba's national hero, helped initiate the final push for independence in 1895. In 1898, the United States entered the conflict after the USS Maine sank in Havana Harbor on February 15 due to an explosion of undetermined origin. In December of that year, Spain relinquished control of Cuba to the United States with the Treaty of Paris. On May 20, 1902, the United States granted Cuba its independence but retained the right to intervene to preserve Cuban independence and stability in accordance with the Platt Amendment. In 1934, the Platt Amendment was repealed. The United States and Cuba concluded a Treaty of Relations in 1934 which, among other things, continued the 1903 agreements that leased the Guantanamo Bay naval base to the United States.

Independent Cuba was often ruled by authoritarian political and military figures who either obtained or remained in power by force. Fulgencio Batista, an army sergeant, organized a non-commissioned officer revolt in September 1933 and wielded significant power behind the scenes until he was elected president in 1940. Batista was voted out of office in 1944 and did not run in 1948. Both those elections were won by civilian political figures with the support of party organizations. Running for president again in 1952, Batista seized power in a bloodless coup 3 months before the election was to take place, suspended the balloting, and began ruling by decree. Many political figures and movements that wanted a return to the government according to the Constitution of 1940 disputed Batista's undemocratic rule.

On July 26, 1953, Fidel Castro, who had been involved in increasingly violent political activity before Batista's coup, led a failed attack on the Moncada army barracks in Santiago de Cuba in which more than 100 died. After defending himself in a trial open to national and international media, he was convicted and jailed, and subsequently was freed in an act of clemency, before going into exile in Mexico. There he organized the "26th of July Movement" with the goal of overthrowing Batista, and the group sailed to Cuba on board the yacht Granma, landing in the eastern part of the island in December 1956.

Batista's dictatorial rule fueled increasing popular discontent and the rise of many active urban and rural resistance groups, a fertile political environment for Castro's 26th of July Movement. Faced with a corrupt and ineffective military--itself dispirited by a U.S. Government embargo on weapons sales to Cuba--and public indignation and revulsion at his brutality toward opponents, Batista fled on January 1, 1959. Although he had promised a return to constitutional rule and democratic elections along with social reforms, Castro used his control of the military to consolidate his power by repressing all dissent from his decisions, marginalizing other resistance figures, and imprisoning or executing thousands of opponents. An estimated 3,200 people were executed by the Castro regime between 1959-62 alone. As the revolution became more radical, hundreds of thousands of Cubans fled the island.

Castro declared Cuba a socialist state on April 16, 1961. For the next 30 years, Castro pursued close relations with the Soviet Union and worked in concert with the geopolitical goals of Soviet communism, funding and fomenting violent subversive and insurrectional activities, as well as military adventurism, until the demise of the U.S.S.R. in 1991.

Relations between the United States and Cuba deteriorated rapidly as the Cuban regime expropriated U.S. properties and moved toward adoption of a one-party communist system. In response, the United States imposed an embargo on Cuba in October 1960, and, in response to Castro's provocations, broke diplomatic relations on January 3, 1961. Tensions between the two governments peaked during the October 1962 missile crisis.

GOVERNMENT

Cuba is a totalitarian state controlled by Fidel Castro, who is chief of state, head of government, First Secretary of the PCC, and commander in chief of the armed forces. Castro seeks to control most aspects of Cuban life through the Communist Party and its affiliated mass organizations, the government bureaucracy, and the state security apparatus. In March 2003, Castro announced his intention to remain in power for life. The Ministry of Interior is the principal organ of state security and control.

According to the Soviet-style Cuban constitution of 1976, the National Assembly of People's Power, and its Council of State when the body is not in session, has supreme authority in the Cuban system. Since the National Assembly meets only twice a year for a few days each time, the 31-member Council of State wields power. The Council of Ministers, through its 9-member executive committee, handles the administration of the economy, which is state-controlled except for a tiny and shriveling open-market sector. Fidel Castro is President of the Council of State and Council of Ministers and his brother Raul serves as First Vice President of both bodies as well as Minister of Defense.

Although the constitution theoretically provides for independent courts, it explicitly subordinates them to the National Assembly and to the Council of State. The People's Supreme Court is the highest judicial body. Due process is routinely denied to Cuban citizens, particularly in cases involving political offenses. The constitution states that all legally recognized civil liberties can be denied to anyone who opposes the "decision of the Cuban people to build socialism." Citizens can be and are jailed for terms of 3 years or more for simply criticizing the communist system or Fidel Castro.

The Communist Party is constitutionally recognized as Cuba's only legal political party. The party monopolizes all government positions, including judicial offices. Though not a formal requirement, party membership is a de facto prerequisite for high-level official positions and professional advancement in most areas, although a tiny number of non-party members have on extremely rare occasions been permitted by the controlling Communist authorities to serve in the National Assembly. The Communist Party or one of its front organizations approves candidates for any elected office. Citizens do not have the right to change their government. In March 2003, the government carried out one of the most brutal crackdowns on peaceful opposition in the history of Cuba when it arrested 75 human rights activists, independent journalists and opposition figures on various charges, including aiding a foreign power and violating national security laws. Authorities subjected the detainees to summary trials and sentenced them to prison terms ranging from 6 to 28 years. Amnesty International identified all 75 as "prisoners of conscience." The European Union (EU) condemned their arrests and in June 2003, it announced its decision to implement the following actions: limit bilateral high-level governmental visits, reduce the profile of member states' participation in cultural events, reduce economic assistance and invite Cuban dissidents to national-day celebrations. See also the Department's Country Report on Human Rights Practices for Cuba.

Although the constitution allows legislative proposals backed by at least 10,000 citizens to be submitted directly to the National Assembly, in 2002 the government rejected a petition known as the Varela Project, supporters of which submitted 11,000 signatures calling for a national referendum on political and economic reforms. Many of the 75 activists arrested in March 2003 participated in the Varela Project. In October 2003, Project Varela organizers submitted a second petition to the National Assembly with an additional 14,000 signatures. Since April 2004, some prisoners of conscience have been released, seven of whom were in the group of 75; all suffered from moderate to severe medical conditions and many of them continue to be harassed by state security even after their release from prison. Moreover, in response to a planned protest by activists at the French Embassy in Havana in late July 2005, Cuban security forces detained 33 opposition members, three of whom had been released on medical grounds. At least 16 other activists were either arrested or sentenced to prison since 2004 for opposing the Cuban Government. There has also been a resurgence of harassment of various activist groups, most notably the "Damas en Blanca," a group of wives of political prisoners.

On July 31, 2006 the Castro regime announced a "temporary" transfer of power from Fidel Castro to his brother Raul, who until that time served as head of the Cuban armed forces and second-in-command of the government and the Communist Party. It was the first time in the 47 years of Fidel Castro's rule that power had been transferred. The transfer took place due to intestinal surgery of an undetermined nature.

Government Leaders

MEMBERS OF THE COUNCIL OF MINISTERS

Raúl Castro Ruz President of the Councils of State and Ministers. First Secretary of the Central Committee of the CCP. Army General. Graduated from Higher Military Training. Birthdate: June 3, 1931
José Ramón Machado Ventura Second Secretary of the Central Committee of the CCP. Politburo member of the PCC. MD. Birthdate: October 26, 1930
Days-Canel Bermúdez Miguel First Deputy Cabinet Member of the Political Bureau of the CPC. electronics engineer. Birthdate: April 20, 1960
Ramiro Valdés Menéndez Vice President of the Councils of State and Ministers. Commander of the Revolution. Politburo member of the PCC. Council Member State. Deputy to the National Assembly of People's Power. Graduated from Higher Military Training.

Birthdate: April 28, 1932
Ricardo Cabrisas Ruiz . Vice President of the Cabinet and its Executive Committee . Bachelor of Political Science Date of Birth: January 21, 1937
Ulises Rosales del Toro Vice President of Council of Ministers and its Executive Committee. Member of the Central Committee of the CCP. Deputy to the National Assembly of People's Power. Graduated from Higher Military Training. Birthdate: March 8, 1942
Antonio Enrique Lussón Battle Vice Cabinet. Member of the Central Committee of the CCP. Division General.
Marino Alberto Murillo Jorge Vice President of the Council of Ministers and member of the State Council. Politburo member of the PCC. Bachelor in Economics. Birthdate: February 19, 1961
Adel Yzquierdo Onofre Rodriguez Minister of Economy and Planning. Vice President of Council of Ministers. Politburo member of the PCC. Mechanical Engineer. Birthdate: June 12, 1945
Abelardo Colome Ibarra Secretary. Vice President of the State Council. Politburo member of the PCC. Corps General. Graduated from Higher Military Training. Birthdate: September 13, 1939
Gustavo Rodríguez Rollero Minister of Agriculture. Agronomist. Birthdate: June 21, 1963
Mary Blanca Ortega Barredo Minister of Domestic Trade. Bachelor in Economics and a Masters in Business Administration. Birthdate: November 17, 1962
René Mesa Villafana

Minister of Construction. Civil Engineer. Birthdate: April 7, 1958
Julian Gonzalez Toledo Minister of Culture.
Ena Elsa Velázquez Cobiella Minister of Education. Deputy of the National Assembly of People's Power. Degree in Chemistry. Birthdate: April 19, 1956
Rodolfo Alarcón Ortiz Minister of Higher Education.
Leopoldo Cintra Frias minister of the Revolutionary Armed Forces. Politburo member of CPC Central Committee and the State Council. Corps General. Bachelor of Political and Social Sciences. Birthdate: July 17, 1941
Lina Olinda Pedraza Rodríguez Minister of Finance and Prices. Member of the Central Committee of the CCP. Deputy of the National Assembly of People's Power. Bachelor of Economic Control. Birthdate: September 16, 1955
Maimir Mesa Ramos . Minister of Communications . regular academic graduate course specializing in Communications at the Academy of FAR Communications Engineer. Birthdate: November 25, 1962
María del Carmen Concepción González Minister of the Food Industry. Member of the Central Committee of the CCP. Deputy of the National Assembly of People's Power. Graduated in History and Social Sciences. Birthdate: September 15, 1957
Salvador Pardo Cruz Industries Minister Engineer technician. Birthdate: December 20, 1947
María Esther Reus González Minister of Justice. Bachelor of Law.

Birthdate: May 23, 1962
Bruno Eduardo Rodriguez Parrilla, Minister for Foreign Affairs. Member of the Central Committee of the CCP. Bachelor in Law Date of Birth: January 22, 1958
Roberto Morales Ojeda. Minister of Public Health. Member of the Central Committee of the CCP. Graduated Medicine. Masters in Public Health. Birthdate: June 15, 1967
Margarita Marlene González Fernández Minister of Labour and Social Security. Industrial Engineering and Master in Human Resources Management. Birthdate: July 20, 1964
Cesar Ignacio Arocha Masid Minister of Transport. Brig. Graduated from Higher Military Training. engineer Railways. Birthdate: February 1, 1959
Manuel Marrero Cruz Tourism Minister. Architect. Birthdate: July 11, 1963
Rodrigo Malmierca Minister of Foreign Trade and Foreign Investment. Member of the Central Committee of the CCP. Bachelor in Economics. Birthdate: October 14, 1956
Ernesto Medina Villaveirán President of Banco Central de Cuba. Member of the Central Committee of the CCP. Bachelor in Economics. Birthdate: July 22, 1955
Elba Rosa Perez Montoya Minister of Science, Technology and Environment.
Alfredo López Valdés Minister of Energy and Mines. Automation Electrical Engineer. Birthdate: April 19, 1945
Ines Maria Chapman Waugh

. President of the National Institute of Hydraulic Resources . Committee Member of the CPC Hydraulic Engineering Date of Birth: September 9, 1965
Julio Christian Jiménez Molina President, National Institute of Sports, Physical Education and Recreation. Bachelor in Political Science. Birthdate: November 12, 1951
Danylo Sirio López president of the Cuban Institute of Radio and Television. director of TV programs. Birthdate: December 24, 1950

PROVINCIAL GOVERNMENT BODIES

Ernesto Barreto Castillo President of the Provincial Assembly of People's Power of Pinar del Río. Deputy to the National Assembly of People's Power. Mechanical Engineer. Birthdate: April 16, 1960
Raul Rodriguez Cartaya President of the Provincial Assembly of People's Power of Artemis. Deputy to the National Assembly of People's Power. standard level Superior. Birthdate: May 22, 1965
David González Yero President of the Provincial Assembly of People's Power Mayabeque.
Marta Hernández Romero . President of the Provincial Assembly of Popular Power in Havana . Deputy of the National Assembly of People's Power . Master of Education Date of Birth: March 19, 1958
Tania Leon Silveira President of the Provincial Assembly of People's Power of Matanzas. Council Member State. Deputy of the National Assembly of People's Power. Agronomist. Birthdate: July 19, 1964
Pestana jorgelina Mederos President of the Provincial Assembly of People's Power of Villa Clara. Deputy of the National Assembly of People's Power.

Bachelor of Law. Birthdate: October 30, 1964
Pernia Mairelis Cordero President of the Provincial Assembly of People's Power of Cienfuegos. Deputy of the National Assembly of People's Power.
Teresita Romero Rodriguez President of the Provincial Assembly of People's Power of Sancti Spiritus. Deputy of the National Assembly of People's Power. Bachelor in Economics and a Masters in Accounting and Finance. Birthdate: May 20, 1965
Victorio Carmenate Raúl Pérez President of the Provincial Assembly of People's Power of Ciego de Ávila. Deputy to the National Assembly of Popular Power BA in Economics. Birthdate: May 21, 1961
Isabel Gonzalez Cardenas President of the Provincial Assembly of People's Power of Camagüey. Deputy of the National Assembly of People's Power
Lilian González Rodríguez President of the Provincial Assembly of People's Power of Las Tunas. Deputy of the National Assembly of People's Power Architect. Birthdate: March 4, 1962
Tellez C. Tamayo Susel the President of the Provincial Assembly of Popular Power in Havana. Deputy of the National Assembly of People's Power
Santiago Manuel Sobrino Martinez President of the Provincial Assembly of People's Power of Granma. Deputy to the National Assembly of People's Power. Industrial Engineer. Birthdate: June 25, 1971
Reinaldo Garcia Zapata President of the Provincial Assembly of People's Power of Cuba Santiago. Deputy to the National Assembly of People's Power. engineer. Birthdate: March 9, 1968
Nancy Acosta Hernández President of the Provincial Assembly of People's Power of Guantánamo. Deputy of the National Assembly of People's Power. Bachelor of Education and Doctor of Pedagogical Sciences.

Birthdate: January 15, 1965
Arelys Casañola Quintana President of the People's Assembly of the Municipality Special Isla de la Juventud. Deputy of the National Assembly of People's Power.

NATIONAL SECURITY

Under Castro, Cuba is a highly militarized society. From 1975 until the late 1980s, massive Soviet military assistance enabled Cuba to upgrade its military capabilities and project power abroad. The tonnage of Soviet military deliveries to Cuba throughout most of the 1980s exceeded deliveries in any year since the military build-up during the 1962 missile crisis.

With the loss of Soviet-era subsidies in the early 1990s, Cuba's armed forces have shrunk considerably, both in terms of numbers and assets. Combined active duty troop strength for all three services is estimated at 50,000 to 55,000 personnel (compared to some 235,000 on active duty 10 years ago) and much of Cuba's weaponry appears to be in storage. Cuba's air force, once considered among the best equipped in Latin America, no longer merits that distinction, though it still possesses advanced aircraft and weapons systems; the navy has become primarily a coastal defense force with no blue water capability. The Cuban army is still one of the region's more formidable, but it also is much reduced and no longer has the considerable resources necessary to project power abroad.

The military plays a growing role in the economy and manages a number of hotels in the tourist sector. The country's two paramilitary organizations, the Territorial Militia Troops and the Youth Labor Army, have a reduced training capability. Cuba also adopted a "war of the people" strategy that highlights the defensive nature of its capabilities. The government continues to maintain a large state security apparatus under the Ministry of Interior to repress dissent within Cuba, and in the last decade has formed special forces units to confront indications of popular unrest.

ECONOMY

Rank	95th
Currency	Cuban peso (CUP) = 100 centavos and Cuban Convertible Peso (CUC) = 24 CUP
Fiscal year	yes
	Statistics
GDP	$72.3 billion $121 billion (PPP)
GDP growth	2.7%
GDP per capita	$10,200 (PPP)
GDP by sector	Agriculture: 4.3%, industry: 21.6%, services: 74%
Inflation (CPI)	1.5% (2009 est.)
Population below poverty line	1.5%
Labor force	5.159 million (Public sector: 78%, Personal sector: 22%)
Labor force by occupation	Agriculture: 20%, industry: 19.4%, services: 60.6%
Unemployment	3.8%
Main industries	Sugar, petroleum, tobacco, construction, nickel, steel, cement, agricultural machinery, pharmaceuticals
	External

Exports	$2.458 billion f.o.b.
Export goods	sugar, medical products, nickel, tobacco, shellfish, citrus, coffee
Main export partners	Canada 17.3% China 16.6% Venezuela 12.7% Netherlands 8.8% Spain 5.8%
Imports	$8.963 billion f.o.b.
Import goods	petroleum, food, machinery and equipment, chemicals
Main import partners	Venezuela 36.4% China 10.5% Spain 8.7% Brazil 5.1% United States 4.2%
Public finances	
Public debt	$19.44 billion (31 December 2009 est.); another $20.8 billion owed to Russia, $0.9 billion owed to Romania and $0.2 billion owed to Hungary
Revenues	$35.01 billion
Expenses	$36.73 billion
Economic aid	$87.8 million

The **economy of Cuba** is a largely centrally planned economy dominated by state-run enterprises overseen by the Cuban government, though there remains significant foreign investment and personal enterprise in Cuba. Most of the means of production are owned and run by the government, and most of the labor force is employed by the state, although in recent years, the formation of cooperatives and self-employment has been encouraged by the Communist Party.

In the year 2000, public sector employment was 76% and private sector, mainly composed by personal property, employment was 23% compared to the 1981 ratio of 91% to 8%. Capital investment is restricted and requires approval by the government. The Cuban government sets most prices and rations goods to citizens. In 2009, Cuba ranked 51st out of 182 with an HDI of 0.863; remarkably high considering its GDP per capita only places it 95th. Public services and transport in Cuba, however, are second-rate compared to more developed counterparts on the mainland. The country's public debt in 2012 was measured at 35.3% of GDP. At the same time, inflation (CDP) was ranked at 5.5%. Furthermore, in the same year, the economy encountered a 3% growth in GDP.

In the 1950s, Cuba had a vibrant but extremely unequal economy, with large capital outflows to foreign investors. The country compared favourably with Spain and Portugal on socioeconomic measures. Furthermore, its income in 1929 was reportedly 41% of the US, thus higher than in some Southern states of the US, such as Mississippi and South Carolina The country has made significant progress towards a more even distribution of income since the Revolution and being placed under economic embargo by the United States. Following the collapse of the Soviet Union, Cuba's GDP declined by 33% between 1990 and 1993, partially due to loss of Soviet subsidies, and partly due to a crash in sugar prices in the early 1990s. Yet Cuba has managed to retain high levels of healthcare and education.

Cubans receive low housing and transportation costs, free education, and health care and food subsidies. Corruption is common, though allegedly lower than in most other countries in Latin

America. However, in their book, *Corruption in Cuba*, Sergio Diaz-Briquets and Jorge F. Pérez-López Servando state that Cuba has "institutionalized" corruption and that state-run monopolies, cronyism, and lack of accountability have made Cuba one of the world's most corrupt states".

The Cuban Government continues to adhere to socialist principles in organizing its state-controlled economy. Most of the means of production are owned and run by the government and, according to Cuban Government statistics, about 75% of the labor force is employed by the state. The actual figure is closer to 93%, with some 150,000 small farmers and another 150,000 "cuentapropistas," or holders of licenses for self-employment, representing a mere 2.1% of the nearly 4.7 million-person workforce.

The Cuban economy is still recovering from a decline in gross domestic product of at least 35% between 1989 and 1993 as the loss of Soviet subsidies laid bare the economy's fundamental weaknesses. To alleviate the economic crisis, in 1993 and 1994 the government introduced a few market-oriented reforms, including opening to tourism, allowing foreign investment, legalizing the dollar, and authorizing self-employment for some 150 occupations. These measures resulted in modest economic growth; the official statistics, however, are deficient and as a result provide an incomplete measure of Cuba's real economic situation. Living conditions at the end of the decade remained well below the 1989 level. Lower sugar and nickel prices, increases in petroleum costs, a post-September 11, 2001 decline in tourism, devastating hurricanes in November 2001 and August 2004, and a major drought in the eastern half of the island caused severe economic disruptions. Growth rates continued to stagnate in 2002 and 2003, while 2004 and 2005 showed some renewed growth. Moreover, the gap in the standard of living has widened between those with access to dollars and those without. Jobs that can earn dollar salaries or tips from foreign businesses and tourists have become highly desirable. It is not uncommon to see doctors, engineers, scientists, and other professionals working in restaurants or as taxi drivers.

Castro's regime has pulled back on earlier market reforms and is seeking tighter state control over the economy. The Cuban Government is aggressively pursuing a policy of recentralization, making it increasingly difficult for foreigners to conduct business on the island. Likewise, Cuban citizens are adversely affected by reversion to a peso economy.

Prolonged austerity and the state-controlled economy's inefficiency in providing adequate goods and services have created conditions for a flourishing informal economy in Cuba. As the variety and amount of goods available in state-run peso stores has declined, Cubans have turned increasingly to the black market to obtain needed food, clothing, and household items. Pilferage of items from the work place to sell on the black market or illegally offering services on the sidelines of official employment is common, and Cuban companies regularly figure 15% in losses into their production plans to cover this. Recognizing that Cubans must engage in such activity to make ends meet and that attempts to shut the informal economy down would be futile, the government concentrates its control efforts on ideological appeals against theft and shutting down large organized operations. A report by an independent economist and opposition leader speculates that more than 40% of the Cuban economy operates in the informal sector. Since 2005, the government has carried out a large anti-corruption campaign as it continues efforts to recentralize much of the economy under the regime's control.

Sugar, which has been the mainstay of the island's economy for most of its history, has fallen upon troubled times. In 1989, production was more than 8 million tons, but by the mid-1990s, it had fallen to around 3.5 million tons. Inefficient planting and cultivation methods, poor management, shortages of spare parts, and poor transportation infrastructure combined to deter the recovery of the sector. In June 2002, the government announced its intention to implement a "comprehensive transformation" of this declining sector. Almost half the existing sugar mills were closed, and more than 100,000 workers were laid off. The government has promised that these workers will be "retrained" in other fields, though it is unlikely they will find new jobs in Cuba's stagnant economy. Moreover, despite such efforts, the sugar harvest continued to decline, falling to 2.1 million tons in 2003, the smallest since 1933. The harvest was not much better in 2004, with 2.3 million tons, and even worse in 2005, with 1.3 million tons.

In the mid-1990s, tourism surpassed sugar as the primary source of foreign exchange. Tourism figures prominently in the Cuban Government's plans for development, and a top official cast it as at the "heart of the economy." Havana devotes significant resources to building new tourist facilities and renovating historic structures for use in the tourism sector. Roughly 1.7 million tourists visited Cuba in 2001, generating about $1.85 billion in gross revenues; in 2003, the number rose to 1.9 million tourists, predominantly from Canada and the European Union, generating revenue of $2.1 billion. The number of tourists to Cuba in 2004 crossed the 2 million mark (2.05 million), including the so-called "medical tourists" from other Latin American countries seeking free medical treatment at Cuban facilities. In 2005 the number of tourists increased to 2.32 million.

Nickel is now the biggest earner among Cuba's goods exports. The nickel industry has been operating close to full capacity and therefore currently stagnant, but it is benefiting from unprecedented increases in world market prices. Revenues have more than doubled from $450 million in 2001 to $1 billion in 2005. The government is making attempts to increase extraction capacity.

Remittances also play a large role in Cuba's economy. Cuba does not publish accurate economic statistics, but academic sources estimate that remittances total from $600 million to $1 billion per year, with most coming from families in the United States. U.S. regulation changes announced in June 2004 allow remittances to be sent only to the remitter's immediate family; they cannot be remitted to certain Cuban Government officials and members of the Cuban Communist party; and the total amount of family remittances that an authorized traveler may carry to Cuba is now $300, reduced from $3,000. (See also the Commission on Assistance to a Free Cuba report at www.cafc.gov, cited below.) The Cuban Government captures these dollar remittances by allowing Cuban citizens to shop in state-run "dollar stores," which sell food, household, and clothing items at a high mark-up averaging over 240% of face value.

Beginning in November 2004, Castro mandated that U.S. dollars be exchanged for "convertible pesos"--a local currency that can be used in special shops on the island but has no value internationally--for a 10% charge. The 10% conversion fee disproportionately affects Cubans who receive remittances from relatives in the U.S.

To help keep the economy afloat, Cuba has actively courted foreign investment, which often takes the form of joint ventures with the Cuban Government holding half of the equity, management contracts for tourism facilities, or financing for the sugar harvest. A new legal framework laid out in 1995 allowed for majority foreign ownership in joint ventures with the Cuban Government. In practice, majority ownership by the foreign partner is nonexistent. Of the 540 joint ventures formed since the Cuban Government issued the first legislation on foreign investment in 1982, 397 remained at the end of 2002, and 287 at the close of 2005. Due in large part to Castro's recentralization efforts, it is estimated that one joint venture and two small cooperative production ventures have closed each week since 2000. Responding to this decline in the number of joint ventures, a spokesperson for the Ministry of Foreign Investment explained that foreign investment is not a pillar of development in and of itself. Moreover, the hostile investment climate, characterized by inefficient and overpriced labor imposed by the communist government, dense regulations, and an impenetrable bureaucracy, continue to deter foreign investment. Foreign direct investment flows decreased from $448 million in 2000 to $39 million in 2001 and were at zero in 2002. In July 2002, the European Union, through its embassies in Havana, transmitted to the Cuban Government a document that outlined the problems encountered in operating joint ventures in Cuba. Titled "The Legal and Administrative Framework for Foreign Trade and Investment by European Companies in Cuba," the paper noted the difficulty in obtaining such basic necessities as work and residence permits for foreign employees--even exit visas and drivers licenses. It complained that the Government of Cuba gave EU joint venture partners little or no say in hiring Cuban staff, often forced the joint venture to contract employees who were not professionally suitable, and yet reserved to itself the right to fire any worker at any time without cause. It noted administrative difficulties in securing financing and warned that "the difficulties of state firms in meeting their payment obligations are seriously threatening some firms and increasing the risk premium which all operators have to pay for their operations with Cuba." The Cuban Government offered no response.

Investors are also constrained by the U.S.-Cuban Liberty and Democratic Solidarity (Libertad) Act that provides sanctions for those who "traffic" in property expropriated from U.S. citizens. More than a dozen companies have pulled out of Cuba or altered their plans to invest there due to the threat of action under the Libertad Act.

In an attempt to provide jobs for workers laid off due to the economic crisis and bring some forms of black market activity into more controllable channels, the Cuban Government in 1993 legalized self-employment for some 150 occupations. This small private sector is tightly controlled and regulated. Set monthly fees must be paid regardless of income earned, and frequent inspections yield stiff fines when any of the many self-employment regulations are violated. Rather than expanding private sector opportunities, in recent years, the government has been attempting to squeeze more of these private sector entrepreneurs out of business and back to the public sector. Many have opted to enter the informal economy or black market, and others have closed. These measures have reduced private sector employment from a peak of 209,000 to less than 100,000 now. Moreover, a large number of those people who nominally are self-employed in reality are well-connected fronts for military officials. No recent figures have been made available, but the Government of Cuba reported at the end of 2001 that tax receipts from the self-employed fell 8.1% due to the decrease in the number of these taxpayers. Since October 1, 2004, the Cuban Government no longer issues new licenses for 40 of the approximately 150 categories of self-employment, including for the most popular ones, such as private restaurants.

In June 2005, 2,000 more licenses were revoked from self-employed workers as a means to reassert government control over the economy and to stem growing inequalities associated with self-employment. The licenses for self-employed workers were typically for service-oriented work, allowing the Cuban people to eke out a small living in an otherwise impoverished state. Moreover, workers in Cuba's tourist sector--at resorts where native Cubans are prohibited unless they are on the job--have been prohibited by a Ministry of Tourism regulation from accepting gifts, tips, or even food from foreigners, in a further attempt at increasing the tourist apartheid that exists on the island.

A 2004 UN Economic Commission on Latin America and the Caribbean (ECLAC) report recommends that Cuba "redesign the parameters of competition in the public, private and cooperative sectors [and] redefine the role of the state in the economy." It recommends more flexibility in self-employment regulations, property diversification, economic decentralization, and a role for the market. The Cuban Government, however, is today reversing the economic liberalization of the 90s and re-centralizing its economy. Evidence of this is found in the decline in the number of firms participating in the *perfeccionamiento empresarial*, or entrepreneurial improvement (EI), program, which is based on capitalist management techniques. EI was instituted in the 1980s as a military-led pilot project, and in 1998, the Cuban Government extended it from military to civilian "parastatals," reportedly to foster capitalist competitiveness. At first, the government highlighted participating companies' achievements in cutting costs and boosting profitability and quality and suggested that the increased autonomy of state managers under EI was producing an efficient form of socialism with a strong link between pay and performance. However, many in the Communist Party, even Castro himself, resisted EI. Many of the original participants have since left the program and participating firms have seen little growth in revenue. The EI program has fallen far short of expectations and the Cuban Government no longer heralds its successes or its future prospects. In 2003 the Cuban Government also tightened foreign exchange controls, requiring that state companies hold money in convertible pesos and obtain special authorization from the central bank before making hard currency transactions. Practically speaking, this restricted companies from using the dollar for internal trade. Following this, in 2004 the government announced that all state entities must stop charging in U.S. dollars and charge only in pesos for any products and services not considered a part of a company's "fundamental social objective." It also recently implemented new requirements to channel imports through monopolistic Soviet-style wholesale distribution companies.

Cuba's precarious economic position is complicated by the high price it must pay for foreign financing. The Cuban Government defaulted on most of its international debt in 1986 and does not have access to credit from international financial institutions like the World Bank, which means Havana must rely heavily on short-term loans to finance imports, chiefly food and fuel. Because of its poor credit rating, an $11 billion hard currency debt, and the risks associated with Cuban investment, interest rates have reportedly been as high as 22%. In 2002, citing chronic delinquencies and mounting short-term debts, Moody's lowered Cuba's credit rating to Caa1 -- "speculative grade, very poor." Dunn and Bradstreet rate Cuba as one of the riskiest economies in the world.

HUMAN RIGHTS

Cuba is an authoritarian state led by Raul Castro, who is president of the council of state and council of ministers, Communist Party (CP) first secretary, and commander in chief of security forces. The constitution recognizes the CP as the only legal party and "the superior leading force of society and of the state." A CP candidacy commission preapproved all candidates for the February 2013 uncontested National Assembly elections, which were neither free nor fair. The national leadership, including members of the military, maintained effective control over the security forces.

The principal human rights abuses included those involving the abridgement of the ability of citizens to change the government and the use of government threats, extrajudicial physical assault, intimidation, violent government-organized counter-protests against peaceful dissent, and harassment and detentions to prevent free expression and peaceful assembly.

The following additional abuses continued: short-term, arbitrary unlawful detentions and arrests, harsh prison conditions, selective prosecution, denial of fair trial, and travel restrictions. Authorities interfered with privacy, engaging in pervasive monitoring of private communications. The government did not respect freedom of speech and press, restricted internet access, maintained a monopoly on media outlets, circumscribed academic freedom, and maintained some restrictions on the ability of religious groups to meet and worship. The government refused to recognize independent human rights groups or permit them to function legally. In addition the government continued to prevent workers from forming independent unions and otherwise exercising their labor rights.

Most human rights abuses were committed by officials at the direction of the government. Impunity for the perpetrators remained widespread.

RESPECT FOR THE INTEGRITY OF THE PERSON, INCLUDING FREEDOM FROM:SHARE

A. ARBITRARY OR UNLAWFUL DEPRIVATION OF LIFE

There were no confirmed reports that the government or its agents committed arbitrary or unlawful killings during the year (see section 1.d.). There was one incident, however, where the violent assault on a pregnant protester may have resulted in the loss of the child. There were no mechanisms readily available to investigate abuses committed by the security forces.

By the end of the year, the government had not responded to calls for an international investigation into the 2012 deaths of opposition activists Oswaldo Paya and Harold Cepero. The government claimed that the two died in a car accident, although in October the driver of that car, Angel Carromero, publicly reiterated his allegation that the car crash that led to their deaths occurred because state security forces followed Paya's vehicle too closely, struck the car, and forced it off the road.

B. DISAPPEARANCE

There were no reports of politically motivated disappearances during the year.

C. TORTURE AND OTHER CRUEL, INHUMAN, OR DEGRADING TREATMENT OR PUNISHMENT

The law prohibits abusive treatment of detainees and prisoners. There were reports, however, that members of the security forces intimidated and sometimes physically assaulted human rights and prodemocracy advocates, dissidents, and other detainees and prisoners both during detention and while imprisoned, and they did so with impunity. Some detainees and prisoners endured physical abuse, sometimes by other inmates with the acquiescence of guards.

There were reports of police assaulting detainees or being complicit in public harassment of and physical assaults on peaceful demonstrators.

Prison and Detention Center Conditions

Prison conditions continued to be harsh. Prisons continued to be overcrowded, and facilities, sanitation, and medical care were seriously deficient. There were a few reports of beatings of prisoners that included beatings by prison officials as well as among prisoners. There were some reports of prisoner-on-prisoner sexual assaults, allegedly due to lax security by prison guards.

Physical Conditions: In 2012, for the first time in decades, the government published the number of prisoners, declaring that 57,337 persons were incarcerated. The government made no similar publication during the year, nor did it provide information regarding the number, location, or capacity of detention centers, which included not only prisons but also work camps and other kinds of detention facilities. Human rights organizations estimated there were more than 65,000 prisoners and detainees.

Men and women were held in separate prisons and police detention facilities. Generally, women reported the same poor prison conditions as men, including inadequate medical care. Women also reported lack of access to feminine hygiene products and inadequate prenatal care. There were reports of inmates as young as 15 in maximum-security prisons.

Prison cells lacked adequate water, sanitation, space, light, ventilation, and temperature control. Although the state provided basic food and some medical care, many prisoners relied on family parcels for food and other basic supplies. Potable water was frequently unavailable. Prison cells were overcrowded, limiting freedom of movement during the day. Prisoners often slept on concrete bunks without a mattress, with some reports of more than one person sharing a narrow bunk. Where available, mattresses were thin and often infested with vermin and insects.

Prisoners, family members, and nongovernmental organizations (NGOs) reported inadequate health care, which led to or aggravated multiple maladies. Prisoners also reported outbreaks of dengue, tuberculosis, hepatitis, and cholera. Prison health workers reportedly reused syringes, raising safety and hygiene concerns.

Political prisoners and the general prison population were held in similar conditions. Political prisoners who refused to wear standard prison uniforms were denied certain privileges, such as access to prison libraries and standard reductions in the severity of their sentence (for example, being transferred from a maximum-security to a medium-security prison). The government sometimes placed healthy prisoners, including political prisoners, in cells with mentally disturbed inmates as punishment. Political prisoners also reported being threatened or harassed by fellow inmates whom they believed were acting on orders of prison authorities.

There were reports of prison deaths from heart attacks, asthma attacks, HIV/AIDS, and other chronic medical conditions, as well as from suicide.

Prisoners reported that solitary confinement was a common punishment for misconduct and that some had been held in isolation for months or even years at a time. In general prisoners in isolation had restrictions on family visits.

Prisoners who criticized the government or engaged in hunger strikes and other forms of protest were subjected to extended solitary confinement, beatings, restrictions on family visits, and denial of medical care. Prisoners had no effective complaint mechanism to seek redress.

Administration: There was no publicly available information about prison administration or recordkeeping in the prison system.

Alternative sentencing was available for nonviolent offenders and for juveniles. Nonviolent offenders may be sentenced to probation. Juveniles may be sentenced to one of 12 Escuelas de Formacion Integral, or Holistic Training Schools, which worked to rehabilitate troubled youth.

A legal department within the Attorney General's Office is empowered to investigate allegations of abuse in the prison system. The results of these investigations were not publicly accessible. By law prisoners and detainees may seek redress regarding prison conditions and procedural violations, such as continued incarceration after their prison sentence has expired. Prisoners reported that government officials refused to allow or accept complaints, or failed to respond to the complaints once submitted.

Prisoners and pretrial detainees had access to visitors, although some political prisoners' relatives reported that prison officials arbitrarily canceled scheduled visits. Some prisoners were able to communicate information about their living conditions through telephone calls to human rights observers and reports to family members.

Prisoners could practice limited religious observance. The Catholic Church and other church groups reported access to prisoners during the year, with services offered in prisons and detention centers in most, if not all, provinces. The interdenominational seminary in Matanzas reported developing a program to train chaplains to offer religious counseling to prisoners. There were isolated reports that prison authorities did not inform inmates of their right to religious assistance, delayed months before responding to such requests, and limited visits to a maximum of two or three times per year.

Independent Monitoring: The government did not permit independent monitoring of prison conditions by international or national human rights groups and did not permit access to detainees by international humanitarian organizations. Although the government pledged in previous years to allow a visit by the UN special rapporteur on torture and other cruel, inhuman, and degrading treatment or punishment, no visit occurred during the year. Unlike in 2013 the government did not invite foreign journalists to tour specific prisons. Independent human rights organizations were not allowed access to prisons during the year.

D. Arbitrary Arrest or Detention

Arbitrary arrest and short-term detention continued to be a common method for the government to control independent public expression and political activity. By law police have wide discretion to stop and question citizens, request their identification, and carry out arrests and searches. The law provides that police officials provide suspects with a signed "act of detention," noting the basis, date, and location of any detention in a police facility and a registry of personal items seized during a police search. There were also reports of short-term detentions following interactions with members of the diplomatic community in Havana. Police officials routinely conducted short-term detentions, at times accompanied by beatings. Arbitrary stops and searches were most common in urban areas and at government-controlled checkpoints located at the entrances to provinces and municipalities. Searches and seizures of property by police officials without providing any record or legal justification were also common practice.

Police and security officials continued to use short-term and sometimes violent detentions to prevent independent political activity or free assembly. Such detentions generally lasted from several hours to several days. An independent domestic monitoring group, the Cuban Commission on Human Rights and Reconciliation (CCDHRN), counted 8,899 through the end of the year, compared with 6,424 in 2013. Long-term imprisonment of peaceful opponents, while rare, did not cease entirely. In February authorities charged, tried, and sentenced more than 50 members of the Santiago-based opposition group Union Patriotica de Cuba (UNPACU) to prison for months or years as punishment for their political activity. In October and November authorities handed down sentences of two to six years to seven individuals who had been held for varying periods without due process. This included independent musician Angel Yunier Remon Arzuaga, who was sentenced to six years' imprisonment, following his alleged assault of a state security agent during a government-organized act of repudiation against Arzuaga in March 2013. He remained in prison at the end of the year.

The law allows up to a four-year detention of individuals before they commit an actual crime, with a subjective determination of "potential dangerousness," defined as the "special proclivity of a person to commit crimes, demonstrated by conduct in manifest contradiction of socialist norms." Mostly used as a tool to control "antisocial" behaviors such as substance abuse or prostitution, authorities also used it to silence peaceful political opponents. While there was no definitive estimate of the number of persons serving sentences for "potential dangerousness," the CCDHRN estimated more than four thousand citizens were held on the charge.

Role of the Police and Security Apparatus

The Ministry of Interior exercises control over police, internal security forces, and the prison system. The ministry's National Revolutionary Police is the country's primary law enforcement organization and was moderately effective in investigating common crimes. Specialized units of the ministry's state security branch are responsible for monitoring, infiltrating, and suppressing independent political activity. The police supported state security agents by carrying out house searches, arresting persons of interest to the ministry, and providing interrogation facilities.

Police routinely violated procedural laws with impunity and often failed or refused to provide citizens with legally required documentation, particularly during arbitrary detentions and searches. Members of the security forces acted with impunity in committing civil rights and human rights abuses.

Although the law on criminal procedure prohibits the use of coercion during investigative interrogations, police and security forces routinely relied on aggressive and physically abusive tactics, threats, and harassment during questioning. Detainees reported that officers threatened them with long-term detention, loss of child custody rights, denial of permission to depart the country, and other intimidation, such as suggesting that an elderly relative might suffer an accident.

There were no mechanisms readily available to investigate government abuses.

Undercover police and agents from the Ministry of Interior were often present and directed activities to disrupt efforts at peaceful assembly (see section 2.b.).

Many state-orchestrated "acts of repudiation" directed against independent civil society groups, including the Damas de Blanco (Ladies in White) and other organizations, were organized to prevent meetings or to shame them publicly. In December 2013 state security agents and affiliated groups staged a protest outside the office of Estado de SATS coordinator, Antonio Enrique Gonzalez-Rodiles. State security brought in buses of schoolchildren to assist in the protest and forced them to watch while state security officers held Rodiles upside down and repeatedly kicked him in the head. Subsequently, Rodiles was briefly detained. Human rights activist and blogger Roberto de Jesus Guerra was reportedly beaten by state security agents on June 11 and warned to stop reporting on human rights abuses. On June 21, during a peaceful protest in Holguin, state police officers allegedly arrested and beat eight-month pregnant Lady in White Magaly Norvis Otero, after which she miscarried.

Arrest Procedures and Treatment of Detainees

Under the criminal procedure code, police have 24 hours after an arrest to present a criminal complaint to a police official called an instructor. The instructor has 72 hours to investigate and prepare a report for the prosecutor, who, in turn, has 72 hours to recommend to the appropriate court whether to open a criminal investigation. Detainees have no right to counsel during this seven-day period.

After the 168-hour detention period, by law detainees must be informed of the basis for the arrest and criminal investigation and have access to legal representation. Detainees facing formal charges must retain counsel within five days of being charged or the state can appoint an attorney on their behalf. Those charged can be released on bail, placed in home detention, or held in continued investigative detention. Once the accused has an attorney, the defense has five days to respond to the prosecution's charges, after which a court date usually is set.

Prosecutors can demand summary trials "in extraordinary circumstances" and in cases involving crimes against state security.

There were reports that defendants met with their attorneys for the first time only minutes before their trials and were not informed of the basis for their arrest within the required 168-hour period.

Bail was available, although typically not granted in cases involving those arrested for political activities. Time in detention before trial counted toward time served, if convicted.

Detainees can be interrogated at any time during detention and have no right to request the presence of counsel. Detainees have the right to remain silent, but officials do not have a legal obligation to inform them specifically of that right.

By law investigators must complete criminal investigations within 60 days. Prosecutors may grant investigators two 60-day extensions upon request, for a total of 180 days of investigative time. This deadline can be waived by the supervising court in "extraordinary circumstances" and upon special request by the prosecutor. In that instance no additional legal requirement exists to complete an investigation and file criminal charges, and a person could be held in detention without charge indefinitely. This exception was invoked often.

Arbitrary Arrest: Officials often disregarded many of the legal procedures governing the arrest process. Authorities often detained suspects much longer than 168 hours without informing them of the nature of the arrest or affording them legal counsel.

In 2012 authorities detained and held without charge for nearly 18 months independent librarian Sonia Garro Alonso; her husband, independent journalist Ramon Munoz Gonzalez; and activist Eugenio Hernandez Hernandez after they engaged in a public protest. In September 2013 authorities charged them with attempted murder, assault, and public disorder. Their trial was postponed on three occasions during the year, but on December 9, Garro, Munoz, and Hernandez were freed with no known conditions.

Pretrial Detention: Detainees were held for months or years in investigative detention, in both political and nonpolitical cases. In nonpolitical cases delays were often due to bureaucratic inefficiencies, a lack of checks on police, and prosecutorial or judicial excesses.

E. DENIAL OF FAIR PUBLIC TRIAL

While the constitution recognizes the independence of the judiciary, the judiciary is directly subordinate to the National Assembly and the CP, which can remove or appoint judges at any time. The judiciary was thoroughly dominated by political considerations, and there was little separation of powers between the judicial system, the CP, and the Council of State.

Civilian courts exist at the municipal, provincial, and Supreme Court levels. Special tribunals are convened for political ("counterrevolutionary") cases and other cases deemed sensitive to "state security" and act behind closed doors. Officials denied entry to trials by some observers during the year. Military tribunals may also have jurisdiction over civilians in cases where any of the defendants were members of the military, police force, or other law enforcement agency.

Trial Procedures

Due process rights apply equally to all citizens as well as foreigners, but courts often failed to protect or observe these rights. The law presumes defendants to be innocent until proven guilty, but authorities often ignored this, placing the burden on the defendant to prove innocence.

Defendants generally have the right to a public trial, but politically motivated trials were often held in secret, citing exceptions for crimes involving "state security" or "extraordinary circumstances." The law does not provide for jury trials. Almost all cases concluded in less than one day and were not open to the press.

The law provides the accused with the right to be present during trial and requires that defendants be represented by an attorney at trial, at public expense if necessary. Defendants' attorneys can cross-examine state witnesses and present witnesses and evidence on the defendants' behalf. The only attorneys licensed to practice in criminal courts are attorneys who work for state collective law offices.

Criteria for admitting evidence was often arbitrary and discriminatory. According to numerous reports, prosecutors routinely introduced irrelevant or unreliable evidence to prove intent or testimony about the revolutionary credentials of a defendant.

Defense attorneys have the right to review the investigation files of a defendant, but not if the charges involve "crimes against the security of the state." In these cases defense attorneys are not allowed access until charges have been filed. Many detainees, especially political detainees, reported that their attorneys had difficulties accessing their files due to administrative obstacles.

In trials of defendants charged with potential dangerousness (see section 1.d.), the state must show only that the defendant has "proclivity" for crime, so an actual criminal act need not have occurred. Penalties can be up to four years in prison. Authorities normally applied this law to prostitutes, alcoholics, young persons who refused to report to work centers, and repeat offenders of laws restricting change of domicile, as well as to political activists who participated in public protests.

The law recognizes the right of appeal in municipal courts but limits it in provincial courts to cases involving lengthy prison terms or the death penalty.

Political Prisoners and Detainees

The government continued to deny holding any political prisoners but refused access to its jails by international humanitarian organizations and the United Nations.

On December 17, the government committed to releasing 53 "prisoners of interest," considered political prisoners by outside observers. At least 10 of the 53 prisoners were released by the end of the year, though some may have been released with conditions, including travel restrictions. While the announcement was made on December 17, some prisoners were released as early as August. Some of the individuals released were later subject to arbitrary short-term detentions when participating in peaceful assemblies and for freely expressing their views.

Accurate numbers of peaceful political prisoners were difficult to determine. Lack of governmental transparency and systemic violations of due process rights obfuscated the true nature of criminal prosecutions and investigations, allowing government authorities to prosecute and sentence human rights activists for criminal violations or "dangerousness." The government used the designation of "CR" (counterrevolutionary) for inmates deemed to be opponents to the regime, but it did not release those numbers. The government continued to deny access to its jails to independent monitors who could help determine the size of the political prisoner population. At least two independent organizations provided estimates on the number of political prisoners being held in prisons. These groups were closely monitored by the government and often faced harassment from state police.

Political prisoners reported being held in isolation for extended periods, even years. Political prisoners were not given the same protections as other prisoners or detainees. In particular they were frequently denied early parole or transfers to lower-security facilities that were commonly granted to other prisoners. Political prisoners also were frequently denied access to home visits, prison classes, telephone calls, and, on occasion, family visits.

Civil Judicial Procedures and Remedies

Although it is possible to seek judicial remedies through civil courts for violations of administrative determinations, lawyers noted that general procedural and bureaucratic inefficiencies often delayed or undermined the enforcement of both administrative determinations and civil court orders. Civil courts, like all courts in the country, lacked an independence and impartiality as well as effective procedural guarantees. No courts allowed claimants to bring lawsuits seeking remedies for human rights violations.

F. Arbitrary Interference with Privacy, Family, Home, or Correspondence

The constitution protects citizens' privacy rights in their homes and correspondence, and police must have a warrant signed by a prosecutor or magistrate before entering or conducting a search. Nevertheless, the government routinely and systematically monitored correspondence and communications between citizens, tracked their movements, and entered homes without legal authority and with impunity. Police searched homes and seized personal goods without the legally required documentation.

In July security forces entered the home of Jorge Luis Perez Garcia "Antunez" without providing legal documentation showing purpose for entering. Security forces struck Antunez and his wife and confiscated documents, including visas, and personal items. Security forces also damaged their furniture and other personal items.

The Ministry of Interior employed a system of informants and block committees, known as Committees for the Defense of the Revolution, to monitor government opponents and report on their activities. Agents from the ministry's General Directorate for State Security subjected foreign journalists, visiting foreign officials, academics, and businesspeople - as well as diplomats - to frequent surveillance, including electronic surveillance.

The CP is the only legally recognized political party, and the government actively suppressed attempts to form other parties. The government encouraged mass political mobilization and favored citizens who actively participated (see section 2.b.).

Family members of government employees who leave international work missions without official permission at times faced government harassment or lost employment, access to education, or other public benefits.

Respect for Civil Liberties

A. Freedom of Speech and Press

The constitution provides for freedom of speech and press only insofar as it "conforms to the aims of socialist society." Laws banning criticism of government leaders and distribution of antigovernment propaganda carry penalties ranging from three months to 15 years in prison.

Freedom of Speech: The government had little tolerance for public criticism of government officials or programs. Public debate of issues considered politically sensitive was limited. During the year state security continuously harassed the organizers of independent fora for debates on cultural and social topics to force them to stop discussing issues deemed controversial. Forum organizers reported assaults by state security, video surveillance installed outside the venue, and detention of panelists and guests on the day they were expected to appear. On several occasions security agents blocked access to personal cell phones and sent false text messages ostensibly from the organizers to program participants to disrupt events.

During the year some religious groups reported greater latitude to express their opinions during sermons and at religious gatherings, although most members of the clergy continued to exercise self-censorship. Religious leaders in some cases criticized the government, its policies, and even the country's leadership without reprisals. The Catholic Church operated a cultural center in Havana that hosted debates featuring participants voicing different opinions about the country's future, at which well-known dissidents were allowed to participate. Some Protestant leaders claimed they were unable to hold debates and openly criticize the government without reprisals. In September the Catholic Church published a pastoral plan for 2014-20 entitled "On the Road to Emmaus," which offered a three-part reflection on the social and political reality on the Church in Cuba and expressed direct criticisms of the government.

Press Freedoms: The government directly owned all print and broadcast media outlets and all widely available sources of information, and it did not allow editorial independence. News and information programming was nearly uniform across all outlets, with the exception of broadcasts of Venezuelan government news programming. The government also controlled nearly all publications and press prints, and the CP must give prior approval for printing of nearly all publications and censored public screenings and performances. The government also limited the importation of printed materials. Foreign correspondents in Cuba had limited access. They were often officially denied interviews and access to gather facts for stories. Despite meeting government vetting requirements, official journalists who reported on sensitive subjects did so at personal risk. *Granma* correspondent Jose Antonio Torres remained in prison at the end of the year; he was sentenced in 2012 to 14 years' imprisonment on charges of espionage for articles he wrote.

Independent journalists faced sustained government harassment, including detention and physical abuse. In December, however, the government accredited an independent journalist affiliated with the independent news organization *14yMedio* to cover an international film festival in Havana.

The Catholic Church received permission to broadcast Christmas and Easter messages as well as religious ceremonies on other holidays on state-run television stations. The Council of Churches, the government-recognized Protestant umbrella organization, was authorized to host a monthly 20-minute radio broadcast.

Violence and Harassment: The government does not recognize independent journalism and subjected some independent journalists to detentions, harassment, equipment seizures, and imprisonment. On June 13, several members of the independent civil action brigade, including independent journalists, were arrested after protesting in Havana for human rights. On September 6, state police arrested Bernardo Arevalo Padron, an independent journalist based in Cienfuegos, because of his reporting for the opposition newspaper *El Cubano Libre, de Hoy*. He was threatened with a four-year jail sentence if he did not leave the country. Several reporters from the organization Hablemos Press, a society for independent journalists, were the targets of threats, including Jose Leonel Silva Guerrero, who was briefly detained and threatened with reprisals against his family if he did not stop working as the Hablemos Press correspondent in Holguin. On June 11, security agents repeatedly punched and stabbed with a pen Roberto de Jesus Guerra, director of Hablemos Press, as he was walking through a Havana residential neighborhood. He suffered a broken nose and a torn ligament.

Censorship or Content Restrictions: The law prohibits distribution of printed materials considered "counterrevolutionary" or critical of the government. Foreign newspapers or magazines were generally unavailable. Distribution of material with political content, interpreted broadly to include the Universal Declaration of Human Rights, foreign newspapers, and independent information on public health, was not allowed and resulted in harassment and, at times, detention. Doctors and religious officials reported government officials threatened and warned them not to discuss public health issues, including outbreaks of diseases, such as cholera, dengue, and chikungunya.

The government sometimes barred independent libraries from receiving materials from abroad and seized materials donated by foreign governments, religious organizations, and individuals. Government officials also confiscated or destroyed cameras and telephones of individuals to prevent them from distributing photographs and videos deemed objectionable, such as those taken during arrests and detentions.

Internet Freedom

There were significant government restrictions on access to the internet and widespread reports that the government monitored without appropriate legal authority the limited e-mail and internet chat rooms and browsing that were permitted. The government controlled all internet access, with the exception of extremely limited facilities provided by a few diplomatic missions and limited but increasing black market facilities.

While the International Telecommunication Union reported that 26 percent of citizens used the internet in 2013, in many cases this access was limited to a domestic intranet that offered only e-mail or highly restricted access to the World Wide Web. Other international groups reported lower internet penetration, with 3 to 5 percent of the population having access to open internet.

The government selectively granted internet access to certain sectors, consisting mostly of government officials, established professionals, some professors and students, journalists, and artists. Others could access limited e-mail and internet services through government-sponsored "youth clubs" or small internet centers approved and regulated by the Ministry for Information, Technology, and Communications. Users were required to purchase prepaid cards and provide personal information in order to access the internet in these centers.

In 2013 the government expanded internet access to encompass 334 computer terminals in 118 computer centers throughout the country. Early in the year, the government-owned telephone company, ETECSA, began offering a limited phone-based e-mail service - but no web access - to its cellular customers. Authorities reviewed the browsing history of users, reviewed and censored e-mail, employed internet search filters, and blocked access to websites considered objectionable. Access cost approximately 4.50 convertible pesos (CUC) ($4.50) per hour, well beyond the means of many citizens, whose average official income was approximately 19 CUC ($19) per month.

While the law does not set specific penalties for unauthorized internet use, it is illegal to own a satellite dish that would provide uncensored internet access. Cuban authorities restricted the importation of wireless routers and reportedly actively targeted private wireless access points and confiscated equipment.

The use of encryption software and transfer of encrypted files are also illegal. Despite poor access, harassment, and infrastructure challenges, a growing number of citizens maintained blogs where they often posted opinions critical of the government, with help from foreign supporters who often built and maintained the blog sites. The government blocked local access to most of these blogs. In addition a small but growing number of citizens could use Twitter, Facebook, Instagram, and other social media channels to report independently on developments in the country, including observations critical of the government. Like other government critics, bloggers faced sustained government harassment, including detention and physical abuse.

Foreigners could buy internet access cards from the national telecommunications provider and use hotel business centers, where internet access could be purchased only in hard currency. Access usually cost between five and 10 CUC ($5 to $10) an hour, a rate well beyond the means of most citizens. Citizens usually could purchase internet access at the national telecommunications provider and use hotel business centers, but they were occasionally prohibited from purchasing access.

Human rights activists reported frequent government monitoring and disruption of cell phone and landline services prior to planned events or key anniversaries related to human rights. ETECSA often disconnected service for human rights organizers in order to disrupt their planned activities.

Academic Freedom and Cultural Events

The government restricted academic freedom and controlled the curriculum at all schools and universities, emphasizing the importance of reinforcing "revolutionary ideology" and "discipline." Most academics refrained from meeting with foreigners, including diplomats, journalists, and visiting scholars, without prior government approval and the presence of a government monitor. Those permitted to travel abroad were aware that their actions, if deemed politically unfavorable, could negatively affect them and their relatives back home. During the year some religious educational centers were allowed greater space to operate.

Outspoken artists and academics faced some harassment and criticism orchestrated by the government. On December 30, authorities detained artist Tania Bruguera and approximately 60 others to prevent Bruguera from staging an open mic performance in the Plaza de la Revolution, a prominent plaza in Havana. Authorities also threatened dozens of other activists with detention or house arrest to prevent them from attending the event. All of those detained were released within three days.

Independent movie theatres, which had shown international films and were common in urban areas, were closed by the government in late 2013 and remained closed.

Public libraries required citizens to complete a registration process before access to books or information was granted. Citizens could be denied access if they could not demonstrate a need to visit a particular library. Libraries required a letter of permission from an employer or academic institution for access to censored, sensitive, or rare books and materials. Religious institutions organized small libraries. Independent libraries, however, remained illegal but continued to exist and faced harassment and intimidation. On August 5, authorities accused the director of an independent library, Rene Rouco Machin, of spreading enemy propaganda, incarcerated him, and then beat him.

B. FREEDOM OF PEACEFUL ASSEMBLY AND ASSOCIATION

FREEDOM OF ASSEMBLY

Although the constitution grants a limited right of assembly, the right is subject to the requirement that it may not be "exercised against the existence and objectives of the socialist state." The law requires citizens to request authorization for organized meetings of three or more persons, and failure to do so carries a penalty of up to three months in prison and a fine. In practice, however, some gatherings were tolerated. Religious groups reported the ability to gather without registering or facing sanctions.

Independent activists faced greater obstacles, and state security forces often suppressed attempts to assemble, even when these were in private dwellings and in small numbers. This trend was particularly pronounced in the eastern part of the country. For example, on August 24, the political opposition group UNPACU reported that state security forces forcibly detained more than 130 activists in Santiago de Cuba during a peaceful protest.

The government continued to organize mobs to assault and disperse those who assembled peacefully. Participants arrived in government-owned buses or were recruited by government officials from nearby workplaces or schools. Participants arrived and departed in shifts, chanted revolutionary slogans, sang revolutionary songs, and verbally taunted the targets of the protest for hours. The targets of this harassment were at times physically assaulted or suffered property damage. Government security officials at the scene, often present in overwhelming numbers, did not arrest those who physically attacked the victims or respond to victims' complaints and instead frequently orchestrated the activities. Reports indicated that officials took direct part in physical assaults.

The government did not grant permission to independent demonstrators or approve public meetings by human rights groups or others critical of any government activity. While the government tolerated the Damas de Blanco's Sunday marches after Mass in the suburbs of Havana, government-organized mobs often broke up marches planned by the Damas in other locations, particularly in Matanzas Province. State security forces also aggressively and arbitrarily detained women to prevent them from marching, sometimes injuring the women in the process. On multiple occasions security forces forced peaceful political protesters into state security vehicles, drove out of town, and released the protesters in remote areas. The government also restricted free assembly by preventing citizens from leaving their homes under threat of arrest. Plainclothes police officers posted themselves in the vicinity of the house to ensure that the citizen could not leave until a public event such as a concert, memorial service, march, or political demonstration was over.

FREEDOM OF ASSOCIATION

The government routinely denied its citizens freedom of association and did not recognize independent associations. The constitution proscribes any political organization not officially recognized. Authorities have never recognized an independent human rights organization, but a number of independent organizations, including opposition political parties and professional associations, operated as NGOs without legal recognition.

Recognized churches, the Roman Catholic humanitarian organization Caritas, the Freemason movement, and a number of fraternal and professional organizations were the only associations legally permitted to function outside the formal structure of the state, the CP, and government-organized organizations. These groups are under the supervision of the CP's Office of Religious Affairs, which has the authority to deny permits for religious activities and exerted pressure on church leaders.

Nonreligious groups must register through the Ministry of Justice to receive official recognition. Authorities continued to ignore applications for legal recognition from new groups, including several new religious groups as well as women's rights and gay rights organizations, thereby subjecting members to potential charges of illegal association.

The government continued to afford preferential treatment for those who took an active part in CP activities and mass demonstrations in support of the government, especially when awarding valued public benefits, such as admissions to higher education, fellowships, and job opportunities.

c. Freedom of Religion

See the Department of State's *International Religious Freedom Report* at www.state.gov/religiousfreedomreport/.

d. Freedom of Movement, Internally Displaced Persons, Protection of Refugees, and Stateless Persons

There were restrictions on freedom of movement within the country, foreign travel, and migration with the right of return. The government also limited internal migration from rural areas to Havana.

In-country Movement: Although the constitution allows all citizens to travel anywhere within the country, changes of residence to Havana were heavily restricted. The local housing commission and provincial government authorities must authorize any change of residence. Persons living in a location without authorization from these bodies may be fined and sent back to their legally authorized place of residence. There were reports of persons who lived in Havana illegally without access to food rations, local identification cards, and other social services. Police occasionally threatened to prosecute for "dangerousness" anyone who returned to Havana after having been expelled. A 2011 decision allowing "illegally present" family members of registered Havana residents to legalize their status to Havana did not improve circumstances for citizens who did not have family members registered as Havana residents.

The law permits authorities to bar an individual from a certain area within the country, or to restrict an individual to a certain area, for up to 10 years. Under this provision authorities may internally exile any person whose presence in a given location is considered "socially dangerous." Some dissidents reported they were prevented from leaving their home provinces or detained by authorities and returned to their homes. One government employee was reportedly fired from his work because of independent political activism but then reinstated and assigned to a different job in a remote area.

Foreign Travel: In January 2013 the government eased restrictions on both migration and temporary foreign travel by eliminating previously required exit permits and replacing them with a system under which citizens are eligible to travel after applying for a two-year passport. The government continued to require several classes of citizens to obtain permission to travel, including highly specialized medical personnel, military or security personnel, many government officials, including academics, and some former political prisoners or well-known activists. On January 26, Manuel Cuesta Morua was one of dozens of activists arrested while organizing an alternative forum to the Community of Latin American and Caribbean States (CELAC) summit. After four days of confinement, the government released him with the charge of "spreading false news against international peace." The government imposed an injunction prohibiting travel abroad pending the conclusion of legal proceedings. In late November the government lifted the travel ban on Cuesta Morua with no explanation.

There were reports of academic officials denied foreign travel permission by the government because of their public statements that CP authorities deemed "unhelpful." Several former political prisoners on supervised release were prevented from traveling.

Emigration and Repatriation: Individuals seeking to migrate legally said they also faced police interrogation, fines, house searches, harassment, and intimidation, including involuntary dismissal from employment. Government employees who applied to migrate legally to the United States sometimes were fired from their jobs when their plans became known. Some family members of government employees who immigrated to the United States lost public benefits or were denied passports to travel and join their family members in the United States.

The law provides for imprisonment of up to three years or a fine of 12 to 80 CUC ($12 to $80) for unauthorized departures from the island, the overwhelming majority of which were by sea. Nonetheless, most persons caught attempting unauthorized departures were detained for no more than two to three weeks and fined. In the case of military or police defectors or those traveling with children, the punishment could be more severe. Jail terms were also more common for persons attempting to flee to the United States through the Guantanamo U.S. Naval Station.

Under the terms of the 1994 U.S.-Cuba Migration Accord, the government agreed not to prosecute or retaliate against migrants returned from international or U.S. waters, or from the U.S. Naval Station at Guantanamo, after attempting to emigrate illegally if they had not committed a separate criminal offense. The government prevented independent monitoring trips of repatriated Cubans outside of Havana. Some would-be migrants alleged harassment and discrimination such as fines, expulsion from school, and job loss, and others reported more severe punishment. Rolando Guerra, brother of civil society activist Roberto de Jesus Guerra, who was incarcerated after his repatriation to Cuba in 2012 on charges of attempting an unauthorized departure, remained in a maximum-security prison ward, without trial.

PROTECTION OF REFUGEES

Access to Asylum: The constitution provides for the granting of asylum to individuals persecuted for their ideals or actions involving a number of specified political grounds. The government has no formal mechanism to process asylum for foreign nationals.

Temporary Protection: On the small number of cases of persons seeking asylum, the government worked with the Office of the UN High Commissioner for Refugees and other humanitarian organizations to provide protection and assistance, pending third-country settlement. In addition the government allowed foreign students who feared persecution in their home countries to remain in the country after the end of their studies, until their claims could be investigated.

Respect for Political Rights: The Right of Citizens to Change Their Government

Citizens do not have the ability to change their government through the right to vote in free and fair elections, and the government retaliated against those who sought peaceful political change.

Elections and Political Participation

Recent Elections: All 612 candidates in the February 2013 National Assembly elections were prescreened by government-run bodies and, once approved by the CP, ran for office uncontested. The president is selected by the National Assembly.

Political Parties and Political Participation: All candidates for office were preapproved by government-run commissions, which rejected independent candidacies without explanation or the right of appeal. All 612 candidates elected in February 2013 and serving in 2014 were either CP members or affiliated and approved by the CP. The government routinely used propaganda campaigns in the state-owned media to criticize opponents.

In the 2012 municipal elections, scores of candidates were summarily refused the opportunity to run. Some independent candidates for municipal positions managed to run, although they were all defeated in nonsecret voting.

Participation of Women and Minorities: There were no official restrictions on women or minorities, and the government actively promoted participation of both in government. President (and CP first secretary) Castro highlighted that the composition of the Central Committee included 47 women (48 percent) and 36 Afro-Cubans (31 percent). The government reported the composition of the National Assembly as approximately 63 percent white, 20 percent black, and 17 percent mixed race.

CORRUPTION AND LACK OF TRANSPARENCY IN GOVERNMENT

The law provides criminal penalties for corruption, and the government was highly sensitive to corruption allegations and often conducted anticorruption crackdowns.

Corruption: All government agencies, especially the Office of the General Comptroller and the Ministry of Interior, were tasked with combating corruption, including through prosecution of government officials, although official media was actively discouraged from investigating corruption.

The law provides for three to eight years' imprisonment for "illegal enrichment" by authorities or government employees. Government officials were not subject to special financial disclosure laws.

In September authorities tried and convicted a prominent foreign businessman of corruption, including bribery, fraud, and tax evasion. The company alleged the government presented weak evidence and denounced the lack of due process in the case. They publicly alleged that they engaged only in common business practices and that the corruption trials were actually hostile takeovers of their businesses.

There were widespread reports of police corruption. Multiple sources reported that when searching homes and vehicles, police sometimes took the owner's belongings or sought bribes in place of fines or arrests. There were numerous reports of law enforcement and other official corruption in enforcement of a myriad of economic restrictions and government services.

Financial Disclosure: The law does not require appointed and elected officials to disclose their assets.

Public Access to Information: The law provides for public access to government information, but requests for information were routinely rejected. The government engaged in limited public outreach activities. It did not conduct training of public officials to encourage effective use of the law granting public access to government information.

GOVERNMENTAL ATTITUDE REGARDING INTERNATIONAL AND NONGOVERNMENTAL INVESTIGATION OF ALLEGED VIOLATIONS OF HUMAN RIGHTS

The government did not recognize domestic human rights groups or permit them to function legally. Several human rights organizations continued to function outside the law, including the CCDHRN, UNPACU, the Christian Liberation Movement, Assembly to Promote Civil Society, and Lawton Foundation for Human Rights. The government subjected domestic human rights advocates to intimidation, harassment, and periodic short-term detentions.

No officially recognized, independent NGOs monitored human rights. The government refused to recognize or meet with any unauthorized NGOs that monitored human rights. Furthermore, there were multiple reports of explicit government harassment of individuals who met with unauthorized NGOs.

The United Nations or Other International Bodies: The government continued to deny international human rights organizations, the United Nations, and the International Committee of the Red Cross access to prisoners and detainees.

In January 2013 the UN Working Group on Arbitrary Detention published a report on the detention of foreign development worker Alan Gross and found his detention to be arbitrary. The government rejected this determination, but on December 17, authorities released Gross and he left the island after a five-year incarceration.

DISCRIMINATION, SOCIETAL ABUSES, AND TRAFFICKING IN PERSONS

The constitution prohibits discrimination based on race, gender, disability, or social status. Racial discrimination, however, occurred frequently in all levels of society, mostly directed at the Afro-Cuban population.

WOMEN

Rape and Domestic Violence: The law criminalizes rape, including spousal rape, and the government enforced the law. Penalties for rape are at least four years' imprisonment, with longer prison terms or death as possible penalties, depending on the circumstances of the rape. The government released some statistics on 2013 arrests, prosecutions, and convictions for violence against women and sexual acts against women and children.

The law does not recognize domestic violence as a distinct category of violence but prohibits threats and violence, including those associated with domestic violence. Penalties for domestic violence are covered by the laws against assault and range from fines to prison sentences of varying lengths, depending on the severity of the offense.

To raise awareness about domestic violence, the government continued to carry out media campaigns. Official television, radio, and print media occasionally discussed issues pertaining to women, including domestic violence. In addition a few government-organized organizations held conferences and worked with local communities to improve services. The UN Children's Fund reported that the government ran counseling centers for women and children in most municipalities, with staff trained in assisting victims of abuse.

Female Genital Mutilation/Cutting (FGM/C): No law prohibits FGM/C, but no evidence indicated the existence of the practice.

Sexual Harassment: The law provides penalties for sexual harassment, with potential sentences of three months' to five years' imprisonment. The government did not release any statistics on arrests, prosecutions, or convictions for offenses related to sexual harassment during the year. Civil society groups reported sexual harassment was underreported. NGOs reported security forces used sexual harassment as a means of repression for women activists in detention.

Reproductive Rights: Couples and individuals have the right to decide the number, spacing, and timing of children; had the information and means to do so; and have the right to attain reproductive health services, free from discrimination, coercion, and violence. Past anecdotal reports noted instances of forced abortion to maintain artificially low infant mortality rates, but no reports of that practice surfaced during the year. Access to information on modern contraception and skilled health attendance during pregnancy, at delivery, and in postpartum care were available, but access to information and contraception to prevent the spread of HIV/AIDS was limited. Individuals had access to emergency health care, including services for the management of complications arising from abortion.

Discrimination: The law accords women and men equal rights and responsibilities regarding marriage, divorce, raising children, maintaining the home, and pursuing a career. The law grants working mothers preferential access to goods and services. The law provides for equal pay for equal work, but there were reports that women are restricted from certain occupations deemed hazardous to their physical or psychological health.

CHILDREN

Birth Registration: Citizenship is normally derived by birth within the country's territory, and births were generally registered promptly. Those who immigrate abroad and have children must request a Cuban passport for the child before re-entering Cuba. Children born outside of Cuba to parents on official business are granted Cuban citizenship.

Child Abuse: According to the government, there was no societal pattern of child abuse. The government operated 174 Guidance Centers for Women and Families, or Casas de Orientacion a la Mujer y la Familia, charged with providing family counseling services. In 2013, the latest year from which data is available, these centers reported they provided assistance to 857 individuals harmed by intrafamilial violence. Nonetheless, some lawyers noted that the country's circa 1975 family code should be modernized to reflect societal changes and new approaches in the legal treatment of violence in families, including child abuse.

Early and Forced Marriage: The legal minimum age of consent for marriage is 18. Marriage for girls as young as 14 and for boys as young as 16 is permitted with parental consent.

Female Genital Mutilation/Cutting (FGM/C): No law prohibits FGM/C, but no evidence indicated existence of the practice.

Sexual Exploitation of Children: Prostitution is legal for 16 year olds and older. While there were numerous reports of underage prostitution, there were no reliable statistics available regarding its extent. In November, however, the government reported that 2,231 children were victims of sexual abuse in 2013. The minimum age of consent for consensual sex is 16. There is no statutory rape law, although penalties for rape increase as the age of the victim decreases. The penal code imposes seven to 15 years' imprisonment for involving minors under 16 in pornographic acts. The punishment may increase to 20 or 30 years or death under aggravating circumstances. The proposal to participate in such acts is punishable with two to five years' imprisonment. The law does not criminalize the possession of pornography, but it punishes the production or circulation of any kind of obscene graphic material with three months' to one year's imprisonment and a fine. The offer, provision, or sale of obscene or pornographic material to minors under 16 is punishable with two to five years in prison. International trafficking of minors is punishable with seven to 15 years' imprisonment.

The government, in cooperation with the British government and a British NGO, maintained centers in Havana, Santiago de Cuba, and Santa Clara for the treatment of child sexual abuse victims. The centers employed modern treatment techniques, including the preparation of children to be witnesses in criminal prosecutions.

International Child Abductions: The country is not a party to the 1980 Hague Convention on the Civil Aspects of Child Abduction.

ANTI-SEMITISM

There were between 1,000 and 1,500 members of the Jewish community. There were no reports of anti-Semitic acts.

TRAFFICKING IN PERSONS

See the Department of State's *Trafficking in Persons Report* at www.state.gov/j/tip/rls/tiprpt/.

PERSONS WITH DISABILITIES

There is no known law prohibiting discrimination against persons with disabilities in employment, education, access to health care, or the provision of other state services. A Ministry of Labor and Social Security resolution accords persons with disabilities the right to equal employment opportunities and equal pay for equal work. There was no information available, however, on compliance with this resolution. There are laws recommending that buildings, communications facilities, air travel, and other transportation services accommodate persons with disabilities, but these facilities and services were rarely accessible to persons with disabilities, and information for persons with disabilities was limited.

The Special Education Division of the Ministry of Education is responsible for the education and training of children with disabilities. Children with disabilities attended school; there were no known patterns of discriminatory abuse in educational facilities or in mental health facilities during the year. The Ministry of Labor and Social Security is in charge of the Employment Program for Persons with Disabilities.

National/Racial/Ethnic Minorities

Although the government's declared policy actively favored racial integration and inclusiveness, Afro-Cubans often suffered racial discrimination, including disproportionate stops for identity checks and searches, and some were subject to racial epithets while undergoing unlawful beatings at the hands of security agents related to political activity. Afro-Cubans also reported employment discrimination, particularly in sought-after positions within the tourism industry and at high levels within the government (see section 7.d.). Afro-Cubans were represented disproportionately in neighborhoods with the worst housing conditions and were economically disadvantaged.

Acts of Violence, Discrimination, and Other Abuses Based on Sexual Orientation and Gender Identity

The law prohibits discrimination based on sexual orientation in employment, housing, statelessness, or access to education or health care. Nonetheless, societal discrimination based on sexual orientation or gender identity persisted.

Mariela Castro, President Castro's daughter, headed the national Center for Sexual Education and continued to be outspoken in promoting the rights of lesbian, gay, bisexual, and transgender (LGBT) persons. Throughout the year the government promoted the rights of LGBT persons, including nonviolence and nondiscrimination in regional and international fora. In May the government sponsored a march and an extensive program of events to commemorate the International Day Against Homophobia and Transphobia. Nonetheless, nongovernmental rights activists asserted the government had not done enough to stop harassment of LGBT persons. Several unrecognized NGOs promoted LGBT issues and faced government criticism, not for their promotion of LGBT issues, but for their independence from official government institutions.

HIV and AIDS Social Stigma

There were reports that some persons with HIV/AIDS suffered job discrimination (see section 7.d.). The government operated four prisons exclusively for inmates with HIV/AIDS. Some inmates were serving sentences for "propagating an epidemic." Special diets and medications for HIV patients were routinely unavailable. Several NGOs lamented that contraceptives and information to prevent the spread of HIV/AIDS was limited.

WORKER RIGHTS

A. Freedom of Association and the Right to Collective Bargaining

The law, including related regulations and statutes, severely restricts worker rights by recognizing only the CP-controlled Workers' Central Union of Cuba (CTC) as the paramount trade union confederation. All trade groups must belong to the CTC to operate legally. The law does not provide for the right to strike. The law also does not provide for collective bargaining, instead setting up a complicated process for reaching collective agreements. The International Labor Organization continued to raise concerns regarding the trade union monopoly of the CTC, the prohibition on the right to strike, and restrictions to collective bargaining and agreements, including that government authorities and CTC officials had the final say on all such agreements.

The government continued to prevent the formation of independent trade unions in all sectors. The CP chose CTC's leaders. The CTC's principal responsibility was to manage government relations with the workforce. The CTC does not bargain collectively, promote worker rights, or advocate for the right to strike. The CTC took a lead role in disseminating information regarding the government's planned large-scale layoffs of government workers and in defending the government's decision to do so.

According to government statistics, approximately 476,000 workers were self-employed during the year, an increase of 12 percent from 2013.

Several small independent labor organizations operated without legal recognition, including the National Independent Workers' Confederation of Cuba, the National Independent Laborer Confederation of Cuba, and the Joint Council of Workers of Cuba; together they comprise the Coalition of Independent Unions of Cuba. These organizations continued to be subjected to police harassment and infiltration by government agents and had a limited capacity to represent workers effectively or work on their behalf.

The government can determine that a worker is "unfit" to work, resulting in job loss and the denial of job opportunities. Persons were deemed unfit because of their political beliefs, including their refusal to join the official union, and for trying to depart the country illegally. Professionals who expressed interest in emigrating were also penalized.

B. PROHIBITION OF FORCED OR COMPULSORY LABOR

The law does not appear to prohibit forced labor explicitly. The law prohibits unlawful imprisonment, coercion, and extortion, with penalties ranging from fines to imprisonment, but there was no evidence that these provisions were used to prosecute forced labor cases.

Compulsory military service of young men was occasionally completed by assignment to an economic entity controlled by the military or assignment to other government services.

The government continued to use some high school students in rural areas to harvest agricultural products (also see section 7.c.).

Also see the Department of State's *Trafficking in Persons Report* at www.state.gov/j/tip/rls/tiprpt/.

C. PROHIBITION OF CHILD LABOR AND MINIMUM AGE FOR EMPLOYMENT

The legal minimum working age is 17, although the labor code permits the employment of children ages 15 and 16 to obtain training or fill labor shortages. The labor code does not permit children ages 15 and 16 to work more than seven hours per day or 40 hours per week or on holidays. Children ages 13 to 18 cannot work in specified hazardous occupations, such as mining, or at night.

There were no known government programs to prevent child labor or remove children from such labor. Antitruancy programs, however, helped ensure that children were in school and not in the labor market. Inspections and penalties were adequate to enforce the law, and it was rare that children under 17 worked. The use of minors in forced labor, drug trafficking, prostitution, pornography, or organ trade is punishable by seven to 15 years' incarceration.

The government used some high school students in rural areas to harvest agricultural products for government cooperatives during peak harvest time. Student participants were not paid but received school credit and favorable recommendations towards university admission. Failure to participate without an excused absence reportedly could result in unfavorable grades or university recommendations, although students were reportedly able to participate in other activities (instead of the harvest) to support their application for university admission.

D. Discrimination with Respect to Employment or Occupation

In December 2013 the National Assembly approved changes to the labor code, which include prohibiting workplace discrimination based on skin color, gender, religious belief, sexual orientation, nationality, "or any other distinction harmful to human dignity." There was no information available on government enforcement of these provisions during the year. The government failed to pass legislation presented during the year that would address discrimination against LGBT persons, including pushing for workplace discrimination protections, antihomophobia demonstrations, and laws for better treatment of transgender individuals.

Discrimination in employment and occupation occurred with respect to persons with HIV and members of the Afro-Cuban population. Leaders within the Afro-Cuban community noted that some Afro-Cubans could not get jobs in sectors such as tourism and hospitality because they were "too dark." The Afro-Cuban leaders explained that jobs in sectors that deal with tourists were filled with fairer-skinned Cubans and were often among the best-paying jobs available. Afro-Cubans were more frequently given menial jobs including cleaning and garbage disposal that excluded them from close contact with tourists, a major source of hard currency.

E. Acceptable Conditions of Work

The monthly minimum wage was fixed at 225 pesos (nine dollars). The minimum wage requirement does not apply to the small nonstate sector. The government supplemented the minimum wage with free education, subsidized medical care (daily pay is reduced by 40 percent after the third day of a hospital stay), housing, and some food. Even with subsidies the government acknowledged that the average wage of 471 non-convertible pesos ($19) per month did not provide a reasonable standard of living.

The standard workweek is 44 hours, with shorter workweeks in hazardous occupations, such as mining. The law provides workers with a weekly minimum 24-hour rest period and 24 days of paid annual holidays. These standards apply to state workers as well as to the small nonstate sector (but not to the self-employed). The law does not provide for premium pay for overtime or prohibit obligatory overtime but generally caps the number of overtime hours at 12 per week or 160 per year. The law provides little grounds for a worker to refuse to work overtime. Refusal to work overtime can result in a notation in the employee's official work history that could imperil subsequent requests for vacation time. The Ministry of Labor has the authority to establish different overtime caps as needed. Compensation for overtime is paid in cash at the regular hourly rate or in additional rest time, particularly for workers directly linked to production or services, and it does not apply to management.

The government sets workplace safety standards, although such standards were outdated. The Ministry of Labor enforced minimum wage and hours of work standards through offices at the national, provincial, and municipal levels, but the government lacked mechanisms to enforce occupational safety and health standards. There was no confirmed information available about the number of labor inspectors. Reports suggested that there were very few inspectors and that health and safety standards frequently were ignored.

Workers complained that overtime compensation was either not paid or not paid in a timely manner. The government maintained the number of trades that could be plied privately (201) and allowed the self-employed to hire labor. Despite criminal penalties for doing so, a significant number of workers participated in the informal economy. Foreign companies operated in a limited number of sectors, such as hotels, tourism, and mining. Such companies operated on the basis of a joint venture policy, in which the government contracted and paid company workers in pesos, an amount that was a small fraction of what the company remitted to the state for labor costs. Most formal employment was only through government employment agencies. Employers, including international businesses and organizations, were generally prohibited from contracting or paying workers directly, although many reportedly made supplemental payments under the table.

The independent and illegal Confederation of Independent Workers of Cuba reported some violations of health and safety laws at worksites throughout the country, including inadequate and poorly maintained equipment and protective gear. The CTC seldom informed workers of their rights and at times did not respond to or assist workers who complained about hazardous workplace conditions. Workers could not remove themselves from dangerous situations without jeopardizing their employment, and authorities did not effectively protect workers facing this dilemma.

FOREIGN RELATIONS

Cuba's once-ambitious foreign policy has been scaled back and redirected as a result of economic hardship and the end of the Cold War. Cuba aims to find new sources of trade, aid, and foreign investment and to promote opposition to U.S. policy, especially the trade embargo and the 1996 Libertad Act. Cuba has relations with over 160 countries and has civilian assistance workers--principally physicians and nurses--in more than 20 nations.

Since the end of Soviet backing, Cuba appears to have largely abandoned monetary support for guerrilla movements that typified its involvement in regional politics in Latin America and Africa, though it maintains relations with several guerrilla and terrorist groups and provides refuge for some of their members in Cuba. Cuba's support for Latin guerrilla movements, its Marxist-Leninist government, and its alignment with the U.S.S.R. led to its isolation in the hemisphere. Cuba is a member of the Organization of American States (OAS), although its present government has been excluded from participation since 1962 for incompatibility with the principles of the inter-American system. Cuba hosted the Non-Aligned Movement (NAM) summit in September 2006 and will hold the NAM presidency until 2009. In the context of the NAM and its ordinary diplomacy, Cuba has developed friendly relations with Iran, North Korea and other rogue states.

Throughout the 1970s and 1980s, Cuba expanded its military presence abroad, spending millions of dollars in exporting revolutions; deployments reached 50,000 troops in Angola, 24,000 in Ethiopia, 1,500 in Nicaragua, and hundreds more elsewhere. In Angola, Cuban troops, supported logistically by the U.S.S.R., backed the Popular Movement for the Liberation of Angola (MPLA) in its effort to take power after Portugal granted Angola its independence. Cuban forces played a key role in Ethiopia's war against Somalia and remained there in substantial numbers as a garrison force for a decade. Cubans served in a non-combat advisory role in Mozambique and the Congo. Cuba also used the Congo as a logistical support center for Cuba's Angola mission. In the late 1980s, Cuba began to pull back militarily. Cuba unilaterally removed its forces from

Ethiopia, met the timetable of the 1988 Angola-Namibia accords by completing the withdrawal of its forces from Angola before July 1991, and ended military assistance to Nicaragua following the Sandinistas' 1990 electoral defeat.

EU-Cuban diplomatic relations have suffered as a result of the March 2003 crackdown on dissidents. In June 2004, EU members imposed restrictive measures on Cuba including inviting dissidents to national day celebrations and suspending high-level meetings between EU members and the Cuban Government. In January 2005, though, the restrictions were suspended in an effort to re-engage the regime as a means of advancing the EU's policy of encouraging reform while preparing for the transition.

Spain is among the most important foreign investors in Cuba. The ruling Zapatero government continues Spain's longstanding policy of encouraging further investment and trade with Cuba. Cuba imports more goods from Spain (almost 13% of total imports) than from any other country. Spanish economic involvement with Cuba is exclusively centered on joint venture enterprises that provide financial benefit to the Cuban Government through state-owned firms. Spain's desire to provide support to its business community often impedes its willingness to pressure the Cuban Government on political reform and human rights issues.

Cuba's bilateral relationship with Venezuela has helped keep the Cuban economy afloat. The "Integral Cooperation Accord" signed by Fidel Castro and Venezuelan President Hugo Chavez in October 2000 laid the groundwork for a quasi-barter exchange of Venezuelan oil for Cuban goods and services that has since become a lifeline for Cuba. For Cuba, the benefits of the cooperation accord are subsidized petroleum and increased hard currency flows. The original agreement allowed for the sale, at market prices, of up to 53,000 barrels per day of crude oil and derivatives (diesel, gasoline, jet fuel, etc.) by PDVSA, Venezuela's state-owned petroleum company, to its Cuban counterpart, CUPET. The number of barrels of oil Venezuela began selling to Cuba has risen to over 90,000 barrels daily. Under the accord, PDVSA extended preferential payment terms to CUPET, including 90-day short-term financing instead of the 30 days offered to its other customers and, in lieu of a standard letter of credit backed by an international bank, PDVSA accepted IOUs from Cuba's Banco Nacional, the central banking entity responsible for servicing Havana's foreign debt. In August 2001, Venezuelan President Hugo Chavez amended the 2000 accord to allow Venezuela to compensate the Cuban Government in hard currency for any and all Cuban products and services originally intended as in-kind payment for Venezuelan oil. As a result, Cuban exports of goods and services to Venezuela climbed from $34 million in 2001 to more than $150 million in 2003. Venezuelan ministries are contracting with Cuba for everything from generic pharmaceuticals to pre-fabricated housing and dismantled sugar mill equipment. On April 28, 2005, Chavez and Castro signed 49 economic agreements in Havana, covering areas as diverse as oil, nickel, agriculture, furniture, shoes, textiles, toys, lingerie, tires, construction materials, electricity, transportation, health, and education. Venezuela is also committed to sending more than $400 million in various products duty free to Cuba and plans to open an office of state-owned commercial Venezuelan Industrial Bank (BIV) in Havana to finance imports and exports between the two countries, while Cuba will open an official Banco Exterior de Cuba in Caracas. Increased economic engagement along with the rapid growth in Cuban sales to Caracas has established Venezuela as one of the island's largest export markets.

A series of recent economic agreements between Cuba and China have strengthened trade between the two countries. Sino-Cuban trade totaled more than $525 million in 2004, according to China Customs statistics. This represents an increase of more than 47% over 2003. Most of China's aid involves in-kind supply of goods or technical assistance. During President Hu-Jintao's visit to Cuba in November 2004, China signed investment-related memorandums of understanding (MOUs) estimated at more than $500 million, according to press reports. If these MOUs are fully realized, they would represent a sharp increase in known Chinese investments in

Cuba. In addition to these MOUs, a number of commercial accords were signed at the first-ever Cuba-China Investment and Trade Forum. China also plans to invest approximately $500 million in a nickel operation in Moa in the eastern province of Holguin. According to the MOU, Cuba will own 51% of the enterprise and Chinese-owned Minmetals the remaining 49%. Chinese and Venezuelan economic support, including investment and direct aid, have given Cuba the space to eliminate many of the tentative open market reforms Cuba put in place during the depth of its mid-1990s economic crisis.

The Russian prime minister visited Cuba in October 2006, signaling a new effort to expand trade and investment, albeit financed by Russian credit. Russia set aside, for the moment, more than USD 20 billion in Soviet-era debt, restructured post-1991 debt, and extended a new credit line to Cuba. The new credit line is for USD 355 million repayable over 10 years at an interest rate of five percent. The new credit is conditioned in that it must be used to purchase Russian cars, trucks, planes, as well as to finance Cuban energy and transport infrastructure projects, including air navigation systems. Russia further agreed to restructure USD 166 million in debt accumulated since 1993. Both nations also signed an agreement on military equipment and technical services.

U.S.-CUBAN RELATIONS

Cuba and the United States restored diplomatic relations on July 20, 2015, which had been severed in 1961 during the Cold War. U.S. diplomatic representation in Cuba is handled by the United States Embassy in Havana, and there is a similar Cuban Embassy in Washington, D.C.. The United States, however, continues to maintain its commercial, economic, and financial embargo, which makes it illegal for U.S. corporations to do business with Cuba, although the U.S. President, Barack Obama, has called for the ending of the embargo but U.S. law requires congressional approval to end the embargo.

As the sway of the Spanish Empire over its possessions in the Americas was crushed in the 1820s as a result of the Spanish American wars of independence, only Cuba and Puerto Rico remained under Spanish rule until the Spanish–American War (1898) that resulted from the Cuban War of Independence. Under the Treaty of Paris, Cuba became a U.S. protectorate; the U.S. gained a position of economic and political dominance over the island, that persisted after it became formally independent in 1902.

Following the Cuban Revolution of 1959, bilateral relations deteriorated substantially. In 1961, the U.S. severed diplomatic ties with Cuba and began pursuing covert operations to topple the Communist regime. Moreover, the U.S. imposed and subsequently tightened a comprehensive set of restrictions and bans vis-à-vis the Cuban regime as retaliation for the nationalization of U.S. corporations' property by Cuba. Meanwhile, several organizations, including a nearly unanimous UN General Assembly, have called for "an end to the United States' decades-long economic, commercial and financial embargo against Cuba."

On December 17, 2014, U.S. President Barack Obama and Cuban President Raúl Castro announced the beginning of a process of normalizing relations between Cuba and the U.S., which media sources have named "the Cuban Thaw." Negotiated in secret in Canada and the Vatican City over preceding months, and with the assistance of Pope Francis, the agreement led to the lifting of some U.S. travel restrictions, fewer restrictions on remittances, U.S. banks access to the Cuban financial system, and the establishment of a U.S. embassy in Havana, which closed after Cuba became closely allied with the USSR in 1961. The countries' respective "interests sections" in one another's capitals were upgraded to embassies on July 20, 2015

AFTER THE COLD WAR

The Cold War ended with the collapse of the Soviet Union in the late 1980s and early 1990s, leaving Cuba without its major international sponsor. The ensuing years were marked by economic difficulty in Cuba, a time known as the Special Period. U.S. law allowed private humanitarian aid to Cuba for part of this time. However, the long standing U.S. embargo was reinforced in October 1992 by the Cuban Democracy Act (the "Torricelli Law") and in 1996 by the Cuban Liberty and Democracy Solidarity Act (known as the Helms-Burton Act). The 1992 act prohibited foreign-based subsidiaries of U.S. companies from trading with Cuba, travel to Cuba by U.S. citizens, and family remittances to Cuba. Sanctions could also be applied to non-U.S. companies trading with Cuba. As a result, multinational companies had to choose between Cuba and the U.S., the latter being a much larger market.

On February 24, 1996, two unarmed Cessna 337s flown by the group "Brothers to the Rescue" were shot down by Cuban Air Force MiG-29, killing three Cuban-Americans and one Cuban U.S. resident. The Cuban government claimed that the planes had entered into Cuban airspace.

Some veterans of CIA's 1961 Bay of Pigs invasion, while no longer being sponsored by the CIA, are still active, though they are now in their seventies or older. Members of Alpha 66, an anti-Castro paramilitary organization, continue to practice their AK-47 skills in a camp in South Florida.

In January 1999, U.S. President Bill Clinton eased travel restrictions to Cuba in an effort to increase cultural exchanges between the two nations. The Clinton administration approved a two-game exhibition series between the Baltimore Orioles and Cuban national baseball team, marking the first time a Major League Baseball team played in Cuba since 1959.

At the United Nations Millennium Summit in September 2000, Castro and Clinton spoke briefly at a group photo session and shook hands. U.N. Secretary-General Kofi Annan commented afterwards, "For a U.S. president and a Cuban president to shake hands for the first time in over 40 years—I think it is a major symbolic achievement". While Castro said it was a gesture of "dignity and courtesy," the White House denied the encounter was of any significance. In November 2001, U.S. companies began selling food to the country for the first time since Washington imposed the trade embargo after the revolution. In 2002, former U.S. President Jimmy Carter became the first former or sitting U.S. president to visit Cuba since 1928.

TIGHTENING EMBARGO

Relations deteriorated again following the election of George W. Bush. During his campaign Bush appealed for the support of Cuban-Americans by emphasizing his opposition to the government of Fidel Castro and supporting tighter embargo restrictions Cuban Americans, who until 2008 tended to vote Republican, expected effective policies and greater participation in the formation of policies regarding Cuba-U.S. relations. Approximately three months after his inauguration, the Bush administration began expanding travel restrictions. The United States Department of the Treasury issued greater efforts to deter American citizens from illegally traveling to the island.

Also in 2001, five Cuban agents were convicted on 26 counts of espionage, conspiracy to commit murder, and other illegal activities in the United States. On June 15, 2009, the U.S. Supreme Court denied review of their case. Tensions heightened as the Under Secretary of State for Arms Control and International Security Affairs, John R. Bolton, accused Cuba of maintaining a biological weapons program. Many in the United States, including ex-president Carter, expressed doubts about the claim. Later, Bolton was criticized for pressuring subordinates who questioned the quality of the intelligence John Bolton had used as the basis for the assertion. Bolton identified the Castro government as part of America's "axis of evil," highlighting the fact that the Cuban leader visited several U.S. foes, including Libya, Iran and Syria.

Following his 2004 reelection, Bush declared Cuba to be one of the few "outposts of tyranny" remaining in the world.

Cuban propaganda poster in Havana featuring a Cuban soldier addressing a threatening Uncle Sam. The translation reads: "Imperialist sirs, we have absolutely no fear of you!"

In January 2006, United States Interests Section in Havana began, in an attempt to break Cuba's "information blockade", displaying messages, including quotes from the Universal Declaration of Human Rights, on a scrolling "electronic billboard" in the windows of their top floor. Following a protest march organized by the Cuban government, the government erected a large number of poles, carrying black flags with single white stars, obscuring the messages.

On September 8, 2006, it was revealed that at least ten South Florida journalists received regular payments from the U.S. government for programs on Radio Martí and TV Martí, two broadcasters that support an opening of Cuban society and multi-party elections in Cuba. The payments totaled thousands of dollars over several years. Those who were paid the most were veteran reporters and a freelance contributor for El Nuevo Herald, the Spanish-language newspaper published by the corporate parent of The Miami Herald. The Cuban government has long contended that some South Florida Spanish-language journalists were on the federal payroll.

On September 12, 2006, the United States announced that it had created five inter-agency working groups to monitor Cuba. The groups were set up after the July 31 announcement that the ailing Cuban leader had temporarily ceded power to a collective leadership headed by his brother Raúl. U.S. officials say three of the newly created groups are headed by the State Department: diplomatic actions; strategic communications and democratic promotion. Another that coordinated humanitarian aid to Cuba is run by the Commerce Department, and a fifth, on migration issues, is run jointly by the National Security Council and the Department of Homeland Security.

On October 10, 2006, the United States announced the creation of a task force made up of officials from several U.S. agencies to pursue more aggressively American violators of the U.S. trade embargo against Cuba, with penalties as severe as 10 years of prison and hundreds of thousands of dollars in fines for violators of the embargo.

In November 2006, U.S. Congressional auditors accused the development agency USAID of failing properly to administer its program to for promoting democracy in Cuba. They said USAID had channeled tens of millions of dollars through exile groups in Miami, which were sometimes wasteful or kept questionable accounts. The report said the organizations had sent items such as chocolate and cashmere jerseys to Cuba. Their report concludes that 30% of the exile groups who received USAID grants showed questionable expenditures.

After Fidel Castro's announcement of resignation in 2008, U.S. Deputy Secretary of State John Negroponte said that the United States would maintain its embargo.

VISION FOR "DEMOCRATIC TRANSITION

In 2003, the United States Commission for Assistance to a Free Cuba was formed to "explore ways the U.S. can help hasten and ease a democratic transition in Cuba." The commission immediately announced a series of measures that included a tightening of the travel embargo to the island, a crackdown on illegal cash transfers, and a more robust information campaign aimed at Cuba. Castro insisted that, in spite of the formation of the Commission, Cuba is itself "in transition: to socialism [and] to communism" and that it was "ridiculous for the U.S. to threaten Cuba now".

In a 2004 meeting with members of the Commission for Assistance to a Free Cuba, President Bush stated, “We're not waiting for the day of Cuban freedom; we are working for the day of freedom in Cuba.” The President reaffirmed his commitment to Cuban-Americans just in time for his 2004 reelection with promises to “work” rather than wait for freedom in Cuba.

In April 2006, the Bush administration appointed Caleb McCarry "transition coordinator" for Cuba, providing a budget of $59 million, with the task of promoting the governmental shift to democracy after Castro's death. Official Cuban news service Granma alleges that these transition plans were created at the behest of Cuban exile groups in Miami, and that McCarry was responsible for engineering the overthrow of the Aristide government in Haiti.

In 2006, the Commission for Assistance to a Free Cuba released a 93-page report. The report included a plan that suggested the United States spend $80 million to ensure that Cuba's communist system does not continue after the death of Fidel Castro. The plan also includes a classified annex that Cuban officials claim could be a plot to assassinate Fidel Castro or a United States military invasion of Cuba, though they have provided no evidence to support this claim.

CONTEMPORARY RELATIONS

Main article: Cuban Thaw

Relations between Cuba and the United States remain tenuous, but since Fidel Castro stepped down from official leadership of the Cuban state and Barack Obama became president of the United States, they have improved.

In April 2009, Obama, who had received nearly half of the Cuban-American vote in the 2008 presidential election, began implementing a less strict policy towards Cuba. Obama stated that he was open to dialogue with Cuba, but that he would only lift the trade embargo if Cuba underwent political change. In March 2009, Obama signed into law a congressional spending bill which eased some economic sanctions on Cuba and eased travel restrictions on Cuban-Americans (defined as persons with a relative "who is no more than three generations removed from that person") traveling to Cuba. The April executive decision further removed time limits on Cuban-American travel to the island. Another restriction loosened in April 2009 was in the realm of telecommunications, which would allow quicker and easier access to the internet for Cuba.

The loosening of restrictions is likely to help nonprofits and scientists from both countries who work together on issues of mutual concern, such as destruction of shared biodiversity and diseases that affect both populations. At the 2009 5th Summit of the Americas, President Obama signaled the opening of a new beginning with Cuba.

Obama's overtures were reciprocated, to some degree, by new Cuban President Raúl Castro. On July 27, 2012, Raúl Castro said that the Government of Cuba is willing to hold talks with the United States government to "discuss anything".On December 10, 2013, at a state memorial service for Nelson Mandela, Barack Obama and Raúl Castro shook hands, with Castro saying in English: "Mr. President, I am Castro." Though both sides played down the handshake (much like the Clinton handshake of 2000), an adviser to Obama said that Obama wanted to improve relations with Cuba, yet had concerns about human rights on the island.

Beginning in 2013, Cuban and U.S. officials held secret talks brokered in part by Pope Francis and hosted in Canada and Vatican City to start the process of restoring diplomatic relations between Cuba and the United States. On December 17, 2014, the framework of an agreement to normalize relations and eventually end the longstanding embargo was announced by Castro in Cuba and Obama in the United States. Cuba and the United States pledged to start official negotiations with the aim of reopening their respective embassies in Havana and Washington.

As part of the agreement, aid worker Alan Gross and an unnamed Cuban national working as a U.S intelligence asset were released by the Cuban government, which also promised to free an unspecified number of Cuban nationals from a list of political prisoners earlier submitted by the United States. For its part, the U.S. government released the last three remaining members of the Cuban Five. Reaction to this change in policy within the Cuban-American community was mixed, and Cuban-American senators Bob Menendez (D-NJ), Marco Rubio (R-FL), and Ted Cruz (R-TX) all condemned the Obama administration's change in policy. However, opinion polls indicated the thaw in relations was broadly popular with the American public.

High-level diplomats from Cuba and the United States met in Havana in January 2015. While the talks did not produce a significant breakthrough, both sides described them as "productive", and Cuban Foreign Ministry official Josefina Vidal said further talks would be scheduled.

Under new rules implemented by the Obama administration, restrictions on travel by Americans to Cuba are significantly relaxed as of January 16, 2015, and the limited import of items like Cuban cigars and rum to the United States is allowed, as is the export of American computer and telecommunications technology to Cuba.

On April 14, 2015, the Obama administration announced that Cuba would be removed from the United States "Terrorist Sponsor" list. The House and Senate had 45 days from April 14, 2015 to review and possibly block this action, but this did not occur, and on May 29, 2015, the 45 days lapsed, therefore officially removing Cuba from the United States' list of state sponsors of terrorism. This move by President Obama further departs the United States from the Cold War conflict and its strain on Cuba-United States relations. On July 1, 2015, President Barack Obama announced that formal diplomatic relations between Cuba and the United States would resume, and embassies would be opened in Washington and Havana. Relations between Cuba and the United States have been formally re-established on July 20, 2015, with the opening of the Cuban embassy in Washington and the U.S. embassy in Havana.

TRADE RELATIONS

Under the Trade Sanctions Reform and Enhancement Act of 2000, exports from the United States to Cuba in the industries of food and medical products are permitted with the proper licensing and permissions from the U.S. Department of Commerce and the United States Department of the Treasury.

The Obama administration eased specific travel and other restrictions on Cuba in January 2011.

A delegation from the United States Congress called on Cuban president Raúl Castro on February 24, 2012 to discuss bilateral relations. The Congress delegation included Patrick Leahy, Democratic Senator from the state of Vermont and chairman of the Senate Committee on the Judiciary, and Richard Shelby, Republican Senator from the state of Alabama and ranking member of the Committee of Banking, Housing and Urban Matters; they went to Cuba as part of a delegation of Senators and Representatives of the Congress of United States.

Travel and import restrictions levied by the United States were further relaxed by executive action in January 2015 as part of the Cuban Thaw

The United States established diplomatic relations with the Republic of Cuba in 1902, opening the first U.S. Embassy in Havana in 1923. The Embassy was closed in 1961 when the United States severed diplomatic relations. During President Carter's administration in 1977, the United States and Cuba signed an agreement establishing the U.S. Interests Section (USINT) in Havana, and the Cuban Interests Section in Washington, DC. Under the formal protection of the Embassy of Switzerland, USINT operated out of the former U.S. Embassy building, which first opened in 1953. On December 17, 2014, President Obama announced the intention to re-establish diplomatic relations with Cuba. After six months of negotiations, the two nations officially renewed diplomatic relations on July 20, 2015, and USINT became U.S. Embassy Havana.

The functions of U.S. Embassy are similar to those of any U.S. government presence abroad: consular services, a political and economic reporting section, a public diplomacy program, law enforcement liaisons through the Regional Security Office and U.S. Coast Guard, a management and administrative office, and other programs to promote coordination with the Cuban government on a growing number of topics of mutual interest.

U.S. Embassy Havana key officers:

Chargé D'affaires: Ambassador Jeffrey DeLaurentis
Deputy Chief of Mission: Scott Hamilton
Political/Economic Chief: Dana Brown
Consul General: Brendan Mullarkey
Management Officer: Jennifer Johnson
Public Affairs Officer: Bruce Kleiner

The U.S. Embassy Havana is located at Calzada between L & M Streets, Vedado, Havana, switchboard: (53-7) 33-3551-3559, fax/general: 33-3700. U.S. Information Service: 33-3967 fax: 33-3869, hours: 8:30 a.m. to 5:00 p.m. Emergencies/after hours: 33-3026.

REFUGEE APPLICATION PROCESS

If a person believes he/she meets the eligibility criteria, that person can apply for refugee status through the Havana Refugee Section.

To apply, an individual person must complete a Preliminary Questionnaire, which can be downloaded from this site, or requested in writing. The written request can be placed in a drop-box located at the gate of the Refugee Section, located at Malecón and J, faxed to (537) 834-4515, or mailed to:

Embajada de los Estados Unidos
Sección de Refugiados
Calzada e L y M
Vedado, La Habana

The application steps are as follows:

Submission of Preliminary Questionnaire

The applicant must submit a completed Preliminary Questionnaire to the Havana Refugee Section. The questionnaire must state the refugee applicant's claim and may include spouse and unmarried children under 21. Individuals over 21 or married must complete their own preliminary questionnaire.

Receipt of Active Case Letter
An individual who appears to meet eligibility criteria will be scheduled for a pre-screen interview in the future. Those who do not qualify will receive a letter informing them that they are not eligible for the program. Applicants are requested not to call or write to check on the status of their application. However, they should inform the Refugee Section by telephone of any change in address or telephone number.

Pre-Screen Interview
When the time has arrived for a pre-screening interview, the applicant will be called or sent a letter asking them to schedule the interview. The purpose of the pre-screening interview is to determine whether an individual meets eligibility criteria. Cases that qualify will have a second interview with a United States Citizenship & Immigration Services (USCIS) officer.

USCIS Interview
A USCIS officer interviews the applicant(s) and makes a determination of refugee status under Section 101(A)(42) of the Immigration and Nationality Act (INA).
For more information about USCIS interviews, please, see the website: http://www.uscis.gov/portal/site/uscis.
For information about requests for reconsideration by USCIS, see the website: http://www.uscis.gov/portal/site/uscis/menuitem.5af9bb95919f35e66f614176543f6d1a/?vgnextoid=c26164337c77e210VgnVCM100000082ca60aRCRD&vgnextchannel=385d3e4d77d73210VgnVCM100000082ca60aRCRD

Security Clearance
Refugee candidates must undergo a security clearance review by U.S. law enforcement agencies.

Departure Documents
Refugee candidates must obtain documents from Cuban officials needed to depart Cuba and enter the United States, including a passport and a medical examination certification.

Flight Departure
Once all security clearances and documents are in order, the Refugee Section will contact the approved refugee to schedule travel.

The Refugee Section will arrange a flight for the refugee(s) from Cuba to the United States. The refugees are required to sign a loan repayment note and pay back transportation costs after arrival in the United States.

TRAVEL AND BUSINESS INFORMATION

The U.S. Department of State's Consular Information Program advises Americans traveling and residing abroad through Consular Information Sheets, Public Announcements, and Travel Warnings. **Consular Information Sheets** exist for all countries and include information on entry and exit requirements, currency regulations, health conditions, safety and security, crime, political disturbances, and the addresses of the U.S. embassies and consulates abroad. **Public Announcements** are issued to disseminate information quickly about terrorist threats and other relatively short-term conditions overseas that pose significant risks to the security of American travelers.

Travel Warnings are issued when the State Department recommends that Americans avoid travel to a certain country because the situation is dangerous or unstable.

For the latest security information, Americans living and traveling abroad should regularly monitor the Department's Bureau of Consular Affairs Internet web site at http://www.travel.state.gov, where the current Worldwide Caution, Public Announcements, and Travel Warnings can be found. Consular Affairs Publications, which contain information on obtaining passports and planning a safe trip abroad, are also available at http://www.travel.state.gov. For additional information on international travel, see http://www.usa.gov/Citizen/Topics/Travel/International.shtml.

The Department of State encourages all U.S citizens traveling or residing abroad to register via the State Department's travel registration website or at the nearest U.S. embassy or consulate abroad. Registration will make your presence and whereabouts known in case it is necessary to contact you in an emergency and will enable you to receive up-to-date information on security conditions.

Emergency information concerning Americans traveling abroad may be obtained by calling 1-888-407-4747 toll free in the U.S. and Canada or the regular toll line 1-202-501-4444 for callers outside the U.S. and Canada.

The National Passport Information Center (NPIC) is the U.S. Department of State's single, centralized public contact center for U.S. passport information. Telephone: 1-877-4USA-PPT (1-877-487-2778). Customer service representatives and operators for TDD/TTY are available Monday-Friday, 7:00 a.m. to 12:00 midnight, Eastern Time, excluding federal holidays.

Travelers can check the latest health information with the U.S. Centers for Disease Control and Prevention in Atlanta, Georgia. A hotline at 877-FYI-TRIP (877-394-8747) and a web site at http://www.cdc.gov/travel/index.htm give the most recent health advisories, immunization recommendations or requirements, and advice on food and drinking water safety for regions and countries. A booklet entitled "Health Information for International Travel" (HHS publication number CDC-95-8280) is available from the U.S. Government Printing Office, Washington, DC 20402, tel. (202) 512-1800.

With the April 2009 directives, the Obama administration removed all travel restrictions for Cuban-Americans to visit and send money to family members in Cuba. However, for those Americans who are not of Cuban descent or have no family in Cuba, there are still ways to travel to Cuba. According to the Cuban Assets Control Regulations, individuals who are subject to U.S. jurisdiction (even if traveling through a third country) must first obtain a license before engaging in travel to, from, and within Cuba.

General licenses are given to certain kinds of travelers including those who are visiting a close relative who is a national of Cuba (including third-country nationals residing in Cuba), journalists and supporting personnel, government officials on official business, members of international organizations (of which the U.S. is a member) traveling on official business, full-time professionals traveling for non-commercial research, full-time professionals traveling for a professional non-commercial meeting or conference organized by an international organization, employees or representative of a U.S. telecommunications services provider, and individuals regularly employed by a producer or distributor of agricultural commodities or medicine.

For those individuals who do not fall under the scope of the general licenses, they may be eligible to obtain a specific license from OFAC. Specific OFAC licenses are given to those who wish to visit a close relative in Cuba who is not a Cuban national, to educational institutions, religious organizations, and other specific licenses are approved on a case-by-case basis.

To apply for a specific license, individuals need to send a letter requesting the specific license and with the details of the potential visit. Academic institutions must send a similar letter and include proof that the institution is accredited by an appropriate association. Religious organizations must send the detailed letter as well and include examples of religious activities they will host in Cuba. The letters must be sent to: Licensing Division, Office of Foreign Assets Control, U.S. Department of Treasury, 1500 Pennsylvania Ave, NW, Washington, DC 20220. More specific guidelines can be found at http://www.treas.gov/offices/enforcement/ofac/programs/cuba/cuba_tr_app.pdf

Once a proper license has been obtained the traveler must have a valid passport and visa. American citizens are issued visas (tourist cards) upon arrival to Cuba or can attain a visa from the Cuban Interest Section in Washington D.C., however make sure to have received the appropriate type of visa for your visit. Additionally, as of May 2010 Cuba requires that all visitors be covered by a non-U.S. medical insurance. Cuba will sell a temporary policy to visitors who do not have a non-U.S. insurer.

Also, keep in mind that credit cards issued by U.S. banks cannot be used in Cuba and the U.S. dollar has not been accepted for commercial transactions since November of 2004. However, there are specially designated Cuban banks that accept major U.S. travelers checks and U.S. dollars can be converted to convertible or non-convertible Cuban pesos (the effective exchange rate including the 10 percent fee for exchanging US dollars to convertible Cuban pesos results in 1 USD = 0.80 CUC) Additionally, keep in mind that there will be a $20 Cuban departure tax that must be paid before leaving the country. The maximum Per Diem rate, or max that can be spent per day of travel in Cuba is $179. Some general and specific licenses, such as for journalists, allow for a higher rate depending on the necessary equipment.

INVESTMENT AND TRADE STRATEGY - PRACTICAL MEASURES AND OBJECTIVES

BASCI TRENDS

MINCEX
Ministry of Foreign Commerce and Investment
www.mincex.cu

CEPEC
Center for promotion of foreign trade and investment
www.cepec.cu

CCRC Chamber of Commerce of the Republic of Cuba
www.camaracuba.cu

The growth rates of Cuba's GDP have been moderate and low, lower that the average for the region. In order to turn this trend around, accumulation rates higher that 20% are required to permit a GDP growth rhythm increase of 5 to 7%.

The Cuban government acknowledges the role played by foreign investment flows in contributing to the economic sustainable development of the country. Therefore we have defined a new Policy to attract foreign investment, taking in general and sectorial principles. The definition of the Policy for Foreign Investment is one of the most important strategic actions within the process of implementing the Economic and Social Policy Guidelines of the Party and the Revolution.

In Extraordinary Session of the National Assembly of the Peoples' Power of March 29th of 2014, Law No. 118 "Law of Foreign Investment" was approved; it was published on April 16th of 2014 in the Official Gazette of the Republic of Cuba in its Special Edition No. 20, also showing its Regulation and a group of complementary norms.

Law No. 118 covers the decision of conceiving of foreign investment as a source for development in activities that are of interest to the country. In certain economic sectors and activities it is considered to be an active and fundamental element corresponding to the short, mid and long range plans for economic and social development.

Foreign investment may be authorized in all sectors except those dealing with the health and education of the population and the armed forces institutions, with the exception of their business systems.

Drawing up a broad-based and diverse Portfolio of Foreign Investment Opportunities that will be updated on a yearly basis allows us to provide an important tool to attract investors at the same time as it summarizes business interests to be developed using foreign capital.

This edition of the Portfolio of Opportunities with Foreign Investment is destined to provide information for potential investors and to invite them to take part in the development of the Cuban economy.

FOREIGN INVESTMENT LEGAL REGIME

Law No. 118/2014: "Law of Foreign Investment"

Decree No. 325/2014: "Regulations of the Law of Foreign Investment" of the Council of Ministers

Resolution No. 46/2014 and No. 47/2014 of the Banco Central de Cuba

Resolution No. 128/2014 and No. 129/2014 of the Ministry of Foreign Commerce and Investment

Resolution No. 16/2014 of the Ministry of Labor and Social Security

Agreement No. 7567, May 2014, of the Council of Ministers

With the passing of Law No. 118 and its complementary norms a favorable business climate has been set up in Cuba. Other advantages are added to tax incentives and these invite foreign investors to choose Cuba as investment territory. Among these advantages:

SECTORIAL POLICIES

Formulation of sectorial policies for identifying investment opportunities with foreign capital that permits access to the Cuban market and its consumers.

Secure and transparent legal framework.

Political, social and legal stability.

Geographical location in the center of an expanding market.

Climate of safety for foreign personnel.

High indicators for education, social security and health of the population.

Highly qualified workforce.

International agreements signed by Cuba with the Latin American Integration Association (ALADI), the Caribbean Community (CARICOM), the Bolivarian Alliance for the Peoples of Our America (ALBA), the Common Market of the South (MERCOSUR), the European Union (EU), the World Trade Organization (WTO).

Governmental policy that prioritizes research and technological innovation.

Promotional institutions at the service of investors with qualified personnel.

Basic infrastructure throughout the country: communications networks; over 20 airports; ports admitting deep-draft vessels; over 95% of national territory with electrical power; rail and highway communication.

INTERNATIONAL AGREEMENT RELATED TO FOREIGN INVESTMENT

Cuba has signed Agreements to prevent Double Taxing with Spain, Barbados, Italy, Russia, Portugal, Qatar, Lebanon, China, Vietnam, Austria, the Ukraine and Venezuela and it has signed

63 agreements for Promotion and Reciprocal Protection of Investments (BITs in the English-language acronym), of these 39 are in force.

FOREIGN INVESTMENT IN CUBA

Law No. 118 establishes the types of business that can be adopted within foreign investment:

Joint enterprise

International economic association contracts including, among others, contracts for hotel management, production or services, contracts to provide professional services, risk contracts to explore nonrenewable natural resources, for construction and agricultural production

Enterprises with 100% foreign capital; foreign investors can set up on national territory as: a) Natural persons acting on their own behalf b) Juridical persons constituting a Cuban affiliate of the foreign entity which they own c) Juridical persons setting up a branch of a foreign entity

At the close of 2013, joint enterprises are the most prevalent, at 51% of total business. The most attractive sectors for foreign capital have been tourism in the top spot, followed by mining and energy.

51% Joint Enterprises 4% Enterprises with 100% Foreign Capital 12% IEA contracts 1% Cooperated Production Contracts 4% Management Production Contracts 28% Hotel Management Contracts

Business with FI by sector -2013

13% Energy and Mining 42% Tourism 10% Industrial 7% Foods 6% Construction 2% Agriculture 4% Transportation 2% Communications 2% Sugar Industry and its byproducts 12% Other Results at the close of the 2013 business year show that associations reported advantages for almost 5 billion CUC with exports representing 69% of the total.

GENERAL FOREIGN INVESTMENT POLICY PRINCIPLES

To conceive of foreign investment as a source for the country's short, mid and long range economic development. Access to cutting edge technologies, securing managerial methods, diversifying and broadening export markets, replacing imports, access to foreign financing, creating new job sources and securing greater incomes on the basis of production linkage with the domestic economy are objectives that should be proposed in order to attract foreign investment.

To secure new managerial methods that contribute to achieving a better market position, increased productivity and profitability, efficiency of complex investment processes and their assimilation by the rest of the economy.

To immediately prioritize foreign investment directed to replacing food imports.

To encourage the development of comprehensive projects generating production linkage in the search for collective efficiency. These projects may be executed with one investor or with several having this mutual interest.

Corresponding to the country's demographic dynamics, foreign investment must allow access to cutting edge technologies that increase productivity and permit efficient use of the workforce.

To contribute to changing the country's energy matrix by taking advantage of renewable energy sources, using solar and wind power and power from agro-industrial waste such as sugar cane, forestry and scrub (marabu) biomass, generation of water and biogas power.

To consider the participation of foreign capital in the complementation of national scientific and technological development projects, preserving intellectual property over the results obtained, especially brand names and patents created by the Cuban Party.

To consider foreign investment in certain economic sectors and activities as an active and fundamental element for growth.

To consider agricultural and foods industry production as prioritized sectors along with tourism, including health, the development of energy sources especially renewable energy, the exploration and exploitation of hydrocarbons and mining resources and construction or improvement of industrial infrastructures.

To guide the greater part of foreign investment towards export sectors. Moreover, to direct it towards eliminating bottle-necks in the production chain, encouraging modernization, infrastructure and changing the technological model in the economy as well as ensuring efficient satisfaction of the country's needs with the aim of replacing imports.

To encourage foreign investment on the basis of a broad-based and diverse Portfolio of Projects. To focus promotion by stages and potential sectors/activities and to encourage diversification in the participation of business people from different countries. To prioritize massive promotion for the Special Economic Development Zones starting with the work by the Special Economic Development Zone of Mariel.

To consider prioritized activities implying transfer of technology, production linkage, carried out in areas having lesser economic development or contributing to increasing the efficiency of the production chain.

In the extraction of natural resources, providing public services, developing biotechnology, wholesale commerce and tourism; Cuban participation will always constitute the majority share.

Among the requirements for approval of foreign investment businesses, introducing criteria planning a balance of payments over time; this element will be considered to be among the decisive indicators for approval.

In foreign investment businesses there shall be no free contracting of the workforce other than in exceptions foreseen by law. The employer-entity will be maintained as a business organization and its aim will be to supply and control the workforce. Salaries will fit the work contributed, efficiency and the added value generated by the enterprise. Payment for the workforce services is negotiated between the employer-entity and the enterprise having foreign capital on the basis of what has been established by the Ministry of Labor and Social Security. To eliminate concepts of salary scales and establish a minimum wage. Contracted employees will earn a salary higher than the minimum wage established.

Foreign investment may be directed selectively towards development of non-state ownership forms with juridical personality, prioritizing the cooperative sector.

State goods will not be transferred in property other than in exceptional cases where they will be destined for purposes of the country's development and they do not adversely affect the political, social and economic foundations of the State.

Exclusivity rights are not granted on the Cuban market; the foreign partner has equality of conditions with third parties and may be supplier and client of the business.

In projects aiming at exporting goods or services, the foreign Party shall guarantee the market.

The country's shortage in construction capacity cannot stop the development of the process of foreign capital investments. Alternatives required to prevent it may be assessed even contracting foreign labor force.

Bidding for design and construction services between foreign and Cuban enterprises whenever the complexity of project so requires, in accordance with regulations in legislation in force about the country's investment process.

To authorize establishing enterprises having 100% foreign capital for executing investment projects having the complexity and important that requires it especially for the development of industrial infrastructure through special turnkey contacts such as: Engineering, Procurement and Construction Contracts (IPC); Engineering, Procurement and Construction Management Contracts (IPCM); Building, Ownership, Operation and Transfer Contracts (BOOT), Building, Transfer and Operation Contracts (BTO).

In principle the setting up of bank accounts abroad will not be authorized nor the acceptance of external guarantees compromising the retaining of Cuban flows in banks abroad.

The economic information requested for foreign investment will be made compatible with international indicators used to measure the results. To publish statistics that will be determined.

Any increase to the investment budget will be assumed by the International Economic Association.

Furthermore, a general principle to grant new tax incentives for joint enterprises and parties in international economic association contracts was approved; The Special Taxation Regime* has been established in the new regulatory framework for foreign investment, as follows:

Taxes	Law No. 118 Foreign Investment	Special Economic Development Zone of Mariel	Law 113 Taxation System
About Profits	0% during 8 years and as an exception for a longer period. Subsequently 15%. 0% on reinvested profits. It may be increased to	0% during 10 years and as an exception for a longer period. Subsequently 12%. Application of Lay No. 118 for profits	35% May increase to 50% for exploitation of natural resources.

	50% for exploitation of natural resources.	reinvestment.	
For using labor force	Exempted	Exempted	Progressive reduction from 20% (2012) to 5% (2016).
Contributions to local development	0% during investment recovery	Exempted	Is being established gradually in the Budget Law
About sales or services	0% during first year of operations, subsequently 50% discount on wholesale sales and on services.	0% during first year of operations, subsequently 1%	2% on wholesale sales and 10% on servicers. New taxable items shall be gradually incorporated.
About personal incomes to partners or Parties	Exempted	Law No. 118 applies	15%
For using or exploiting	50% discounts during	Law No. 118 applies	For the use of beaches,
natural resources and	investment recovery		waste disposal into
preserving the			hydrographic basins and
environment (5 taxes)			terrestrial waters: defined in the annual Budget Law. Use of bays and forestry resources according to taxable items in Law 113
Customs	Exempted during the investment process	Exemptions for importation of means, equipment and goods are exempted	Taxable items are established in the Customs Duties

*Joint enterprises and international economic associations are governed by what has been established in legislation in force (Law No. 113 of the Taxation System), with the adjustments of this special regime. Enterprises with 100% foreign capital pay taxes according to legislation in force. In the case of International Economic Association Contracts for Production, Services and Professional Services Management, this is governed by what has been established in legislation in force (Law No. 113 of the taxation System) with the adjustments of this special regime, especially the tax on profits in the gross incomes type, 4%.

Taxes Applicable to Enterprises with 100% Foreign Capital

Profit Tax 35% that may go up to 50% for exploitation of natural resources,

or up to 50% of the 35% that is the tax type established. Workforce Tax It is gradually reduced until 5% in 2016. Sales Tax 5% on wholesale sales, 10% on retail sales. Gradual application until 2016. Services Tax 10% gradual application until 2016. Special Products and No tax is paid on sales, especially for products and on services Services Tax for:

(1) goods constituting raw material for industrial production and for goods and (2) services destined for exportation Environmental Tax For the use or exploitation of beaches, for approved waste disposal in hydrographic basins, for the use and exploitation of bays, for the use and exploitation of forestry resources and wildlife and for the right to use terrestrial waters: gradual application of these taxes and the majority of their taxable types shall be established in the Annual Budget Law

Territorial Contribution Gradually established in the Budget Law. Customs Tax To be set in the Customs Tariffs.

The Article 47 of Law 1128 establishes: "The Ministry of Finances and Prices, having heard the opinion of the Ministry of Foreign Commerce and Investment, taking into account the benefits and the amount of the investment, capital recovery, indications provided by the Council of Ministers for prioritized sectors of the economy, as well as the benefits it may bring to the national economy, may grant total or partial exemptions, on a temporary or permanent basis, or grant other tax benefits according to what has been established in taxation legislation in force, for any of the types of foreign investment recognized in this Law".

SPECIAL ECONOMIC DEVELOPMENT ZONE OF MARIEL

The Special Economic Development Zone of Mariel (ZED Mariel in the Spanish acronym) is located close to west Havana and covers an area of 465.4 square kilometers. It takes in six municipalities in the province of Artemisa, with a population of 60,471.

Its general vision is to show Cuba's new face to the world in investment, building, production, economic and social matters in a harmonious setting where production using top technologies, environmental sustainability, formation and training of the workforce come together under a special regime that provides incentives to encourage these intentions. This endeavor is imbued with the optimism and confidence of the Cuban government on the basis of the technical and intellectual capacities created by our country.

ADDED VALUE GOODS AND SERVICES

During the initial period Sector A will be developed: it covers approximately 43 square kilometers (9% of the total area of the Zone) and is located on the western edge of Mariel Bay. For improved operations, it has been subdivided into 11 areas.

In Sector A we have developed significant modern works for port facilities, highways and rail and water supply infrastructures in order to provide power and to deal with information-communications. For establishing themselves in the Zone, investors will be provided with leveled-terrain lots having the required basic services.

INDUSTRIAL AND LOGISTICS ACTIVITIES ZONE OF MARIEL (ZIALM) TERRITORIAL COMPOSITION

Highways – First-class Existing Roadways – Second-class Existing Roadways – Proposed First-class Roadways – Proposed Second-class Roadways – Work under construction – Urban Settlements – Rural Settlements

ZIALM: Zoning

Code	Name	Extentions Km2
A-	Reserve Zone	6 8
A-	West Ecological Park	
A-	High-Tech Industrial Park	6
A-	Oil Activities Zone	
A-	Logistical Activities Zone	87
A-6	Narrow Rail Complex	6
A-7	Port Activities Zone	6
A-8	Agro-Foods Processing Zone	
A-	Agricultural Development Zone	8 7
A-	Technopark	8
A-	Mangrove Area	
	Are Tootal	43.72

These important advantages combined with the development of a Logistical Activities Zone will encourage the creation of a favorable milieu to establish production and services projects.

CONTACT INFORMATION:

Desamparados No. 166 e/Habana y Compostela, Oficina 302, Habana Vieja, La Habana, Cuba. Tel. (537) 864-4240 al 47 Email: ventanillaunica@zedmariel.co.cu

• Technical specifications for Foreign Investment

Manufacturing radial tires

Description	Setting up a plant running on clean cutting edge technology to manufacture 1.2 million radial tires, 56% for light automobiles and 44% for heavy transport, for the domestic market and exportation (400,000 units).
Investment Type	Joint Enterprise
Cuban Party	Company associated with Grupo Empresarial de la Industria Química (GEIQ)
Estimated Investment Amount	223 million USD
Location	Sector A. Zone A-10
Contacts	Vicepresidencia GEIQ Email: lage@geiq.cu Tel: (537) 207 -6823

Manufacturing aluminum cans

Description	Setting up a plant running on clean technology to replace imports of aluminum cans for beverages (beer, soft drinks, malt drinks, juice, etc.) at levels over 600 million units per year. Estimated area of 4500 square meters.
Investment Type	Joint Enterprise
Cuban Party	Company associated with Grupo Empresarial de la Industria Sidero Mecánica (GESIME)

Estimated Investment Amount	40 million USD
Location	Sector A. Zone A-10
Contacts	Vicepresidencia GESIME Email: cherrera@sime.cu Tel: (537) 263 3429

Manufacturing air conditioning equipment Manufacturing project for glass bottles for beverages

Description	Setting up a plant running on clean cutting edge technology to manufacture air conditioning equipment for central systems, commercial and home air conditioning equipment and the production of parts, spare parts and accessories and post-sale and warranty service, to replace imports supported by new investment projects for the development of tourism and a considerable amount
	of equipment for installed air conditioning to be replaced yearly.
Investment Type	Joint Enterprise
Cuban Party	Company associated with Grupo Empresarial de la Industria Sidero Mecánica (GESIME)
Estimated Investment Amount	15 million USD
Location	Sector A. Zone A-10
Contacts	Vicepresidencia GESIME Email: cherrera@sime.cu Tel: (537) 263 3429
Description	Setting up a plant running on clean technology to replace imports of glass bottles for beverages (beer, foods, rum), for medicines and food conserves, at over 210 million units yearly, thereby allowing us to cover 95% of the current domestic market. The plant must be designed with a daily melting capacity of 220 tons/day in 2 furnaces (one for 120 tons/day of amber and green glass bottles and the other furnace for 100 tons/day for clear glass).
Investment Type	Joint Enterprise
Cuban Party	Company associated with Grupo Empresarial de la Industria Quimica (GEIQ)
Estimated Investment Amount	70 million USD
Location	Sector A. Zone A-10
Contacts	Vicepresidencia GEIQ Email: lage@geiq.cu Tel: (537) 207 -6823

Manufacturing various glassware items Manufacturing commercial footwear

Description	Setting up a plant running on clean cutting edge technology to manufacture various assortments of tableware, glassware, goblets, water jars, destined as replacements for imports; the main client will be the hotel and out-of-hotel tourism sector.
Investment Type	Joint Enterprise
Cuban Party	Company associated with Grupo Empresarial de la Industria Ligera
	(GEMPIL)
Estimated Investment Amount	10 million USD
Location	Sector A. Zone A-10

Contacts	Vicepresidencia GEIQ Email: lage@geiq.cu Tel: (537) 207 -6823

Description	Setting up a plant running on clean and cutting edge technology to manufacture commercial footwear to replace imports, approximately 47 million pairs of shoes per year. Estimated investment amount is 20 million USD.
Investment Type	Joint Enterprise
Cuban Party	Company associated with Grupo Empresarial de la Industria Ligera (GEMPIL)
Estimated Investment Amount	20 million USD
Location	Sector A. Zone A-10
Contacts	Vicepresidencia GEMPIL Email: trujillo@minil.cu Tel: (537) 263 - 3605

AGRO-FOODS SECTOR

Production of fresh vegetables to be sold in the Special Economic Development Zone of Mariel (ZEDM) and for exportation, by setting up 2 covered growing house modules

Description	Setting up two covered growing house modules to produce and commercialize fresh vegetables for domestic consumption and export. We foresee setting up the modules in two stages: an initial stage will set up a 5-hectare module in the first year and, depending upon results and demand, the second module would be set up subsequently.
Investment Type	Joint Enterprise
Cuban Party	Empresa de Cítricos Ceiba
Estimated Investment	6 million USD
Amount	
Location	Sector A. Zone A-9
Contacts	Director de Empresa de Cítricos Ceiba Email: ilio@citricosceiba.cu Tel: (53-47) 31 1106/311100

Hog production for channeled commercialization, finished products, genetic animals and hog semen

Description	Building and setting up facilities running on clean, modern technologies, controlled environments, waste treatment and solar panels that are efficient in their use of energy resources, for the primary production of hogs, their slaughter and industrial processing, with vacuum-packing system, refrigeration chambers and freezers as well as genetic development, semen production and the production of 675,000 metric tons of balanced feed for the animals. The competitive productive pyramid will be based on the genetics of Yorkshire, Landrace, Duroc and CC21 breeds and their breeding to obtain F1 Yorkland sows to guarantee the efficiency of the commercial production of on-the-hoof hog meat, destined to replace imports and for exportation. Commercial production will have 3000 breeders with the aim of producing 7200 metric tons of hoof weight pork; slaughtered hogs will have live weights of 100-

	120 Kg transformed into channeled pork with an installed capacity of slaughtering 300 hogs per day; at 270 working days per year we will be able to slaughter up to 81,000 hogs each year. The processing plant will have a capacity of 59 metric tons per day.
Investment Type	Joint Enterprise
Cuban Party	Empresa Nacional Génetica Porcina -Coralsa.
Estimated Investment Amount	190 million USD
Location	Sector A. Zone A-9
Contacts	Dirección General del Grupo de Producción Porcina Email: norberto@minag.cu Tel: (537)8847253/8847254 (53)5263 1788 (cel.) Dirección de Negocios y Colaboración Email: prod4por@minag.cu Corporación Alimentaria S.A. (CORALSA) Email: negocios@coralsa.com.cu Tel: (537) 202-1194/202 7388/205-9093

Soy Processing (Refined Oil Factory)

Description Setting up a plant running on clean technology, energy efficiency and levels of productivity and efficiency that are competitive on the international level, to mill 500,000 tons of soy beans per year in

	order to obtain 85,000 tons of refined oil and 375,000 tons of soy flour for animal consumption. The refined oil will be distributed in 1/2, 1, 4 and 20 liter sizes, eliminating all current domestic distribution of bulk refined oil. Currently, both refined soy oil and soy flour production for animal consumption is below the country's level of demand.
Investment Type	Joint Enterprise
Cuban Party	Corporación Alimentaria S.A (CORALSA)
Estimated Investment Amount	149 million USD
Location	Sector A. Zone A-8
Contacts	Corporación Alimentaria S.A. (CORALSA) Email: negocios@coralsa.com.cu Tel: (537) 202-1194/202 7388/205-9093

Development for producing top quality confectionary goods, candies, sherbets, fine, sweet, soda and cream biscuits and breakfast cereals with the emphasis on nutritional value

Description	Setting up a plant running on clean technology, energy efficiency and high quality standards to produce confectionary goods (sherbets, sweet, salty, soda and filled biscuits, candies and breakfast cereals, etc.) in different formats and assortments, in order to replace imports, for the tourism sector, domestic market and export.
Investment Type	Joint Enterprise

Cuban Party	Corporación Alimentaria (CORALSA)
Estimated Investment Amount	15.3 million USD
Location	Sector A. Zone A-8
Contacts	Corporación Alimentaria S.A. (CORALSA) Email: negocios@coralsa.com.cu Tel: (537) 202-1194/202 7388/205-9093

Production of instant dry yeast

Description Setting up a plant running on clean technology, energy efficiency and high quality standards to produce 6,000 tons per year of instant dry yeast for tourism, the domestic market and export.

Investment Type	Joint Enterprise
Cuban Party	Corporación Cuba Ron S.A.
Estimated Investment Amount	14.5 million USD
Location	Sector A. Zone A-8
Contacts	Corporación Cuba Ron S.A Email: cubaron@cubaron.co.cu Tel: (537) 27301 02/ 204 73 17

BIOTECHNOLOGICAL SECTOR: DEVELOPING AND PRODUCING MEDICINES VACCINE PRODUCTION PLANT

Description	Building a closed cycle plant to obtain bacterial vaccines from pathogenic micro-organisms, enteric vaccines, and vaccines based on external membrane protein, attenuated and conjugate vaccines. This plant will be designed under Good Production Practices regulations. Some of the vaccines to be produced: cholera, meningococcal, meningococcal conjugate and salmonella variants, etc.) This project must be conceived as a vaccine production complex with several production lines of pharmaceutical ingredients and finished products. Production is fundamentally for export.
Investment Type	International Economic Association
Cuban Party	Vacunas Finlay S.A., Centro de Investigación-Producción de Sueros y Vacunas
Estimated Investment Amount	65 million USD
Location	Sector A. Zone A-3
Contacts	Dirección General del Centro de Investigación-Producción de Sueros y Vacunas. Email: ccampa@finlay.edu.cu Tel: (537) 2080976 / 2086086

Homeopathic products production plant Plant for producing natural products based on powders and fluid extracts

Description	Building a production complex for homeopathic compounds in liquid presentations of the different lines of Vacunas Finlay S.A. products (homeopathic complexes and nosodes). The lines will
	cover all existing branches (PrevengHo, AliviHo, TratHo, EstimulHo) to be produced on an industrial basis for domestic

	consumption and for exportation agreements. A plant should also be built to have areas for formulation, dynamo dilution, filling and final bottling. It will also have warehouses for initial raw materials, inflammable substances (alcohol) and finished products as well as areas for the services for generating purified water and pure steam.
Investment Type	International Economic Association
Cuban Party	Vacunas Finlay S.A., Centro de Investigación -Producción de Sueros y Vacunas
Estimated Investment Amount	15 million USD
Location	Sector A. Zone A-3
Contacts	Dirección General del Centro de Investigación -Producción de Sueros y Vacunas. Email: ccampa@finlay.edu.cu Tel: (537) 2080976 / 2086086
Description	Production and commercialization of natural products based on powders and fluid extracts from medicinal plants destined for the domestic market and export. The objective of proposed investment project is to create a production infrastructure for processing medicinal plants and obtaining medicines from natural products based on powders, capsules and fluid extracts. It also includes the machinery and infrastructure to process drying and improvements in the field.
Investment Type	International Economic Association
Cuban Party	Vacunas Finlay S.A., Centro de Investigación -Producción de Sueros y Vacunas
Estimated Investment Amount	35 million USD
Location	Sector A. Zone A-3
Contacts	Dirección General del Centro de Investigación -Producción de Sueros y Vacunas. Email: ccampa@finlay.edu.cu Tel: (537) 2080976 / 2086086

Plant for producing monoclonal antibodies Plant for oral solid medicines (tablets and capsules)

Description	Building an industrial biotechnological facility to produce monoclonal antibodies for therapeutic use in cancer and other chronic diseases (capacity of 100 Kg per year), from the active pharmaceutical ingredient right up to the final product. Including warehouses, offices and technological services. Production is basically for export.
Investment Type	International Economic Association
Cuban Party	Cimab S.A. Centro de Inmunología Molecular
Estimated Investment Amount	90 million USD
Location	Sector A. Zone A-3
Contacts	Dirección General del Centro de Inmunología Molecular. Email: lage@cim.sld.cu Tel: (537) 271 4335
Description	Building a plant to manufacture generic medicines in solid oral forms. We plan a production plant having a nominal capacity of

	4500 million tablets and 500 million capsules per year. Production is fundamentally for export.
Investment Type	International Economic Association
Cuban Party	Empresa Laboratorios Medsol
Estimated Investment Amount	100 million USD
Location	Sector A. Zone A-3
Contacts	Dirección General de la Empresa Laboratorios Medsol. Email: alarcon@ms.medsol.cu Tel: (537) 271 3423

Plant for producing antiretroviral medicines

Description	Building a plant to produce generic antiretroviral medicines in solid oral form, with a nominal capacity of 300 million units per year. Production is fundamentally for export.
Investment Type	International Economic Association
Cuban Party	Empresa Laboratorios Medsol
Estimated Investment Amount	25 million USD
Location	Sector A. Zone A-3

Contacts Dirección General de la Empresa Laboratorios Medsol. Email: alarcon@ms.medsol.cu Tel: (537) 271 3423

Plant for contraceptive products

Description	Designing and building a plant to manufacture oral and hormone contraceptive pills and their principal active ingredients (hormones and antihormones), classified to levels of contention 5 (OEL5) including activities "in process" and control testing of production underway. The new plant will fulfill the following process requirements: • Capacity : 500,000,000 pills per year • Forms : 7 different forms Production is fundamentally for export.
Investment Type	International Economic Association
Cuban Party	Empresa Laboratorios Medsol
Estimated Investment Amount	25 million USD
Location	Sector A. Zone A-3
Contacts	Dirección General de la Empresa Laboratorios Medsol. Email: alarcon@ms.medsol.cu Tel: (537) 271 3423

Blood-based products plant Plant to produce injectable medicines

Description	Building a production plant to process 100,000 liters of plasma a year, with yields of 18 gr to 23 gr of protein/liter of plasma. Incorporation via transference technology of producing Blood-Clotting Factor VIII and Factor IX. Production is fundamentally for export.
Investment Type	International Economic Association

Cuban Party	Empresa de Sueros y Productos Hemoderivados "Adalberto Pesant"
Estimated Investment Amount	160 million USD
Location	Sector A. Zone A-3
Contacts	Dirección General de la Empresa de Sueros y Productos Hemoderivados "Adalberto Pesant". Email: mcayiz@pesant.biocubafarma.cu Tel: (537) 202 0551
Description	Building a production plant for injectable liquids, complying with Drug Industry Good Manufacturing Practices, of the following: • Injectable ampoules • Injectable liquid bulbs • Pre-filled syringes Installation plans are for a production capacity of 20 million ampoules per year, 20 million vials with liquid and lyophilized products and 10 million pre-filled syringes per year for an assortment including sterilized products obtained by aseptic processing and terminal sterilization. Production is basically for exportation.
Investment Type	International Economic Association
Cuban Party	Empresa Laboratorios AICA+
Estimated Investment Amount	160 million USD
Location	Sector A. Zone A-3
Contacts	Dirección General de la Empresa Laboratorios AICA+ Email: teresita@aica.cu Tel: (537) 271-2576

Plant to produce measured dosage sprays Plant to produce solid oral medicines (tablets, caplets and capsules)

Description	Building a pharmaceutical plant to manufacture dose-inhalers, basically bronchodilator products to treat asthma, allergic respiratory diseases and chronic obstructive pulmonary diseases (COPD). Technological transfer of nationally produced products and the introduction of new products for COPDs. Production is destined basically for exportation.
Investment Type	International Economic Association
Cuban Party	Empresa Laboratorios Medsol
Estimated Investment Amount	55 million USD
Location	Sector A. Zone A-3
Contacts	Dirección General de la Empresa Laboratorios Medsol. Email: alarcon@ms.medsol.cu Tel. (537) 271 3423
Description	Building a plant to produce solid forms from natural products. For the Cuban and Latin American markets
Investment Type	International Economic Association
Cuban Party	Laboratorios DALMER S.A.
Estimated Investment Amount	40 million USD
Location	Sector A, Zone A-3
Contacts	Dirección General de Laboratorios DALMER S.A. Email: blanca@cnic.edu.cu Tel: (537) 208254/ 208 5835

Plant to produce cephalosporins and carbapenemas (injectable)

Description	Building a plant to produce cephalosporins and carbapenemas (injectable) with a capacity to obtain up to 21 million ampules per year. Production will be destined to satisfy domestic demands and the rest will be for exportation.
Investment Type	International Economic Association
Cuban Party	Empresa Farmacéutica 8 De Marzo
Estimated Investment Amount	60 million USD
Location	Sector A, Zone A-3
Contacts	Dirección General de la Empresa Farmacéutica 8 De Marzo. Email: nancy@8marzo.biocubafarma.cu Tel: (53) 052866741

Plant to produce oral penicillin-based antibiotics

Description	Building a plant to produce and sell oral penicillin-based antibiotics for oral suspensions with and without beta-lactamase inhibitors, with a capacity in the first stage of 500 million capsules and 20 million bottles for suspensions, produced on the basis of imported active principles. Production is for exportation and domestic sales to satisfy the demands for these medicines.
Investment Type	International Economic Association
Cuban Party	Empresa Farmacéutica 8 De Marzo
Estimated Investment Amount	30 million USD
Location	Sector A. Zone A-3
Contacts	Dirección General de la Empresa Farmacéutica 8 De Marzo. Email: nancy@8marzo.biocubafarma.cu Tel. (53) 052866741

Energy Sector Installation and operation of Photovoltaic Solar Farms

Description	Installation and operation of photovoltaic solar parks with capacities between 5 and 15 MWp. All the energy delivered to the Sistema Electrico Nacional will be by the Union Eléctrica through an Energy Sale Contract.
Investment Type	100% Foreign Capital Company
Cuban Party	Union Eléctrica
Estimated Investment Amount	Depending on the installed capacity (between 1.5 and 2.0 million USD per MW of installed power)
Location	Selected areas of the ZEDM
Contacts	Dirección de Negocios de la Unión Eléctrica Email: pedrob@oc.une.cu Tel. (53) 879-0268

OTHER PROJECTS BEING PROMOTED BY CUBAN ENTITIES IN THE SPECIAL DEVELOPMENTZONE OF MARIEL

1. MANUFACTURING LIGHT AUTOMOBILES

We need to identify a potential partner to guarantee financing and markets for setting up a new plant using clean cutting edge technology to assemble and manufacture a minimum of 10,000 light automobiles per year, for the domestic market and exportation, associated with industries in Havana in order to manufacture parts, spare parts and accessories as well as a network of countrywide technical services. Investment Type: Joint Enterprise. Cuban Party: Grupo Empresarial de la Industria Sidero Mecánica (GESIME).

2. Production of valves for pressure bodies

We need to identify a potential partner to guarantee financing and markets for setting up a new plant using clean cutting edge technology to manufacture valves for

pressure bodies such as extinguishers, gas cylinders, oxygen and acetylene tanks, etc., in order to replace imports. Investment Type: Joint Enterprise. Cuban Party: Grupo Empresarial de la Industria Sidero Mecánica (GESIME).

3. Project to manufacture raffia cloth, large-sized bags (woven and not-woven and thermo-formed)

We need to identify a potential partner to guarantee financing and markets for setting up a new plant using clean cutting edge technology to produce raffia cloth, large- sized bags (woven and not-woven and thermo-formed) in order to replace imports. Investment Type: Joint Enterprise. Cuban Party: Grupo Empresarial de la Industria Ligera (GEMPIL).

4. Engineering and technological projects company

We need to identify a potential partner with the potential for creating a joint enterprise to develop engineering, supplies and construction job management projects, setting up and starting up industrial, agro-industrial, waste water treatment and renewable energies projects as well as post-sale services for the domestic market and the exportation of services. Investment Type: Joint Enterprise. Cuban Party: Grupo Empresarial de la Industria Sidero Mecánica (GESIME).

5. Plant for the production of biodrugs to treat cancer and other chronic diseases

Building a new industrial biotechnology facility to produce recombinant proteins for treating cancer and other chronic diseases, from the active pharmaceutical ingredient (10 kg/year capacity). Including warehouses, offices and technological services. Production will be basically for exportation. Investment Type: International Economic Association. Cuban Party: Cimab S.A. Centro de Inmunología Molecular.

6. Good Manufacturing Pratices Plant (BPF in the Spanish acronym) for development and production of oral biological medicines

Building a plant to manufacture oral biological medicines with a fermentative capacity of 500 L, with the potential for manufacturing anti-salmonella vaccines and cholera probiotics. Production is basically for exportation. Investment Type: International Economic Association. Cuban Party: DALMER S.A. Laboratories.

7. Investment associations providing auxiliary services

Investment projects providing auxiliary and support services for the drug industry:

Metrology and validation of measuring equipment laboratory and production areas.

Specialized engineering services workshop for refrigeration, water treatment systems, diagnostics for maintenance systems, etc.

Specialized treatment plant for solids, liquid and gas waste.

Water and steam treatment service plant.

Logistical services for warehouses for imported products and the movement of

importation/exportation loading. Investment Type: International Economic Association. Cuban Party: BioCubaFarma

TRADE STRATEGY AND BUSINESS OPPORTUNITIES BY SECTOR

Sector		Location	Quantify
	Mariel	Rest of the country	Total
Agro-food	5	32	37
Sugar Industry		4	4
Biotechnology and medicines	13		13
Wholesale Business		1	1
Construction		6	6
Renewable Energy	1	13	14
Industry	6	10	16
Mining		10	10
Oil		86	86
Transportation		3	3
Tourism		56	56
Total	25	221	246

AGRICULTURE FORESTRY AND FOOD SECTOR

The Boyeros Agricultural Fair (FIAGROP in its Spanish acronym) is a platform for promoting opportunities for commercialization, introducing new firms, joint enterprises and other forms of businesses for an agro-foods market with non-stop growth.

Agriculture is a factor adding dynamics to the Cuban economy since it requires growth in the other branches that complement the cycle of its products.

To promote sector performance, the Cuban government has implemented agricultural policies regarding economic incentives and access for the producers to financing, consumables, agricultural markets, technology, etc.

Land ownership remains to a large degree in the hands of the State even though only 29.4 % of the land is managed by state entities while 70.6 % is managed by non-state formats such as Basic Production Units (UBPCs), Credit and Service Cooperatives (CCSs) and Agricultural Production Cooperatives (CPAs).

Land Distribution by Forms of Management 29% State 27% UBPCs 8% CPAs 36% CCSs and Private Management	Land Ownership 78% State ownership 7% Cooperative ownership 15% Small Farmers

The sector has strengths and identified opportunities that can be strengthened by foreign investment.

Availability of agricultural land with uncultivated areas permitting expansion of the current productive limits within a short time. The country has 6.3 million hectares of agricultural land; of this only 2,640,000 hectares are being cultivated.
Potential for increasing areas under irrigation on the basis of recovering systems or new projects. According to National Statistics Office information for 2012, there is a 7 billion cubic meter capacity for water extraction, of which 55% goes to agriculture.
Structured systems for plant and animal protection with nationwide networks and effective border controls. Cuba is a zone that is free of Type 1 diseases existing in the area.
Access to the domestic market, increased demands and good strategic position for access to markets in the area. Domestic market potential according to importation levels is around 1,900 million USD. Cuba also has natural advantages to promote exports mainly to areas in the Caribbean.
The agricultural system has drawn up development programs of the principal products to the year 2020. It also foresees logistical investment projects in production chains, from producer consumables to final clients.

Approximately 13.2% of the country's working-age population works in the agricultural system. Of a total 924,817 workers, 56% are employed in the cooperative sector.

Qualified Workforce

University-educated	23.478	Middle Technicians	48,170
Of these: Agronomist Engineers	6,047	Of these: Agronomists	12,000
Agricultural Engineers	546	Veterinary Animal Technicians	9,466
Veterinary Doctors	4,726		

We have 342 teaching institutions providing agriculture and forestry degree courses, in the specialties of agricultural engineering, veterinary medicine, middle technician in veterinary animal medicine, etc.

The sector's scientific and innovative work is backed by institutions providing services associated with soil conservation and use, plant health, veterinary medicine, overall livestock and land control such as the National Center for Livestock Control, the National Center for Plant Health, the National Center for Land Control, the Soils Institute and the Institute of Veterinary Medicine.

Leading Products:

Tobacco: Cuban Premium tobacco (cigars) is internationally recognized for its unbeatable quality and advantageous position among the competition. It is a product in great demand among smokers in the upper economic range market. Associated with the prestige of its portfolio of brands and Cuban tobacco leaves, we are developing other export products such as mechanized products and cigarettes. Citrus fruits: Fresh citrus fruits (oranges and grapefruits), concentrated and simple juices and essential oils are products with experience and consolidated markets.

Fruit: the main types are fruit pulp, especially mango and pineapple juice.

Coffee: Exports basically include Superior Arabica (Crystal Mountain, Extraturquino, Turquino and Altura). The main client is Japan and we also sell to France, the UK, New Zealand, Australia, Germany and other European countries.

Cacao: This product has great export potential; currently it is being exported to European countries such as Switzerland and Belgium.

Honey production: This is a product with great foreign market potential and it has many benefits. There are possibilities for assortments of specific types of honeys (organic honey) and to diversify the formats besides exporting soft extract and dry pollen and diversified products such as beauty crèmes based on honey.

Other products: There is potential for vegetable charcoal, pine resin, vegetables and garden vegetables and seeds.

SECTORIAL POLICY:

To promote comprehensive agro-industrial projects that increase food production, encourage sustainable development and increase efficiency, quality and competitiveness in the different forms of production management at work in this sector, in the aim of replacing food imports and to increase and diversify exports.

Foreign investment shall be fundamentally directed towards fruit, vegetables, grains and cereals, beef, pork, poultry, animal food and milk, as well as integral products including intensive management of forestry products having a commercial nature.

It excludes tobacco agricultural products and the Premium cigar industry. Land ownership shall not be transferrable. In joint business ventures the contribution of the Cuban Party may include the real right of usufruct for the land.

Contact Information: Dirección de Negocios del Ministerio de la Agricultura Tel: (537) 884-7697 y (537) 884-7508 Email: secrenegocios@oc.minag.cu negocios@oc.minag.cu

The Foods Industry in Cuba deals with activities that transform raw materials and obtain products from milk, meat, fruit, vegetables, coffee, flour, beverages, oil, cacao and fishing products.

The Business System is made up of 108 enterprises of which 11 are International Economic Associations and it is directed through the Business Group of the Foods Industry (GEIA), the Cubaron Corporation (CUBARON) and Corporation Alimentaria S.A (CORALSA).

We have a National Center for Quality Inspection, the Foods Industry Research Institute, the Fishing Research Center and the Maritime Fishing Institution which support work in the sector.

SALES INCOMES

28% Tourism 27% Hard Currency Markets 9% Domestic Commerce 22% Exports 14% Other
Source: Ministry of the Foods Industry

The labor force is composed of 83,000 workers; of these 62% are university graduates, technicians and pre-university level, 38% have below Grade 12 educations. We have 2 institutes training technicians and professionals.

The foods industry generates average income of 954 million CUC with tourism and hard currency markets being the main destinations for the products.

The Foods Production Division aims to transform:

Spirits and alcohols into: varying grades of quality rum, wine (including dry wine), vinegar, etc.

Sugar and its byproducts: carbonated beverages and candy

Hops and barley into: beer and malt drinks

Wheat flour into: bread, crackers, sherbets, etc.

Soy beans into: refined oil

Cacao into: cocoa, candy "africanas", chocolate-covered products, etc.

It is interested in foreign investment for the technological modernization of production of soy oil, cookies and crackers, sherbets, waters, carbonated beverages, wheat flour, candies, other chocolate and confectionary products.

Among the main imported raw materials are soy beans, hops, beer, flavorings, coloring agents, conserving agents, etc.

There is potential for increased exports of products derived from chocolate, rum, beer, malt drinks, soy bean flour for animal consumption and wheat flour for the bread industry.

The Agro-Foods Production Division aims to transform:

Dairy milk and soy bean into: pasteurized milk, condensed milk, sterilized milk, soft cheeses, semi-soft cheeses, hard cheeses, ice cream, yoghurt, butter, etc.

Beef and pork into: beef, sausages (sausages and hot dogs), beef products (shaped products such as hamburgers, meat balls and croquettes), salted meats, smoked meats, etc.

COFFEE BEANS INTO ROASTED COFFEE

Fruits and vegetables into: pulp, juice, nectar, sweetened fruit in syrup, sterilized vegetables, pickled vegetables.

It is interested in foreign investment for the technological modernization of production of meat products and sausages, long-life dairy products and soy milk byproducts.

Among the main imported raw materials we are powdered milk, additives, flavoring, material for bottles and packaging, conserving agents, synthetic tripe, etc.

There is potential for increased exports of products such as tinned fruit, juice and nectar.

Cuban Parties associating in foreign investment businesses:

CubaRon Corporation: over 20 years of experience in the production and commercialization of rum and other alcoholic beverages of varying types and quality, spirits, alcohol and its byproducts. Its main aim is to increase exports of rum, low-alcohol-content beverages and juices.

Corporacion Alimentaria S.A. CORALSA: Created in 1995 to participate as shareholder in foreign enterprises based in Cuba or abroad, associated with foods industry activities. It has experience in developing meat products, ice cream, flour for bread production and semolina, beer and malt drinks, water and soft drinks, chocolate products and other cacao byproducts.

Sectorial Policy:

To promote integral projects generating linked productions and encourage efficiency throughout the chain. Excluded is anything dealing with the capture and industrialization of lobster.

Contact Information:

Dirección de Negocios del Grupo Empresarial de la Industria Alimentaria. Email: minal@minal.cu negocios@coralsa.com.cu

TECHNICAL SPECIFICATIONS ON FOREIGN INVESTMENT OPPORTUNITIES

Production of beef, its industrial processing and commercializing special cuts (2 projects)

Description	To increase beef production on the basis of exploiting 100% of installed capacities for fattening up steer. The aim is to fatten up steer of over 400 Kg hoof weight at 24 months old. As part of the infrastructure we require technological modernization in the slaughterhouses to transform and industrialize channels for special cuts incorporating added value to the product, improve its quality and appearance to be sold on the tourism market and in the hard-currency shops, thereby ensuring that imports are replaced. This project can be undertaken in Matanzas and/or Ciego de Avila, as the investor prefers. The project will allow for growth of cattle genetics, it will recover agricultural areas for raw material production for animal fodder and strengthen the production chain with the participation of agricultural cooperatives.
Investment Type	Joint Enterprise
Cuban Party	Livestock Genetics Enterprise
Estimated Investment Amount	10.0 million USD
Location	In Livestock Genetic Enterprise areas in Matanzas and Turiguano (Ciego de Avila).
Market Potential	The project provides a replacement for imports and ensures special cuts of beef for tourism and local consumption markets.
Estimated Anticipated Results	5,000 metric tons of beef for special cuts incorporating added value to the product, improving quality and appearance for it to

	be sold to the tourism and local markets thereby ensuring that imports are replaced.
Contacts	Dirección General Grupo de Producción Porcina (GRUPOR). e-mail: norberto@minag.cu e-mail: prod4por@minag.cu Tel.: (537) 884-7253 and (537) 884-7254.

Pork Production for channeled commercialization and finished pork products (5 projects)

Description	This project may be undertaken in Cienfuegos, Villa Clara, Matanzas, Pinar del Rio or Artemisa, as the investor prefers. Its aim is to increase pork production on the basis of exploiting all installed capacities. We foresee attaining 3,000 breeders in the aim of producing 7,200 metric tons of hoof weight hogs. Slaughtered hogs will have hoof weights of 100-120 Kg, transforming into channeled hogs in an abattoir to be built as part of the infrastructure. The abattoir will have an estimated installed slaughter capacity of 300 hogs per day; with 270 working days per year we will be able to slaughter up to 81,000 hogs each year. Channeled hogs will be industrialized in a processing plant to be built as part of the enterprise's infrastructure for the aim of producing finished products and byproducts including sausages, shaped products and smoked meats incorporating added value to the product and improving its competitive edge. We foresee developing the genetics of the Yorkshire, Landrace, Duroc and CC21 breeds; fodder production for hogs; semen production; providing breed-improvement services; recovering agricultural areas to produce raw materials to be used for animal fodder production and strengthening the chain with agricultural cooperatives.
Investment Type	Joint Enterprise
Cuban Party	EMPRESA PORCINA & CORALSO
Estimated Investment Amount	120.0 million USD
Location	In Empresa Porcina areas close to the area where the Joint Enterprise will be located in Cienfuegos, Villa Clara, Matanzas, Pinar del Rio and Artemisa.
Market Potential	The project replaces imports and will ensure demands for finished pork products and byproducts for the tourism and local markets.
Estimated Anticipated Results	108,000 metric tons of finished products and byproducts including pork sausages, shaped pork products and smoked pork
Contacts	Dirección General Grupo de Producción Porcina (GRUPOR). email: norberto@minag.cu; prod4por@minag.cu Tel.: (537) 884-7253 and (537) 884-7254.

Buffalo Cattle Production for industrialization and the commercialization of milk and its byproducts

Description	To increase buffalo milk production on the basis of exploiting 100% of installed capacities; for this purpose we shall have to activate 22 dairies with the aim of producing 4.7 million liters of buffalo milk per year. The milk will be industrialized in an existing plant in Nazareno, Havana Province, which requires technological modernization for a line of industrializing buffalo milk in order to produce Mozzarella cheese, yoghurt and butter incorporating added value to the product, improving quality and appearance in various formats to be sold on the tourism and local markets as replacements for imports. We hope to develop buffalo genetics, recover agricultural areas for the production of raw materials to become animal fodder and strengthen the productive chain with participation of agricultural cooperatives.
Investment Type	Joint Enterprise
Cuban Party	Empresa Pecuaria Genetica Bufalina El Cangre and CORALSA.
Estimated Investment Amount	55.2 million USD
Location	In Empresa Pecuaria Genetica Bufalina areas in Mayabeque Province.
Market Potential	The project replaces imports of milk, cheese, mozzarella, yoghurt and butter for tourism and local markets.
Estimated Anticipated Results	70.5 million liters of buffalo milk
Contacts	Dirección General Grupo de Producción Porcina (GRUPOR). email: norberto@minag.cu; prod4por@minag.cu Tel.: (537) 884-7253 and (537) 884-7254

Poultry Meat Production and its channeled commercialization (9 projects)

Description	To increase production of poultry (chicken) on the basis of exploiting installed production capacities. For this purpose we will have to activate production of fertile eggs and their incubation. The aim is to produce 10,000 metric tons of channeled chicken per year. Chickens slaughtered will have live weight of 2 kg at 38 days, with food/live weight conversion of 1.75 Kg. We require acquisition of equipment for technological modernization in the line of slaughtering 3000 chickens per hour, representing slaughtering 24,000 chickens per day in the abattoir. This project can be undertaken in Pinar del Rio, Artemisa, Matanzas, Villa Clara, Cienfuegos, Sancti Spiritus, Camaguey, Holguin and Granma, as the investor prefers. The enterprise will allow developing the genetics for high reproduction breeds, incubation, recovering agricultural areas for the production of raw materials destined to produce animal feed and strengthen the productive chain with participation of agricultural cooperatives.
Investment Type	Joint Enterprise
Cuban Party	Empresas Avicolas
Estimated Investment Amount	35.5 million USD
Location	In Empresas Avicolas in Pinar del Rio, Artemisa, Matanzas, Villa Clara, Cienfuegos, Sancti Spiritus, Camaguey, Holguin and Granma.
Market Potential	The project replaces imports and ensures channeled chicken for the tourism and local markets.

Estimated Anticipated Results	150,000 metric tons of channeled chicken
Contacts	Dirección General Unión de Empresas del Combinado Avícola Nacional (UECAN). email: dirección@uecan.minag.cu; prod4por@minag.cu Tel.: (537) 884-7306, (537) 884-7307, (537) 884-7253 and (537) 884-7254.

Rice Production in the southern part of Artemisa and Mayabeque Provinces

Description	To increase national production of rice by applying proper techniques in agricultural exploitation, adapted to the climate and local soil conditions, using correct fertilization, phytosanitary and post-harvest systems.
Investment Type	Joint Enterprise
Cuban Party	Empresa Agroindustrial de Granos José Martí
Estimated Investment Amount	37.06 million USD
Location	Empresa Agroindustrial de Granos José Martí in San Cristobal municipality, Artemisa Province.
Market Potential	Sales on the national market to replace imports, for tourism and eventual exportation.
Estimated Anticipated Results	10.0 MTM yearly average
Contacts	Dirección del Grupo Agroindustrial de Granos email: contabilidadgaia@minag.cu Tel.: (537) 884-7600

Peanut Production

Description	To develop peanut production with participation of agricultural cooperatives and individual farmers in order to replace imports. We hope to obtain yields between 2.5 and 3 tons per hectare on the basis of satisfying the nutritional needs of the plant with adequate seeds. We foresee using the agricultural areas of the former sugar mills where infrastructure and agricultural practices exist for exploring growing possibilities.
Investment Type	Joint Enterprise
Cuban Party	Empresa Agroindustrial de Granos Jovellanos
Estimated Investment Amount	70.5 million USD
Location	Jovellanos municipality, Matanzas province.
Estimated Anticipated Results	7,400 metric tons per year
Contacts	Dirección del Grupo Agroindustrial de Granos. Email: contabilidadgaia@minag.cu Tel.: (537) 884-7600

Processing and commercialization of Elite quality conventional coffee

Description	To efficiently process the production of Cuban coffee from selected special micro-regions in the hills of Guantanamo to create a leading brand on the international level. The scope of the investment includes updating technological coffee processing techniques in order to increase acceptance levels for the dry healthy product, ensuring good conservation, handling, storage and commercialization, to improve levels of knowledge in the

	coffee-growing areas and to update them thereby improving the quality of high-grade assortments of coffees and increasing the available amounts for the foreign market.
Investment Type	International Economic Association Contract
Cuban Party	Empresa Procesadora de Café Asdrubal Lopez Vazquez of Guantanamo
Estimated Investment Amount	10.3 million USD
Location	Empresa Procesadora de Café Asdrubal Lopez Vazquez is some 1.7 Km to the west of the Guaso River and the same distance from the Jaibo River in the southern area of the city of Guantanamo (the industrial zone) at the intersection of the southern ring-road and the highway that leads to the Nicaragua warehouses.
Market Potential	Coffee production will be destined for exportation, for the Elite Quality market.
Contacts	Dirección de Negocios y Desarrollo del GEAM. Email: ddesarrollo@geam.minag.cu Tel. (537) 884-7456 and (537) 884-7457

Making use of Scrub (marabú) Biomass for the production of vegetal charcoal and increasing intensive forestry management plantations (4 projects)

Description	To annually produce, on an industrial basis, 3000 metric tons of vegetal charcoal and 2600 metric tons of charcoal activated from marabú scrub, as well as replanting 3300 hectares free of marabou. In addition, we would produce vegetal charcoal briquettes for export. The scope of the investment includes equipment needed for harvesting and transportation of marabú, thereby ensuring stable sustained supplies of the biomass required for charcoal production as well as acquiring equipment and machinery for forest replanting, with intensive management of the areas being cleaned up. This project can be undertaken in Granma, Holguin, Camaguey and Ciego de Avila, as the investor prefers.
Investment Type	International Economic Association Contract
Cuban Party	Empresas Forestales Integrales
Estimated Investment Amount	4.1 million USD (each project)
Location	Companies in Granma, Holguin, Camaguey and Ciego de Avila, locations of the vegetal charcoal and activates production industry. Areas of marabu and forest plantations to be promoted cover several municipalities no further away than 30 Km from the project site.
Market Potential	Foreign market, basically Europe. Surplus electricity generated will be delivered to the Sistema Electroenergetico Nacional.
Estimated Anticipated	Vegetal Charcoal – 3000 metric tons annual average
Results	Activated Charcoal – 2600 metric tons annual average Briquettes – 1050 metric tons annual average Sales of electrical power
Contacts	Dirección de Negocios y Desarrollo del GEAM Email

	ddesarrollo@geam.minag,cu Tel.: (537) 884-7456 and (537) 884-7457

Development of agro-industrial production of citrus fruit and other fruit in the Contramaestre region

Description	To increase production, improve quality and commercialize concentrated and simple juices, essential citrus oils and pulp, juices and conserves of other tropical fruit. The citrus fruit line has the capacity of processing a maximum of 75,000 tons per year of fruit; currently less than 1% is being handled. We wish to process 45,000 tons/year of fruit; for this purpose we will replace the other tropical fruit current line that processes less than 1.5 tons per hour with another line that processes 6 tons per hour.
Investment Type	International Economic Association Contract
Cuban Party	Empresa Citricos America Libre
Estimated Investment Amount	6.9 million USD
Location	Contramaestre Municipality in Santiago de Cuba. Province is a region with a long citrus-growing tradition, with excellent geographical location where, because of the type of soil and the climate, fruit present a higher content of soluble solids and less acidity thereby making them ideal for consumption as fresh fruit and being industrially processed.
Market Potential	Foreign market, basically Europe. Domestic market: fresh fruit will be marketed and its byproducts will be industrialized in small formats such as nectar, fruit in syrup, creams and marmalades, in the tourist sector of Holguin and Santiago de Cuba. The principal client for tropical fruit pulp is the Ministry of Foods Industries (MINAL) tinning industry.
Estimated Anticipated Results	To produce 6,450 tons/year of concentrated and simple juice, 90 tons of essential oils, 13,870 tons of pulp, juice and other conserves. The processing operation will be able to process 9,230 tons/year of fresh fruit.
Contacts	Dirección General Empresa Cítricos América Libre. Email: guillermo@enet.cu Tel. (5322) 58-7432

Development of the production of citrus and other fruit, such as fresh fruit and industrialized products in the Empresa Citricos Ceiba

Description	The project is designed for installation of an industrial plant to process fruit and to encourage the region's Future Development Program. It will indirectly tie in the agricultural cooperatives as suppliers of the raw material thereby ensuring the production chain. We need to finance the production to guarantee acquisition of high quality seedlings, consumables, services and technical assistance.
Investment Type	Joint Enterprise
Cuban Party	Empresa Citricos Ceiba
Estimated Investment Amount	9.0 million USD
Location	Empresa Citricas Ceiba is located at KM 9 ½ of the Doble Via de

	Ceiba, Caimito municipality in the province of Artemisa.
Market Potential	Products will be for the domestic market (10%) and exportations (90%). The domestic market will basically include tourism and local markets.
Estimated Anticipated Results	2 tons/day of chopped fruit, 10,000 liters/day of juice, 5 ton/hour of pulp and conserves as well as increased exports
Contacts	Dirección Empresa Cítricos Ceiba email: ilio@citricosceiba.cu Tel. (5347) 31-1100 and (5347) 31-1106.

Increased Production Potential for Shrimp Farming

Description	To increase shrimp production by improving the technology being used today to grow-out the larva and reduce costs during this phase. The possibility of seeding +8 mg postlarvae in the hatchery stage, up to +300 mg, to subsequently transfer them to the nursery stage and to introduce probiotics and other technologies to handle the ponds will produce fewer days per productive cycle and therefore increase the rotation rate of hectares per4 year, decrease food consumption (tons of feed per ton of harvested shrimp); average harvested weight gain; percentage survival increase in the grow-out pond stage.
Investment Type	Joint Enterprise
Cuban Party	CORALSA
Estimated Investment Amount	19.9 million USD
Location	Granma province, Rio Cauto municipality
Market Potential	Export market, principally Asia.
Estimated Anticipated Results	Obtaining technology guaranteeing improved efficiency in order to improve growing hectare rotation and other cutting edge technologies to handle the ponds and resulting in operations costs similar to those on an international level with a strategy for management as well as spare parts and mastery of the technology. International market quality demands are satisfied and at the same time, solutions will be implemented to increase disease control and achieve sustainable development that is harmonious with the environment.
Contacts	Corporación Alimentaria S.A (CORALSA). Calle 14 No 115, entre 1ra y 3ra, Playa, La Habana, Cuba. email: negocios@coralsa.com.cu Tel.: (537) 202-1194, (537) 202-7388 and (537) 205-9093

Production and commercialization of fresh, filled pasta (lasagna, cannelloni, ravioli, tortellini, panzerotti and gnocchi) and their accompanying sauces

Description	To increase the availability of fresh filled pastas and sauces. Activating this industry will also make it possible to decrease the current proportion of imported fresh filled pastas now on the local market. Orienting production capacities has been estimated according to the composition of the current demands of the hotel sector in Cuba, depending on each type of product: lasagna 39.0%, cannelloni 22.0%, ravioli 15.0%, tortellini 13.0 %,

	panzerotti 6.0 %, gnocchi 5.0%
Investment Type	Joint Enterprise
Cuban Party	CORALSA
Estimated Investment Amount	2.0 million USD
Location	Havana province or Villa Clara
Market Potential	Production will be destined to satisfy demands of the principle tourism areas in the country and the local market.
Estimated Anticipated Results	We have calculated that demand will increase over the next few years as tourism grows, reaching a total of over 300 tons per year. We plan for sales for the 15-year period that are over 25.5 MMUSD; therefore we would like to produce and commercialize 1000 kg per day of fresh filled pasta and 20 kg per day of sauces.
Contacts	Corporación Alimentaria S.A (CORALSA). Calle 14 No 115, entre 1ra y 3ra, Playa, La Habana, Cuba. email: negocios@coralsa.com.cu Tel. (537) 202-1194, (537) 202-7388 and (537) 205-9093

Production of carbonated drinks and bottled water

Description	To increase availability of carbonated drinks and bottled water by setting up a cutting edge technology line in the country's central region for production and distribution in that zone and in the eastern part of the country. It will also make possible the creation of a distribution network destined to satisfy demands in the central and eastern parts of the country. The investment project also seeks to replace today's bulk soft drink and syrup commercialization.
Investment Type	Joint Enterprise
Cuban Party	CORALSA
Estimated Investment Amount	12.3 million USD
Location	Ciego de Avila municipality, Ciego de Avila province
Market Potential	Local and tourism markets
Estimated Anticipated Results	500, 000hl per year of carbonated drinks and bottled water
Contacts	Corporación Alimentaria S.A (CORALSA). Calle 14 No 115, entre 1ra y 3ra, Playa, La Habana, Cuba. email: negocios@coralsa.com.cu Tel. (537) 202-1194, (537) 202-7388 and (537) 205-9093

Industrial processing of cacao and increased production of chocolate-based products

Description	To modernize the existing cacao processing plant with a view to obtaining various chocolatier products. Currently the industry demands 2,500 tons of cacao and only receives 1,500 tons that satisfy 60% of formats and assortments for the domestic market in CUC. According to MINAGRI estimates, we can attain a national cacao seed production of approximately 3,500 tons for the year 2020.

Investment Type	Joint Enterprise
Cuban Party	CORALSA
Estimated Investment Amount	16.8 million USD
Location	Guantanamo province, Baracoa municipality
Market Potential	Tourism, local market and export. Replacing imports.
Estimated Anticipated Results	Processing 1,000 tons per year of cacao (liquor, butter and cocoa) with high-productivity technology, automation and efficient energy consumption, as well as reduced environmental impact with the quality specifications demanded by international standards.
Contacts	Corporación Alimentaria S.A (CORALSA). Calle 14 No 115, entre 1ra y 3ra, Playa, La Habana, Cuba. email: negocios@coralsa.com.cu Tel. (537) 202-1194, (537) 202-7388 and (537) 205-9093

Production of Confectionary and Cereals

Description	To diversify production of confectionary (candies, sherbets, fine biscuits, sweet, cream and soda crackers) and breakfast cereal mixes in different formats and assortments with an emphasis on nutritional values.
Investment Type	Joint Enterprise
Cuban Party	Corporation Alimentaria S.A. (CORALSA), mercantile company with 100% Cuban capital, whose corporate purpose is shareholder participation in joint enterprises in the foods sector.
Estimated Investment Amount	15.3 million USD
Location	Villa Clara province, Caibarien municipality
Market Potential	Tourism and local markets and part for exportation
Estimated Anticipated Results	Current demands, with a view to replace imports, reaches an annual total of approximately 18 to 20 million USD.
Contacts	Corporación Alimentaria S.A (CORALSA). Calle 14 No 115, entre 1ra y 3ra, Playa, La Habana, Cuba. email: negocios@coralsa.com.cu Tel. (537) 202-1194, (537) 202-7388 and (537) 205-9093

Soy processing plant to produce refined oil

Description	To mill 500,00 tons of soy beans per year
Investment Type	Joint Enterprise
Cuban Party	CORALSA
Estimated Investment Amount	149.0 million USD
Location	Artemis or Cienfuegos province
Market Potential	Sales to the local market. Oil distribution will take in up to Holguin province, with Santiago de Cuba production (where the country's only soy processing plant and oil refinery is located) covering the rest of the eastern provinces. Today, refined oil production (28.000 tons) and soy flour for animal consumption (85,000 tons) does not meet demand levels.
Estimated Anticipated Results	85,000 tons of refined oil and 375,000 tons of soy flour for animal

	consumption.
Contacts	Corporación Alimentaria S.A (CORALSA). Calle 14 No 115, entre 1ra y 3ra, Playa, La Habana, Cuba. email: negocios@coralsa.com.cu Tel. (537) 202-1194, (537) 202-7388 and (537) 205-9093

SUGAR INDUSTRY SECTOR

The identifying roots of our nation were formed in the old sugar mills (bateyes). Since sugarcane was introduced to Cuba, the sugar industry sector has always been the most important one for Cuban agro-industrial production.

ZERUS S.A. is the mercantile company ensuring the agro-industrial sector of sugar and its byproducts in its search for new joint businesses using foreign capital and developing existing businesses.

AZCUBA is the sugar industry group in charge of managing the entities that make up the sugar agro-industry for developing sugar productions, electrical energy, sugarcane byproducts and agricultural and industrialized foods.

There are 14 Sugar Industry Enterprises throughout Cuba, as well as 8 companies supporting the sugar agro-industry with activities including the commercialization of sugar, its byproducts and agricultural products, technical services, construction services, industrial set up, automation and mechanical production, exporting equipment and technical assistance, etc.

Sector Principal Infrastructure	
56 sugar mills	
7 refineries	
12 distilleries	
35 animal food plants	
2 board factories	
10 rum companies	
3 CO_2 plants	
Agricultural and technological equipment, aggregates and spare parts workshops	
Available area	800,000 hectares
Area under exploitation	600,000 hectares
% mechanized harvesting	90
Number of workers	70,000

Heirs to a long tradition, the human capital at work in the sugar agro-industry is experienced, well-trained and with excellent quality. It includes 10,000 university-educated workers, 16,000 middle technicians and 13,000 qualified laborers.

There are 2 research centers (one is industrial and the other is agricultural) and a training center guaranteeing research development with results for obtaining new technologies and products as well as for the growing use of automated and computerized systems.

National Center Sugar Industry Training was founded in 1978 and it is the first school in Cuba responsible for managerial and technical training.

For five decades, the Cuban Institute for Sugarcane Byproduct Research (ICIDCA) has carried out scientific-technical and technical innovation work as evidenced by the significant awards won. Web site: www.icidca.cu

The Sugar Cane Research Institute provides its clients with a range of technologies, equipment and services to cover their most pressing needs regarding research as applied to the growing of sugarcane. Website: www.inica.minaz.cu

LEADING PRODUCTS

Raw Sugar: we have the tradition and knowledge of our workers and our professionals' technical capacities.

Ecological Sugar (organic): there is a growing export market as well as for the byproducts with organic fruit, honey and alcohol and rum byproducts.

Alcohol, rum, spirits and liqueurs: prestigious high-quality products are exported and can be the leaders in some countries.

Sorbitol-FOS: High-quality and in-demand product with growing export possibilities. Our knowledge and acquired know-how for its production with glucoses from various origins could become an exportable service.

Technical Assistance: The experience and high-quality of Cuban sugar industry technicians encourages exporting technical assistance.

SECTORIAL POLICY:

Businesses with foreign capital in this sector should promote projects directed towards modernizing and increasing the use of installed capacities, promoting their efficiency and yield, the quality of the sugar, growth and diversification of exportable funds, byproduct availability and the growth of byproduct production with a focus on energy. Businesses to manage the production chain are being prioritized.

Technical Specifications for Foreign Investment Sugar Mill Production Management (4 projects)

Description	In the 1980s, proposed sugarcane production of this type was around 90,000 tons of sugar on average or more, during at least 150 harvest days with a yield of 65 tons per hectare. (T/ha). The aim of investing in sugar mills is to recover those figures, identifying a "Management" foreign partner who would deal with finding the necessary financing and contribute with modern business administration tools and the necessary resources. The aim is to: • Recover capacities of original sugar mill designs. • Gradually increase sugarcane and sugar production. • Introduce new production and managerial technologies • Improve sugar production efficiency, its quality and reducing costs. • Self-finance the recovery.
Investment Type	International Economic Association Contract for Production Management
Cuban Party	Sugar industry companies owning each sugar mill

Estimated Investment Amount	40.0 million USD (each project)
Location	The following sugar mills: Mario Muñoz in Matanzas province, 30 de Noviembre in Artemisa, Batalla de las Guásimas in Camagüey and Majibacoa in Las Tunas.
Market Potential	Exportation and the local market
Contact:	Dirección de Negocios de ZERUS Email: jorge.lodos@zerus.azcuba.cu Tel: (537) 838-3194 ext. 237

INDUSTRIAL SECTOR

The industrial sector is related to the production of bottles and packaging, recycling raw materials, manufacturing electronic equipment and electrical appliances, chemical products and its byproducts, medical equipment, textiles, clothing and accessories, hygiene products, perfumes and cosmetics, all of which will be helped by foreign investment in the aim of generating production linkage, allowing imports to be replaced and exports to be increased.

Therefore, priorities are set for modernizing the metals industry, industries producing steel byproducts, electrical appliances, manufacturing aluminum and glass containers for beverages and medicines, increasing capacities for the design and manufacture of metal structures, comprehensive handling of solid waste and other recyclable materials as well as various products that constitute consumption goods for the population.

The international industrial convention and exhibition CUBAINDUSTRIA is to be held twice a year; the first edition was held in 2014 proving to be an excellent place for scientific, academic and professional exchanges among Cuban and foreign specialists in the sector. CUBAINDUSTRIA provides an ideal opportunity to learn about products, equipment, machinery, new technologies, parts and components and to draw up trade agreements, strategic alliances, development covenants, associations and contracts for new supply alternatives.	The sector has a total of 205 companies, production centers and services spread throughout Cuba employing a total of 86,284. It significantly identifies itself with 25% of mechanical engineers and an equitable distribution of general technical specialties such as mechanical engineering, industrial engineering chemical engineering, etc.

Contact Information:

Dirección de Inversiones y Cooperación MINDUS Email: forcada@industrias.cu Tel. (537) 263-3215

SECTORIAL POLICY:

To promote projects to modernize and create new capacities in the aim of covering national demand, replace importations and generate exportations. It includes the branches of Mechanical-Metal, Light, Chemical and Electronics Industry.

Electronics, Informatics, Automation and Telecommunications Industry

The Electronics, Informatics, Automation and Telecommunications Industry is a very dynamic sector and so it requires flexible industries and highly qualified personnel that are able to quickly reconvert processes and give added value to products.

We have drawn up our 2014-2017 Development Program and we now have our own designs for LCD to LED TVs, induction stoves, UPS, LED lighting and other electronic applications. We provide design and manufacturing capacities for various installations: solar panels, STB for digital land TV, self-supporting and reinforced communications towers, lighting, antennae and other electronic equipment. We have plastic injection lines that permit massive production of electrical appliances.

PRINCIPAL PRODUCTS:

Solar Panels: an outstanding item in the renewable energy sources sector.

LCD to LED TVs: we have our own designs and decoding boxes for digital land TV.

Protectors, home and industrial lighting, electronic transformers and LED lighting: since 1998 we have manufactured over 1.5 million voltage protectors as well as over 500,000 home and industrial lighting of all kinds; this has allowed us to significantly replace importing these items into the country. We have also designed electronic transformers, an item that is competitive and allows us to take the step towards manufacturing other types of lighting such as LED T 8 and street lighting LEDs.

We have certified training centers thereby allowing us to increase training personnel through ties with leading electronics technology entities on a world-wide level, such as ESAC, CEDAI and Cubatel and GEDEME.

Investment opportunities in the sector are directed towards manufacturing high-efficiency LED lighting, cell phones, PC tablets, optical supports, etc.

CONTACT INFORMATION:

Dirección de Negocios del Grupo Empresarial de la Industria Electrónica Email: eldris@cubaelectrónica.cu Tel. (537) 204-5630 ext. 127

Technical Specifications on Foreign Investment Opportunities Production and commercialization of products and services for Informatics Solutions

Description	To produce and commercialize products and services for Informatics Solutions (standard desktop PC, machine systems without MSD discs, PC tablets, Laptops and Minilaptops). The aim of the project is to cover the growing demand of the domestic market for informatics solutions, to replace imports of informatics equipment having the backing of parts and spare parts in order to provide warranty and post-sale services including software and nationally manufactured applications.
Investment Type	Joint Enterprise
Cuban Party	Empresa Industrial para la Informática, las Comunicaciones y la Electrónica (GEDEME) belonging to the Grupo Empresarial de la Industria Electrónica
Estimated Investment Amount	9.6 million USD
Location	Callejon de Andrade y Prensa Latina Km 1 ½, Marianao municipality, La Habana province

Market Potential	Current annual demand is estimated at 75,000 computers, and in 10 years the figure should be approximately one million. Basic clients are hotels, retail shops, universities, schools, state entities, non-state sector and the new investment projects being developed in the country.
Contacts	Dirección General de GEDEME. Email: jcarlos@gedeme.co.cu Tel: (537) 260-4028

LIGHT INDUSTRY

Light industry includes over 600 factories and workshops organized into 10 production branches throughout the country.

Textile Garment Industry: Main products: clothing, textiles for decorations, uniforms, accessories for clothing and labels, socks, men's and ladies' underwear, bathing suits and t-shirts. The principal exportable item is GUAYABERA CUBANA, a typical Cuban garment that has won numerous awards at FIHAV under the brand name of "Criolla".

Textile Industry: Main products: cotton and polyester/cotton fabrics, towels, cleaning rags, covers, sheets, bedspreads, sewing thread, jute and propylene sacks, henequen rope and string. We have a large capacity to produce ecologically-friendly containers.

Furniture Industry: Main products: wooden, metal and fiber furniture, box spring and foam mattresses, pillows, decorative and industrial lamps, doors and windows, utilitarian and decorative ceramics, humidors and wooden elements for flooring.

Printing Industry: Main products: books, magazines, newspapers, pamphlets, serviettes, envelopes, catalogues, conventional and self-sticking labels, covers, packages and packing, cigar rings, accessories for cigars, assorted cards, printed paper products in continuous formats, assorted advertisements.

Cleaning Products and Cosmetics Industry: Main products: soap, cosmetics, perfumes, toothpaste, deodorants, shampoo, home and industrial detergents, air fresheners and other products tor hygiene and cleaning including mini-packages for hotels.

Matches, Leatherwork, Footwear and the Paint Industry: Main products: leatherwork, men's and ladies' footwear in all the different styles, decorative candles, surgical gloves, matches, lighters and different kinds of paint and varnish.

This industry is mainly interested in foreign investment to modernize existing technology in order to develop products that will replace imports on a large scale such as hygienic/sanitary disposable products, footwear, packaging and packing in general as well as encouraging exports.

Contact Information:

Dirección de Negocios del Grupo Empresarial de la Industria Ligera. Email: yoyi@minil.cu Tel. (537) 260-3443

Technical Specifications on Foreign Investment Opportunities Production and Commercialization of Mesh Sacks

Description	Most of production is for agricultural produce sacks for the domestic market. By acquiring technological equipment for the production processes, encouraging the replacement of imports.
Investment Type	Joint Enterprise
Cuban Party	Empresa Luis A. Turcios Lima SAREX, belonging to the Grupos Empresarial de la Industria Ligera
Estimated Investment Amount	4.5 million USD
Location	UEB TEXORO belonging to the National Empresa Luis A. Turcios Lima legally domiciled at Caretera Central Via Santiago de Cuba km 848, Bayamo municipality, Granma province.
Market Potential	Current demands on domestic industry taking into account Ministry of Agriculture state enterprises total 10 million sacks for agricultural produce; this does not take into account the growing demands of the new non-state market.
Contacts	Dirección General email: javier@sarex.co.cu Tel.:(5342) 27-1789

PRODUCTION AND COMMERCIALIZATION OF FOOTWEAR

Description	Production, distribution and commercialization of footwear for the local market on the basis of acquiring cutting edge technology, installing production capacities for 6 million pairs of shoes per year, in 8 production lines, to manufacture three types of shoes: sport, casual and sandals. A small part of production will be for export.
Investment Type	Joint Enterprise
Cuban Party	COMBELL footwear company, belonging to the Grupo Empresarial de la Industria Ligera
Estimated Investment Amount	12.6 million USD
Location	Via Blanca and Avenida Monumental, Habana del Este municipality, La Habana
Market Potential	Domestic demand is estimated at 47 million pairs of shoes per year
Contacts	Dirección General de la Empresa de Calzado COMBELL. email: Guillermo@combell.com.cu Tel: (537) 881-2442

Chemical Industry

The Chemical Industry is developing the manufacture and commercialization of environment-friendly petro-chemical products. We have a development program whose implementation via the required investments would allow us to technologically modernize and gradually replace the chemical industry's high volumes of imports.

INDUSTRIAL GASES: Main Products: medical and industrial oxygen, acetylene, nitrogen, argon and carbon dioxide both liquid and gas as well as nitrous oxide and compressed air to satisfy domestic demands. FERTILIZERS AND PESTICIDES: We have a Quality management System endorsed by the Cuban Vessel Registry (RCB) and a receiving base for cryogenic ammonia with modern technology. Among our products the outstanding ones are ammonium nitrate (technical and fertilizers), calcium nitrate and physical NPK mixes (nitrogen, phosphorus, potassium). A great variety of these products does not satisfy domestic demands, and for this reason we are in the process of studying and assessing the investments required to gradually replace current imports. PAPER: This branch has nine plants located throughout the country. Some of the products offered ate corrugated cardboard packaging, pads, corrugated cardboard separators, multilayer sacks (valves and open), egg trays and containers, Testliner (150 to 200 g/m^2), wrapping paper (reams and spools), culture paper (127 to 200 g/m^2), cards (230 to 600 g/m^2), buffet boxes (1/2 and 1 lb), school notebooks, files, pay envelopes, cores (40 to 200 Mm), tissue paper, toilet paper and serviettes. CHEMICALS: Empresa Electroquimica de Sagua (ELQUIM) is dedicated to producing liquid chlorine, sodium hypochlorite, caustic soda, chlorhydric acid, hydrogen, aluminum sulfate and liquid sodium silicates. RUBBER: Fundamentally dedicated to the manufacture of new tires with diagonal technology, retreading and producing technical rubber articles (ATG). Production of new agricultural and general transportation tires is for the domestic market basically for agriculture.

Retreading tires is done at five (5) plants located in Havana, Santa Clara, Camaguey, Holguin and Santiago de Cuba. This is a high-impact service for the economy because of the savings it represents and the extending of the useful life of tires. Manufacture of technical rubber articles is destined to satisfy the needs of the economy and renewable energy programs, etc. GLASS: Manufacture and commercialization of glassware and ornamental glass. We incorporate flat glass manufacture, with cutting, polishing, beveling, engraving, stained glass and combinations of all of these. Installed production capacity no longer satisfies current demands. The country also produced laboratory glassware, consumables for health and decoration including flasks, culture tubes, pipettes, burettes, funnels, etc. Installed production capacity satisfies 50% of domestic laboratory demands for glassware.

We have a CHEMICAL ENGINEERING AND RESEARCH CENTER (CIIQ) whose main mission is to undertake scientific research, provide high-quality scientific-technical and engineering services such as process analyses and controls, graphic design, applied research, specialized products, validation and feasibility studies.

The principal working strategies to be developed with foreign investment concentrate on manufacturing newsprint and Bond, tissue paper, radial tires, etc.

Contact Information:

Direcci6n de Negocios del Grupo Empresarial de la Industria Química email: marileida@quimica.minbas.cu Tel. (537) 204-1142

Technical Specifications on Foreign Investment Opportunities Production and Commercialization of Newsprint and Bond Paper

Description	To execute technological reconversion and start-up operations of the Fine Paper Plant in order to produce 60,000 tons per year of paper distributed in 40,000 tons per year for printing and writing and 20,000 tons per year for newspapers via the modernization of facilities and the continuous introduction of advanced technologies to replace imports and for exportation purposes.
Investment Type	Joint Enterprise
Cuban Party	QUIMI S.A. belonging to the Grupo Empresarial de la Industria Química
Estimated Investment Amount	107.2 million USD
Location	Finca Palmarito S/N, Jatibonico municipality, Sancti Spiritus province.
Market Potential	The investment would be directed to satisfy domestic demand for

	40,000 tons and would destine some 20,000 tons for exportation
Contacts	Director General de la Empresa del Papel. email: gatell@pappyrus.minem.cu Tel: (537) 203-8944

PRODUCTION AND COMMERCIALIZATION OF TISSUE PAPER AND ITS CONVERSION

Description	Installation and startup of a new tissue paper plant having the capacity to produce 20,000 tons per year to satisfy the domestic market and to encourage exportations. We would like to modernize our facilities, acquire new advanced technologies and ensure stable supplies of raw materials, consumables and spare parts.
Investment Type	Joint Enterprise
Cuban Party	QUIMI S.A. belonging to the Grupo Empresarial de la Industria Química
Estimated Investment Amount	73.1 million USD
Location	Cardboard Factory of Santa Cruz del Norte, Mayabeque province.
Market Potential	We foresee that domestic demand for tissue paper will reach 20,000 tons per year. We plan to establish a niche in the export-market to Latin America.
Contacts	Director General de la Empresa del Papel. Email: gatell@pappyrus.minem.cu Tel: (537) 203-8944

METAL-MECHANICAL INDUSTRY AND RECYCLING

Plans for strategic alliances point towards the development of the iron and steel industry, recycling, mechanical industry, the automotive sector and equipment for the agricultural sector. Priority is given to the investment projects dealing with steel, manufacturing containers as well as complex products for agriculture and transportation, etc.

Main products for the domestic and export markets:

Carbon steel, wire rod and wire byproducts, electrical conductors, various refractories, transportation systems for sugarcane, farm implements, irrigation systems and components, various agricultural tractor trailers, 220 liter barrels, tin cans for food preserves, accumulator batteries, bus assembly and repairs, forklifts, automotive parts and spare parts, railway repairs and reconstruction and their spare parts, heavy and light metal structures, aluminum frame working, electrical appliances, hydro-sanitary accessories, medical and clinical-surgical instruments, doctor office and food industry furniture, scales, steam generating equipment, gas extraction systems, high pressure recipients, cold chambers, air-conditioning and refrigeration equipment, solar heaters, parts and spare parts for elevators for different uses. We are distinguished by our comprehensive system of recycling scrap metal and non-metal waste that adds value and allows us to reduce the cost of our products.

Our plans included association with foreign enterprises for items such as producing and commercializing long and special stainless steel products, production and commercialization of car batteries and UPS, production and commercialization of aluminum can, production and commercialization of metal structures as well as comprehensive solid urban waste handling systems.

Contact Information:

Vicepresidencia de la Dirección de Negocios del Grupo Empresarial de la Industria Sideromecánica. email: cherrera@sime.cu Tel. (537) 263-3429

Technical Specifications on Foreign Investment Opportunities Solid Urban Waste Handling Integrated System (SIGRSU in its Spanish acronym)

Description	The project's principal aim is to gradually reduce total volumes of generated waste to minimum levels thereby avoiding negative impact on the environment and human health; today waste is sent to dumps or sanitary landfills. SIGRSU includes all the stages of the process beginning with proper selection, collection, treatment, recycling and energy assessment to generate electricity and heat and to produce organic fertilizers. Only the inert unrecyclable waste that has no value will be sent to the landfill centers, although in later stages studied could be made about some uses for this inert portion of waste. Currently there is no SIGRSU in Cuba. The project's scope would cover the entire country and be carried out in stages. It will begin in the western area, specifically in La Habana province since its waste generation levels are estimated at 2,585.01 tons per day. The first priority would be to broaden the project and build similar plants in the center and eastern parts of the island.
Investment Type	Joint Enterprise
Cuban Party	An enterprise subordinated to the Union of Raw Materials Recovery Enterprises (UERMP) attached to the Grupo Empresarial de la Industria Sidero Mecanica.
Estimated Investment	First stager: 115.0 million USD for investing in a
Amount	Comprehensive RSU Processing Plant including several lines and improvement to the collection and dumping system.
Location	A zone in Havana, Cuba.
Market Potential	Markets for the resulting products will be: Secondary raw materials: domestic industry and the excess will be exported; today 16 groups of products are processed. The basic ones are steel scrap, molten iron, stainless steel, copper, aluminum, bronze, lead, paper and cardboard, plastics, glass bottles, glass, electronic scrap and others. The gas generated is required by the Sistema Electroenergetico Nacional to generate energy. 100% of the fertilizer generated can be used by the Ministry of Agriculture.
Contacts	Dirección General UERMP email: jorgeluis@uermp.cu, estela@uermp.cu Tel: (537) 205-1042

Production and Commercialization of Long Products made of Stainless Steel and Alloys

Description	To create production capacities for long products made of stainless steel and alloys, basically directed to exportation, to a nominal capacity of 180,000 tons per year, by modernization and enlarging equipment in the Acinox Tunas steel plant and installing a new laminator to cover domestic demands and encourage exports.
Investment Type	Joint Enterprise
Cuban Party	"Acinox Tunas" Stainless Steel Enterprise belonging to the Grupo Empresarial de la Industria Sideromecanica.

Estimated Investment Amount	222.5 million USD
Location	Circunvalante Norte Km 2 ½, Zona Industrial, Las Tunas, La Tunas province.
Market Potential	Promoting exports of stainless steel and alloys in Latin America and the Caribbean and in Europe and satisfying domestic demands for an estimated 4,000 tons per year.
Contacts	Dirección de Acinox Tunas email: rosendo@acinoxtunas.co.cu Tel: (5331) 34-6512

PRODUCTION AND COMMERCIALIZATION OF METAL STRUCTURES

Description	To insert production of metal structures in the existing plant in Metunas into a global chain to manufacture construction systems, to increase efficiency in the production of metal structures up to 25,200 tons per year by modernizing existing facilities and capacities and continuously introducing advanced technologies.
Investment Type	Joint Enterprise
Cuban Party	Empresa Mecanica del Transformado del Acero belonging to the Grupo Empresarial de la Industria Sideromecanica.
Estimated Investment Amount	25.8 million USD
Location	UEB METUNAS, Camino del Oriente Km 2 ½ Zona Industrial, Las Tunas municipality, Las Tunas province.
Market Potential	In the next 10 years we foresee that the demand for metal structures in Cuba will be well over 200,000 tons.
Contacts	Dirección de UEB METUNAS email: eraldo@metunas.co.cu Tel: (5331) 34 -5351

PRODUCTION AND COMMERCIALIZATION OF CAR BATTERIES AND UPS

Description	To increase production capacities of car batteries and UPS by at least 300,000 equivalent units per year by modernization of the existing facility, promoting the replacement of imports.
Investment Type	Joint Enterprise
Cuban Party	Empresa de Acumuladores “XX Aniversario” (CUBAT) belonging to the Grupo Empresarial de la Industria Sideromecanica.
Estimated Investment Amount	13.8 million USD
Location	Zona Industrial Faxas, Vuelta del Caño, Ciudad de Manzanillo, Granma province, Cuba.
Market Potential	Satisfying domestic demands estimated at some 315,000 batteries per year
Contacts	Dirección de CUBAT email: esanchez@acunet.co.cu Tel: (5323)-5301112

PRODUCTION AND COMMERCIALIZATION OF ALUMINUM CANS IN THE EASTERN AREA OF THE COUNTRY

Description	Production plant for aluminum cans in the countries requiring repairs and outfitting as well as technological modernization of the existing equipment do the aim of increasing the production capacity to 300 million cans per year.
Investment Type	Joint Enterprise

Cuban Party	Empresa de Envases de Aluminio (ENVAL) belonging to the Grupo Empresarial de la Industria Sideromecanica.
Estimated Investment Amount	21.8 million USD
Location	Carretera Vieja vía a San Germán, Km. 3 y 1/2, Zona Industrial Sur, Ciudad de Holguín, Holguín province.
Market Potential	Estimated 2014 demand is 577 million cans, reaching 605 million physical units in the year 2022; the principal clients are the joint enterprises Bucanero S.A. and Los Portales S.A. and the Union de Conservas.
Contacts	Dirección General de Envases de Aluminio Holguín email: aristides@envalhlg.co.cu Tel: (5324) 42-2417

TOURISM SECTOR

Cuba is the largest island in the West Indies and, setting it apart from other destinations in the Caribbean, it has a tourism product characterized by the hospitality of its people, exceptional natural attractions, local historic heritage, rich artistic and cultural life, unique healthcare situation, political stability and safety for tourists.

The website www.cubatravel.cu provides precise details about Cuban tourism's attractions, products, varieties, accommodations, etc.; it is updated on a daily basis in the English, Spanish and German languages, and will soon include Russian and French editions.

In 2013 2,852,527 visitors arrived in Cuba. Daily income per client averaged 100 USD, totaling 2 billion 315 CUC.

For 20 years the formation of the principal in-hotel and out-of-hotel profiles has been assumed by the Professional Training for Tourism Employees System, under the FORMATUR acronym, with 13 Hotel and Tourism schools throughout the country.

The tourism high season in Cuba is during the period between November and April.

GRAN CARIBE	With 20 years of experience in the Cuban tourist industry, it operates 45 tourist facilities divided into All Inclusive, Family, Historical, Business/City, Beach and Cays categories. It services can be found under the following g brand names: Hola Club, Club Premium and Classic.
CUBANACAN	Since 1987 its business has grown to include associations with prestigious international hotel chains. Besides city hotels it has secured these commercial Sun and Beach brand names: Brisas and Cub Amigo Horizontes and Horizontes, with hotels that are located in natural settings.
GAVIOTA	With 25 years of experience today this is the fastest growing organization in Cuban tourism. This tourism group has among its aims to promote and sell hotel and tourism services as well as specialty packages for health, boating, fishing, diving and others.
CUBAGOLF	Newly created, CUBAGOLF S.A., belonging to the Grupo Empresarial Extra Hotelero Palmares looks after the development of the Cuban project to promote the island as a golf-holiday destination. Currently it is in negotiations with several foreign partners to incorporate joint ventures to build, manage and run tourism-real estate golf complexes throughout the country.

Overall Hotel capacity is more than 61,000 rooms. 65% of the rooms are under 4 and 5-star categories.

The International Tourism Fair of Cuba (FITCUBA) is the most important annual event for the Cuban tourism industry. Edition thirty-five of FITCUBA will be held on May 7, 2015 at the Cayo Coco island destination "Jardines del Rey" and it will be dedicated to Italy.

Rooms by categories

SECTORIAL POLICY:

Foreign investment participation in the sector will be directed to promote new hotels through new building projects, or reconstructions, of accommodations facilities as well as the complementary infrastructures.

In out-of-hotel activity it will be promoting real estate development associated with golf courses and others that will be complemented by 100% Cuban marinas and also building high-the theme parks. Not included are dolphinariums, foods services, marinas and complementary services.

Another aim will be to diversify the management and commercialization of tourist facilities by renowned foreign chains.

Priorities will include the Guardalavaca area in the north of Holguin province, the South Central Coast specifically Cienfuegos and Trinidad, Playa Santa Lucia in the northern part of Camaguey and the Covarrubias Tourist Resort Area in the north of Las Tunas province. Investor participation will be the exception in Havana and Varadero. Commitments have already been made with Habana Vieja, Playas del Este de La Habana and the northern cays.

TECHNICAL SPECIFICATIONS ON FOREIGN INVESTMENT OPPORTUNITIES

Building and commercializing top-quality hotel and villa capacities in the Cienfuegos Resort Area

Cienfuegos, known as the Pearl of the South, has attractive destinations for cultural tourism, boating, nature and "sun and beach" tourism. The historical center of town, declared World Heritage Center in 2005, impresses visitors for its historical-cultural and architectural importance. It provides a good site for events with its facilities for congresses, business and working meetings complemented by a generous network of roads and the airport infrastructures. Investment Type: Joint Enterprise. Cuban Party: Gran Caribe hotel group. Market Potential: The traditional markets attracted to this resort area come from Canada, France, Germany, the UK, Holland and Italy. We would like to increase numbers from these same countries. Developing markets are Argentina, the US, Belgium, Luxemburg and Denmark. Potential markets are Russia, Venezuela, Chile, Brazil and China.

Contact Information:

Dirección de Negocios Email: rubenf@grancaribe.gca.tur.cu Tel: (537) 204-0567 Website: www.gran-caribe.cu Address: Ave. 7ª Nº 4210, Miramar, La Habana, Cuba.

Lots in the North Sector

	Hotel del Mar 1	Hotel del Mar 2

Estimated Investment* (M USD)	$23,750	$23,750
Rooms	125	125
Area (hectares)	1.0	1.0
Estimated Annual Results		
Rooms Existing Days (UNO)	45,625	45,625
Occupancy rate (%)	75	75
Rooms Days Occupied (UNO)	34,219	34,219
Occupancy density	1.9	1.9
Tourists Days (UNO)	65,016	65,016
Average Tourist Income (USD)	$90	$90
Tourism Income (USD)	$5,851,406	$5,851,406

Lots in the South Sector

	Hotel Puesta de Sol 1	Hotel Puesta de Sol 2
Estimated Investment *(M USD)	38,000	33,250
Rooms	200	175
Area (hectares)	0.75	0.75
Estimated Annual Results		
Rooms Existing Days (UNO)	73,000	63,875
Occupancy rate (%)	75	75
Rooms Days Occupied (UNO)	54,750	47,906
Occupancy density	1.9	1.9
Tourists Days (UNO)	104,025	91,022
Average Tourist Income (USD)	$90	$90
Tourism Income (USD)	$9,362,250	$8,191,969

Lots in the Pasacaballo Sector

	Hotel Punta Milpa
Estimated Investment* (M USD)	$38,000
Rooms	200
Area (hectares)	1.0
Estimated Annual Results	
Rooms Existing Days (UNO)	73,000
Occupancy rate (%)	75
Rooms Days Occupied (UNO)	54,750
Occupancy density	1.9
Tourists Days (UNO)	104,025
Average Tourist Income (USD)	$90
Tourism Income (USD)	$9,362,250

*Calculated on cost per room, totaling 190 M USD

Building and commercializing top-quality hotel and villa capacities at the Covarrubias Resort Area in Las Tunas

A newcomer to the tourist scene in Cuba Las Tunas province, known as the Balcony of Oriente, provides a new area for visitors with its beautiful beaches and nature-based tourism based on the richness of its medicinal waters. It also has spots for exploring caverns. The northern coast has one of the loveliest beaches, Covarrubias; it has a comfortable hotel infrastructure protected by virgin vegetation and beaches averaging 8 meters in width. Of course there is also the 6 km long coral reef. Investment Type: Joint Enterprise

Cuban Party: Cubanacan S.A.

Market Potential: we are seeing a strong Canadian presence at this destination. We are looking for other markets that would make operations possible in the low season (May to October).

Contact Information:

Dirección de Negocios. Email: dirmixtas@cubanacan.tur.cu Tel: (537) 833-40 90 ext. 600 Website: www.cubanacan.cu Address: Calle 23 Nº 156, Vedado, La Habana.

Lots at the Covarrubias Sector

	Villa Covarrubias	Villa Real Covarrubias
Estimated Investment* (M USD)	$85,000	$98,600
Rooms	500	580
Area (hectares)	8.0	9.1
Estimated Annual Results		
Rooms Existing Days (UNO)	182,500	211,700
Occupancy rate (%)	70	70
Rooms Days Occupied (UNO)	127,750	148,190
Occupancy density	1.8	1.8
Tourists Days (UNO)	229,950	266,742
Average Tourist Income (USD)	$80	$80
Tourism Income (USD)	$18,396,000	$21,339,360

*Calculated on cost per room, totaling 170 M USD

Building and commercializing top-quality hotel and villa capacities at the Guardalavaca Resort Area in Holguin

The Holguin resort area is one of the destinations having the best service and highest satisfaction rates in the country. The eastern part of Cuba assembles a group of characteristics which, besides beautiful beaches and exuberant nature, includes a rich historical and cultural heritage, a range of mainly four and five-star hotels and well-qualified professional staffs. We offer Sun and Beach, Nature, Boating, Diving, Health, Business, Events and Cultural types of tourism. We preserve the zone where America was discovered and the archeological capital of Cuba; we are also the ideal destination for visitors looking for fun, cultural exchanges, peace and safety. Investment Type: Joint Enterprise Cuban Party: Cubanacan S.A. Market potential: We are looking for the objective of consolidating already existing markets that show growth such as Canada, the UK, Holland and Italy, of recovering markets showing decreasing or steady numbers and which have air connections with this destination such as Germany and Finland and of attracting new potential markets such as Spain, Scandinavia, Russia, Mexico and South America.

Contact Information: Dirección de Negocios. Email: dirmixtas@cubanacan.tur.cu Tel: (537) 833-40 90 ext. 600 Website: www.cubanacan.cu Address: Calle 23 N° 156, Vedado, La Habana.

Lots in the Guardalavaca North Sector

	Lot 9 Hotel	Lot 11 Villa/Bungalows	Lot 12 Villa/Bungalows
Estimated Investment* (M USD)	$125,500	$45,000	$45,000
Rooms	502	180	180
Area (hectares)	8.0	9.1	
	Estimated Annual Results		
Rooms Existing Days (UNO)	183,230	$65,700	$65,700
Occupancy rate (%)	80	80	80
Rooms Days Occupied (UNO)	146,584	52,560	52,560
Occupancy density	2.0	2.0	2.0
Tourists Days (UNO)	293,168	105,120	105,120
Average Tourist Income (USD)	$80	$95	$95
Tourism Income (USD)	$23,453.440	$9,986,400	$9,986,400

*Calculated on cost per room, totaling 250 M USD

Building and commercializing top-quality hotel and villa accommodations in the Santa Lucia Resort Area of Camaguey

Northern Camaguey province had two tourist development centers: Playa Santa Lucia and the city of Camaguey. The former caters to Sun and Beach tourism and the latter is part of the Cuba Circuit with optional Playa Santa Lucia; it has great potential for events, cultural and historical tourism because of its remarkable heritage. Investment Type: Joint Enterprise Cuban Party: Cubanacan S.A. or the Gran Caribe Hotel Group Market Potential: Canada is the largest market for Playa Santa Lucia maintaining significant growth in numbers of arrivals concentrated mainly during the high season (November to April). We would like to diversify the markets and recover the numbers for Germany, Italy and Argentina. Also, developing hotel investment projects will contribute to strengthening markets such as Mexico, Spain and Holland in the aim of getting a better position for the product by increasing arrivals to this destination.

Contact information:

Dirección de Negocios de Cubanacán. Email: dirmixtas@cubanacan.tur.cu Tel: (537) 833-40 90 ext. 600 Website: www.cubanacan.cu Address: Calle 23 N° 156, Vedado, La Habana.	Dirección de Negocios de Gran Caribe. Email: rubenf@grancaribe.gca.tur.cu Tel: (537) 204-0567 Website: www.gran-caribe.cu Address: Ave. 7ª N° 4210, Miramar, La Habana.

Lots in the La Boca Sector

	Lot 36 Villa	Lot 36 Villa A	Lot 38
Estimated Investment* (M USD)	$47,850	$44,550	$42,900
Rooms	290	270	260
Area (hectares)	8.97	8.28	7.91
Estimated Annual Results			

Rooms Existing Days (UNO)	105,850	98,550	94,900
Occupancy rate (%)	75	75	75
Rooms Days Occupied (UNO)	79,388	73,913	71,175
Occupancy density	1.9	1.9	1.9
Tourists Days (UNO)	150,836	140,434	135,233
Average Tourist Income (USD)	$80	$80	$80
Tourism Income (USD)	$12,066,900	$11,234,700	$10,818,600

Lot at Residencial Tararacos

	Lot 10 Hotel
Estimated Investment* (M USD)	$41,250
Rooms	250
Area (hectares)	5.7
Estimated Annual Results	
Rooms Existing Days (UNO)	91,250
Occupancy rate (%)	75
Rooms Days Occupied (UNO)	68,438
Occupancy density	1.9
Tourists Days (UNO)	130,031
Average Tourist Income (USD)	$80
Tourism Income (USD)	$10,402,500

*Calculated on cost per room, totaling 165 M USD

Building and Commercializing top-quality hotel accommodations in the Trinidad Resort Area in Sancti Spiritus

"Trinidad de Cuba" is the name under which this tourism destination is commercialized in the world and it includes the following types of tourism: city, sun and beach, ecological, cultural, health, boating, hunting and fishing, speleology and nature. It has a large array of hotel and out-of-hotel services and an infrastructure to support tourism thereby reinforcing its potential. Since it is a consolidated product it has a competitive edge on other destinations, with two colonial cities Trinidad and Sancti Spiritus, the third and fourth oldest villas founded by the Spanish in Cuba. Investment Type: Joint Enterprise. Cuban Party: Cubanacan S.A. Market Potential: This investment project would be directed towards the main markets basically covered by the traditional markets studied in the Trinidad area: Canada, Germany, Russia and France. Developing potential markets are Argentina, Brazil, Uruguay, Chile, the UK, Italy, Spain, Belgium, Holland and Austria.

Contact Information:

Dirección de Negocios. Email: dirmixtas@cubanacan.tur.cu Tel: (537) 833-40 90 ext. 600
Website: www.cubanacan.cu Address: Calle 23 Nº 156, Vedado, La Habana.

Lots in the Ancon Resort Area

	Lot 3 Hotel	Lot 1 Hotel	Lot 9 Hotel
Estimated Investment* (M USD)	$80,000	$20,000	$60,000
Rooms	400	100	300
Area (hectares)	11.3	8.5	5.1
Estimated Annual Results			
Rooms Existing Days (UNO)	146,000	36,500	109,500
Occupancy rate (%)	75	75	75
Rooms Days Occupied (UNO)	109,500	27,375	82,125
Occupancy density	1.9	1.9	1.9
Tourists Days (UNO)	208,050	52,013	156,038
Average Tourist Income (USD)	$90	$90	$90
Tourism Income (USD)	$18,724,500	$4,681,125	$14,043,375

	Lot 11 Hotel	Lot 13 Hotel	Lot 14 Hotel	Lot 17 Hotel
Estimated Investment* (M USD)	$120,000	$80,000	$60,000	$60,000
Rooms	600	400	300	300
Area (hectares)	11.5	10	7.5	3.5
	Estimated Annual Results			
Rooms Existing Days (UNO)	219,000	146,000	109,500	109,500
Occupancy rate (%)	75	75	75	75
Rooms Days Occupied (UNO)	164,250	109,500	82,125	82,125
Occupancy density	1.9	1.9	1.9	1.9
Tourists Days (UNO)	312,075	208,050	156,038	156,038
Average Tourist Income (USD)	$90	$90	$90	$90
Tourism Income (USD)	$28,086	$18,724	$14,043	$14,043

*Calculated on cost per room, totaling 200 M USD

Real Estate Development associated with the Golf Course at El Faro/El Jagüey. Rancho Luna Pasacaballos Resort Area

Description	Development of the Golf Real Estate Tourism Complex at the El Faro/El Jagüey Lot, Cienfuegos province on an area of about 517 hectares that will include 2 18-hole golf courses, 1 practice course, 1 Clubhouse, 2 5-star hotels with a total of approximately 240 rooms and Spa, 3,600 real estate units (360 houses or villas and 3240 apartments) for sales In Perpetua, sports areas, shops and service areas, etc.
Investment Type	Joint Enterprise
Cuban Party	CUBAGOLF, S.A.
Estimated Investment Amount	580.00 million USD
Location	Cienfuegos province

Market Potential	The market for future real estate owners and hotel, house and apartment clients and guests will basically be Canada, Europe and Latin America chiefly Brazil, Argentina, Colombia and Mexico.
Expected Estimated Results	Prices for a game of golf are estimated to be between 70 and 85 USD. Average hotel prices are estimated at 130 USD per person with a density of 1.6 and 70% average occupancy rate. Residential units may be rented for 200 to 300 USD per day, estimating a 33% occupancy rate, signifying incomes of 70.8 million USD of which 60% will be paid to the owners and the remaining 40% will be incomes for the joint enterprise. Other incomes will be coming in for foods services, recreation and rental of shops.
Contacts	President's Office Emails: dir.golf@palmares.tur.cu; ep.golf@palmares.tur.cu Tel: (537) 272-2318 and 272-2311 Address: Calle 13 No. 18006.esquina a 5ta Ave Miramar, Municipio Playa, La Habana, Cuba.

Real Estate Development associated with the Golf Course at Loma Linda

Description	Development of the Golf Real Estate Tourism Complex at Loma Linda, Holguin province that will include two (2) 18hole golf courses, one (1) practice course, one (1) Clubhouse, one (1) 5-star hotel with a total of approximately 170 rooms and Spa, 1,300 real estate units (400 houses or villas and 900 apartments) for sales In Perpetua, sports areas, shops and service areas, etc.
Investment Type	Joint Enterprise
Cuban Party	CUBAGOLF, S.A.
Estimated Investment Amount	380.00 million USD
Location	Cienfuegos province
Market Potential	The market for future real estate owners and hotel, house and apartment clients and guests will basically be Canada, Europe and Latin America chiefly Brazil, Argentina, Colombia and Mexico.
Expected Estimated Results	Prices for a game of golf are estimated to be between 70 and 85 USD. Average hotel prices are estimated at 130 USD per person with a density of 1.6 and 70% average occupancy rate. Residential units may be rented for 200 to 300 USD per day, estimating a 33% occupancy rate, signifying incomes of 70.8 million USD of which 60% will be paid to the owners and the remaining 40% will be incomes for the joint enterprise. Other incomes will be coming in for foods services, recreation and rental of shops.
Contacts	President's Office Emails: dir.golf@palmares.tur.cu; ep.golf@palmares.tur.cu Tel: (537) 272-2318,272-2311 Address: Calle 13 No. 18006.esquina a 5ta Ave Miramar, Municipio Playa, La Habana, Cuba.

Management and Commercialization of 33 Hotel Facilities

At the close of 2013, 17 foreign companies were operating in Cuba, managing over 31,000 rooms through 64 Hotel Management and Commercialization Contracts. With a view to continue promoting this type, we provide details about the facilities that may be object of management and commercialization.

In operating hotels we foresee the possibility of including financing by the managing foreign company for reconstruction of the facility.

Existing Hotel Facility Management and Commercialization

Province	Resort Area	Facility	Product	Category	Rooms
Gran Caribe					
La Habana	Monte Barreto	Neptuno-Triton Complex	City	3*	266 + 266
	Vedado	Vedado-Saint John's complex	City	3*	203 + 88
	Traditional Downtown	Deauville	City	3*	144
Varadero	Varadero	Kawama	Beach	4*	336
	Varadero	Villa Tortuga	Beach	3*	292
	Varadero	SunBeach	Beach	3*	272
Cienfuegos	Cienfuegos	Jagua	City	4*	149
	Cienfuegos	La Union	City	4*	49
	Cienfuegos	Rancho Luna-Faro Luna Complex	City	3*	222 + 46
Cubanacan					
La Habana	Playas del Este	Tropicoco	Beach	2*	188
	Monte Barreto	Chateau Miramar	City	4*	50
	Marina Hemingway	Acuario & villas	Boating	3*	381
	Marina Hemingway	El Viejo y El Mar	Boating	3*	190
Varadero	Varadero	Aguas Azules	Beach	3*	411

Management and Commercialization of New Hotel facilities under construction

Province	Resort Area	Facility	Product	Category	Rooms	Opening
Gaviota						
Ciego de Avila	Cayo Guillermo	Punta Playuelas	City	5*plus	158	Apr-16
Ciego de Avila	Cayo Guillermo	Punta Rasa Hotel 1	Beach	5*	500	May-16
Matanzas	Varadero	Las Conchas I	Beach	5*	827	May-16
Villa Clara	Cayo Las Brujas	Farallon Este	Beach	5*	516	Aug-/16
Ciego de Avila	Cayo Guillermo	Punto Rasa Hotel II	Beach	5*	500	Aug-16
Ciego de Avila	Cayo	Pilar I	Beach	5*plus	245	Oct-16

	Guillermo					
Ciego de Avila	Cayo Paredon Grande	Roca Este 2	Beach	5*	700	2016
Villa Clara	Cayo Las Brujas	Farallon Oeste	Beach	5*	660	Jan-17
Villa Clara	Cayo Las Brujas	San Agustin	Beach	5*plus	252	Apr-17
Camagüey	Cayo Cruz	Quebrada 17	Beach	5*	550	Apr-17
Camagüey	Cayo Cruz	Quebrada 21	Beach	5*	700	June-17
Villa Clara	Cayo Las Brujas	La Salina Suroeste	Beach	4*	574	2017
Ciego de Avila	Cayo Paredon Grande	Roca Centro	Beach	5*	600	2017
Ciego de Avila	Cayo Paredon Grande	Roca Este 1	Beach	5*	600	2017
Villa Clara	Cayo Las Brujas	La Salina Noreste	Beach	4*	680	2018
Camagüey	Cayo Cruz	Quebrada 24	Beach	5*	675	2018
Camagüey	Cayo Cruz	Punta Cocina Lot 32	Beach	5*	895	2018
Ciego de Avila	Cayo Paredon Grande	Roca Norte 1	Beach	5*	700	2018
Ciego de Avila	Cayo Paredon Grande	Roca Norte 2	Beach	5*	600	2018

ENERGY SECTOR

OIL

Geologically speaking, to the south of Cuba there is the volcanic Caribbean arc and to the north the southern rim of the North American platform. The greater part of oil production in Cuba is found in a sector between La Habana and Matanzas provinces where the largest field possessing geological reserves of around 6,000 million barrels is located. Almost all of Cuban territory, some 100,000 km^2, is a prospect for oil exploration besides the zone of shallow waters and its extension towards the deep water zone.

In Cuba we have discovered several dozens of oilfields most of them extra-heavy oil although there is also light, medium and very light oil. The oilfields are basically found at sea and can be reached from land with horizontal drilling; this permits us to not only reach the fields but also to attain greater productivity.

Cuba's Exclusive Economic Zone (EEZ) in the Gulf of Mexico shares the same scenarios, the same parent rock, reservoirs and seals of the prolific oil basin of the Gulf of Mexico where gigantic oilfields have been discovered and one of the greatest world-level industries has been developed.

ECONOMIC INFORMATION

Total oil and gas production is equivalent to approximately 4 million tons per year (25 million barrels a year); of these 3 million tons per year (10 million barrels per year) are crude oil and approximately 1,100 million cubic meters of natural gas per year.

There are 20 prospects in the EEZ capable of producing between 10,000 and 20,000 extractible barrels in the zone.

Cuban Party associated with foreign capital business

Cupet logo The Union Cuba- Petróleo (CUPET) is the Cuban state organization in charge of satisfying the supply of fuels and lubricants to the domestic market. It is a highly specialized entity made up of 41 enterprises of which 5 are joint enterprises. It is authorized to undertake all UPSTREAM and DOWNSTREAM operations on its own behalf or in association with foreign enterprises.
CUPET Awards and Recognizance Premio Calidad de la Unión Cubapetróleo (2004), Premio Calidad de la Unión Cubapetróleo (2005), Premio Calidad de la Unión Cubapetróleo (2006), Premio Ministerial de la Calidad del MINBAS (2006), Galardón Estrella Internacional Categoría Oro del World Quallity Commitment BID (2006), Premio Giraldillas a la Calidad de la Gestión Empresarial (2007).

Training of Personnel

There are over 24,000 employees; 73% are men and 27% are women. From 2006 to the present the Centro Politecnico del Petróleo has graduated over 31,603 employees. It has 5 schools throughout the country.

Specialties:
Oil Engineering
Safety and Health on the Job and in the Environment
International Operators' Certification
Managerial Courses
Leadership Techniques

The Centro de Investigacion del Petróleo (CEINPET) is dedicated to training personnel in drilling, extraction, refining and application of oil methods.

Training Personnel Abroad

CUPET personnel has received training at important prestigious training centers abroad in countries such as Canada (NAIT), Mexico (Noria and Teximpet), Venezuela (PDVSA and AIVEPET), Trinidad and Tobago (FTW), Brazil (PETROBRAS), China (CPTDC), Argentina (LAAPSA) and Norway (PETRAD).

Infrastructure

There are 13 commercializing entities, 3 oil producing companies, 4 refineries and 16 companies providing various services. There is a complex and all-encompassing system of producing fields, refineries, loading and unloading systems, warehousing facilities and gas-ducts that demonstrate CUPET's enterprising will to answer the country's energy demands.

SECTORIAL POLICY:

To create, broaden and modernize production capabilities. To promote projects for exploration and production of hydrocarbons.

Technical Specifications on Foreign Investment Opportunities

Oil Exploration at risk and shared production in blocks in national territory shallow waters (8 Blocks)

Description	To define the potential of oil and gas in determinate shallow water areas and in the event that this is positive, to start exploiting those energy resources.
Investment Type	International Economic Association Contract at risk for exploration of hydrocarbons and its production
Cuban Party	Union Cuba Petroleo (CUPET)
Location	The 8 blocks available are situated to the north of the provinces of Pinar del Rio, Matanzas, Villa Clara and Sancti Spiritus and also to the south of Pinar del Rio, Artemisa, Mayabeque, Matanzas, Ciego de Avila, Camaguey and Granma. EXPLORATION BLOCKS IN SHALLOW WATERS LEGEND CONTRACTED LOTS AVAILABLE BLOCKS BLOCKS WHERE CUPET IS OPERATING BLOCKS UNDER NEGOTIATION AND/OR ASSESSMENT
Market	First, the domestic market and should there be surpluses, these would be exported
Contacts	Dirección General de Comercial Cupet S.A Email: business@cupetsa.co.cu Tel: (537) 831-4752

Oil Exploration at Risk and shared production in blocks of the Exclusive Economic Zone in the Gulf of Mexico (52 Blocks)

Description	To define the potential for oil and gas in the ZEE and in the event this is positive, start exploitation of these energy resources
Investment Type	International Economic Association Contract at risk for the exploration for hydrocarbons and their production
Cuban Party	Union Cuba Petroleo (CUPET)

Location

The EEZ takes in an area of 112,000 sq. km in deep waters of the Gulf of Mexico, to the north of the provinces of Pinar del Rio, Artemisa, Mayabeque and Matanzas where 52 blocks are available for negotiation. The Port of Mariel located in the Special Economic Development Zone of Mariel has conditions to be a logistical base for supporting offshore operations. EXPLORATION BLOCKS IN DEEP WATERS OF THE GULF OF MEXICO LEGEND Cuba-USA Maritime Border - Cuba-Mexico Maritime Border CONTRACTED BLOCKS PDVSA (VENEZUELA) SONANGOL (ANGOLA) ROSNEFT-ZARUBEZHNEFT AVAILABLE BLOCKS

Market	First for the domestic market and should there be surpluses these will be exported
Results	For a block, with contract length of 30 years and using an average price of 128.2 USD/Bbl and a updating rate of 10%, we estimate a VAN of 1241.2

	million USD, a TIR of 18.5% and recovery period of 7.5 years.
Contacts	Dirección General de Comercial Cupet S.A Email: business@cupetsa.co.cu Tel: (537) 831-4752

Oil Exploration at Risk and shared production in terrestrial blocks on national territory (25 Blocks)

Description	To define the oil and gas potential on land area of national territory and should this prove to be positive, to start exploitation of these energy resources
Investment Type	International Economic Association Contract at risk for the exploration of hydrocarbons and their production
Cuban Party	Union Cuba Petroleo (CUPET)
Location	There are 25 available blocks, throughout national territory, except urban areas and some excluded areas in protected areas or those reserved for other prioritized interests of the country TERRESTRIAL BLOCKS FOR EXPLORATION LEGEND AVAILABLE BLOCKS SHERRIT BLOCKS WHERE CUPET IS OPERATING PETROVIETNAM M.E.O.AUSTRALIA BLOCKS BEING ASSESSED AND/OR NEGOTIATED
Market	In the first place, for the domestic market and should there be surpluses, this would be for exportation
Results	For one block, with a contract length of 25 years and using an average price of 122.6 USD/Bbl and an updating rate of 12%, we estimate VAN of 191.7 million USD, TIR of 44% and a recovery period of 3.4 year
Contacts	Dirección General de Comercial Cupet S.A Email: business@cupetsa.co.cu Tel: (537) 831-4752

Secondary Recovery in exploitation oil fields

Description	To increase the recovery coefficient of existing oil reserves in determinate oilfields where it is not possible to extract them with conventional exploitation methods
Investment Type	International Economic Association Contract at risk for secondary recovery of hydrocarbons
Cuban Party	Union Cuba Petroleo (CUPET)
Location	Oilfields currently open for negotiations are located in the North Havana-Matanzas strip and in the central basin in the province of Ciego de Avila. It is possible that in the future other oilfields will be proposed where it would be advisable to apply secondary recovery methods
Market	First the domestic market and should there by surpluses they would be exported
Results	We estimate for a block with a contract length of 30 years: Average price for the project = 95.1 USD/Bbl VAN = 142.4 million USD, TIR = 46.3% Investment recovery (once production has started) = 2.1 years Updating rate=12%
Contacts	Dirección General de Comercial Cupet S.A Email: business@cupetsa.co.cu Tel: (537) 831-4752

Renewable Energy Sources

Use of Renewable Energy Sources is one of the principal priorities for the country and it is essential for achieving the following objectives:

Modify the energy matrix of generation and consumption of electricity.

Decrease the inefficiencies in the electrical system.

Reduce dependence on fossil fuels.

Contribute to environmental sustainability.

Increase competitiveness of the economy as a whole.

Decrease the high cost of energy delivered to consumers due to fuel prices.

Only 4.3% of energy in Cuba is obtained from renewable sources.	Facilities using renewable energy sources at the present time: 4 wind farms 9476 solar panels 7 11 MW solar parks 10,595 solar heaters 57 sugar mills with 470 MW 827 biogas plants 9343 windmills 169 hydroelectric facilities
Making use of Renewable Energies is part of the country's Economic and Social Development Program.	

IPROYAZ of AZCUBA and INEL of the Electrical Union engineering enterprises, the Grupo Empresarial de la Industria Sideromecanica, enterprises of the Ministry of Agriculture and the Ministry of Foods Industry have highly qualified personnel to execute these programs and they have plants and workshops for the purpose.

The country has over 10 universities with highly trained scientific-technical personnel offering degree courses in technical specialty engineering, and in the branches of the economy and social sciences, etc. Postgraduate courses, diploma courses, masters and doctorates are also taught.

Biomass:

The participation of this Renewable Resource is top priority for the country in changing its Energy Matrix.

With the objective of increasing sale of electricity to the Sistema Electroenergetico Nacional , we have studied and planned to install 755MW at 19 Bioelectric Plants at Sugar Mills with the best parameters for pressure and temperature in order to operate for more than 230 days per year with Sugarcane Biomass and Forestry Biomass, basically marabu scrub, available in the areas close to these facilities. A large number of these will be done with foreign capital.

The 19 Bioelectric plants will produce over 1900 GWh/year and they will stop issuing approximately 1,700,000 tons of CO_2 into the atmosphere; studies are now underway to indicate project feasibility.

As part of the development for the Bioelectric Program we plan to modernize AZCUBA's Boiler Factory in the central part of the country in order to satisfy the demand for high and middle pressure boilers, as well as workshops to manufacture ventilators, over-heaters and other components. The Grupo Empresarial de la Industria Sideromecanica factories will be able to supply structures, pumps and other components.

This link-up will permit us to reduce installation costs for the Bioelectric Plants at the sugar mills and will provide an opportunity to set up production alliances with foreign partners in order to provide supplies for this important program.

Wind Power Resource:

We executed the Prospect Project and characterization of Cuban wind power potential; it dealt with installing a network of 88 automatic measuring stations for the wind parameters to heights of up to 50 meters in 32 zones throughout the country and a network of 12 reference meteorological stations for measurements up to 100 meters in height.

We have the endorsement of the Garrad Hassan & Partners International Consultants (Garrad Hassan Iberica branch) on the basis of the Technical Project Assessment for Wind Power Prospects and the estimate for yield in 10 zones and with the experience acquired in installation and exploitation of 4 demonstration wind farms, with a total of 11.7 MW. Of these, those installed in the north of Holguin province (9.6 MW) have reached an annual capacity factor that is more than 27%.

On the basis of available wind resources, the Union Electrica has studied the installation of 633 MW in 13 Wind Farms, with capacity factors over 30% which will produce over 1000

WIND POWER PROGRAM – LOCATIONS

We foresee linking up with National Industry to manufacture air-generator towers and other installation components and the opportunity to set up production alliances with foreign partners to provide supplies for these components for the Wind Farm Program.

Photovoltaic Energy:

The potential of solar radiation recorded in this country is approximately 5KWh per square meter per day. We have studied installation up to 2030 of 700 MWp en Photovoltaic Solar Parks (PSFV) connected to the National Electrical System. Macro or micro-locations are defined in areas where the PSFV will be built, connected to the network and we have drawn up the corresponding Opportunity Studies. We prioritize the PSFVs that can be installed in the isolated electrical systems of tourism cays.

Once all the foreseen PSFV potential has been installed, we will be producing over 1000 GWh/year thereby stopping harmful emissions into the atmosphere of over 874,000 tons of CO_2.

The country has one Solar Panel Manufacturing Plant to produce 150 and 240 Wp photovoltaic panels; it is in Pinar del Rio and has an annual production capacity of 14 MWp that provides the opportunity to set up production alliances with foreign partners in order to increase these productions. National industry also has the capacity to manufacture the table structures needed for installing the foreseen PSFVs.

Hydroenergy:

On the basis of reservoirs already built in the country and the water available in canals and bodies of water, we have drawn up a program to build 74 small hydroelectric plants (PCHE) with over 56 MW. We have drawn up the corresponding Opportunity Studies. Once all the planned power has been installed, the program will produce 274 GWh generated power per

HYDROENERGY PROGRAM – LOCATION OF 74 NEW PLANTS

In order to produce small hydroelectric turbines there are capacities in a Plant with the experience of manufacturing hydraulic turbines up to 325 kW and other components and parts for these facilities. We foresee modernizing this plant for the purpose and for setting up production alliances with foreign partners in order to decrease investment costs.

Biogas:

Currently the country's Development Programs for pork, beef and poultry production include obtaining significant volumes of organic waste, likewise waste obtained from foods industry factories and the sugar industry, figures on the rise with the development plans underway. Currently the potential for organic waste is over 490 million m^3, coming from animal production, the foods industry and solid urban waste.

It is top priority for the country to eliminate the pollution of rivers and hydrographic basins, making use of this waste for energy purposes. The foods industry and pork production require this kind of technology because of the volumes of waste they produce and this is an opportunity to set up alliances with foreign partners to achieve that objective.

SECTORIAL POLICY:

To create, enlarge and modernize production capacities. To promote projects to generate energy from renewable sources.

Technical Specifications on Foreign Investment Opportunities Generating Energy from Forestry Biomass

Description	To build and set up plants to generate electricity (bioelectrical plants) in Empresas Forestales Integrales areas of Macurije and Minas de Matahambre, both in the province of Pinar del Rio, capacity 7MWh and 3 MWh respectively on the basis of the forestry biomass obtained from agro-industrial waste associated with exploitation of forest plantations, the industrial processing of wood harvested and the shredding of the biomass from areas infested with marabu scrub. The scope of the investment considers encouraging and exploiting energy forests guaranteeing stable and sustained supplies of the forestry biomass in demand by bioelectrical plants, as well as the acquisition of equipment and machinery for harvesting, shredding

	and transporting the wood waste.
Investment Type	Joint Enterprise
Cuban Party	Empresas Forestales Integrales
Estimated Investment Amount	Macurije 32.3 million USD Minas de Matahambre 14.4 million USD
Location	Macurije, Guane municipality, beside the existing sawmill Pons, Minas de Matahambre municipality, beside the existing sawmill
Market Potential	Electricity will be delivered directly to the Sistema Electroenergetico Nacional at the points where they interconnect with the sawmill in order to replace imports
Estimated Anticipated Results	The generation capacity of the two plants annually will be 54.9 GWh. The plant's exploitation regime will be 24hours a day, 365 days a year with a technical availability of 89%, signifying 7,008 H of generation every year. We anticipate that with the building of these bioelectrical plants, the replacing of 14.3 thousand tons of fossil fuel will annually save 7.9 million USD. The price for the sale of electricity will correspond to the purchase price of the UNE.
Contacts	Dirección de Negocios y Desarrollo del GEAM. Email ddesarrollo@geam.minag.cu Tel.: (537) 884-7456 and 884-7457

Bioelectrical Plants with 30MW to 60MW capacity (10 projects)

Description	To install 30MW to 60MW capacity bioelectrical plants to generate electricity, high pressure and temperature steam, using for this the bagasse during harvest as fuel and converting it into technological steam for heating via cogeneration. The surplus electricity not used by the mill is delivered to the national electrical energy system; besides the harvest, other biomass (not sugarcane) can be used. The bioelectrical plant shall be attached to a mill and may be associated to a Production Administration Contract for that mill in order to guarantee greater amounts of biomass (bagasse) and to9 improve its efficiency.
Investment Type	Joint Enterprise
Cuban Party	ZERUS S.A.
Estimated Investment Amount	Considering a cost of 2,400 USD/kW, the investment amounts would be between 72 and 144 million USD
Location	The bioelectrical plants will be attached to existing mills with a capacity of 4000 to 7000 tons of sugarcane per day or more, located in the provinces of Ciego de Avila, Sancti Spiritus, Holguin, Camagüey, Las Tunas, Granma, Mayabeque and Santiago de Cuba. The names of the mills and their possible potential for installation are: Ecuador (35 MW); Uruguay (50MW); Urbano Noris (50MW); Cristino Naranjo (35MW); Brasil (50MW); Antonio Guiteras (50MW); Majibacoa (35MW); Grito de Yara (35MW); Héctor Molina (35MW) and Julio Antonio Mella (35MW).

Market Potential	The electricity produced would be destined for national consumption to replace oil imports used in the production of electricity at the thermoelectric plants. The electricity client would be the Union Nacional Electrica (UNE) via sales agreements for all the electricity that would be sold to the national electrical energy system.
Anticipated Results	Acceding to modern technologies and financing, reducing kWh production costs, increasing energy supplies guaranteed for the country and reducing local and global environmental pollution. Accelerating the rhythm of replacing electricity produced with oil consumption thereby at the same time guaranteeing payments with the value of the saved oil for these thermoelectric plants.
Contacts	Dirección de Negocios ZERUS Email: jorge.lodos@zerus.azcuba.cu Tel. (537) 838-3194 ext. 237

Maisi Wind Farm Project for 174 MW

Description	To develop a project with regional scope to install a power of 174 MW, along the coastal strip of the Maisi Peninsula. For this purpose, to set up contiguous 4 wind parks (PE), developing 2 of 51 MW on the basis of 200 m of the coastline and the other 2 of 35 MW further inland and behind the first two. Each PE of 51 MW would have 34 air generators (AG), nominal unit power of 1.5 MW and axle box height of 70 m or more. Each PE of 36 MW would have 24 units of the same power. As an option, we could install a similar range of total power using a proportional number of air generators in ranges of unit power greater than 1.5 MW. The project will include installing electrical networks and internal communications and exit substation(s) for linkage with the National Electric System network (SEN). Electricity generated is delivered by the enterprise at the interconnecting point, under a energy sale Contract (PPA) signed by UNE for a term of 20 years.
Investment Type	100% Foreign Capital Enterprise. The Enterprise would carry out the investment under the COO contract type to be signed with UNE; this will permit completing preliminary studies, financing, engineering, contracting, building and setting up, operation and maintenance of the wind park as well as financing for the networks associated with the evacuation of energy produced at the aforementioned farms.
Cuban Party	Union Electrica (UNE)
Estimated Investment Amount	Investment estimated for the 174 MW at 285 million USD
Location	Region of the Maisi Peninsula, Maisi municipality, Guantanamo province. Strip almost parallel to the coast.
Market Potential	Electricity will be generated for the Sistema Electroenergetico Nacional with the purpose of decreasing the use of fossil fuels, reducing pollutant gas emissions and contributing to the safety and energy independence of the country.
Contacts	Dirección de Negocios de la UNE Email: pedrob@oc.une.cu Tel: (537) 879-0268

Banes Wind Farm Project for 102 MW

Description	To develop a project with regional scope to install a power of 102 MW, along the coastal strip of the Lucrecia Peninsula, between Cabo Lucrecia on the north and Punta de Mulas further south and in the center of the peninsula. For this purpose, to set up contiguous 2 wind parks (PE), each having 51 MW power; each PE of 51 MW would have 34 air generators (AG), nominal unit power of 1.5 MW and axle box height of 70 m or more. As an option, we could install a similar range of total power using a proportional number of air generators in ranges of unit power greater than 1.5 MW. The project will include installing electrical networks and internal communications and exit substation(s) for linkage with the Sistema Electroenergetico Nacional network (SEN). Electricity generated is delivered by the enterprise at the interconnecting point, under a energy sale Contract (PPA) signed by UNE for a term of 20 years.
Investment Type	100% Foreign Capital Enterprise. The Enterprise would carry out the investment under the COO contract type to be signed with UNE; this will permit completing preliminary studies, financing, engineering, contracting, building and setting up, operation and maintenance of the wind park as well as financing for the networks associated with the evacuation of energy produced at the aforementioned farms.
Cuban Party	Union Electrica (UNE)
Estimated Investment Amount	200 million USD
Location	Region of the Lucrecia Peninsula, Banes municipality, Holguin province.
Market Potential	Electricity will be generated for the Sistema Electroenergetico Nacional with the purpose of decreasing the use of fossil fuels, reducing pollutant gas emissions and contributing to the safety and energy independence of the country.
Contacts	Dirección de Negocios de la UNE Email: pedrob@oc.une.cu Tel: (537) 879-0268

MINING

Regulatory Framework

Law 76 "Law of Mines" of 1994 Decree Law 222 "Regulations of the Law of Mines" Law 81 "Law of the Environment"

The Cuban archipelago has a broad range of diversity in metal raw materials as well as industrial rock and minerals. This is due to the fact it is constituted by a mosaic of geological structures which include sequences of the continental margin, volcanic island arcs and oceanic crust, put together into a unique ensemble as the result of the geological processes of subduction and collision.

At the present time 45% of national territory is organized into geological maps to the scale of 1/50.000 and 100% of Cuban land area has been geophysically surveyed by air.

The principal value of Cuban minerals, based on the fact that they lie close to the surface and can be exploited in open pit mines at a cost relatively lower than that of extraction in subterranean depths.

Upon this mosaic there is a succession of young sedimentary rock formed during the last 40 million years in a tectonic regime of platforms. Among the principal mineral metal resources are: Fe, Ni, Co, Cu, Pb, Zn, Au, Ag, Mn, W and Cr.

Curious Fact:

The Matahambre Mine (Pinar del Rio) in its time was the deepest mine in the Americas and its processing plant was one of the world's most efficient. It became a school of mining and generations of Cuban geologists and miners passed through its doors. After being closed in 1997 it was declared a National Monument.

In the case of Industrial Rock and Minerals (RMI) of non-metal minerals, in Cuba we have identified resources of laterite clay, asbestos, sand, quartz sand, barite, basalt, bentonite, limestone, quartzite, quartz, kaolin, cyanite, calcarenite, feldspar, phosphorite, garnets, gabbros, graphite, marble, magnesite, mica, olivine, semiprecious stones, mineral salt, serpentine, talcum, tobes, plaster and zeolite.

INFRASTRUCTURE

The Grupo Empresarial Geominsal has companies for developing geology and mining distributed throughout the country; they have a high degree of experience in the sector: Empresa GeoMinera Pinar del Rio; Empresa GeoMinera Isla de la Juventud; Empresa GeoMinera Centro; Empresa GeoMinera Camagüey; Empresa GeoMinera Oriente; Empresa Minería de Occidente; Empresa de Ingeniería, Construcción y Mantenimiento; and Empresa Central de Laboratorios "José Isaac del Corral".

In the case of the nickel and cobalt industry the Grupo Empresarial Cubaniquel has two production plants and other companies giving services to producers; some of these are mechanical products maintenance and construction, port services, employment agency, employee services, engineering research center and others.

TRAINING PERSONNEL

The mining sector has highly qualified personnel in specialties of geology, geophysics, mines, metallurgy and other similar degree specialties. We have a large group of excellent professionals trained at the technical and university levels.

We have a Research Center for the Metallurgic-Mining Industry (CIPIMM), an offshoot of the Centro de Investigaciones Mineras de Occidente (CIMO). For the nickel and cobalt industry we have the Centro de Investigaciones Niquel (CEDINIQ) in the municipality of Moa. New professionals are trained at the Instituto Superior Minero Metalurgico of Moa where research in this branch is also being carried out.

Cuban Parties associated in foreign investment businesses

GeoMinera S.A.	Geominera S.A. has over 20 years of experience in exploitation and commercialization of solid minerals from Cuban deposits. It operates under a Quality Management System satisfying the requirements established in the NCISO 9001: 2008 norms duly endorsed by certification issued by the Oficina Nacional de Normalizacion de Cuba on July 10, 2013. It has been present at projects in countries in the Americans and Africa.
Caribbean Nickel S.A.	Commercial Caribbean Nickel S.A. (CCN) has the priority of finding financing, markets and technologies for the sustaining and development of the nickel industry and to create new production capacities. For over 25 years, CCN has promoted businesses with companies in the sector and has undertaken projects with organizations from China, Russia, Canada, Australia, Belgium, the UK and others.

SECTORIAL POLICY

To create, broaden and modernize production capacities. To promote projects for exploration, extraction and processing minerals.

Foreign Investment Opportunity Specifications

Projects in the Recognizance and Geological Investigation Phase (Prospecting – Exploration) for precious metals (gold and silver), base metals (copper, lead, zinc) and other minerals of interest

Description: Development of projects in the Recognizance and Geological Investigation Phase (Prospecting – Exploration) for precious metals (gold and silver), base metals (copper, lead, zinc) and other minerals of interest in the following regions:

Central Cuba

Ciego – Camaguey – Tunas

Holguin and Macizo Sagua – Baracoa

• Sierra Maestra Preferred Investment Type: International Economic Association Contract at risk for Recognizance and Geological Investigation (Prospecting-Exploration) for precious metals (gold and silver), base metals (copper, lead, zinc) and other minerals of interest. Prospects identified with sufficient advances in their degree of studies may be up for the possibility of establishing a joint enterprise or not. Cuban Party: GeoMinera S.A. Estimated Investment: It must be defined by the size of each project and the work methodology selected for each one of them, depending on the mining activity phase it is in: Recognizance or Geological Investigation. Market: If during the validity of the International Economic Association Contract a deposit is discovered that is economically viable (deposit) it would go over to the creation of a Joint Enterprise whose aim would be the exploitation, processing and commercialization of the minerals extracted. Its commercialization in concentrated forms of metals or others would be done directly on the foreign market. It could also mean significant savings for the country in terms of replacing imports should this occur.

Contact Information:

Dirección de Negocios GeoMinera S.A. Email: gustavo@gmsa.cu Webpage:www.gmsa.cu Tel: (537) 690-2741 ext.115

The Central Cuba Region takes in the territory of the provinces of Santa Clara, Cienfuegos, Sancti Spiritus and Ciego de Avila. It presents a clear geo-tectonic zoning characterized south to north by the following sequences: terrain on the continental border of SW Cuba (Escambray made up of metamorphosed continent boarder sequences); volcanic island arc sequences of the Lower and Upper Cretaceous; and a belt of mafic rock and ultramafic oceanic rock placed inside each other as the result of the collision of the volcanic island arc against the continental border sequences if he Bahamas-Florida block.

From the metallogenic point of view, the region exhibits an ample variety of deposit models: in the Escambray massive sulfurous deposits are inside Irish-type sediment; in the volcanic island arc sequences –and the associated intrusive sequences- VMS felsic (Kuroko type) predominate and the porfidic type. In the mafic and ultramafic rock hills Au orogenic and VMS mafic-ultramafic sequences predominate.

PROSPECTS OF INTEREST:

Carlota-Victoria Guachinango	Raw Materials: Cu,Zn, Au, Co Type of mineralization: Massive sulfurs in Cu –Zm ± Co, Au, Ag Irish type Degree of study: Carlota, Victoria & Guachinango: Exploration, still
	having minerals without borders. Recognizance in Siguanea & San Narciso. Other manifestations (Guachinango Este, Furnia I & II, Guamo, La Batea, etc.) not studied. Work Phase to be undertaken: Exploration in the known deposits and prospecting in the rest of the mineral district.
Cobre Arimao-	Raw Materials: Cu, Mo, Au, Ag
Las Breñas	Type of mineralization: Low or middle sulfuration meso-epithermal and Cu – Mo ± porfidic Au, accompanied by Cu skarn Degree of study: Arimao: Exploration. Area of the silicificated zone and the zones rich in magnetite with high associated laws of Cu and Au, still undetermined. Macagua: Prospecting: mineral zone Work Phase to be undertaken:
Tuinicú-Fortuna	Raw Materials: Cu, Zn, Au, Ag Type of mineralization: felsic polymetal VMS (Kuroko) abnd Cu – Mo ± porfidic Au Degree of study: Recognizance Work Phase to be undertaken: Recognizance
La Moza-	Raw Materials: Cu, Au, Ag
Yagrumal	Type of mineralization: Cu-Mo ± Porfidic Au and Cu-Au mesothermal Degree of study: Survey Work Phase to be undertaken: Recognizance
San Fernando-Antonio	Raw Materials: Cu, Zn, Au, Ag Type of mineralization: Felsic type (Kuroko) VMS polymetal Degree of study: Exploration in San Fernando and Antonio. Recognizance in Independencia, San Fernando Sur, Santa Rosa, Central Sector and Zambumbia Este. Work Phase to be undertaken: Exploration in San Fernando and its flanks and Antonio. Prospecting in San Fernando Sur, Santa Rosa, Central Sector and Zambumbia Este. Recognizance in the rest of the area.
Corralillo-	Raw Materials: Au, Ag. Possible Cu, Zn, Pb
Cifuentes	Type of mineralization: Au in quartz veins and orogenic Au type carbonates, also possible the presence of mafic-ultramafic (Cyprus type) VMS. Degree of study: Regional geochemical studies done in the framework of the geological surveys to the scale of 1:50 000 and a geochemical sampling campaign was done by a junior company in 1996-1997 with a total of 598 samples, among these 376 soil samples. We

	know of no deposits or manifestation in the area. Work Phase to be undertaken: Recognizance
Sancti Spiritus Norte	Raw Materials: Au, Ag, possible Cy, Zn Pb Type of mineralization: Au-Ag in orogenic type quartz veins Degree of study: Lote Grande in exploration. The rest of the manifestations lack studied details Work Phase to be undertaken: Complete exploration in Lote Grande and recognizance in the rest of the area
Venegas	Raw Materials: Au, Ag, Cu Type of mineralization: Au-Ag orogenic type, Possible Cu –Au VMS mafic-ultramafic (Cyprus) type Degree of study: Recognizance in some manifestations Work Phase to be undertaken: Prospecting in La Mas Buena, recognizance in the rest

The Ciego-Camagüey-Tunas Region partially takes in the provinces of Ciego de Avila, Camagüey and Las Tunas and is very favorable for mineralization of gold and silver. Small deposits of gold and iron were exploited here at the beginning of the twentieth century.

Geologically speaking, the region is characterized by well-developed island arc magmatism, of calco-alkaline and alkaline composition, whose nucleus is identified by a well-expressed principal magmatic axis, east-west orientation and constituted by intrusive rock. Effusive sequences are found on its flanks.

In the intrusive nucleus there are outstanding associations of granodiorite, gabbro-sienite and gabbro-plagiogranite, principally represented by the polyfasic intrusive hills of Gaspar, Las Parras and Sibanicu-Las Tunas. According to its petrochemical characteristics these plutonic rocks can be divided into three series: 1) normal calco-alkaline, 2) sodic calcoalkaline and 3) alkaline.

Due to the depth of the occurrence, volcanism presents varia from deep submarine in the K1 volcanic island arc (Albian-Santonian) to the sub-aerial explosive in the K2 volcanic island arc (Campanian). The volcanogenic-sedimentary sequences are along both flanks of the magmatic axis. The most prospective zones are related to the South flank sequences even though the north flank also appears interesting, such as Loma Jacinto.

Mineralization in this last case seems connected to intrusive acidic and alkaline bodies. Nevertheless, in other sequences to the south of the magmatic axis such as Golden Hill, mineralization is associated with volcano-tectonic structures, apparently connected to the other secondary magmatic axis that does not come up to the surface.

The most important types of deposits present in this region are the high-sulfuration and lowsulfuration epithermals, as well as Cu – Mo ± Au porfidic type sequences. There are also Cu skarn type deposits (Tamarindo mineral district) and other models of deposits could appear such as the Fe, porfidic Fe and Torio-Tierras Raras veins.

To the north of the volcanic island arc sequences there is a belt of mafic and ultramafic rock sequences in which the San Felipe ophiolitic hill stands out. These sequences just like in the central region are found in allochthonous position. Here there are laterite deposits of Fe – Ni

– Co as well as Cyprus-type VMS.

Prospects of Interest:

El Pilar	Raw Materials: Au Type of mineralization: high-sulfuration epithermal Au Degree of study: prospecting Work Phase to be undertaken: exploration
Caunao	Raw Materials: Au, Ag Type of mineralization: epithermal Au - Ag Degree of study: regional geological survey Work Phase to be undertaken: Recognizance in the entire area
Jagüey – La Catuca	Raw Materials: Au, Ag, possible Cu, Zn, Th and Tierras Raras Type of mineralization: epithermal Au – Ag and auriferous skarn. Possible Th veins Degree of study: Recognizance in Jagüey La Caridad, La Mina and Catuca Work Phase to be undertaken: additional works of Recognizance to definitively establish prospects, or not, of the three principal known manifestations. Recognizance work in the rest of the area.
Guaimaro -Jobabo	Raw Materials: Cu, Mo, Au, Ag. Possible Fe Type of mineralization: High sulfuration, low sulfuration and low alkaline sulfuration epthermal deposits. Porfidic deposits of Cu-Mo±Au and alkaline Au, with possible presence of other types of deposits. Degree of study: Exploration in Florencia and Maclama. Prospecting in the Jobabo district. Recognizance in Guaimaro, Palo Seco and Tres Casas I. Work Phase to be undertaken: Exploration of the Golden Hill flanks. Completing exploration of Maclama, Florencia and its flanks. Prospecting of porfridic deposits of Gauimara, Palo Seco and Tres Casas. Recognizance of the rest of the area.
Jacinto – La Sola	Raw Materials: Au, Ag Type of mineralization: los alkaline sulfuration epithermal Au-Ag. Possible epithermal Au – Ag and Cu – Mo ± porfidic Au and porfidic alkaline Cu-Au Degree of study: Exploration in Jacinto. Sparsely studied in the rest of the area. Work Phase to be undertaken: Complete exploration of Jacinto and its flanks. Recognizance in the rest of the area.
La Tunas W –	Raw Materials: Cu, Au, Ag, possible Mo and Zn
Tamarindo	Type of mineralization: Recognizance in Cañada, Asientos de Tamarindo, Manicaragua and Tamarindo 5. Serveys in the rest of the area. Degree of study: Cu-Au skarn. Possible epithermal deposits of porfidic Cu-Mo ± Au Work Phase to be undertaken: Prospecting in objective with recognizance completed and recognizance in the rest of the area.
Las Sureñas	Raw Materials: Possible Au, Ag, Cu, Mo Type of mineralization: High and low epithermal sulfuration and/or intermediate meso-epithermal sulfuration Degree of study: Geological mapping at scale of 1”250 000 Work Phase to be undertaken: Regional recognizance in the entire area.

The Holguín and Macizo Sagua -Baracoa Region is made up of a steep allochthonous sequence of volcanogenic-sedimentary and ophiolitic rock (known as “Zona Aura”) in close and overlapping tectonic contact by transcurrent and over the top faults. This sequence, heavily layered and folded, rests on the North American continental border (Bahamas-Florida block). The principal models of deposits present in the zone are Mother Lode –type auriferous, orogenic copper-gold-silver and Cyprus-type VMS.

The greatest possibilities to locate mineral deposits are found in the sites where the over the top and transcurrent faults are cut by transversal faults going north and north-east, as where the over the top sequence is cut by subvolcanic bodies, of basic to middle composition and often acid.

In the region, metallic mineralization presents spatial and genetic association with the subvolvanic bodies and the tectonic zones. We can see a clear tectonic-magmatic control. In the territory we can clearly distinguish two groups of hydrothermal alterations related to the useful and associated mineralization: one of them with subvolcanic bodies and the other with the ophiolitic and tectonic zones.

Prospects of Interest:

Holguín Oeste	Raw Materials: Au, Ag and Cu, possible Ti Type of mineralization: Mother Lode type orogenic Au-Ag and massive orogenic sulfurs. Possible orogenic mineralization in sequences of the continental border. Degree of study: Recognizance in the two prospects (Monte Rojo and Las Cuevas). Surveys in the rest of the area. We underline that the degree of study of the manifestations and mineral occurrences (30) present in the area, except Floro Perez is very poor therefore the area could, be considered practically virgin. Work Phase to be undertaken: prospecting in the two prospects and recognizance in the rest of the area.
Aguas Claras –	Raw Materials: Au - Ag
Guajabales	Type of mineralization: Orogenic type gold Degree of study: prospecting and exploration Work Phase to be undertaken: Exploration in Reina Victoria, Nuevo Potosi, Agrupada and Holguinera and prospecting in the rest of the satellite manifestations.
Santa Maria –	Raw Materials: Cu, Zn, Au, Ag, possible EGP
Charco Prieto	Type of mineralization: massive orogenic sulfurs of Cu – Zn – Au - Ag Degree of study: Recognizance Work Phase to be undertaken: prospecting of the four prospects and recognizance in the rest of the area
Cuatro Palmas	Raw Materials: Au and Ag Type of mineralization: Mother Lode type orogenic Au – Ag Degree of study: Recognizance Work Phase to be undertaken: prospecting the Cuatro Palmas prospect and recognizance of the rest of the area.

The Sierra Maestra Region extends to the west of the city of Santiago de Cuba. It presents good prospects for locating precious metals (gold and silver), base metals (copper, lead, zinc) and magnesium. The territory has a great number of mineral deposits: among the most important we recognize the El Cobre deposit in the province of Santiago de Cuba.

The Sierra Maestra, principal geographical accident in the eastern part of Cuba, extends on a line parallel with the coast, basically to the west of the city of Santiago de Cuba. It extends to the east where it is known as the Sierra de la Gran Piedra.

Geologically speaking, this region is constituted mainly by the Paleocene Volcanic Island Arc which has numerous outstanding volcanic-tectonic structures, intrusive and subvolcanic bodies. This arc is fundamentally underwater and is currently represented by a monoclinal anticlinal tilt to the north, affected by three main systems of fractures: one that is sublatitudinal (for example, the El Cobre fault with which the deposit of the same name is associated) and the other two going NW and NE.

The region is distinguished by a metalogenic zoning in the south-north direction. To the south intermediate sulfuration mesoepithermal deposts are developed (copper-copper and gold), copper molybdenum porfidic deposits with gold and skarn (iron with/without copper and gold); felsic VMS (Kuroko type) continue to appear and to the north there are the vulganogenic magnesium deposits.

Prospects of Interest:

Marea del Portillo	Raw Materials: Cu. Au. Ag, possible Zn Type of mineralization: Intermediate mesoepithermal sulfuration, possible felsic VMS (Kuroko

	type) Degree of study: Geological survey Work Phase to be undertaken: Recognizance in the entire area
Vega Grande – Juanica	Raw Materials: Cu, Ag, Au, Possible Zn Type of mineralization: Degree of study: Recognizance in La Cristina, La Nicolasa (Sector Vega Grande) and Juanica. Surveys in the rest of the area. Many of the manifestation described present mining work from the past. Work Phase to be undertaken: Prospecting in La Cristina, La Nicolasa and Juanica. Recognizance in the rest of the area.
Esperanza – El Cobre	Raw Materials: Cu, Au, Ag, Zn, Pb and Cd. Possible Mo Type of mineralization: felsic VMA (Kuroko) and Cu – Mo ± porfidic Au Degree of study: El Cobre has been explored. Prospecting in Bueycabon. Recognizance in the other manifestations. Work Phase to be undertaken: El Cobre: checking (complementary exploration) and feasibility study to recommence exploitation of the deposit. Prospecting in Bueycabon and recognizance in the other manifestation.
Hierro Santiago	Raw Materials: Fe, Cu, Au, garnet, possible Zn and Ag Type of mineralization: Fe and Fe-Cu Au skarn. Possible epithermal Au-Ag Degree of study: Fe deposits in the Distrito Mineral Hierro Santiago have been explored with many of them open pits. However this high degree of study is essentially oriented to the evaluation of Fe ores; it is insignificant for Au. In contrast, manifestation has been barely studied. Work Phase to be undertaken: Checking resources and exploration for Au and base metals in deposits of Fe – Cu – Au and Fe in the Distrito Mineral Hierro Santiago. Recognizance in the rest of the area.
Sierra del Purial Oeste	Raw Materials: Cu, Au, Ag, possible Zn, Ni and Co Type of mineralization: Cu – Ni orogenic sulfurs and possibly felsic VNS (Kuroko type) more or less modified by the regional metamorphism. Degree of study: Prospecting in the Eleccion and Jobito prospects, recognizance in the manifestations. Work Phase to be undertaken: prospecting in Eleccion and Jobito. Recognizance in the rest of the area.
Sierra del Purial Este	Raw Materials: Cu, Zn, Au, Ag Type of mineralization: mafic-ultramafic (Cyprus type) VMS. Mesoepithermal Au – Ag modified by regional metamorphism Degree of study: Surveys Work Phase to be undertaken: Recognizance in the entire area
Mn Cuba Oriental	Raw Materials: Mn. Possible Cu, Zn, Au, Ag Type of mineralization: Mn volcanogenic or "Cuban Mn type volcanogenic deposits" (D.L.Mosier and N.J. Page, 1988, U.S. Geological Survey Bulletin, 1822). Possible presence of VNS felsic (Kuroko type). Degree of study: Prospecting and exploration work. Mostly exploited. Work Phase to be undertaken: recognizance in the entire area, oriented towards locating new deposits not at the surface and checking for possible presence of massive sulfurs under the deposits of Mn, known and/or to be discovered.

Geological investigation (Prospecting-Exploration) at risk in various deposits of Mica and Kaolin on the Isle of Youth

Description	The Isle of Youth is the mecca of Cuban kaolin; here we find dozens of deposits and manifestations of this mineral, most of it with some degree of study, even some with resources assessed at high categories.

Investment Type	International Economic Association Contract (AEI) at risk, to do geological investigation (Prospecting and Exploration) for mica and kaolin. In the case of obtaining positive economic results, a Joint Enterprise would be created to undergo assimilation of one or several deposits after drawing up the corresponding Feasibility Study.
Estimated Investment	Total investment is estimated around 5.3 million USD, a value to be defined once the corresponding projects for required investigations are done.
Location	All the mineral deposits in this project are on the Isle of Youth.

Prospects of Interest:

Mica prospects, "El Aleman", (0.46 km^2) at some 10 Km SW of the city of Nueva Gerona.

Mica prospects, "Ciro Redondo", (2.25 km^2) at some 15 Km west of the city of Nueva Gerona.

Mica prospect,"El Bobo", (5.25 km^2) at some 10 km west of the city of Nueva Gerona.

Kaolin prospect, "Rio del Callejon", (1.8km^2) at some 18 km to the SW of the city of Nueva Gerona and 2 km NE of the town of La Demajagua.

Kaolin prospect, "Km 13" (0.23 km^2) at 13 km south of the city of Nueva Gerona and 2 km north of the town of Santa Fe.

Kaolin prospect, "Santa Barbara-Buena Vista" (10.12 km^2) at some 25 km to the SE of the city of Nueva Gerona and 3 to 4 km NE of the town of La Demajagua.

Kaolin prospect, "La jungla" (1.14 km^2) at some 30 km south of the city of Nueva Gerona and 10 km W of the town of Santa Fe.

Geological investigation (Prospecting-Exploration) at risk for the Wolfram "Lela" prospect on the Isle of Youth

Description	Prospect "Lela" was submitted to Search and Exploration work in the 1980s when the two systems of veins were sufficiently assessed and another two were partially assesses and the rest of the systems were only mapped. It is characterized by high geological complexity and a relatively low degree of study. Officially assessed resources are at around 794,200 tons of mineral (0.61% WO3) I the category of Indicated and 1,250,400 tons of mineral (0.26% WO3) in the category of Inferred; this is not sufficient to industrially assimilate this deposit. The principal objective of this business is to undergo Geological Investigation (Prospecting-Exploration) at risk within the framework of a Geological Investigation Concession (sub-phases of Prospecting and/or Exploration), to unify and organize all existing information as well as the additional jobs that lead to the elevation of category of the already assessed resources and the discovery of new bodies of wolframite mineral. The final objective would be to start up a mining operation and the corresponding processing plant for exploiting the mineral, with the obtaining of WO3 concentrates; should it turn out to be economically attractive the cupriferous and/or molybdic mineralization being investigated would also be considered for the mining operation. This objective would have to be carried out within the framework of a Joint Enterprise and be

	supported by the corresponding Feasibility Study.
Investment Type	International Economic Association at Risk Contract – in those prospects identified as mature we could assess the possibility of directly creating a Joint Enterprise.
Estimated Investment	6.8 million USD
Location	The proposed zone is in the Lomas de Siguanea some 50 km SW of New Gerona and 2 km E of the Hotel Colony, Isle of Youth. Its area is around 9.5 km2. The relief is hilly with maximum slopes of 80 to 100 m. Access to the zone is by the Gerona-Hotel Colony highway and internal movement can be done using the network of roads and embankments, preferably in 4-wheel drive vehicles.

Exploitation, processing and commercialization of products obtained from the "Hierro Mantua" copper deposit, Mantua municipality of Pinar del Río.	
Description	The Hierro Mantua deposit is the principal reserve of cuprous minerals in Cuba. The deposit is highly complex due to its mineralogical composition and its geology; different technologies are being successfully studied in Cuba and in other countries such as Rumania, Chile, Canada, etc. Completion of technological studies and drawing up the Feasibility Study for the copper deposit in the Mantua zone in Pinar del Río are among the objectives pursued by this Project. We are also developing mining activities and the exploitation of authorized minerals in the mining concession and the processing and commercialization of Grade A copper cathodes.
Investment Type	Joint Enterprise
Cuban Party	Geominera S.A
Estimated Investment Amount	The investment total amount is estimated at around 157,4 million USD.
Location	The "Hierro Mantua" copper deposit is found in the municipality of Mantua in the western region of the province of Pinar del Río, 262 km by highway from Havana and 147 km from the provincial capital, Pinar del Río, covering an area of 760.01 hectares.
Market Potential	The current international market is suffering a shortage of copper supplies thereby maintaining high prices. We foresee that the project will produce 18,000 tons of 99.99% pure copper cathodes a year. We expect to have 6,000 tons per year covering domestic demands in Cuba's mechanical and electrical industry since currently we are importing this product as raw material. The rest of production will be exported.
Contacts	Dirección de Negocios GeoMinera S.A. E-mail: gustavo@gmsa.cu Tel. (537) 690-2741 ext.115

Deposits at Cajalbana, San Felipe and Colas Roja de Moa

Cuba has over 70 years of experience in the exploitation of deposits for the recovery of nickel (Ni) and cobalt (Co).

Until the end of 2013, Cuba had produced over 2.95 million tons of Ni and Co, aiming at surpassing the 3 million mark by this year of 2014.

On national territory we know of 43 deposits of nickel. The majority of which to the north of the eastern provinces; resources total 1130 million tons with content and this places it among the three leading countries that have this mineral.

Besides the aforementioned Ni and Co, deposits to be explored are characterized by their high content of iron (Fe), magnesium (Mg) and silicon (Si) and the existence of metals in the platinic group will be studied along with the presence of rare metals.

In the case that concentrations justifying recovery of rare and platinic group metals should be determined, new production capacities must be built since the country does not have the suitable facilities for the concentrated production of these metals.

Investment opportunities are presented below, directed to the development of projects in the Geological Investigation Phase in the deposits of Cajalbana, San Felipe and Moa.

Cajalbana Project, Pinar del Rio Province

Description	In this zone there are deposits of some 52 million tons of laterite nickel and cobalt mineral that can be processed in order to obtain nickel and cobalt products for commercialization.
Investment Type	Preferably International Economic Association Contract using the type of at risk contract for the EFTE elaboration stage. After this has been concluded, a Joint Enterprise will be set up in charge of the execution of the project, the procuring, building and start up and operation for the factory. Another alternative is setting up the Joint Enterprise from the beginning, including the EFTE elaboration.
Cuban Party	Commercial Caribbean Nickel S. A.(CCN)
Estimated	Only studies on a laboratory level have been done at Cajalbana;
Investment	technology for its processing has not be confirmed and so the figures can only be taken as a reference since they must be confirmed by geological and metallurgical studies and future accounting calculations. 500 to 700 million USD will be needed for building the plant and starting it up.
Location	La Palma municipality, Pinar del Rio province
Market	The nickel and cobalt market should be growing in the next decades due to the growth of emerging countries and their demands on stainless steel; manufacturing hybrid automobiles and the great demand for batteries for them; and the continued development of nanotechnology that needs both nickel and cobalt.
Anticipated results	Production capacity: 10,000 – 12,000 tons/year of nickel and cobalt. Mineral resources: 51 million tons
Contacts	Dirección de Commercial Caribbean Nickel S. A Email: mcabello@ccn.co.cu Tel: (537) 862-4601 ext. 110

San Felipe Project, Camagüey Province

Description	Some 300 million tons of laterite nickel and cobalt mineral are deposited in this zone; it can be processed in order to obtain nickel and cobalt products for commercialization' The project's objectives include doing studies for the development and future exploitation of the deposit, including geological investigation, development of technology, elaboration of basic engineering and the Technical Economic Feasibility Study.
Investment Type	Preferably International Economic Association Contract using the type of at risk contract for the EFTE elaboration stage. After this has been concluded, a Joint Enterprise will be set up in charge of the execution of the project, the procuring, building and start up and operation for the factory. Another alternative is setting up the Joint Enterprise from the beginning, including the EFTE elaboration.
Cuban Party	Commercial Caribbean Nickel S. A. (CCN)
Estimated	Up to the present, a study on the conceptual scale had been done;
Investment	its figures need to be confirmed by geological and metallurgical studies and future accounting calculations. We estimate a total of 59.7 million USD for the first stage and a total project cost of between 4,000 to 4,500 million USD (with a 15% contingency factor).
Location	Municipality of Camagüey, province of Camagüey.
Market	The nickel and cobalt market should be growing in the next decades due to the growth of emerging countries and their demands on stainless steel; manufacturing hybrid automobiles and the great demand for batteries for them; and the continued development of nanotechnology that needs both nickel and cobalt.
Anticipated results	Annual production of 50,000 to 60,000 tons of nickel and cobalt, metallurgical recovery: Ni: 88%, Co: 86%. Mineral Resources: 300.0 million tons (0.9% Cut Off for Ni).
Contacts	Dirección de Commercial Caribbean Nickel S. A Email: mcabello@ccn.co.cu Tel: (537) 862-4601 ext. 110

Colas Rojas Project, Moa

Description	Development of a Project for the treatment and use of Moa's "red tails" the result of processing laterites in order to obtain nickel with acid technology (PAL). The objective is to extract iron and other elements containing the tails and the mitigation of the environmental impact produced by them. It is necessary to complete technological, laboratory and pilot plant studies and to determine which products will be the most suited for the market. Besides iron, the tails contain Al_2O_3, Cr_2O_3, SiO_2, MgO, MnO, P_2O_5 and others in lesser proportions. "Red tails" are being produced and stored since 1961 with an accumulated volume estimated at 80 million tons. They will continue being produced at an annual rhythm of over 3 to 4 million tons in the next 30 years. We need to find or identify investors or international contractors with the financial, technological and market capacities to be able to make use of or dispose of these tails.
Investment Type	Any of the forms foreseen in Law 118 of Foreign Investment
Cuban Party	Commercial Caribbean Nickel S. A
Estimated	Without counting on the technology for its processing, it is not
Investment	possible to determine the fundamental economic indicators. The business includes drawing up risk studies for the development of technology or developing solutions and facilities for being handled and shipped by sea to

	foreign markets.
Location	Moa municipality, Holguín
Market	Exportation for the use of iron concentrate obtained as a cargo material for foreign steelworks or for domestic consumption to replace domestic scrap in Cuban steelworks.
Contacts	Direcci6n de Commercial Caribbean Nickel S. A Email: mcabello@ccn.co.cu Tel: (537) 862-4601 ext. 110

TRANSPORTATION SECTOR

The first railroad in Spanish America, one of the first airlines to issue in the era of commercial flights, one of the oldest naval industries on the continent are some of the elements that make up the roots and traditions of the Cuban transport sector. They have played an important role in all the stages of Cuban history.

After an intense period of development during the first years of the Revolution, transport in Cuba suffered from the impact of the difficult years following the collapse of the socialist bloc during the 1990s and not until the beginning of the new century did recovery of the main services take place, corresponding to the advances being felt in the national economy.

Principal Regulatory Provisions:

Law 109 of the Roads Safety Code of September 17, 2010
Law 115 of the Inland Waters Navigation of October 2, 2013.
Decree Law 168 on Transport Operation Licensing of November 26, 1996
Decree Law 180 on Railroads of December 15, 1997
Decree Law 230 on Ports of September 13, 2002
Decree Law 255 on Civil Aviation of October 5, 2007
Decree 278 of the Air and Sea Search and Rescue System of December 30, 2006.

Cuba has a broad-based transport infrastructure that includes the branches of automotive, rail, maritime-port and air transportation and is currently being organized, modernized and technologically updated, being improved by human resources and materials available and to improve the efficiency in its use as well as in the overall development of all the branches to coordinate with the country's economic-social growth within the context of the world economy.

It is important to insert foreign investment into this sector in order to accelerate the attaining of these objectives and with it to achieve the needed competiveness of transport both in cargo and passengers, demanded by the various production spheres and national economy services; all of the foregoing supported by the presently existing strengths as follows:

• Qualified human resources in a wide range of transport specialties, in all branches, with the education base necessary to quickly assimilate new technologies and develop transportation products and services (sailors, plane crews, rail specialists, planners, scientists, etc.)

Workforce by Education

To Grade 9: 17,498
Grades 9 to 12: 26,754
Middle Technicians: 24,179

University Graduates: 8,194

Vast roadways network of over 60,000 kilometers of roadways for automobile transportation and over 8,000 kilometers of rail lines interconnecting by Loading and Unloading Centers that exist throughout the country and that even though they require technical improvement also interconnect the main economic and population centers with a network of ports and national and international airports that in turn have all the port and airport services available according to world standards.

Cuban Ports

Installed capacity for ship repairs in the more than 40 shipbuilding facilities and dry docks all over the country which, although they need to be modernized, are an important departure point for taking advantage of existing opportunities for this service in the Caribbean; this is complemented by the existence of International Quality Classifying Company "Registro Cubano de Buques" having over thirty years of experience in this sector.

Installed capacity of workshops and industries for automotive and rail transportation that can be modernized and adapted to new technologies with minor investments in order to develop the manufacture of spare parts and accessories for transport in all its branches.

Strategic location in Latin America and the Caribbean region for developing transport services and products.

Growing domestic market for passenger and merchandise transport as well as for their auxiliary and connected services.

OBJECTIVES FOR FOREIGN INVESTMENTS

Management for shipbuilders for the development of the naval industry both for attention to the domestic fleet for crossings and auxiliary services and to broaden exportations of products and services in this activity.

Management of wholesale commercialization of spare parts and accessories in the different branches of transport, including the development of local manufacturing and/or repairing of components having the greatest rotation on the domestic market and their possible exportation.

Efficient management of specialized transport services of cargo and passengers, both on national territory and internationally, including exploitation and technical assurance.

Efficient management of services related to commercial and agricultural aviation oriented towards both the domestic and international markets.

Management of transport products and services (including activities of training, research, project and administration) in Cuba and in third countries.

Cuban Parties associated with foreign capital businesses:

CDC S.A. is a company providing naval repairs and construction services; repairs and maintenance of fuel storage tanks; production of bottled oxygen and acetylene and all the technical services satisfying the needs of domestic and international clients both in the naval and industrial sectors. Its Quality Management system is registered by Lloyd's Register of the UK and the Oficina Nacional de Normalizacion.

Empresa Comercializadora AXESS is a company that commercializes on a wholesale basis both imported products and those purchased in Cuba. With over 30 years of experience in the wholesale market of automotive spare parts, parts and accessories in Cuba, it is the best commercializing company within the automotive sector. It has a network of stores and warehouses distributed all over the country.

Empresa Provincial de Transporte de La Habana is a company that provides passenger public transportation services in Havana using tis fleet of over 900 buses of different categories (articulated and rigid) grouped at 16 bases distributed over Havana. It also has facilities dedicated to repairing spare parts and accessories.

Empresa de Transporte de Trabajadores in a company providing transport services for tourism employees all over the country. It operated a total of 998 buses distributed over 21 bases. The company provides services not only to employees directly connected to the tourism industry but also to employees of other companies and government organizations.

SECTORIAL POLICY

To develop port infrastructure, the building and repairing of vessels in shipbuilding companies, the purchase and/or management of ships, technical assurance activity and the exploitation of automotive transport, manufacture and repairing of spare parts and accessories, management of workshops and other rail system activities and in everything regarding commercial and agricultural aviation.

Technical Specifications on Foreign Investment Opportunities Building, remodeling, operations and management of Astillero Casablanca

Description	To provide naval repair and construction services; repairs and maintenance of fuel storage tanks; production of bottled oxygen and acetylene and all the technical services satisfying the needs of domestic and international clients both in the naval and industrial sectors and carrying out the following objectives: a) diversification and extending services to new export markets b) access to advanced technologies, replacing a large part of them for their operations c) developing linkups with other products of national economy goods and services
Investment Type	Joint Enterprise
Cuban Party	CDC S.A.
Estimated Investment Amount	34.8 million USD
Location	Eastern end of Havana Bay on Carretera del naval No. 9, Reparto Casablanca, Regla municipality, La Habana
Market Potential	In the Gulf of Mexico, Central America, Caribbean and South American region they sail ships of small, medium and large sizes, approximately 1125 ships in one year, of these around 225 vessels came into Cuban ports in 2013, with a total 75 ship-owners. With the opening of the container terminal at the Special Development Zone of Mariel ship repairs in the medium and

	large size range will be promoted. Among the national market sectors identified as potential market: industrial sector, hotel sector especially in terms of construction and repairs of fuel storage tanks and in the repairs and/or renovations to all types of systems (pipes, electricity, etc.) throughout the country.
Estimated Anticipated Results	1. Promoting replacement of imports and constituting a saving by not having Cuban ships in dry-dock abroad. 2. Maximizing exportations of services on the basis of repairing foreign ships. 3. Generating income in foreign currencies for other sectors of the national economy providing services needed by ships and foreign ships' crews during their stay while their ships are being repaired in Cuba. 4. Newly constructed docks will be able to be used at all times for minimal maintenance costs during the investment recovery period. 5. Updating the country's technology in matters dealing with naval repairs and construction.
Contacts	Dirección de Relaciones Internacionales del Ministerio del Transporte. email: ivan.ne@mitrans.co.cu Tel: (537) 884-1196

Comprehensive Management of an Urban Transportation Base in Havana

Description	To organize the services of the public transportation of passengers according to international operations standards, with suitable maintenance and repairs schedules and the necessary logistics system allowing for the proper yield of principal assets, fundamentally the transportation means and greater efficiency in management. To ensure that itineraries approved by the Dirección General de Transporte Provincial de La Habana for the selected bases are carried out, along with the quality levels for this service, fulfilling the following aims, among others: • Improving utilization of the existing fleet on the basis of recovering vehicles that are not in service and adequate sustainability of the functioning fleet. • Providing opportune financing necessary for the resources required by the management including what is necessary for gradual replacement and increasing the size of the fleet in use. • Obtaining means and technological equipment necessary for fleet maintenance and repairs and for the training of specialized personnel for both operations and technical needs.
Investment Type	International Economic Association Contract for Services Management
Cuban Party	Empresa Provincial de Transporte de La Habana
Estimated Investment Amount	4.8 million USD
Location	To the south of the city of Havana, a base in the town of Mulgoba, Boyeros municipality, Havana
Market Potential	The public transportation of passengers market in Havana is suffering shortages; there is sufficient demand to triple the service level being provided today if it is developed efficiently. Experiences acquired can be extended to other transportation bases of the city and all over the country.
Estimated Anticipated Results	• Accelerated recovery for buses that are paralyzed for long periods of time • Improved quality and service levels for passenger transportation • Using the knowledge and principal standards of how a Urban Transportation Base should operate to subsequently use this at all public transportation bases in Havana • Decreased exploitation costs because of improved maintenance schedules • Improved efficiency and organization in general in the management of a Bus Base.

Contacts	Dirección de Relaciones Internacionales del Ministerio del Transporte. Email: ivan.ne@mitrans.co.cu Tel: (537) 884-1196

Comprehensive Management for a Base for Tourism Employee Transportation in the cays of the central region of Cuba

Description	To organize transportation services for employees of the tourism industry who are working in the hotel network in the central cays region according to the international operations standards for this type of service, with proper maintenance and repairs schedules and the necessary logistics system allowing for the proper yield of principal assets, fundamentally the transportation means and greater efficiency in management. To ensure that itineraries approved by the Dirección General de Transporte Provincial de La Habana for the selected bases are carried out, along with the quality levels for this service, fulfilling the following aims, among others: • Improving utilization of the existing fleet on the basis of recovering vehicles that are not in service and adequate sustainability of the functioning fleet. • Providing opportune financing necessary for the resources required by the management including what is necessary for gradual replacement and increasing the size of the fleet in use. Obtaining means and technological equipment necessary for fleet maintenance and repairs and for the training of specialized personnel for both operations and technical needs.
Investment Type	International Economic Association Contract for Services Management
Cuban Party	Empresa de Transporte de Trabajadores del Turismo
Estimated Investment Amount	9.5 million USD
Location	A base for transport in the province of Santa Clara belonging to the Empresa de Transporte de Trabajadores del Turismo
Market Potential	Transportation of tourism industry employees, not only those working in the hotel network but also those working in out-of-hotel networks in the resort area of the northern cays in the province of Santa Clara, has growing potential at a time when we are planning for increased hotel capacities in this region. Experience acquired at this first Transportation base can then be applied to other tourist resort areas in Cuba.
Estimated Anticipated Results	• Quantity and quality of transportation services for employees is guaranteed for the requirements of tourism in the central region of Cuba • Knowledge and the principal standards of how an Employee Transportation Base should function • Decreased exploitation costs because of improved maintenance schedules • Improved efficiency and organization in general.
Contacts	Dirección de Relaciones Internacionales del Ministerio del Transporte. Email: ivan.ne@mitrans.co.cu Tel: (537) 884-1196

DRUG AND BIOTECHNICAL INDUSTRY SECTOR

The Drug and Biotechnological Sector industry produces medicines, equipment and high technology services on the basis of the country's scientific-technical development, for the improvement of the health of the Cuban people and the generating of exportable goods and services.

The Grupo de las Industrias Biotecnologica y Farmaceutica, BioCubaFarma, is made up of:

16 large manufacturing enterprises with 78 production facilities

8 commercializing enterprises

11 enterprises abroad

Establishments in all the provinces of Cuba

Over 21,000 employees are at work; of these 58% have higher and middle higher education levels. Over 900 have their Masters of Sciences and approximately 600 are taking their Masters. Over 250 are Doctors of Sciences and approximately 150 are in the process of getting their Doctors of Sciences degrees.

PRODUCTS:

Among the principal products there are prophylactic vaccines against infectious diseases, biodrugs for the treatment of cancer (including monoclonal antibodies and therapeutic vaccines), products for the prevention and treatment of cardiovascular conditions as well as for the treatment of ulcers in diabetic foot.

We also manufacture generic products and new generation drug compounds as well as systems for early diagnosis and prevention of malignant tumors, malformations, hereditary-metabolic diseases and others. We also offer natural and traditional medicine products and agricultural research as well as advanced technology medical equipment, nanotechnology, neurosciences and neurotechnology.

In Cuba, BioCubaFarm has health registrations for 592 drug products and 28 biological products; abroad, its enterprises have over 800 health registrations in different countries.

In general, it develops 91 products / projects directed towards the principal diseases:

33 projects and products against infectious diseases	7 projects and products for diabetes and other pathologies
33 oncological projects and products	18 cardiovascular projects and products

Comprehensive Programs for patients for high impact on their health:

Prevention program for diseases with prophylactic vaccines.

Program for early diagnosis and treatment of different cancer pathologies.

Program for investigation and treatment of diabetes and its complications such as ulcers of the diabetic foot.

Program for diagnosing and evaluation different diseases (cardiology, neurology, etc.) with new medical equipment.

Program for the detection of hereditary-metabolic malformations and diseases.

The total number of patents awarded abroad is more than 1400; among these are included medicines recognized on international levels such as Heberprot-P which is used for the treatment of the ulcers of the diabetic foot and the monoclonal antibody Nimotuzumab for the treatment of tumors in the head and neck, esophagus and brain.

BioCubaFarm exports to more than 50 countries and its Program of Clinical Development abroad includes 40 Clinical Tests in 24 countries.

IN its international expansion this sector uses various types of business, among these the most outstanding are joint development of research and development projects, distribution and representation agreements, transfer of technology agreements and joint enterprises outside of Cuba and other enterprises that are 100% Cuban capital abroad. It also promotes the direct foreign investment in Cuba that will be significant in the Special Development Zone of Mariel.

SECTORIAL POLICY:

To promote projects in Cuba with strategic partners for the production of the finished forms and active pharmaceutical ingredients in generic medicines. In the case of biotechnological products we will assess specific business to complement national projects, keeping intellectual property rights and looking after the proper use of what the joint enterprise could produce as well as the creation or enlarging of production capacities.

HEALTH SECTOR

Cuba has a tradition of over 285 years of medical education, with 134,400 doctors having been trained in the last 50 years, both Cubans as well as those coming from over 120 countries. The Island has become one of the nations of the world with the best health indicators. Its strengths are quality and specializations with a growing development of the infrastructure of services and human capital.

Basic Information

11,000 doctors' offices
497,021 health workers
451 polyclinics
18 research institutions
126 old age homes
243 community seniors' centers
142 maternity homes
152 hospitals
1,215 dentistry services

Training Human Capital	Development of Science	Basic Medicines
• 13 universities.	and Technology	• 888 items.
• 13 independent	• 44 science and	• 296 are imported.
medical sciences	technological innovation	• 592 are nationally produced.

faculties and 26	entities.	
affiliates.	• 18 research institutes and	
• University campuses in	centers.	
all the country's	• 15 scientific-technological	
municipalities.	development centers.	
• National School of	• 2241 categorized	
Public Health.	researchers, of these 867	
	are doctors in sciences.	

Cuban Party associated in businesses with foreign capital

– Cuban Medical Services Marketing Entity (SMC)

The Comercializadora de Servicios Medicos Cubanos is in charge of marketing and promoting medical health services in Cuba and the world.

Among its business lines there are Medical Care Services in Cuba for which there are 47 institutions in the national health system, 8 international clinics, 4 anti-drug villas and more than 600 hospital beds. To develop this line of business the enterprise works on searching for agencies, syndicate and insurance companies that want to use these clinics to send them patients to receive medical care in Cuba.

It has already signed contracts with 31 travel agencies and travel agents form 17 countries; more than 20,000 medical care services have been provide to patients coming from 71 countries. Over 150 programs are commercialized in its services portfolio.

The SMC also offers among its services the possibility of medical care for the employees of foreign entities based in Cuba, medical services abroad through agreements with institutions, governments and municipalities, promoting academic training programs in the medical sciences in Cuba and abroad.

We also offer technological programs or packages which include services by health professionals and technicians combined with biotechnological products, among which are:

Prevention, diagnosis and treatment of cancer.

Comprehensive care of diabetic patients including prevention, diagnosis and treatment actions for Diabetes Mellitus.

Services for the diagnosis and rehabilitation of cardiovascular diseases.

Comprehensive care for hearing disorders.

Early detection of children's neuro-developmental disorders.

Comprehensive study of challenged persons.

Ophthalmologic program.

Contact Information: www.smcsalud.cu smc@smcsalud.cu

SECTORIAL POLICY:

To promote foreign investment with the objective of achieving development of exportations of Cuban medical and health services.

Opportunities in the sector are being designed.

CONSTRUCTION SECTOR

The construction sector takes in, among other activities, engineering-geological research applied to construction, drawing up designs for construction and setting up activities, construction of civil state works, industrial works, engineering works, docking and dredging works as well as production and commercialization of construction materials and products.

Professionals in the Sector

Civil Engineers
Architects
Mechanical Engineers
Hydraulic Engineers
Electrical Engineers
Economy and Accounting Degrees
Industrial Engineers
Others

The sector has a workforce of approximately 106,000; of these 20% are technicians and 59% are laborers. The number of professionals is over 11,000 distributed in the specialties of Civil Engineering, Architecture, Mechanical Engineering, etc.

1727 workers provide construction services and technical assistance in 19 countries.

The International Construction Fair (FECONS) is a window to the world showing off Cuba's construction prowess. Held every two years, the Fair is the ideal event for exchanges with exhibiters form different countries and for promoting products and services for export. FECONS has managed to occupy a significant place on the international business scene as a specialized event. **The sector has a Quality Management System certified in 130 organizations, for a 72% total.**

LEGAL FRAMEWORK

Resolution 328/96 for the creation of the Comision Nacional de Contratacion y Licitacion de Obras Proyectos y otros servicios de la Construccion and the creation of the Registro nacional de Constructores, Proyectistas y Consultores de la Republica de Cuba and its regulations.

Some Projects Already Executed
Study, conception and execution of the Viaducto de la Farola which connects the cities of Guantanamo and Baracoa. Considered among the seven marvels of civil engineering of Cuba.
Construction of highways in the sea (causeways) as access routes to the cays for tourism exploitation.

Development of stone bases with continuous sediment grain-size analysis, using asphalt mixes and concrete pavements.
Research, introduction and generalization of different types and qualities of Portland cement and Portland with natural Cuban pozzolana additives, electric arc furnace dregs, and hydrofuge and also calcium-pozzolana agglomerate.
Transfer and development of the construction technology of great earthwork dams, notable elevating levels of the dams and preventing flooding in prolonged periods of rainfall and during hurricanes.
Development of construction materials such as domestically manufactured cement-based paints, textured plastering, single layer mortar, D-10 cement-based weatherproofing, ceramic low-water-consumption bathroom fixtures, solar heaters for social works, etc.
Drawing up engineering-geological maps of the regions having special importance for construction

SECTORIAL POLICY:

To accede to new technologies to improve efficiency in construction, increase production of materials, spare parts and recover and complete general repairs plants. To promote the construction of infrastructure and industrial maintenance works fundamentally for the nickel, oil and cement industries as well as designing and constructing hotels for tourism and real estate complexes associated with golf courses.

Technical Specifications on Foreign Investment Opportunities Production of calcinated plaster, blocks and plaster-based products for construction

Description	The project is designed to produce calcinated plaster and calcinated interlocking plaster blocks as construction elements for building interior walls and partitions. A later phase is foreseen to carry out other calcinated plaster-based products for constructions such as false plaster ceilings and decorative elements such as capitals, cornices, corners, soffits, gradients, mortars and plaster. The plant which is part of this business project has the equipment and technology to manufacture gypsum, with the installed capacity to produce 10,000 tons/year of modeling plaster and 10,000 tons/year for construction. This proposal will achieve an increase of 6,800 tons/year destined for the production of plaster blocks.
Investment Type	International Economic Association Contract
Cuban Party	Empresa de Materiales de la Construcción de Ciego de Avila
Estimated Investment Amount	3.3 million USD
Location	UEB Maximo Gomez in the municipality of Chambas, Ciego de Avila province, near the country's largest plaster deposits.
Market Potential	Domestic demands for these products, in the construction of interior walls in tourism buildings, in the construction of homes built by private individuals as well as in other economic and social objectives. All this would reduce costs due to importing the plasterboards, structures and accessories, on the basis of manufacturing the aforementioned blocks in Cuba with Cuban plaster and domestic production of plaster glue. We also note the existence of growing demands for plaster blocks in Central America and the Caribbean, therefore we foresee exports going

	to those places.
Estimated Anticipated	Annual sales: 1,524,240 USD (Domestic market 66% -
Results	Exports 34%) Annual savings in the case of importing similar products: 2,369,516 USD. Investment Recovery Period: 5 years and 7 months.
Contacts	Dirección de Negocios del Ministerio de la Construcción Email: presidente@uneca.co.cu Tel. (537) 209-6067 and (537) 209-4582

Production of Asphalt Cloth

Description	The objective of the project is the production of self-protected asphalt cloth with granular slate or ceramic mineral, unprotected asphalt cloth, paint and asphalt-based putties to satisfy annual domestic demands and for export to Central and South America of the self-protected cloths. We foresee the installation of 3 production lines.
Investment Type	Joint Enterprise
Cuban Party	Empresa de Impermeabilizantes IMPERASFAL
Estimated Investment Amount	18.3 million USD
Location	At the facilities belonging to the Empresa de Impermeabilizantes IMPERASFAL in El Cano, La Lisa municipality, Havana province.
Market Potential	This investment project is conceived to satisfy required sales of asphalt cloth, asphalt-based paint and putty on the domestic market and we foresee exportation of the production surpluses in self-protected asphalt cloth to countries in Latin America and the Caribbean where we have noted a growing demand for these products.
Estimated Anticipated Results	Savings because of import replacement: 3,744,000.00 USD/year Investment Recovery period: 7 years
Contacts	Dirección General de la Empresa de Impermeabilizantes, IMPERASFAL Email: fernando@imp.perdurit.com.cu Tel. (537) 202-0033 and (537) 272-0911

Production of smooth sheets

Description	Production of smooth sheets for reinforced panels in order to replace imports of cement agglomerate boards for interior walls, exterior walls, mezzanines and roofs.
Investment Type	Joint Enterprise
Cuban Party	Empresa de Fibrocemento de Artemisa
Estimated Investment Amount	18.1 million USD
Location	Facilities of the Empresa de Fibrocemento Perdurit (UEB Artemisa) at Finca Santa Teresa, Las Cañas, Artemisa.
Market Potential	This investment project is conceived to satisfy the demands for light panels for homes, social works, tourism sites and real estate

	on the domestic market.
Estimated Anticipated Results	Installation of technology that does not exist in the country that allows for the production of an element that today is being imported. Investment Recovery Period: 6 years
Contacts	Director de la empresa de Fibrocemento Perdurit rvargas@perdurit.com.cu Tel: (537) 836-5510 and (537) 835-7081

Production of PVC systems for Construction

Description	The project's objective is to manufacture PVC systems for construction in the production of sanitary and electrical built-ins, adhesives, cleaner and primer; tubes for networks in the electrical industry sector and PVC communications and construction systems.
Investment Type	International Economic Association Contract
Cuban Party	Empresa de Impermeabilizantes IMPERASFAL
Estimated Investment Amount	36.8 million USD
Location	At the IMPERASFAL facilities in El Cano, La Lisa Municipality, Havana province.
Market Potential	There is growing interest in PVC products. We foresee the exportation of production surpluses to countries in Latin America and the Caribbean.
Estimated Anticipated Results	Savings of 2.8 million USD/year because imports will be replaced. Investment Recovery Period: 4 years
Contacts	Dirección General de IMPERASFAL Email: fernando@imp.perdurit.com.cu Tel. (537) 202-0033 and (537) 272-0911

Nuevitas Cement Factory

Description	This proposal's objective is to build a new plant to manufacture 1.1 million tons of clinker. Exportation, distribution and commercialization of cement, clinker and other hydraulic binders and their byproducts, also able to carry out connected activities related to manufacture, distribution and sales of hydraulic lime, paper bags, aggregates and concrete, cement artifacts and other construction materials as well as research and providing services associated with the principal product.
Investment Type	Joint Enterprise
Cuban Party	GECEM Internacional S.A.
Estimated Investment Amount	410.0 million USD
Location	Near today's Nuevitas cement plant to the north of the aforementioned city in Camagüey province.
Market Potential	Production is conceived for domestic consumption and exportation. We foresee that 80% of clinker production will be destined for the production of cement for export and the rest will be for the domestic market.
Estimated Anticipated Results	Estimated annual sales after reaching 100% foreseen capacity

	will be 112,651.1 MUSD Investment Recovery Period: approx. 13 years
Contacts	Dirección de Negocios del Ministerio de la Construcción. Email: presidente@uneca.co.cu Tel. (537) 209-6067 y (537) 209-4582

Gibara Cement Factory

Description	Design, construction and operation of a new technological line with the production capacity of 1.1 million tons of grey clinker per year, with modern dry processing technology to achieve greater energy efficiency and low impact levels on the environment.
Investment Type	Joint Enterprise
Cuban Party	GECEM Internacional S.A.
Estimated Investment Amount	430.0 million USD
Location	Gibara municipality close to the entrance to town in that area known as "Catucos" in Holguin province
Market Potential	Production is conceived for domestic consumption and export. We foresee 80% of clinker production will be for the production of cement for exportation and the rest will be for the domestic market.
Estimated Anticipated Results	Estimated annual sales after achieving 100% of foreseen capacity will be 112,651.1 MUSD Investment Recovery Period: approx. 13 years
Contacts	Dirección de Negocios del Ministerio de la Construcción. Email: presidente@uneca.co.cu Tel. (537) 209-6067 y (537) 209-4582

BUSINESS SECTOR

Wholesale business in Cuba is the activity of selling nationally produced or imported goods wholesale, destined for production entities, retail or wholesale commercializing entities, industrial and institutional consumers and natural persons.

Among the enterprises operating in this sector are those subordinated to the Grupo de Productos Industriales y de Servicios, the Grupo de Empresas Mayoristas de Alimentos y Otros Bienes de Consumo, the Grupo de Administracion Empresarial, the Grupo Empresarial de la Industria Ligera (GEMPIL) and the Grupos Empresarial de la Agricultura (GELMA) as well as the COPEXTEL and CIMEX corporations.

By 2014 there are over 2000 entities participating in wholesale business in Cuba. The current infrastructure of the sector is precarious and insufficient and therefore needs investment projects that guarantee access to new technologies.

Businesses in this sector are mainly directed to ensure the distribution of widely-used products and families of national and imported products that are most in demand in the country; therefore supplies are stabilized with efficacy and efficiency and logistical high costs are minimized.

Contact Information:

Dirección de Comercio Mayorista del Ministerio del Comercio Interior Tel: (537) 861-0949

SECTORIAL POLICY:

To develop wholesale business by appropriating financial resources, advanced managerial methods, marketing technologies and techniques.

To establish foreign investment in strategic areas, under the varieties of joint enterprises and international economic association contracts with majority Cuban participation. In retail business some business can be established with majority Cuban participation.

Technical Specifications on Foreign Investment Opportunities

Wholesale Importation and commercializing automotive spare parts, parts and accessories

Description	To encourage opportune supplies of automotive spare parts, parts and accessories for the national transportation system through the combination of importation and developing wholesale business, creating a valuable chain for repairs and manufacturing to be carried out in domestic industry. To assimilate cutting edge systems of warehousing, distribution and commercialization with a high degree of automation, guaranteeing the necessary infrastructure to carry out operations. Raw materials will be supplied to domestic manufacturers with whom contracts will be signed and their products will be bought. Imports and national products will be sold wholesale on the domestic market. National producers will also have access to the newest technological packages for manufacturing that guarantees high work productivity and decreased production costs.
Investment Type	Joint Enterprise
Cuban Party	Empresa Comercializadora AXESS
Estimated Investment Amount	8.7 million USD
Location	Kilometro 1 ½ Autopista Nacional, Ampliacion de Coyula, Reparto D'Beche, Guanaboacoa, La Habana
Market Potential	The domestic market for spare parts and accessories would be in the order of 124 million USD. The demand for buying automotive select brand name spare parts and accessories for MITRANS for 2015 is in the order of 68 million USD.
Estimated Anticipated Results	We would like to reach a significant increase in competitiveness in the importation value chain, wholesale commercialization and distribution of automotive spare parts, parts and accessories in Cuba, achieving new and effective production link-ups between the different actors in the chain that will first guarantee the development and sustainability of the country's transportation system and in the second phase will assure national producers growing participation in the international market.
Contacts	Dirección de Relaciones Internacionales del Ministerio del Transporte. Email: ivan.ne@mitrans.co.cu Tel: (537) 884-1196

IMPORTANT GOVERNMETN CONTACTS

Ministries of Cuba

There are numerous official agencies, businesses and industries controlled by various ministries in Cuba, all under the umbrella of the centrally controlled Cuban government.

We have compiled a complete list of Ministries in Cuba for you. However, the Cuban government is in the process of reorganizing Cuban ministries.

Structure of Administration and Business Groups in Cuba

The Economic and Commercial Office of Spain in Havana at the Spanish Embassy in Cuba published this detailed list of the structure and relationship between businesses and ministries in Cuba courtesy of CubaPolidata.com

CENTRAL BANK OF CUBA

To issue the national currency and seek for its stability.
To contribute to the macroeconomic balance and orderly development of the economy.
To keep custody of the country's international reserves.
To propose and implement a monetary policy which allows to attain the economic goals established by the country.
To ensure normal internal and external payment operations.
To dictate mandatory regulations.
To exercise the functions related to the discipline and supervision of the financial institutions and representative offices authorized to establish themselves in the country and of any other entrusted to it by the laws.
Besides the aforementioned classical functions, Banco Central de Cuba must undertake other challenges:

to improve the monetary system, in such way, that it can make feasible execution of the economic activity, enable its accurate measure, contribute to making efficiency analysis on real basis and encourage the efficacy of the economy in general and, particularly, work productivity and to
normalize the external financial relations of the country – including the foreign debt issue - and support credit management of banks integrating the national system and of Cuban enterprises by means of bilateral contacts with other central banks, export credit insurance companies and other official and private financial institutions.
Cuban Civil Aviation Institute

Calle 23 # 64, Vedado, Municipio Plaza de la Revolución, Ciudad de La Habana, Cuba
Telefono: 33 4949 Fax:334553 iacc@avianet.cu

The Cuban Civil Aviation Institute is the body responsible for directing, implementing and monitoring state and government policy related to air transportation, civilian air navigation and its auxiliary and connected services.

CUBAN RADIO AND TELEVISION INSTITUTE

The Cuban Radio and Television Institute is the body responsible for directing, implementing and monitoring state and government policy related to television and radio broadcasting.

National Institute of Sports, Physical Education and Recreation

The National Institute of Sports, Physical Education and Recreation is the body responsible for directing, implementing and monitoring state and government policy related to sports, physical education and recreational programs.

NATIONAL HYDRAULIC RESOURCES INSTITUTE

Address: Humbolt 106 esq. P. Plaza. Ciudad Habana. Cuba
infoinrh@hidro.cu
The National Hydraulic Resources Institute is the body responsible for directing, implementing and monitoring state and government policy related to the country's water resource operations.

MINISTRY OF AGRICULTURE

Agencia de Información y Comunicación para la Agricultura de Cuba
Ave. Boyeros y Conill, Edif. MINAG, Plaza, Ciudad de La Habana 10600, Cuba
Voz: (537)884-5427; Fax: (537)881-2837 gestion@agrinfor.cu

The Ministry of Agriculture is the body responsible for directing, implementing – within its jurisdiction – and monitoring state and government policy related to:

The use, conservation and improvement of land used for cultivation and the ownership and possession of agriculture and forestry land
Plant Health
Veterinary medicine
The conservation, management, rational use and sustainable development of forest resources and the country's wild flora and fauna
The protection and growth of the country's cattle stocks
The mechanization and irrigation of production programs within its jurisdiction
The production of agricultural crops other than sugar cane, livestock and forestry
The cultivation and production of rice, tobacco, citrus fruits, apicultural products, poultry, feed, forestry products, and others for which it is given responsibility by the Executive Committee of the Council of Ministers
The harvesting and use of agricultural and forestry product
Ministry of Auditing and Control

The Ministry of Auditing and Control is the body responsible for administering, implementing and monitoring the way government and state policies concerning the prevention and detection of, and fight against incidences of administrative corruption are applied.

It is also responsible for auditing the government, for governmental regulation and control and for methodologically regulating, organizing administering and controlling the National Auditing System.

MINISTRY OF BASIC INDUSTRY

The Ministry of Basic Industry is the body responsible for directing, implementing and monitoring state and government policy related to the following activities:

The generation, transmission, distribution and marketing of electrical energy

The production and distribution of fuel and lubricants
The prospecting, exploration and extraction of oil and gas
The prospecting, exploration, extraction and exploitation of solid minerals
The production of fertilizers, chemical fibers, industrial gases, plastic articles, pesticides, paints, colorants, varnishes and other chemical products
The production of tires, inner tubes and rubber products
The production and conversion of paper, cardboard and wood pulp
The production of glass and glass products
Ministry of Construction

Ave: Carlos Manuel deCéspedes y 35, Plaza de la Revolución, La Habana, Cuba CP 106000
Fax: 55-5303 despacho@micons.cu

The Ministry of Construction is the body responsible for directing, implementing – within its jurisdiction – and monitoring state and government policy related to:

Geological engineering explorations for construction purposes
The drafting of designs for construction and installation projects
Civil construction and industrial installation
Maintenance and repair of housing and urban developments
Building maintenance
The development of civil, industrial, road, waterway and dredging projects, which are of benefit to the state
The manufacturing of concrete and asphalt and prefabricated concrete products
The implementation of measures for monitoring the application of the General Housing Act and the housing supply, including the pronouncement or proposal of necessary regulation

MINISTRY OF CULTURE

Calle 2, entre 11 y 13, Vedado, CP 10400 Plaza de la Revolución, Ciudad de La Habana, Cuba
atencion@min.cult.cu

The Ministry of Culture is responsible for directing, guiding, monitoring and implementing, within its jurisdiction, the application of state and government cultural policy.

It is also responsible for guaranteeing the protection, preservation and enhancement of Cuba's cultural heritage.

MINISTRY OF DOMESTIC TRADE

The Ministry of Domestic Trade is the body responsible for directing, implementing and monitoring the application of state and government policy related to domestic wholesale and retail commerce in foods, other goods and services for personal and commercial consumption.

MINISTRY OF THE ECONOMY AND PLANNING

20 de Mayo e/. Territorial y Ayestarán. Plaza de la Revolución
Teléfono: 881 8789 mep@ceniai.inf.cu

The Ministry of the Economy and Planning is the body responsible for directing, implementing and monitoring the application of state and government policy related to the economy, planning, statistics, standardization, measurement and quality control, community services, physical planning and industrial design.

MINISTRY OF EDUCATION

The Ministry of Education is the body responsible for directing, implementing and monitoring the application of state and government policy related to education, with the exclusion of higher education.

MINISTRY OF FINANCE AND PRICES

Obispo # 211 esquina Cuba

sdinformacion@mfp.gov.cu phone: 867 1920 or 867 1800 ext.4033 y 4034

The Ministry of Finance and Prices is the body responsible for directing, implementing and monitoring the application of state and government policy related to finance, taxes, prices, auditing and insurance.

It is responsible for giving advice concerning these policies and directing and monitoring the organization of state finances and the utilization of financial resources.

MINISTRY OF THE FISHING INDUSTRY

5ta. Ave entre 246 y 248 # 24606.
Barlovento. Playa. Ciudad de la Habana. Cuba.

Telef. Pizarra: 209-7930, 209-7949, 209-7987, 209-7999
Fax: 204-9168 info@fishnavy.inf.cu

The Ministry of the Fishing Industry is the body responsible for directing, implementing and monitoring state and government policy related to the exploration, conservation, extraction, cultivation, processing and marketing of fishing resources and the merchant fleet.

Ministry of the Food Industry

The Ministry of the Food Industry is the body responsible for directing, implementing and monitoring state and government policy related to the production of:

The dairy industry
The meat industry
Vegetable preserves
Flour and its derivatives
Oils and fats
Snack foods
Alcoholic and non-alcoholic beverages

CUBA TRADE POLICY AND AGREEMENT - STRATEGIC INFORMATION AND DEVELOPMENTS

BASIC INFORMATION

Cuba's foreign trade exerts a strong and decisive impact on the economy of the country, for this reason among its objectives are diversifying their business partners, working to achieve a realignment of trade policy in pursuit of favorable markets for its exports, diversity and competitiveness of their export items, as well as import substitution. The Ministry of Foreign Trade and Foreign Investment is responsible in the Republic of Cuba, for directing, implementing and monitoring the implementation of the policy State and Government as to the activities of trade, investment and cooperation abroad. With regard to the external sector, it can be noted that in 2010 exports at constant prices of goods grew by 56.3% while services one 1.8%.

The growth of imports of goods was 38.5% and the growth in imports of services was 8.2%, also at constant prices. America has become the main trading partner with 58.9% of total trade in goods in 2010, followed by Europe with 19.8% and Asia with 18.3%. Within Cuba's main trading partners are Venezuela, China, Canada, Spain and Brazil. Since the 90s, the export of services has had an increasing role in the Cuban economy, occupying more than 75% of the Cuban PIC, which expresses its increasingly important role in the results of foreign trade influence. Sales of professional services, especially in health, engineering, information technology and biotechnology are consolidated as the largest source of foreign exchange.

EXPORT AND IMPORT REGIME

Cuba regime does not apply to any export or import licenses, regulations, quotas or other that may impede trade.

It is possible to trade only through Cuban foreign trade or international associations created under Act 77, which will be granted the right to export and / or import by Ministry of Foreign Trade and Foreign Investment, and international trade transactions, for the nomenclature of products that fits with its objects, excluding those products that are listed in the nomenclature negative export and / or import, approved by the MINCEX, unless they are specifically authorized by the Agency itself.

Today there are other regulations such as those related to preserving the national heritage and bans on drugs and narcotics, as well as health and other related environmental protection, protection of endangered species, transboundary movements of wastes and other hazardous materials, to whose exports and / or imports of additional authorizations required by the competent authorities.

REGULATIONS FOR THE ESTABLISHMENT OF BRANCHES AND AGENTS

The establishment of foreign companies in Cuba is subject to compliance with the requirements of Decree 206 of 1996 of the Executive Committee of the Council of Ministers, through which authorized the establishment of offices of companies or foreign individual entrepreneurs interested in maintaining a branch in the country to directly address their business with Cuban companies and organizations.

Also, for those foreign entities or individual entrepreneurs who wish to have a representative in the country, without actually opening an office, the possibility to be represented, following the granting of an agency contract, by a national entity legally authorized to act as agent.

There is a National Register of Branches and Agents of Foreign Corporations, attached to the Chamber of Commerce of the Republic of Cuba. The inscription on it is an essential requirement for entities or entrepreneurs who wish to establish an office or have an agent in the country. The document proving the authorization to set the license is issued by the registrar.

By Resolution No. 550 of 2001, supplementing the decree, establishing the basic principles to be considered for enrollment authorization on the National Register of Branches and Agents of Foreign Corporations, among which the presentation of the last balance sheet Company, duly audited by an independent entity, extract from Register, issued no more than 6 months prior to the filing date of the application, and establishes an annual volume less than half a million USD during the last 3 years of operations with Cuba.

Decree Law 250 of 30 July 2007 was the Cuban Court of International Commercial Arbitration Court continues the Foreign Trade Arbitration, which was created in 1963, and yielded information and apply commercial arbitration long before most Latin American countries.

It is noteworthy that with the entry into force of Decree Law 250 is open the door to a new service, mediation, which by Regulation, Resolution 13/2007 of the President of the Chamber of Commerce of the Republic of Cuba, constitute an alternative dispute resolution in the Cuban Court of International Commercial Arbitration. To this end, the Court has a list of mediators who will be responsible for providing this service and who were authorized by the Chamber of Commerce of the Republic of Cuba.

Within the Model Clause Arbitration and Mediation, it suggests that "the parties shall comply with the contract in good faith. Any discrepancy in his performance, or agreements arising or in connection therewith, shall be settled through friendly negotiations or mediation if necessary. Parties do not reach an agreement, agree to submit such dispute to the Cuban Court of International Commercial Arbitration, by arbitration, subject to its Rules of Procedure. "

Similarly, the statutes of the Cuban Court of International Commercial Arbitration set out in Resolution 11/2007 of the Chamber of Commerce of the Republic of Cuba and its government functions and the court.

CUSTOMS REGIME

Cuban customs legislation provides for all customs procedures referred to in the International Convention on the simplification of customs procedures, also known as the Kyoto Convention, adopted by the Customs Cooperation Council in 1973. These are:

· Customs Warehouse

· Customs Transit

· Entry for home use

· Temporary Admission of goods for re-export in the same state

· Temporary Admission of Goods for inward

· Temporary exportation of goods for outward processing

· Temporary Export of Goods for re-importation in the same state

· Drawback duty drawback or

· Replacement warranty

· Transshipment

· Processing of goods for home use

· Export final

· Cargo

In the case of Cuba, according to the Customs Law (Decree No. 162) and its complementary standard (Resolution No. 31 of 2005 of the Chief of the General Customs of the Republic of Cuba), may request the enjoyment of Customs warehousing commercial importers, branches of foreign corporations and foreign corporations agents, who must submit to the Chief of the General Customs of the Republic application of the regime to which are appended the documents required by the legislation.

TARIFF SYSTEM

The Tariff Trade of the Republic of Cuba, enacted by Decree-Law No.124 of 1990 taken as supporting the Harmonized System Nomenclature Product Classification (SACLAP). Until November 2012, was in effect the SA-08 and from December 2012 came into effect on SA-2012, containing a 5th. Amendment of the Harmonized System. The SACLAP 2012, is enforced by Resolution No. 196/2012 of the Onei. Link.

The Cuban regime has two tariff preference schemes:

A group of goods from the countries of the Global System of Trade Preferences (GSTP) debits are granted tariff lower than those corresponding to the most favored nation. The European Union grants trade preferences to developing countries within its Generalised System of Preferences (GSP). The latest revision of the SGP provided a list of the 12 countries of the European system will tariff advantages for having been cataloged in recent years as economies of upper-middle income by the World Bank, which lies between Cuba, rising to force to cleave 2014.

Also free access is granted or lower tariffs than those for most favored nation traded products under trade agreements in the context of the member countries of the Latin American Integration Association (ALADI).

The member countries of the Association who have signed these agreements are: Argentina, Bolivia, Brazil, Chile, Colombia, Ecuador, Mexico, Paraguay, Peru, Uruguay, Venezuela and Panama. Moreover, Guatemala and the Caribbean Community (CARICOM).

As part of the commitments made in the framework of ALADI, our country began participating in the Regional Tariff Preference, involving the granting of mutual preferences among member countries to products that are not traded on the agreements, except for those included lists of exceptions each. The Chamber of Commerce of the Republic of Cuba extends ALADI certificates of origin to exporters Cuban request.

Furthermore Cuba unilaterally opened its market to a specific list of industrial products preferably from Bolivia, Ecuador and Paraguay, less developed countries relative LAIA with differential treatment within the association.

Also, our country is part of the Agreements on Cultural Property Seeds and signed by members of ALADI, whereby tariff repealing debts for a group of products included in these agreements.

INDUSTRIAL PROPERTY

The Cuban Industrial Property Office (CIPO) is under the Ministry of Science State organ, Technology and Environment, blamed the establishment of the legal system, politics, administration and management of industrial property in the country, as providing services inherent in matter.

In addition to services associated with the registration of industrial property, the CIPO also provides specialized services in the field to facilitate the marketing of different ways to get involved in the negotiating processes; Others include: consulting, valuation of intangibles of Industrial Property, the Industrial Property Organization through an internal system of specialized research and service modalities of industrial property. It also publishes the monthly OCPI Official Bulletin of Industrial Property , technical and legal content according to existing national and international standards for this type of publication and magazines, brochures and other materials in digital format. The legal aspects comprising the National System of Industrial Property of the Republic of Cuba, are available on the WEB site www.ocpi.cu , as previously mentioned publications.

Our country is member of the following arrangements, treaties and conventions administered by the World Intellectual Property Organization:

Convention Establishing the World Intellectual Property Organization (1967), from March 27, 1975.

Paris Convention for the Protection of Industrial Property (1891), from November 17, 1904.

Madrid Agreement concerning the repression of false or misleading indications of origin on products (1891), from January 1, 1905.

Protocol Relating to the Madrid Agreement Concerning the International Registration of Marks since 1995.

Nice Agreement Concerning the International Classification of Goods and Services for the International Registration of Marks since 1995.

Lisbon Agreement on Protection of Appellations of Origin and their International Registration (1958).

Patent Cooperation Treaty (PCT) (1970), from July 16, 1996.

Strasbourg Agreement, in force since November 9, 1995.

Vienna Agreement Establishing an International Classification of the Figurative Elements of Marks (1973), since 1997.

Budapest Treaty on the International Recognition of the Deposit of Microorganisms for the Purposes of Patent Procedure (1977), in force since February 19, 1994.

Nairobi Treaty on the Protection of the Olympic Symbol, since 1984.

Locarno Agreement Concerning the International Classification for Industrial Designs since 1998.

Berne Convention for the Protection of Literary and Artistic Works in force since February 20, 1997.

Treaty on the Law of Trademarks, signed on October 28, 1994.

Treaty on the Law of Patents, signed on June 2, 2000.

STANDARDS, METROLOGY AND QUALITY

The activities of standardization, metrology and quality in Cuba are regulated by the Decree Law No. 182 "Standardization and Quality" , the Law No. 183 "On Metrology" Decree (both adopted on 23 February 1998), the Decree 62 Law "On the implementation of the International System of Units" , the Decree No. 270 Regulation of Decree Law "On Metrology" , the Executive Committee of the Council of Ministers; which it aims to regulate those set out in the Law No. 183, "metrology" Decree, so the objectives, general principles and definitions given in the same underlying regulations that document, and Decree 271 " of infringements of the regulations established in metrology " .

The National Bureau of Standards, recognized as NC, is the National Standards Body of the Republic of Cuba which represents the country at the International and Regional Organizations for Standardization. This body represents Cuba at the International Organization for Standardization (ISO), the International Organization of Legal Metrology (OIML), the Codex Alimentarius Commission (CODEX), the General Conference on Weights and Measures (GFCM), Technical Barriers to Trade World Trade Organization (WTO / TBT) , the Eurasian Cooperation Metrological Institutions (COOMET) and the Pan American Standards Commission (COPANT), among others.

The national standardization, procedures of conformity assessment (certification, quality inspection, testing, etc.) and the National Metrology Service (SENAMET) are developed based on the principles and recommendations of international organizations and regional referred, particularly those arising from the WTO.

Decree Law No.182 "Standards and Quality" recognizes the NC National Certification Body in accordance Systems Management, Products, Processes and Services regarding the requirements specified in standards, technical regulations and other normative documents .

Accreditation

The ONARC (National Accreditation Authority of the Republic of Cuba) is responsible for developing and approving the assessment and recognition of the competence of the entities that carry out the conformity assessment, including testing laboratories are included and calibration and inspection bodies, with the aim of contributing to national and international recognition of the activities developed in the field of conformity assessment. For more information: http://www.onarc.cubaindustria.cu

FOREIGN TRADE REGULATIONS

LAWS

--Commercial Code--

Law No. 59/87 --Code Civil--

Law No. 77/95 of Extranjera-- Investment

DECREES LAWS :

Decree-Law No. 15/78 Basic - General for Economic - Contracts

Decree-Law No. 22/79 - Customs Tariff for commercial imports without - character

Decree-Law No. 124/90 of Customs - Tariff

Decree-Law No. 162/96 - Of Customs

Decree-Law No. 177/97 - On Insurance system

Decree-Law No. 182/98 - Reorganization legal basis for standardization and quality, taking into account trends OMC

Decree-Law No. 184/98 - The seal for Export

Decree-Law No. 226/01 - Register of Companies

Decree-Law No. 250/07 - Of the Cuban International's Commercial Arbitration Court

Decree-Law No. 264/09 - Fusion MINCEX-MINVEC, creation of the Ministry of Foreign Trade and Foreign Investment.

Decrees:

Decree No. 109/82 - Regulation Decree No. 53/79 of the General Conditions of Contract Supply -

- Regulation Decree No. 206/96 of the National Register of Branches and Agents of foreign - Trading Companies

Decree No. 277/05 - Of the Customs Administrative Offences - **Resolutions of the Ministry of FOREIGN TRADE AND FOREIGN INVESTMENT:**

YEAR	N or	DATE OF DISPOSITION	CONTENT OF LEGAL PROVISION	GAZETTE N or
1994	153	11/05/1994	Creates the National Registry of Exporters and Importers attached to the Chamber of Commerce.	GOO N or 7 29/06/94
1996	35	06/02/1996	It lays down rules on the importation of motor vehicles and marketing, as well as institutions empowered to make such import.	GOO N or 11 09/04/96
	200	04/06/1996	It enforces the Regulations for the Processing of Applications for import or export of goods Eventually.	GOO N or 28 20/09/96
	338	09/16/1996	Import policy of firearms destined for the bodies of protection, hunting and sporting use.	
1997	27	08/01/1997	It sets out the principles to act as agent of foreign firms and enforces the pro forma Agency Agreement.	02/28/97 No 3 GOO
1999	404	21/09/1999	It enforces the General Standards for the acquisition of machinery and equipment used.	GOO N or 63 09/24/99
2000	40	7/2/2000	Enforces the Methodological Notes for the conclusion of contracts of sale of goods using the group or category "C" of the INCOTERMS in force.	GOO N or 16 02/08/00
2001	190	03/05/2001	Enforces the Regulations on the import and export activity.	GOExt. N or 5 04/05/01
	339	6/7/2001	Indications enforces the import of biological products, raw materials, medicines for human and animal use, diagnosticians and cosmetics containing bovine or its components, as well as the import of feed components of flour, powder and pellets or crustaceans.	GOO N or 52 16/07/01
	550	13/11/2001	It enforces the procedure for processing of records by the National Registry of Branches and Agents of Foreign Corporations.	GOO N or 80 16/11/01

2003	385	14/4/2003	It enforces the regulations for the proper application, use, management, inspection and supervision of the National Warranty Seal Cuban Snuff.	GOO N or 26 07/22/03
	774	15/12/2003	It enforces the methodology for the calculation of the execution cycle of the Commercial Operation, Efficiency Indicator import activity of the companies implementing the Business Improvement.	GOO N or 11 15/03/04
2004	69	26/2/2004	Sets Offer Application Procedure, Preparation of tender documents Concurrency and Price Analysis.	GOO N or 26 04/30/04
	231	7/7/2004	Enforces the procedure for monitoring compliance with the technical requirements Products Import and Export.	GOO N or 51 3/9/2004 P. 824
	550	29/12/04	Establishes offenses and measures to be applied to authorized to engage in foreign trade entities.	GOO No 8 16/3/2005 P. 117
2005	339	15/08/05	Extends the application of Resolution No. 231 of 2004 on international economic associations created under Law No. 77 of Foreign Investment Law.	GOO No. 50 27/10/05 P. 811
	472	28/11/05	Establishes measures for the efficient extraction and transportation of import cargo to its final destination.	GOE No. 34 26/12/05
	480	12/07/05	Modifies the methodology for calculating the cycle commercial operation.	
2006	30	12/01/06	Sets the information required by the MINCEX for the purpose of implementing the Operational Planning System and Weekly Monthly imports.	
	4. 5	18/01/06	Approves the procedure for importing companies for chartering ships and contracts when no appropriate action charter.	

	258	30/06/06	Replaces Annex No. 1 of Joint Resolution No. 1/06 MINCEX-MITRANS "Procedure for weighing the import goods."	GOO No. 73 3/10/06
	332	29/08/06	Establishes measures for planning the Trans-Port-Internal Economy, on the importation of goods chain.	GOE No. 29 06/09/06
	358	13/09/06	It establishes guidelines for the import of machinery, equipment and transport technology, and systems and facilities.	GOE No. 32 18/09/06
	475	20/12/06	Regulation of the National Group of Technical Regulations to Trade.	GOO No. 11 23/01/07
2007	77	13/03/07	Enacts the Disciplinary Regulations Branch	GOO No. 25 29/03/2007
	248	16/07/07	It sets parameters for the successful completion of the execution of commercial operation.	GOO No.53 03/08/2007
	263	08/01/07	It enforces the Guidelines on Trade-Related Aspects of Internal Control and related contracts and consignment commission for the sale of goods imported on consignment.	GOO No. 59 Pag. 927 03/09/2007
	402	14/11/07	Procedure for granting classifications to entities subject to Law No. 77 "Foreign Investment Law".	GOO No.82 Pag. 1581 17/12/2007
2008	68	20/02/08	Enforces the "Procedure for issuance, amendment and cancellation of powers of foreign trade, as well as the classifications of authorized products, state enterprises and commercial companies 100% Cuban capital."	
2009	65	24/04/09	Regulates the participation of the Coordinating Committees Purchasing and import of products, hereinafter Commodity Committees.	
	66	24/04/09	Purchasing Coordinating Committee and Import of aluminum.	

	67	24/04/09	Purchasing Coordinating Committee and Import generators.	
	68	24/04/09	Purchasing Coordinating Committee and Import of Plastic Raw Materials.	
	69	24/04/09	Purchasing Coordinating Committee and Import Metal.	
	70	24/04/09	Purchasing Coordinating Committee-Import Automotive Media and some of its parts.	
	71	24/04/09	Purchasing Coordinating Committee and Import of timber and timber products.	
	72	24/04/09	Purchasing Coordinating Committee and Import Tire.	
	176	07/08/09	Regulates the import of goods without running commercial representations of foreign entities in the country.	
2011	86	28/02/2011	Create the Coordination Committee for the import of equipment and instruments for laboratories.	

Application instructions MINCEX activity:

Instruction No. 2/07 --Procedimiento for opening, inspection and reception of import goods in containers-

Joint Instruction No. 1 / 06- Implementation of Joint Resolution No. 1/2005 MINCEX-MITRANS on compulsory weighing of import goods.

--About 777 OM Regulation of the National Register of Sucursales--

--About OM-1549 requesting documentation to suppliers extranjeros--

OM-1680 -Indicaciones approvals of Operations Comerciales--

OM-2182 -Precisiones in quality and inspection to consider the operations of import-

OM-2216 --Indicaciones on the role of the customer in the importaciones--

OM-2246 -Principles activity Import-

BASIC TRADE AND INVESTMENT AGREEMENTS

No.	Partners	Status	Date of signature	Date of entry into force
1	Algeria	Signed (not in force)	22/09/1999	
2	Argentina	In force	30/11/1995	01/06/1997
3	Austria	In force	19/05/2000	25/11/2001
4	Barbados	In force	19/02/1996	13/08/1998
5	Belarus	In force	08/06/2000	16/08/2001
6	Belize	In force	08/04/1998	16/04/1999
7	BLEU (Belgium-Luxembourg Economic Union)	Signed (not in force)	19/05/1998	
8	Bolivia, Plurinational State of	In force	06/05/1995	23/08/1998
9	Brazil	Signed (not in force)	26/06/1997	
10	Bulgaria	In force	16/12/1998	24/05/2000
11	Cambodia	Signed (not in force)	26/09/2001	
12	Cape Verde	In force	22/05/1997	08/01/2003
13	Chile	In force	10/01/1996	30/09/2000
14	China	In force	24/04/1995	01/08/1996
15	Colombia	Signed (not in force)	16/07/1994	
16	Croatia	Signed (not in force)	16/02/2001	
17	Denmark	Signed (not in force)	19/02/2001	
18	Dominican Republic	Signed (not in force)	15/11/1999	
19	Ecuador	Terminated	25/05/1995	15/08/1997
20	Finland	Signed (not in force)	17/12/2001	
21	France	In force	25/04/1997	06/11/1999
22	Germany	In force	30/04/1996	22/11/1998
23	Ghana	Signed (not in force)	02/11/1999	
24	Greece	In force	18/06/1996	18/10/1997

25	Guatemala	In force	20/08/1999	10/08/2002
26	Guyana	Signed (not in force)	22/10/1999	
27	Honduras	Signed (not in force)	09/08/2001	
28	Hungary	In force	22/10/1999	24/11/2003
29	Indonesia	In force	19/09/1997	29/09/1999
30	Italy	In force	07/05/1993	23/08/1995
31	Jamaica	Signed (not in force)	31/05/1997	
32	Lao People's Democratic Republic	In force	28/04/1997	10/06/1998
33	Lebanon	In force	14/12/1995	07/01/1999
34	Malaysia	In force	26/09/1997	27/10/1999
35	Mexico	In force	30/05/2001	29/03/2002
36	Mongolia	In force	26/03/1999	18/10/2000
37	Mozambique	In force	20/10/2001	26/02/2002
38	Namibia	Signed (not in force)	27/06/1997	
39	Netherlands	In force	02/11/1999	01/11/2001
40	Panama	In force	27/01/1999	11/05/1999
41	Paraguay	In force	21/11/2000	06/12/2002
42	Peru	In force	10/10/2000	25/11/2001
43	Portugal	In force	08/07/1998	18/06/1999
44	Qatar	Signed (not in force)	06/11/2001	
45	Romania	In force	27/01/1996	22/05/1997
46	Russian Federation	In force	07/07/1993	08/07/1996
47	San Marino	Signed (not in force)	01/01/2002	
48	Slovakia	In force	22/03/1997	05/12/1997
49	South Africa	In force	08/12/1995	07/04/1997
50	Spain	In force	27/05/1994	09/06/1995
51	Suriname	Signed (not in force)	07/01/1999	
52	Switzerland	In force	28/06/1996	07/11/1997
53	Trinidad and Tobago	In force	26/05/1999	07/01/2000
54	Turkey	In force	22/12/1997	23/10/1999

55	Uganda	Signed (not in force)	01/01/2002	
56	Ukraine	In force	20/05/1995	04/12/1996
57	United Kingdom	In force	30/01/1995	11/05/1995
58	Venezuela, Bolivarian Republic of	In force	11/12/1996	15/04/2004
59	Viet Nam	In force	12/10/1995	01/10/1996
60	Zambia	Signed (not in force)	22/01/2000	

STRATEGIC INFORMATION FOR CONDUCTING BUSINESS

The Republic of Cuba is an archipelago formed by the island of Cuba, with an extension of 106,007 km2, the Isle of Youth, with 2 200 km2 of surface, and around 4 200 keys and small islands. It's total surface covers 110 922 km2, lying at the entrance of the Gulf of Mexico, in the Caribbean Sea. It limits to the north with the peninsula of Florida (United States of America), at a distance of 180 km; to the south with Jamaica, at 140 km; to the east with Haiti, at 77 km, and to the west with the Yucatan peninsula (Mexico), which lies 210 km away.

Flat lands which cover 70% of its territory make Cuba an essentially plain territory, with three big mountain chains: Sierra de los Organos, in the western region; Sierra del Escambray, in the center of the island, and Sierra Maestra in the eastern part, the latter including the main height in the country, Pico Real del Turquino, with 1 974 meters (5 933 feet) above sea level.

Cuba's climate is considered subtropical moderate, with predominance of tropical maritime conditions. The average annual temperature is 25,2 degrees Celsius (77 degrees F) in summer and 22 degrees C (71,6 degrees F) in winter, with two very well defined seasons: the dry season, from November through April, and the rainy season, from May through October.

Average rain fall totals 1 059 mm during the rainy season and 316 mm in the dry season, for an annual average of 1 375 mm.

The Cuban coasts have a length of 5 746 km, the north coast being the largest with 3 209 km. The coastal zones have numerous excellent beaches as well as bays, ports and cities.

According to estimated figures, Cuba's population reaches 11,2 M inhabitants, with an annual growth rate of 0,6 per 100. Since the decade of the 90s, a gradual aging of the population has become evident, the number of persons over 60 years of age now reaching 12,9% of the total.

Spanish is Cuba's official language, while English is used extensively in commercial and cultural circles as well as in international contacts.

Politically and administratively, Cuba is divided into 14 provinces, 158 municipalities and one special municipality.

From west to east, the provinces are Pinar del R¡o, La Habana, Ciudad de La Habana, Matanzas, Villa Clara, Cienfuegos, Sancti Spiritus, Ciego de Avila, Camagüey, Las Tunas, Holguín, Granma, Santiago de Cuba, Guantánamo y Las Villas. The special municipality of Isla de la Juventud (Isle of Youth) consists of that island, located south of the province of La Habana.

Ciudad de La Habana is Cuba's capital. Also important because of their economic development and population are the cities of Santiago de Cuba, Holguín, Camagüey, Cienfuegos, Matanzas, Pinar del Río, Ciego de Avila, Bayamo and Guantánamo.

Cuba is a socialist State of workers, independent and sovereign, organized as a unitary and democratic republic.

The National Assembly of People's Power is the supreme organ of power of the State, having constituent and legislative power in the Republic of Cuba as parliamentary regime.

The Council of Ministers is the highest executive and administrative organ and constitutes the government of the Republic of Cuba.

The country has only one political party: the Communist Party of Cuba.

The State is ruled by the Constitution of the Republic of Cuba, approved on February 24, 1976, with reforms introduced in July, 1992.

Education is free of cost at all levels, as well as the teaching materials. There are no illiterates in the country, which has 300 000 teachers more, 47 higher education centers and 300 OOO students.

There are universities or university faculties in all the provinces, as well as medium level, specialized, polytechnical and other educational centers.

Cuba's health care system, covering the whole country, is considered unique in Latin America. Medical services are free of cost for all Cuban citizens.

Cuba possesses the lowest infant mortality rate in Latin America and one of the lowest in the world. 7.2 out of 1000 born alive. Life expectancy reaches 75.2 years.

According to the Ministry of Public Health, in 1997 Cuba had 62624 doctors (56.8 / 10000 inhabitants) being 28855 family doctors (26.2 / 10000 inhabitants), 9816 dentists (26.2/ 10000inhabitants) 81333 nurses and assistants; 283 hospitals, 12 investigation institutes 440 policlinics, 166 dentist clinics, 26 blood banks, 164 medical offices, 220 mother's homes, 196 aged clinics and 27 homes for the physical disabled.

THE DOMESTIC POLITICAL SITUATION IN THE 1990S

During the mid-1990s the overriding domestic policy concern for Cuban leaders was to arrest the economic free-fall caused by the breakup of the Council of Mutual Economic Assistance (CMEA) and the Soviet Union and to establish a basis for future growth without significantly altering the current political regime. The economic crisis of the early 1990s, in which Cuba's Gross Domestic Product (GDP) declined by almost half, and already low living standards plummeted, was the greatest challenge to ever face Fidel Castro and the communist leadership. Faced with a sharp worsening of economic conditions on the island and the reemergence of small, isolated pockets of domestic opposition, the government resorted in the early 1990s to a dual policy of liberalization of the external economic sectors and heightened repression in an effort to head off an impending political crisis.

The political component of the regime's survival strategy began to take shape in 1991, when Fidel Castro dismissed any significant moves toward political liberalization at the PCC's Fourth Party Congress. At that Congress, Castro prepared the country for the so-called "zero-option," a strategy of economic autarchy designed to address the worst case scenario of a total cutoff of oil imports from Russia, to whom Cuba owed US$28 billion. The contingencies foreseen in the zero option were extreme. According to the plan, most motorized vehicles would be replaced by human and animal-powered transport, and Cuban farmers would resort to organic agriculture to compensate for an absence of fertilizer. Hundreds of thousands of urban dwellers would be compelled to move to the countryside to procure their own food. Under the logic of the zero-option plan, the prospects for legalization of an organized opposition became more remote than ever, given the purported need for absolute unity in a time of dire crisis. As part of a crackdown on dissidents and government opponents, the government established Rapid Reaction Brigades--civilian mobs organized by the Directorate of State Security (*Seguridad del Estado*) to intimidate and physically assault dissidents in so-called "acts of repudiation."

As economic conditions on the island continued to worsen and hopes for a democratic transition faded, the most desperate individuals--mainly young men in their twenties and thirties--began to take to the sea on homemade rafts bound for the United States. The number of rafters (*balseros*) rescued at sea by the United States Coast Guard rose nearly tenfold in three years, from 466 in 1990 to 4,169 in 1993.

In late 1993 and early 1994, there were growing signs of unrest and indications that the regime was losing its ability to maintain law and order. Nightly blackouts encouraged a rash of urban crime, and for the first time since the early 1960s the neighborhoods of Havana reverberated with the clanging of pots and pans in noisy antigovernment protests. In July 1993, a civil disturbance broke out in the fishing town of Cojímar, when residents attacked police who had fired on Cubans trying to escape the island. In October 1993, a second civil disturbance broke out in the Havana suburb of Regla, during the funeral of a man who had been shot and killed by police in another escape attempt.

Dramatic refugee departures continued to mount in early 1994, sparking an intensification of police presence in coastal areas and increased coastal patrols. In the first half of the year, thirteen boats were hijacked and diverted to the United States. Several aircraft, including an airliner and a military transport helicopter, were also hijacked and diverted to southern Florida. Some of the escape attempts produced violent clashes between police and the escapees. Alarmed over the thefts of state property and concerned that word of the dramatic refugee escapes would destabilize the regime, the government embarked on a crackdown against refugees caught attempting to flee the country.

On July 13, 1994, Cuban government fire boats rammed and sank a tugboat with 72 refugees aboard. Forty-one refugees, including 12 children, drowned as a result of the ramming which broke the tugboat in half. According to survivors, before the ramming, high pressure water hoses had been used against persons found above deck. After the boat sank, the pursuing government boats refused for more than 30 minutes to lend assistance to the survivors in the water. Only after a passing foreign vessel was seen observing the drama did Cuban Coast Guard boats attempt to rescue the survivors. In the aftermath, the Cuban government portrayed the incident as an accident, but the regime's actions were condemned as deliberate by Amnesty International and the Inter-American Commission on Human Rights. Shortly after the incident, Pope John Paul II sent a private message of condolence and solidarity to the families of the victims.

Social tension reached a peak on August 5, 1994, when several hundred (by some estimates more than a thousand) people rioted in a seafront Havana district. Videotape footage of the event showed rioters looting shops, battling police, and shouting anti-government slogans. This was the first major civil disturbance to take place in Havana since the consolidation of the regime in the early 1960s. Although the police regained control of the situation in a matter of hours, Cuban officials later admitted that they were badly shaken by the disturbance. Appearing on state-run Cuban television, Fidel Castro declared that Cuba would no longer prevent "illegal" departures from the island. During the next several weeks, tens of thousands of people congregated on the northwestern coast of Cuba seeking opportunities to emigrate from the island by sea. During August and early September, the United States Coast Guard intercepted more than 30,000 people in the Florida Straits attempting to flee Cuba on homemade rafts. A large number of empty rafts were also found at sea, suggesting that several hundred (by some estimates several thousand) people may have drowned while traveling on unseaworthy vessels.

Responding to the uncontrolled mass exodus and seeking to curb unsafe departures by raft, on August 19 the Clinton administration announced that Cubans intercepted at sea would no longer be granted automatic political asylum in the United States, but would instead be given safe haven at the United States Naval Base at Guantánamo Bay, Cuba. The flow of refugees continued unabated until September 9, 1994, when the Cuban and United States governments reached a migratory agreement to stem the exodus. In the September 9 agreement, Cuba agreed to use mainly "persuasive" means to prevent unsafe departures in exchange for United States approval of 20,000 visas annually to legal Cuban "migrants" (despite Cuba's commitment to employ nonviolent means to avoid departures, "attempted illegal departure" remains a felony carrying a 2-year prison sentence). The United States in turn would adopt a "wet feet vs. dry feet" policy toward Cuban refugees. Hereafter, Cuban refugees who make it to U.S. shores would be released to family and relatives in the United States, whereas those intercepted at sea by the U.S. Coast Guard would be immediately returned to Cuba unless a very strong claim for political asylum could be made.

In the aftermath of the August 1994 riot and the *balsero* crisis, the Cuban government took additional steps to alleviate shortages and stabilize the political situation. The most significant changes were the reestablishment of the farmers markets that had been shut down in 1986 and the authorization of individual self-employment in about 100 trades. In the meantime, the Cuban government continued to maintain a strict clampdown on independent civic organizations and opposition political activity.

GOVERNMENT STRUCTURE

COUNCIL OF MINISTERS

The Council of Ministers is a large cabinet-like body that comprises the leadership of all of the national-level ministries, state committees, and national institutes. The Council incorporates both the executive and the high-level administrative leadership of the national government. Article 98 of the 1976 constitution stipulates the broad powers of the Council of Ministers. These include the issuance of administrative regulations, the submission of a draft national budget to the National Assembly of Popular Power (Asemblea Nacional de Poder Popular--ANPP), and the handling of foreign policy. In addition, the Council of Ministers is responsible for "organizing and conducting the political, economic, cultural, scientific, social, and defense activities of the state as outlined by the National Assembly."

The Council of Ministers consists of a president, who is considered the head of government, a first vice president, and the heads of major ministries and central government agencies. Ministers are appointed by the ANPP at the initiative of the Council of State, headed by Fidel Castro. Within the Council of Ministers, there exists an Executive Committee comprising the president, the first vice president, the executive secretary, and five vice presidents. This group forms the inner cabinet within the Council of Ministers and is the highest administrative and executive authority of the Cuban state. Prior to a major cabinet reorganization in 1994, each Executive Committee member had oversight authority over a group of functionally related ministries. All Executive Committee members are also members of the PCC Politburo. By virtue of his dual presidency of the Council of Ministers and the Council of State, and his status as PCC first secretary and commander in chief of the armed forces, Fidel Castro is the most powerful figure in the Executive Committee and has a disproportionate influence over all executive decision making.

In April 1994, the central state apparatus was thoroughly reorganized in an effort to streamline the cumbersome bureaucracy and consolidate the activities of functionally related agencies. The reorganization of the bureaucratic framework established during the 1970s was most pronounced among the agencies dealing with economics, foreign trade, science and technology, and tourism--areas where supply-and-demand considerations were being introduced. These changes were a prelude to a systematic government downsizing that was begun in the summer of 1995.

The bureaucratic reorganization, carried out under the terms of Decree Law 147 of April 22, 1994, abolished several state committees and national institutes formerly belonging to the Council of Ministers and subsumed their operations under existing or new ministries. Significantly, the state committee structures that were abolished or absorbed were part of the central planning apparatus of the Cuban state. In addition, the reorganization law consolidated the National Academy of Sciences and the Executive Secretariat of Nuclear Affairs under a newly created Ministry of Science, Technology, and the Environment. The decree law also upgraded the National Tourism Institute to ministerial status.

A total of seven new ministries were created, while the organizational category of state committee was abolished and the number of national institutes was reduced. The newly established ministries are Economy and Planning; Finances and Prices; Foreign Investment and Economic Cooperation; Labor and Social Security; Metallurgy and Electronics Industry; Science, Technology, and the Environment; and Tourism.

The Executive Committee of the Council of Ministers was also reorganized. Two of seven vice presidencies were abolished and the oversight authority of vice presidents over clusters of ministries was revoked. Instead, vice presidents would chair interagency task forces and committees, but would not necessarily exercise executive authority beyond their respective ministries. This latter provision, which is apparently intended to reduce potential turf battles among ministers, also reduces the chances that any single individual might develop an inter-bureaucratic power base from which to challenge Castro's authority.

In January 1995, the Cuban government announced a second major cabinet reshuffle, this time affecting only the economics and trade-related ministries. Eight cabinet-level officials, including two vice presidents of the Council of Ministers, were removed in an effort to place reform-minded technocrats in high-level economic posts. The appointments were widely believed to have been taken at the initiative of Carlos Lage, the recently appointed secretary of the Council of Ministers and a key figure in Cuba's economic reform process. In an interview published by the official daily, Granma, in January, Lage described the cabinet changes as "favoring the reorganization of the state apparatus with the participation of other valuable cadres" with the objective of making the state "more rational, more energetic, more efficient, less costly and adjusted to the conditions we face today."

COUNCIL OF STATE

The Council of State serves as the permanent committee of the ANPP when the Assembly is not in session. The Council of State, which is comparable to the Presidium of the Supreme Soviet of the former Soviet Union, can issue decree laws, propose legislation and constitutional reforms, and appoint and dismiss ministers. All of these activities are closely coordinated with the PCC. The Council of State has thirty-one members, elected from among ANPP deputies who are also top PCC leaders. Thus, Fidel and Raúl Castro, as well as most of the PCC Politburo, are periodically elected to the Council of State in orchestrated Assembly votes.

The Council of State includes a president, a first vice president, five vice presidents, a secretary, and twenty-three regular members. According to the constitution, the Council of State president is officially the head of state. This position, along with the presidency of the Council of Ministers, has always been held by Fidel Castro. By virtue of his dual status as head of state and government, and his authority as PCC first secretary, Castro is able to control and coordinate executive and legislative decision making. Castro's presidency of the Council of State also gives him legal authority to appoint and remove government ministers. Castro's presidential authority thus complements his control over personnel and policy decisions as PCC first secretary. As president, Castro may also assume personal command of any government ministry during a crisis. A 1992 amendment to the constitution made explicit the president's authority to assume direct command over the armed forces under conditions of national emergency, thereby reaffirming Castro's status as commander in chief.

There is a pronounced overlap of membership in the Council of State and the PCC Politburo, with sixteen out of thirty-one Council of State members being Politburo members as well. The majority presence of Politburo members within the Council of State guarantees that all internal decisions, decided by majority vote, coincide with PCC directives. The Council of State thus serves, along with the Council of Ministers, as a fail-safe legal channel for PCC control of the state.

The Council of State also usurps the legislative authority of the National Assembly. The Council of State's decree law authority renders the ANPP little more than a rubber stamp parliament, convened during brief biannual sessions in order to ratify directives from the PCC leadership. As a permanent committee of an elected National Assembly, the Council of State provides a thin democratic façade to authoritarian rule by Fidel Castro and the top leadership of the PCC.

NATIONAL ASSEMBLY

The National Assembly of People's Power (Asamblea Nacional del Poder Popular--ANPP) was established by the 1976 constitution as the unicameral national legislature.

The Assembly, which currently has 589 members representing territorial districts nationwide, is directly elected every five years. Elections to the ANPP are noncompetitive, with the nominating and voting process under the control of the local PCC organizations, such as the Committees for the Defense of the Revolution (CDRs) and other mass organizations. Campaigning is prohibited, and the main criterion for electibility is commitment to the Revolution under the direction of the PCC and the leadership of Fidel Castro. Candidates are usually nominated on the basis of their personal popularity and their "active integration" into the political system. The latter quality is essential to being placed on the candidate list because dissidents, regime opponents, and even mild critics of the regime are systematically shut out of the nominating process. Seventy percent of the current Assembly membership are either PCC members or members of PCC-affiliated organizations, and all appear to be loyal to the status quo.

Although it is legally empowered by the constitution to debate and pass legislation, in practice the ANPP general chamber abdicates all substantive decision-making authority to the Council of State, whose thirty-one members are elected from among the Assembly's ranks. The debility of the Assembly is assured by the infrequency and short duration of its biannual plenary sessions, which last no more than two weeks. Although the Assembly has eight standing committees, they do not exercise any effective authority to publicly debate or modify bills. During its biannual plenums, the Assembly plays a passive role as audience for various government speakers. Once the Council of State's legislative proposals have been presented, they are summarily ratified by unanimous or near unanimous vote of the general chamber.

ANPP deputies, who are predominantly young and politically inexperienced PCC members with minimal background in parliamentary procedure, are little inclined to challenge the party leadership in public debate. Moreover, deputies are amply aware that--proclamations of collegiality notwithstanding--any attempt to challenge the leadership on substantive issues is paramount to political and professional suicide. Like membership in the PCC Party Congress, an ANPP deputyship is generally considered an honorific position, usually granted as a reward for loyalty and valuable service to the Revolution. Moreover, the remarkably high rate of turnover within the ANPP--83 percent in the last election--prevents deputies from forging an independent power base. Perhaps the most telling indicator of parliamentary weakness is the ANPP's lack of a permanent meeting place. During its brief sessions, the ANPP convenes in the Havana Convention Center, while the historic national Capitol building, towering formidably over the city center, houses a government ministry.

The Council of State is not representative of the Assembly membership, but consists instead of high PCC officials, including members of the Politburo, who also hold ANPP seats. Thus, Fidel Castro, who holds a deputyship from Santiago de Cuba and has been president of the Council of State since the office was created, is periodically reelected by unanimous vote of the general chamber. Under the supervision of the ANPP president, a position currently held by Politburo member Ricardo Alarcón, Castro's nominees for the remaining thirty seats in the Council of State are ratified by unanimous or near-unanimous vote. Among the top Politburo members elected to the Council of State, Raúl Castro customarily occupies the first vice presidency.

JUDICIARY

Article 120 of the 1976 constitution establishes the People's Supreme Court as the nation's high court and authorizes the creation of lower courts. The Supreme Court is organized into five chambers: criminal, civil and administrative, labor, state security, and military. The lower court system comprises fourteen people's provincial courts and 169 people's basic courts at the municipal level.

Under Cuba's Marxist-Leninist legal system, the judiciary is not recognized as an independent branch of government but is instead subordinate to the Council of State and the ANPP. In practice, the courts are nearly powerless to defend individuals against acts of the state, especially when dealing with politically relevant cases. There is no known instance of a revolutionary Cuban court ruling against the government in a political trial. Moreover, the Court is not authorized to decide on constitutional matters, a prerogative legally held by the ANPP. The Court is thus limited to ruling on individual civil and criminal cases.

Justices of the People's Supreme Court--about half of whom are PCC members--are nominated by the Council of State and are elected by the ANPP. Lower court judges are nominated by the Ministry of Justice and are elected by their respective provincial and municipal assemblies. In addition to its 700 professional judges, the Cuban judiciary employs 14,000 "lay judges," who share the bench with the professionals. The ostensible purpose of the lay judges is to inject popular attitudes and values into the administration of justice. In practice, lay judges are used to pack the courts with PCC loyalists. In this manner, the regime undermines the judiciary's institutional autonomy and ensures that all judicial rulings are sympathetic to the government and the PCC.

CUBAN COMMUNIST PARTY

Since the mid-1960s, Cuba's sole legally recognized political party, the PCC, has been the paramount institution of the regime. In the early 1990s, the PCC claimed almost 1.5 million members, or approximately 10 percent of the population. The party is rooted in an uneasy alliance among the core leaderships of fidelista veterans of the "26 of July" movement and members of the former Popular Socialist Party (Partido Socialista Popular--PSP), Cuba's pro-Soviet communist party. Although Fidel Castro declared his allegiance to Marxism-Leninism in the early 1960s, it was not until the ratification of the constitution of 1976 that the PCC's hegemony over society and the political system came to resemble that of Soviet and East European communist regimes. Article 5 of the constitution of 1976 recognizes the PCC--whose organization and activities intrude on practically all aspects of Cuban life--as the "organized vanguard of the Cuban nation" and "the supreme guiding force of society and the state."

The PCC performs many roles within Cuban society. Among them, the most important is that of ideological "rudder" of the regime. As the sole institution with exclusive authority to decide fundamental political, economic, and social issues, the PCC determines the parameters within which all other institutions--most notably the state--may operate. Working in concert with a network of mass organizations under its control, the PCC is also a vital intermediary between the regime and society, bearing principal responsibility for propaganda, socialization, and elite recruitment. The PCC's capacity to act as the exclusive intermediary between regime and society derives from its singular influence over the state (the country's only legal employer), the mass media, and the education system.

Through its Committees for the Defense of the Revolution (Comités por la Defensa de la Revolución--CDRs), the PCC also serves as the regime's most important instrument of control over society. The CDRs, which consist of approximately 80,000 neighborhood block committees, are one of the key totalitarian components of the political system. They keep civil society atomized and weak by usurping its functions and preventing its resurgence through surveillance, intimidation, and constant interference in the private sphere. The mass organizations also hinder the development of civil society by monopolizing the public sphere and claiming exclusive representation of officially recognized social and occupational groups.

PARTY CONGRESS

Following the practice of the former Soviet Union and East European communist parties, the PCC convenes party congresses every five years to review and adjust its policies and institutions and to map out national strategy for the next five-year period. Party congresses, typically lasting one to two weeks, are large gatherings of hundreds of delegates from all sectors of the PCC, as well as the top party leadership. The PCC held party congresses in 1975, 1980, 1986, 1991 and, most recently, in February 1997.

Like other large representative gatherings in Cuba, party congresses serve mainly as a forum for the introduction of new initiatives by the top PCC leadership, rather than as an arena for debate of fundamental issues. The general chamber does not formulate policy, but merely ratifies decisions made in advance by the PCC leadership. In preparation for the congress, working groups may be assembled to elaborate the new party program, but these tend not to contravene the policy preferences of the top leadership. Whereas the working groups may discuss in closed session issues beyond the scope of the leadership's agenda, only proposals approved in advance by the Politburo are brought to the floor of the general chamber. In the final reckoning, a party congress only goes as far to initiate reform as it is allowed to go by Fidel Castro and the top Politburo membership.

Despite their theatrical character, the congresses draw the attention of domestic and international observers because they portend significant change in PCC institutions and policies. The First Congress, held in 1976, ratified the current constitution and marked the beginning of the "institutionalization" of the regime along Soviet lines; the Second Congress in 1980 emphasized improving economic efficiency and accepted minor concessions to economic rationality by authorizing the formation of the farmers' markets. The Third Congress in 1986 initiated the process of "rectification," wherein the Party was exhorted to return to its socialist ideological roots and the farmers' markets experiment was discontinued.

The Fourth Party Congress was especially significant because it coincided with the crisis and collapse of Soviet and East European communism and the disbanding of the Council of Mutual Economic Assistance (CMEA) trade and aid system. These extraordinary events presented a formidable challenge to Cuba's political and economic institutions. In the wake of the collapse of its key trading partners and the international repudiation of its totalitarian political model, the regime faced its most severe test of survival since the early 1960s.

Prior to the Fourth Congress, a number of observers had speculated that Fidel Castro might accept incremental political and economic reforms as a tactical move to relegitimize the regime and avoid a violent Romania-style rupture. Instead, Castro--who had opposed Mikhail Gorbachev's policy of restructuring (perestroika) in the Soviet Union--reaffirmed single-party rule and rejected the possibility of legalizing alternative political organizations. In the economic arena, however, the Congress approved a constitutional amendment that allowed the return of foreign direct investment (after a thirty-year hiatus) and authorized self-employment in a limited number of service sector occupations. In addition, the PCC announced an end to discrimination against Roman Catholics and other religious groups by allowing religious believers to join the party. Finally, Castro conceded to changing external circumstances and disavowed any further attempts to spread revolution to the Third World. Thus, Jorge Domínguez observes that the Fourth Party Congress:

> in short, was not responsive to the wishes of those who wanted to liberalize and democratize Cuba substantially, but it was responsive to some of the wishes of its core constituency, the middle-level cadres who staffed the regime and on whose personal prestige, the polls showed, the allegiance of ordinary citizens rested.

The Fourth Party Congress also produced significant institutional change within the PCC. Pursuing a policy of political retrenchment, Castro engineered a far-reaching purge of reform-minded leaders within the party and strengthened his own position as the central figure in the regime. The Fourth Congress also approved a high turnover of Politburo and Central Committee members in a process whereby young and inexperienced cadres replaced more established leaders who could potentially challenge Castro's authority. Upon Castro's initiative, the Congress abolished the PCC Secretariat and eliminated candidate membership in the Politburo. By absorbing some of its former candidate members and adding several new members, the Politburo was expanded to twenty-five posts.

CENTRAL COMMITTEE

The principal institution of the PCC between party congresses is the Central Committee. The Committee, which consists of 150 high-ranking party members (including the PCC Politburo), oversees party activities at all levels of the state and society and is responsible for carrying forward the programs initiated at the congresses. In addition to the top PCC political leadership at the national and provincial levels, the current Central Committee also includes members of the armed forces, municipal party secretaries, leaders of mass organizations, the heads of large state enterprises, and a variety of PCC activists from the fields of economics, education, medicine, the sciences, and sports.

Central Committee members are selected from among delegates to the party congresses. Although the general chamber of the Central Committee delegates day-to-day governing authority to the Politburo, membership in the larger body confers high prestige and is a stepping stone toward appointment to the highest organizations of the party and the state.

In October 1990, the Central Committee's bureaucracy was cut back as part of a broader effort to reduce waste and excessive interference by the PCC in administrative affairs. The Committee's nineteen departments were consolidated into nine, and its work force was cut by half. However, the Committee was given special powers to circumvent local, provincial, and national state and party organs in the event of a national emergency requiring rapid popular mobilization. The Central Committee was also authorized, through the Politburo, to override the decisions of government ministries in situations of national emergency.

POLITBURO

The Politburo, which is appointed from the ranks of the Central Committee, is the highest authority of the Cuban political system. It not only sets party policy, but also "recommends" legislative and executive action to be taken by the state. The coordination of party and state policies is facilitated by the overlapping partisan, legislative, and executive responsibilities of key leaders in the Cuban political system, most notably Fidel Castro.

Castro's indefinite tenure as "Maximum Leader" is recognized in the preamble to the constitution, which mentions him by name as the founder and head of the Cuban revolutionary process being carried forward by the PCC. His legal authority over the "party-state" stems from his dual occupancy of the highest party and government posts, as reflected in his formal titles of president of the Council of State and of the Council of Ministers, first secretary of the PCC Politburo, and commander in chief of the Revolutionary Armed Forces. Castro is thus the unchallenged head of state, head of government, and chairman of the PCC. This arrangement is consistent with the organic concept of the state promoted by the constitution, which accepts the tutelary role of the PCC in the affairs of state.

In addition to Fidel and Raúl Castro, the Politburo includes influential government ministers, provincial PCC party secretaries, the leaders of some of the mass organizations, and high-ranking military officers. The Fourth Party Congress approved substantial structural and personnel changes to the Politburo. Veteran revolutionary leaders such as Minister of Culture Armando Hart Dávalos and Women's Federation president Vilma Espín were replaced by younger Castro loyalists, such as former Union of Young Communists General Secretary Roberto Robaina González, President of the Writers' and Artists' Union Abel Prieto Jiménez, and presidential staff member Carlos Lage Dávila. In all, eleven of the Politburo's twenty-five members have been appointed since 1991. Of the eleven new members, none was older than forty-nine at the time of his or her appointment.

Castro's courting of young fidelistas at the expense of senior party leaders appeared to fulfill a dual purpose. First, it strengthened Castro's relative authority by reducing the amount of collegiality within the inner policymaking elite. Instead of having to deal with fellow "historic figures" (históricos)--who, as Castro's contemporaries, hold significant independent authority--Castro would preside over a cabinet containing far more junior subordinates. Lacking the standing of their predecessors and owing their political rise to Castro, these new Politburo members are considered less likely to challenge the "Comandante's" initiatives or to question his judgment in internal policy debates.

A second reason for Castro's overtures to young cadres stems from his desire to reverse widespread alienation among Cuban youth from the political culture of the Revolution. By promoting popular young leaders such as Roberto Robaina, the regime appeared to revitalize itself, despite the fact that, as Castro's foreign minister, Robaina exercised little independence in formulating policy. The appointment of a young foreign minister was also designed to elicit a favorable reaction in the foreign media. However, despite their youth, there is little indication that the new crop of revolutionary leaders is any more inclined to introduce fundamental political reform than their predecessors--at least not while Castro remains in office.

In contrast to the stagnation he has imposed on political affairs, Castro has yielded to economic necessity by allowing his chief economic advisor, Carlos Lage, to pursue limited economic reforms. The dire shortage of foreign exchange since the collapse of the CMEA has forced Castro grudgingly to accept the introduction of joint ventures with foreign corporations, primarily in the tourism industry. Since the approval of a constitutional amendment allowing foreign direct investment and the legalization of dollar transactions and limited self- employment in 1993, Lage's economic team has cautiously proceeded with reforms intended to steer foreign hard currency into state coffers and bring the large black market economy under profitable regulation by the state (see Economy). However, reforms of the domestic economy have lagged far behind those of the external sectors, providing only minimal relief to the Cuban population.

DECISION MAKING

Within Cuba's totalitarian political system, state-society relations follow Fidel Castro's well-known maxim: "Within the Revolution everything; outside the Revolution nothing." Thus, the regime is somewhat receptive to currents of opinion within its own ranks and within the broader "revolutionary family" (the PCC and the mass organizations under its control). However, regime leaders do not recognize the rights of expression of individuals who are not "integrated" or those whose dissenting views surpass established limits.

Within the hierarchical structure of the PCC, the main organizing principle is that of "democratic centralism," wherein the lower levels of the party are accountable to the higher levels, which presumably rule by popular mandate. The PCC proclaims the sovereignty of the people and goes to extraordinary lengths to generate the appearance of mass participation. Consequently, it generates great fanfare over its theatrical electoral processes, and it employs sophisticated polling techniques to discern the popularity of its policies. "Participation" in the Cuban context generally does not entail open, adversarial debate on substantive issues.

Instead, consultation between the party hierarchy and the rank-and-file more often than not involves orchestrated ratification of the leadership's agenda. Instances of public disagreement on fundamental political issues are rare, and these usually result in the purging of the offending subordinate if he or she happens to be on the "wrong" side of an issue of importance to the top leadership (such was the suspected fate of former Foreign Minister Roberto Robaina, who was replaced in 1998 and subsequently disappeared from public view). As a result, deviation from the official line on matters submitted for discussion does not take the form of a rejection of the leadership's objectives or a questioning of its motives, but is framed in the form of "suggestions" relating to peripheral issues. Thus, even within the PCC rank and file, communication is constrained by self-censorship and the prevailing attitude among the lower levels is one of complacency.

Public opinion is not considered by government leaders in deciding matters pertaining to the fundamentals of the political system or in addressing issues of vital interest to the top leadership. Thus, for example, when Fidel Castro decided in 1986 that the highly popular farmers' markets introduced earlier in the decade were undermining socialism and the regime's economic control capabilities, he decreed their closure without the benefit of public debate. The regime is not completely unresponsive to currents of public opinion, however. It is willing to accommodate, in certain instances, some of the demands of the PCC-affiliated mass organizations. In the past, mass organization leaders have expressed reservations over policies of the central administration that adversely affect their constituents. Nevertheless, most such disagreements are voiced discreetly in private and are always carefully worded to avoid any implied criticism of Fidel or Raúl Castro.

REPRESSION OF DISSENT

Whereas the regime demonstrates some flexibility in accommodating the demands of its partisans, its response to public dissidence and opposition has consistently been uncompromising and repressive. During the first two decades of the Revolution, thousands of regime opponents, including many individuals who today would be classified as prisoners of conscience, were executed by firing squad or "disappeared" in prison. During the 1960s, the Castro regime's campaign to destroy the autonomous institutions of civil society produced a raft of excesses, including mass deportations and imprisonments, and--during the mid-1960s--the internment of opponents and suspicious individuals in agricultural labor camps. During the 1970s, it is estimated that Cuba's prison system held more than 40,000 long-term political prisoners, giving Cuba one of the world's highest per capita rates of political incarceration.

During the late 1970s and early 1980s, approximately 20,000 political prisoners were freed on condition that they immediately leave the country. In its 2000 Annual Report, Amnesty International classifies approximately 300 imprisoned Cubans as political prisoners, but acknowledges that its estimates are conservative. Amnesty International and Human Rights Watch/Americas have consistently reported ill treatment of detainees in prisons and police stations, and frequent short-term detention and harassment of human rights and political activists.

In 1992 Freedom House documented dozens of cases of political detainees being subjected to unnecessary psychiatric treatments, including multiple doses of electroshock therapy, in efforts to alter their personalities and as a method of torture. Political prisoners are regularly subjected to physical and psychological torture, including beatings, neglect, and isolation in cramped, unventilated cells. Political prisoners are also frequently housed alongside common criminals, including violent felons. Prison conditions are known to be extremely poor through testimonial evidence and through evidence gathered by the United Nations Commission on Human Rights (UNCHR).

From 1991 until 1997, the UNCHR designated a Special Representative (upgraded in 1992 to Special Rapporteur) to investigate the human rights situation in Cuba. The Cuban government consistently denied the Special Rapporteur permission to enter the country and refused to respond to the Rapporteur's written inquiries on human rights matters. Based on reports from Cuba's independent human right groups, every year but one since 1991, the UNCHR has adopted resolutions condemning Cuba's human rights record. For example, in 1995, the Commission approved a resolution that regretted profoundly Cuba's violations of basic human rights and fundamental freedoms and expressed "particular concern at prevailing intolerance for freedom of speech and assembly in Cuba."

Government encroachment on the rights of Cuban citizens is systematic. Rights violations are carried out within the parameters of the legal system and at the behest of the highest political authorities. The Cuban constitution of 1976 recognizes only "social rights," and prioritizes these over the civil liberties of individuals. The Cuban Penal Code does not meet international standards of due process and protection of individual rights. Among the felonies listed in the code are thought crimes such as "dangerousness," "illegal association," and "dissemination of enemy propaganda." These charges, which carry sentences ranging from one to fifteen years, are often lodged against nonviolent political dissidents and human rights monitors. More vocal opponents who call for fundamental political change may be charged with "rebellion," which carries sentences exceeding fifteen years and, in some cases, may warrant capital punishment. Individuals who are convicted of insulting the commander in chief face prison sentences of up to three years, and Cubans caught attempting to emigrate illegally may be imprisoned for up to two years. Trial procedures are skewed against defendants, who do not enjoy the right of habeas corpus and are usually not assigned a public defender until the actual date of their trial.

The regime not only violates basic civil liberties, but also uses political criteria to discriminate in the provision of employment, education, and social services. Thus, for example, individuals who display "antisocial" tendencies may be denied promotions or may be dismissed altogether from their jobs, or their children may be expelled from universities. Human rights monitors and independent journalists who attempt to report on Cuban human rights conditions have had their telephone service and other utilities disconnected and their communications equipment confiscated. These and other sanctions provide the government with a broad range of lesser coercive mechanisms to dissuade the discontented from joining opposition groups.

During crisis situations, the regime has used emigration as a "safety valve" to rid itself of dissatisfied elements of society. The result has been a diaspora of more than 1.5 million people during the past four decades. Most refugees have fled to the United States, Canada, Spain, and several countries of Latin America. The majority of Cuban refugees have settled in the United States, mostly in southern Florida, home to the largest Cuban exile community.

OFFICIAL CORRUPTION

Despite official rhetoric extolling egalitarianism and the regime's purported commitment to "the new socialist man," corruption and clientelism are endemic to Cuban institutions, almost all of which are controlled by the state. Like a well-oiled urban political machine, the regime relies on the allocation of goods and services based on demonstrated political loyalty to maintain the support of the military and the Communist Party rank and file. In the circumstances of scarcity that pervade life in Cuba, and with the discrediting of Communism as the legitimizing ideology of the regime, government largesse has become a highly effective method of maintaining the support of traditional regime loyalists within the Communist Party (PCC).

High PCC functionaries and military officers constitute a privileged class (mayimbes) within Cuban society. They enjoy a variety of perks, including luxury housing, priority access to scarce transportation resources, freedom to travel overseas and to import foreign luxury items duty free, and access to segregated medical and recreational facilities. Moreover, the children of high party functionaries enjoy superior educational opportunities and are exempted from the military draft and from agricultural labor.

In 1997 Forbes magazine placed Fidel Castro among the world's richest individuals, with a personal fortune estimated at US$1.5 billion. Many observers have suggested that this is a conservative estimate. It is rumored that Castro maintains more than a dozen residences across Cuba, as well as large tracts of land for personal recreational use.

In addition to traditional forms of corruption, strong evidence emerged during the 1980s of Cuban involvement in international organized crime. Evidence from that period suggests that high-ranking officials, most notably Armed Forces head, Raul Castro, knowingly allowed Cuban territory and military facilities to be used for the transshipment of narcotics into the United States

The 1989 drug scandal that led to the trial and execution of Division General Arnaldo Ochoa Sánchez and several other high-ranking military officers provided a wealth of information on the lifestyles of Cuban officials and on alleged government- sponsored participation in drug trafficking. Testimonies from the trial corroborated allegations by Cuban government defectors that Cuban officials, under the direction of Minister of Interior José Abrantes and with the tacit consent of Raúl Castro had cooperated with the Colombian Medellín Cartel in transshipping cocaine bound for the United States.

CUBA ECONOMY: STRATEGIC INFORMATION

Currency	Cuban peso (CUP) = 100 centavos
Fiscal year	yes
	Statistics
GDP	$125.5 billion
GDP growth	4.3%
GDP per capita	$9,500
GDP by sector	Agriculture: 4.6%, industry: 26.1%, services: 69.3%
Inflation (CPI)	3.6%
Population below poverty line	1%
Labor force	4.853 million (Public sector: 78%, Private sector: 22%)
Labor force by occupation	Agriculture: 21.2%, industry: 14.4%, services: 64.4%
Unemployment	1.9%
Main industries	Sugar, petroleum, tobacco, construction, nickel, steel, cement, agricultural machinery, pharmaceuticals
	External
Exports	$3.231 billion f.o.b.
Main export partners	Netherlands 21.8%, Canada 21.6%, China 18.7%, Spain 5.9%
Imports	$10.86 billion f.o.b.
Main import partners	Venezuela 26.6%, China 15.6%, Spain 9.6%, Germany 6.4%, Canada 5.6%, Italy 4.4%, US 4.3%, Brazil 4.2%
	Public finances
Public debt	$16.79 billion (convertible currency); another $20.8 billion owed to Russia $0.9 billion owed to Romania and $0.2 billion owed to Hungary
Revenues	$35.01 billion
Expenses	$36.73 billion
Economic aid	$87.8 million

The **economy of Cuba** is a largely state-controlled, centrally planned economy overseen by the Cuban government, though there remains significant foreign investment and enterprise in Cuba. Most of the means of production are owned and run by the government and most of the labor force is employed by the state. In the year 2000, the public sector employment was 76% and the private sector at 23% compared to the 1981 ratio of 91% to 8%. Capital investment is restricted and requires approval by the government. The Cuban government sets most prices and rations goods to citizens. The present Cuban Minister of Economy and Planning is Marino Murillo.

In the 1950s, Cuba had a one-crop, backward economy whose domestic market was constricted and whose population was characterized by chronic unemployment and deep poverty. The country has made significant progress since the Revolution, with its rate of economic growth exceeding the rest of Latin America Cubans receive low housing and transportation costs, free education and health care, and food subsidies.

Corruption is common. Preferential treatment exists for those who are members of the Communist Party or who hold positions of power within the government

The Cuban economy is still recovering from a decline in gross domestic product of at least 35% between 1989 and 1993 due to the loss of 80% of its trading partners and Soviet subsidies

This era was referred to as the "Special Period in Peacetime" later shortened to "Special Period". A Canadian Medical Association Journal paper states that "The famine in Cuba during the Special Period was caused by political and economic factors similar to the ones that caused a famine in North Korea in the mid-1990s. Both countries were run by authoritarian regimes that denied ordinary people the food to which they were entitled when the public food distribution collapsed; priority was given to the elite classes and the military." Cubans had to resort to eating anything they could find, from Havana Zoo animals to domestic cats. Because of the overthrow of the Soviet Union and other socialist countries, Cuba experienced economic difficulties, which led to a drop in calories per day from 3052 in 1989 to 2600 in 2006.

The government has undertaken several reforms in recent years to stem excess liquidity, increase labour incentives, and alleviate serious shortages of food, consumer goods, and services. To alleviate the economic crisis, the government introduced a few market-oriented reforms including opening to tourism, allowing foreign investment, legalizing the U.S. dollar, and authorizing self-employment for some 150 occupations. (This policy was later partially reversed, so that while the U.S. dollar is no longer accepted in businesses, it remains legal for Cubans to hold the currency.) These measures resulted in modest economic growth. The liberalized agricultural markets introduced in October 1994, at which state and private farmers sell above-quota production at free market prices, have broadened legal consumption alternatives and reduced black market prices

Government efforts to lower subsidies to unprofitable enterprises and to shrink the money supply caused the semi-official exchange rate for the Cuban peso to move from a peak of 120 to the dollar in the summer of 1994 to 21 to the dollar by yearend 1999. Living conditions in 1999 remained well below the 1989 level. New taxes introduced in 1996 have helped drive down the number of self-employed workers from 208,000 in January 1996

Havana announced in 1995 that GDP declined by 35% during 1989-93, the result of lost Soviet aid and domestic inefficiencies. The drop in GDP apparently halted in 1994, when Cuba reported 0.7% growth, followed by increases of 2.5% in 1995 and 7.8% in 1996. Growth slowed again in 1997 and 1998 to 2.5% and 1.2% respectively. One of the key reasons given was the failure to notice that sugar production had become dramatically uneconomic. Reflecting on the Special period Cuban president Fidel Castro later admitted that many mistakes had been made, “The country had many economists and it is not my intention to criticize them, but I would like to ask why we hadn’t discovered earlier that maintaining our levels of sugar production would be impossible. The Soviet Union had collapsed, oil was costing $40 a barrel, sugar prices were at basement levels, so why did we not rationalize the industry?"

RECOVERY

Due to the continued growth of tourism, growth began in 1999 with a 6.2% increase in GDP Growth in recent years has picked up significantly, with a growth in GDP of 11.8% in 2005 according to official Cuban information In 2007 the Cuban economy grew by 7.5%, below the expected 10%, but higher than the Latin American average rate of growth. Accordingly, the cumulative growth in GDP since 2004 stood at 42.5 %.

POST-FIDEL REFORMS

In 2007, Raúl Castro's administration hinted that the purchase of computers, DVD players and microwaves would become legal. However, monthly wages remain less than 20 U.S. dollars. Mobile phones, which have been restricted to Cubans working for foreign companies and government officials, have become legalized. The new program could put phones in the hands of hundreds of thousands of Cubans.

ENERGY PRODUCTION

Due to the reliance on declining Soviet era electricity generators, many areas of Cuba suffered frequent blackouts and brownouts for extended periods, creating additional pressure on society. To counter these problems, the government has put Cuba through "Energy Revolution", which has placed increased emphasis on the efficient use of electrical energy and more efficient small-power generators linked in a synchronized network. The country has increased the number of solar- and wind-powered generators Though development was hampered by large-scale damage created by Hurricane Dennis and Hurricane Wilma, which cut Cuba's electricity generation capacity by half in the areas most affected, Cuba now exceeds the government set demand in electricity production. Raul Castro told Cubans in his July 26 speech in 2007, that the Special Period is not yet over.

GOVERNMENT POLICIES

Rationing in Cuba refers to the system of food distribution known in Cuba as the *Libreta de Abastecimiento* ("Supplies booklet"). The system establishes the rations each person is allowed to buy through that system, and the frequency of supplies.

On top of rationing, the average wage at the end of 2005 was 334 regular pesos per month ($16.70 per month) and average monthly pension was $9.

A person can get more jail time for killing a cow (10 years in prison) than killing a human. Those who sell beef without government permission can get three to eight years in prison. Eaters of illegal beef can get three months to one year in prison.

After the 1959 Cuban Revolution, citizens were not required to pay a personal income tax (their salaries being regarded as net of any taxes). However, from 1996, the State started to impose income taxes on Cubans earning hard currency, primarily the self-employed.

In their book, *Corruption in Cuba*, Cuban American authors Sergio Diaz-Briquets and Jorge F. Pérez-López claim that the Communist regime institutionalized corruption; "Castro's state-run monopolies, cronyism, and lack of accountability turned Cuba into one of the world's most corrupt states". On the other hand, the Corruption Perceptions Index ranks Cuba 65th (from best to worst) out of 180 countries, better than most other countries in Central or Latin America.

As in other former socialist countries, few citizens hesitate to steal from the government when given opportunity. Since the vast majority of people are in state jobs and the state makes up much of the economy, petty crime is widespread.

Sociolismo also known as amiguismo meaning "friend-ism" or "partner-ism" is the informal term used in Cuba to describe the reciprocal exchange of favors by individuals, usually relating to circumventing bureaucratic restrictions or obtaining hard-to-find goods. It comes from the Spanish word *socio* which means business partner or buddy, and is a pun on *socialismo*, the Spanish term for socialism. It is analogous to the *blat* of the Soviet Union.

The term is particularly associated with the black market economy, and perceived cronyism in Cuba's state controlled command economy. *Socios* can be black market operators who "facilitate" (steal) goods that are officially reserved for the state. They can also get someone a job or obtain paperwork.

AGRICULTURE

As a result of inefficient state-run agriculture, Cuba imports up to 80% of its food. After coming to power, Raúl Castro, Fidel Castro's brother, has ridiculed the bureaucracy that shackles the agriculture sector.

Before 1959, Cuba boasted as many cattle as people. Today meat is so scarce that it is a crime to kill and eat a cow without government permission. Cuban people even suffered from starvation during the Special Period.

Agriculture in Cuba has played an important part in the economy for several hundred years. Agriculture contributes less than 10 percent to the gross domestic product (GDP), but it employs roughly one fifth of the working population. About 30 percent of the country's land is used for crop cultivation

The inefficient communist system that shackles the agriculture sector was ridiculed by Raúl Castro in a July 2007 speech. Cuba now imports about 80% of the food it rations to the public. The rationing program accounts for about a third of the calories the average Cuban consumes

URBAN AGRICULTURE AND CROPS

Due to the shortage of fuel and therefore severe deficiencies in the transportation sector a growing percentage of the agricultural production takes place in the so-called urban agriculture. In 2002, 35,000 acres (140 km^2) of urban gardens produced 3.4 million tons of food. Current estimates are as high as 81,000 acres In Havana, 90% of the city's fresh produce come from local urban farms and gardens. In 2003, more than 200,000 Cubans worked in the expanding urban agriculture sector

SUGAR

Until 1960, the USA received 33% of their sugar imports from Cuba. However, the sugar production has fallen from approx. 8 million tons to approx. 3.2 million tons in the 1990s.

TOBACCO

Cuba has the second largest area planted with tobacco of all countries worldwide Tobacco production in Cuba has remained about the same since the late 1990s. Cigars are a famous Cuban product worldwide and almost the whole production is exported The centre of Cuban tobacco production is the Pinar del Río Province . Tobacco is the third largest source of hard currency for Cuba The income derived from the cigars is estimated at 200 M US$ The two main varieties grown in Cuba are Corojo and Criollo. 85% of the tobacco grown in Cuba is produced by National Association of Small Farmers members
See also: Cuban cigars

CITRUS

Cuba is the world's third largest producer of grapefruit. 60% of the citrus production are oranges, 36% grapefruit. In the citrus production the first foreign investment in Cuba's agricultural sector took place: In 1991, the participation of an enterprise from Israel in the production and processing of citrus is the *Jagüey Grande* area, approx. 140 km east of Havana, was officially recognized The products are mainly marketed in Europe under the brand name *Cubanita*.

RICE

Rice plays a major role in the Cuban diet. Rice in Cuba is mostly grown along the western coast. There are two crops per year. The majority of the rice farms are state-farms or belong to co-operatives Cuba has been a major importer of rice. Recently, the annual rice imports have approached 500 000 tonnes of milled rice. The production of rice is limited due to the shortage of water and similar to other industries in Cuba the lack of fertilizers and modern agricultural technology. The yield per hectare remains lower than the average of Central American and Caribbean countries

POTATO

The per capita consumption of potatoes in Cuba amounts to 25 kg per year. Potatoes are mainly consumed as French fries. The potato production areas (in total 37,000 acres) are concentrated in the Western part of Cuba. The main variety grown in Cuba is the Désirée Seed potatoes are partly produced locally. Some 40,000 tons of seed potatoes are imported annually from New Brunswick, Canada and the Netherlands

CASSAVA

Some 260,000 acres (1,100 km^2) are planted with cassava The cassava originates from the Latin American and Caribbean region and is grown in almost every country of the region. Cuba is the second largest producer of cassava in the Caribbean with a production of 300,000 t However, the yield per hectare is the lowest of all Caribbean countries. Most of Cuba's production is used directly for fresh consumption Part of the cassava is processed to sorbitol in a plant near Florida, Central Cuba.

TROPICAL FRUITS

Plantains and bananas account for over 70 percent of production with plantain 47% and banana 24% of the local production. Both are only produced for domestic consumption Other tropical fruits produced in Cuba are mango, papaya, pineapple, avocado, guava, coconut, and anonaceae (sugar apple family).

INDUSTRY

In total, industrial production accounted for almost 37% of the Cuban GDP, or US$6.9 billion, and employs 24% of the population, or 2,671,440 people, in 1996.
More recently Cuba's world-class biotechnology and pharmaceutical industry is gaining in its importance to the economy. It has been claimed that soon it will become Cuba's main source of foreign exchange. Among the products sold internationally are vaccines against various viral and bacterial pathogens, and promising anti-cancer vaccines are undergoing exhaustive clinical trials. Some Cuban scientists, like V. Verez-Bencomo, have been awarded international prizes for their contributions in biotechnology and Sugar Cane. Cuban vaccines are sold, among other countries, in Russia, China, India, Pakistan, and several Latin American countries.

TOURISM

In the mid 1990s tourism surpassed sugar, long the mainstay of the Cuban economy, as the primary source of foreign exchange. Tourism figures prominently in the Cuban Government's plans for development, and a top official cast it as the "heart of the economy". Havana devotes significant resources to building new tourist facilities and renovating historic structures for use in the tourism sector. Cuban officials estimate roughly 1.6 million tourists visited Cuba in 1999 with about $1.9 billion in gross revenues. In 2000, 1,773,986 foreign visitors arrived in Cuba. Revenue from tourism reached US $1.7 billion.

The rapid growth of tourism has had widespread social and economic repercussions in Cuba. This has led to speculation of the emergence of a two-tier economy and the fostering of a state of tourist apartheid on the island. This situation was exacerbated by the influx of dollars into the Cuban economy during the 1990s, potentially creating a dual economy based on the dollar (the currency of tourists) on the one hand, and the peso on the other. Scarce imported goods - and even some of local manufacture, such as rum and coffee- could be had at dollars-only stores, but were hard to find or unavailable at peso prices. As a result, Cubans who earned only in the peso economy, outside the tourist sector, were at an economic disadvantage. Those with dollar incomes based upon the service industry began to live more comfortably. This widened the gulf between Cubans' material standards of living, in conflict with the Cuban Government's long term socialist policies.

RETAIL

Cuba has a very poorly developed retail sector. There are no large shopping centers and the commercial districts that existed before the revolution are largely shut down. Those that remain carry few and poorly made products that are priced in dollars and are too expensive for the average Cuban to purchase. The majority of the stores are small dollar stores, bodegas, agro-mercados (farmers' markets), and street stands.

POVERTY

Typical wages range from factory worker's 400 non-convertible Cuban pesos a month to doctor's 700. That is only around 17-30 U.S. dollars a month. After Cuba lost subsidies in 1991, malnutrition resulted in an outbreak of diseases. Cuba's poverty level is one of the lowest in the developing world, ranking 6 out of 108 countries, 4 in Latin America, and 48 among all countries. Pensions are among the smallest in the Western hemisphere at $9.50. In 2009, Raul Castro increased minimum pensions by 2 dollars, which he said was to recompense for those who have "dedicated a great part of their lives to working... and who remain firm in defence of socialism".

SELF-EMPLOYMENT

To provide jobs for workers laid off due to the economic crisis, the government was having difficulty providing, and to try to bring some forms of black market activity into legal - and therefore controllable - channels, Havana in 1993 legalized self-employment for some 150 occupations. The government tightly controls the small private sector, which has fluctuated in size from 150,000 to 209,000, by regulating and taxing it. For example, owners of small private restaurants (*paladares*) can seat no more than 12 people and can only employ family members to help with the work. Set monthly fees must be paid regardless of income earned and frequent inspections yield stiff fines when any of the many self-employment regulations are violated. Rather than expanding private sector opportunities, in recent years, the government has been attempting to squeeze more of these private sector entrepreneurs out of business and back to the public sector. Many have opted to enter the informal economy or black market. In recent years there has developed what is called "urban agriculture", production which takes place on small parcels of land in the cities. Growing organopónicos (organic gardens) in the private sector has been attractive to city dwelling small producers who get to sell their products in the same place where they produce them, avoiding taxes and enjoying a measure of government help from the Ministry of Agriculture (MINAGRI) in the form of seed houses and advisors.

INTERNATIONAL TRADE

The Netherlands receive the largest share of Cuban exports (24%), 70 to 80% of which through Fondel Finance, a company owned by the Van 't Wout family who have close personal ties with Fidel Castro. Currently, this trend can be seen in other colonial Caribbean communities who have direct political ties with the global economy. (e.g. British West Indies, United States Virgin Islands, French outer-territories, etc.) The second largest trade partner is Canada, with a 22% share of the Cuban export market.

CONNECTION WITH VENEZUELA

The relationship cultivated between Cuba and Venezuela in recent years has resulted in agreements that Venezuela provide cheap oil in exchange for Cuban "missions" of doctors which aid and help to improve the Venezuelan health care system. Cuba, with the second-highest per capita number of physicians in the world (behind Italy), sends tens of thousands of doctors to other countries as aid, as well as for obtaining favorable economic terms of trade.
While Venezuela says that Cuba is paying part of the bill with the professionals, medicines, books and other items that Cuba sends, some independent analysts say the numbers don't add up. Havana would have to be collecting about $80,000 per year per Cuban worker in Venezuela to cover the costs of its oil imports, the analysts say. Instead, Cuban doctors in Venezuela receive about $3,000 per year, according to three Cuban doctors who defected from the program (see also Mission Barrio Adentro). The White House's point man on plans for a post-Castro transition, Caleb McCarry, recently told The Miami Herald that U.S. estimates of total Venezuelan subsidies to Cuba per year "are up to the $2 billion figure." This can be compared to the $4 billion to $6 billion that Moscow once pumped into Cuba per year

FOREIGN INVESTMENT

Since the Special Period, Cuba has actively courted foreign investment. All would be foreign investors are required to form joint ventures with the Cuban government. The sole exception to this rule are Venezuelans, who are allowed to hold 100% ownership in businesses due to an economic agreement between Cuba and Venezuela. Cuban officials said in early 1998 that there were a total of 332 joint ventures. Many of these are loans or contracts for management, supplies, or services normally not considered equity investment in Western economies. Investors are constrained by the U.S.-Cuban Liberty and Democratic Solidarity Act which provides sanctions for those who "traffic" in property expropriated from U.S. citizens. As of March 1998, 15 executives of three foreign companies have been excluded from entry into the United States. Over a dozen companies have pulled out of Cuba or altered their plans to invest there due to the threat of action under the Libertad Act.

US DOLLAR

In 1993 the Cuban Government made it legal for its people to possess and use the U.S. dollar. From then until 2004, the dollar became a major currency. To capture the hard currency flowing into the island through tourism and remittances - estimated at $500–800 million annually - the government set up state-run "dollar stores" throughout Cuba that sold 'luxury' food, household, and clothing items, compared with basic necessities, which were bought using the Cuban peso. As such, a gap in the standard of living developed between those with access to dollars and those without. Jobs that could earn dollar salaries or tips from foreign businesses and tourists became highly desirable. It was common to meet doctors, engineers, scientists, and other professionals working in restaurants or as taxicab drivers.

However, in response to stricter economic sanctions by the US, and because the authorities were pleased with Cuba's economic recovery, the Cuban government decided in October 2004 to remove the American dollar from circulation. In its place, the Cuban convertible peso is now used, which although not internationally traded, has a value pegged to that of the dollar. As a source of additional revenue, a 10% surcharge is levied for conversions from US dollars to the convertible peso; this surcharge does not apply to other currencies, so it acts as an encouragement to tourists to bring currencies like Euros, pounds sterling or Canadian dollars into Cuba. Indeed, an increasing number of areas rich in tourism now also accept Euros directly for many transactions.

ECONOMY AND ECONOMIC DEVELOPMENT - MAIN OBJECTIVES

- Growth of 5 % rate of the Gross Domestic Product.
- An advance in the most important indicators of economic efficiency, as the main support to economic and social development.

  Work Productivity : 4,3 %
  Energy intensity: -2,6 %
- Rate of growth of investments by approximately 14 %.
- Developing tourism, to reach 2 millions of visitors, and 15% in terms of total gross income.
- A growth of industrial production of 7,4 %.
- Sugar industry will have a 3,7 million tons sugar harvest.
- Equivalent production of petroleum and gas is planned to reach 4 millions tons. Generation of electricity on the base of domestic fuel will rise to 90 %.
- Constructions will grow 18 % and non sugar cane agriculture around 10 %.
- In industry, important growths are planned in nickel production, to reach 75 thousand tons (increase 5%), steel production 15%, and stainless steel will also be duplicated.
- Increase exports more than 20 % specially bent tobacco and rum. Imports will growth more than 4 %. These projections will support a reduction of the balance of trade deficit.
- Internal financial balance will be maintained, decreasing the liquidity as a proportion of the GDP.
- A fiscal deficit of 779 million pesos, which in terms of the proportion of the Gross Domestic Product represents 2,7 % .

PUBLIC FINANCES IN CUBA

PUBLIC FINANCES

The Ministry of Finances and Prices is the State's Central Administration Institution in charge of the management, implementation and control of the application of the fiscal, financial, taxes, prices, auditing and insurance policy of the State and the Government. It also provides advice on these policies to these Institutions of the administration of the country and manages and controls the organization of public finances and the use of financial resources.

As part of the arrangement of public finances, Law Decree 192 **"On Financial Administration of the State"**, was endorsed in April 1999 as one of the most outstanding steps in the arrangement of public finances. Its objective is to impart more clearness, arrangement and organicity to the process of planning, implementation and control of public finances so as to meet the goals and policies set by the state.

Law-Decree 192 substitutes Act 29 "Organic Act of the State Budget" in force since 1980, but now obsolete because it could not meet overall current conditions of the economy in general neither those of finances particularly approached.

The law-decree defines and covers a group of principles, standards, systems, institutions and management procedures which make it possible to gather public resources and use them to meet state goals, endeavoring to meet the needs of society. It is made up by the following systems:

a. Taxes
b. Budget
c. Treasury
d. Public credit
e. Government accountancy

The System of Taxes is ruled by special legislations, mostly Act 73 **"On the System of Taxes"** passed by the Cuban Parliament in 1994 and by other provisions. These legislations are gradually applied with the elementary principles of social justice to protect low-income sectors and stimulate work and production and control cash liquidity.

The act mentioned above acknowledges eleven (11) taxes, three rates (3) and one (1) contribution which are applied based on the principles of generality and equity of taxes, in line with the economic capacity of people that should pay for them.

Taxes:

- Tax on gross profits
- Tax on personal incomes
- Tax on sales
- Tax on special products
- Tax on public services
- Tax on the property or possession of certain goods
- Tax on land transport
- Tax on the transfer of goods and heritage
- Tax on documents
- Tax on the use of labor force
- Tax on the use and exploitation of natural resources and for the protection of the environment

Contributions:

- Contribution to social security

Rates:

- Rate for tolls

Rate for airport and travelers service

- Rate for the settlement of adds and commercial propaganda

Taxes put in force has been introduced gradually in line with conditions set for that end.

The system has achieved consolidation and institutionalization and in a short term it has been able to reestablish a tax paying oriented mind, the timely collection of taxes and the collection of non-tax incomes payable to the state by legal and natural persons.

The **budget systems** keeps up with the accomplishments in this issue derived from the previous act and introduces new principles according to the most common international practice in the issue of budgeting and register. Stress is made on the principles of non-compensation of expenditures and incomes and the register of expenditure by earning.

Classifiers of financial resources and uniform expenditures were established for all the system. They provide the necessary information for control and efficiency in the management of public resources at the different levels of the budget.

Although Cuba is a unitary republic by definition of its Constitution, the system of government was structured after 1976 by a central government, 14 provincial governments and 169 municipal governments in line with the political and administrative division of the country. Consequently, for each level of the government there is a budget that is the financial basis for the fulfillment of its role of top authority of the state within the limits of the corresponding territory. This gives rise to the Budget System made up by 200 budgets:

The combination of a central management principle, which recognizes and gives powers to the local bodies of the, People´s Power is present in the Cuban budget system so that they can extensively participate in working out, implementing and liquidation of budgets.

Legislative and normative functions of all the system are concentrated in the central bodies as well as the necessary proceedings to achieve macroeconomic stability and guarantee timely financial support of crucial tasks of the economic development. And the distribution of financial resources that might provide for equity and implementation of programs, regardless of economic development in the territories is also accomplished through the concentration of the functions above mentioned

Local bodies of the government concentrate a large share of financial resources that guarantee the implementation of the economic policy together with the corresponding autonomy for planning and use of resources. The end is to join the interest of every territory and those of society as a whole. The relation between the central budget with the provincial budgets is further explained.

The budget of the state is discussed and endorsed by the Cuban Parliament every year during its sessions at the end of the year and this budget rules from January 1st to December 31st every year.

Working out starts during May-June once the Council of Ministers issue its guidelines and top priorities. Then, the Ministry of Finances and Prices works out specific guidelines considering the characteristics of every sector, branch, activity or territory based on the considerations of the Council of Ministers. These specific guidelines are the basis on which bodies linked to the Central Budget and to Provincial and Municipal Budgets work out preliminary plans and present them before the Ministry of Finances and Prices in October. A process of analysis, evaluation and negotiation of figures for further submittal before the Council of Ministers starts after this date

After the analysis, the Council of Ministers submits the project before the National Assembly of People's Power (Cuban Parliament) that approves it by the following items:

a. The Budget of the State, by the total amount of financial resources and expenditures and within them, by its main sources and ends and in its opening, by current budgets and capital budgets.
b. The Central Budget divided into current budget and capital budget and consigning the main sources of financial resources, the total sum of expenditures and the detachment of its destination.
c. The Budget for Social Security, by the total amount of its financial resources and expenditures.
d. The percentages of participation of provincial budgets in the incomes of the Central Budgets
e. Direct transfers to grant to provincial budgets, bearing on the Central Budget

After the endorsement of the Budget of the State, the Ministry of Finances and Prices gives notice with the corresponding figures to the agencies related to it and periodically allots budgetary credits.

During implementation, there can be changes and adjustments made by the different organizations and institutions if they do not affect limits set forth in the notices.

The Ministry of Finances and Prices has the power to implement changes as long as they do not affect the balance of incomes and expenditures, i.e., they can not change the Fiscal Deficit endorsed by Parliament.

Periodically, the different organizations and institutions are compelled to report on the implementation of the budget. This provides for the evaluation of fulfillment and at the end of the fiscal year they should present the liquidation that serves as the basis for the rendering of accounts of the Ministry of Finances and Prices before the Government and the Parliament

Concerning the System of the Treasury, its implementation has been propelled by requirements needed not only by an efficient financial management including the flow of funds but also, by the reform sped up in the banking system of the country.

Though it is not valid to speak of a system of the treasury, certain basic principles are being applied. The most outstanding are: working out a budget for payments; monthly financial programs of budget distribution; shortening the terms to hand budgetary credits.

All the territories have created mechanisms to operate under the principles of treasury set by the Law - Decree and to manage the accounts of the Central Budget in the different territories.

And parallel to this, work has been done on the System of Government Accounting. The establishment of income and uniform expenditure classifiers has been crucial for this end.

Accountancy of management entities was worked out and introduced, establishing heritage and budget control. These are the basis to know efficiency and economy of public expenditure management and the proper use of funds allotted by the State budget

Though the Law - Decree authenticates the legal frame for the introduction of the System of Public Credit it will not come into force in a short term because it is conditioned by other factors.

RELATIONS OF BUDGET WITH PUBLIC BUSINESS

The changes that have occurred as a result of the crisis and the restatement needed in the organization and management of public administration and the endorsement of Act 73 on the Tax System conditioned a change in the relations between public business and the Budget of the State. This change provides for a clearer concept of the state in its double role of Treasury and owner.

Under this concept, all public business is compelled to pay taxes, rates and contributions to the Treasury, in line with Act 73. Commitments with the Treasury are compulsory and failure to comply under the terms and amounts set leads to penalties established by law.

Profits after honoring the Treasury can be used for different ends previously defined by the representatives of the State. The most important are the contribution to the budget by the yield of the state investment, the capitalization and finance of investments and stimulation to workers teams.

The system conceives a closest link of the business with the result of its economic management when it grants autonomy on the issue of financial management. It favors the capacity and initiative of business managers and strengthens their responsibility for the work they carry out.

In this sense, the system allows for the creation of reserves and provisions from the gross income to cover eventual losses and risks as well as provisions for voluntary expenditures aimed for general repairs.

Besides profits, the use of other sources for financing such as decentralized resources from the accumulated depreciation, the sale of active assets and bank credits are recognized to start a process of investments. In this way, agencies and institutions are progressively separated from the Budget on the issue of finance for investments, increase of working capital, stimulation to workers and other plans for development.

Due to state needs there is public business producing under conditions that can not cover expenditures with profits. They are unprofitable. In this case, the State Budget subsidizes their production based on a plan endorsed under the guidelines of the Annual Law of Budget

RELATIONS OF THE CENTRAL BUDGET WITH THE PROVINCIAL BUDGETS

The Central Budget allots budgets to the provinces based on certain criteria of distribution and in line with the policy of decentralization of resources explained in the Budgetary System for organizations and institutions of the local bodies of the government so that they can efficiently manage their budgets. The criteria for budget allotment are the following:

Incomes transferred or owned: These incomes come from institutions managed by local bodies of the government or linked to collections from a past or future expenditure that should be paid by the community e.g. the reproduction and education of labor force causes expenditures in education, public health, recreation and cultural and social ones. It is for this reason that the Tax on the Use of Labor Force is fully transferred to the provinces and municipalities regardless of subordination of the institution that pays.

Participative incomes: These incomes are derived from taxes at the central level collected in the provinces / municipalities, with rates ranging from 10 to 20% on the Tax of Circulation and the Tax on Profits of business of national subordination

The Central Budget allots Direct Transfers as subsidies to balance fiscal capacities between provinces and municipalities and are not aimed to finance any particular expenditure. Likewise, Direct Transfers are made to finance investments in programs of the infrastructure, housing and road construction and social and cultural works.

Consequently, local governments and the institutions subordinated to them are responsible for the management and use of financial resources allotted. This makes it possible to increase efficiency and efficacy in the service of these institutions.

Decentralization in the management of public expenditures to the provinces / municipalities guarantees an effective application of the social policy established. It also provides for a more active performance since the institutions of local governments have the power to define and approve the objectives of expenditures, considering the needs and characteristics of every territory according to the established limits of their budgets.

During the fiscal year and according to the implementation, they can transfer financial resources from one thing to another by way of budgetary changes without permission from higher budgetary organizations. This provides more flexibility in the decentralized management of budget and a more efficient allotment and use of resources and the timely attention to financial needs.

MAIN CHARACTERISTICS OF BUDGET FOR THE YEAR 2000

State Budget for the year 2000 has regarded that in spite of a favorable forecast for next year's economy, external financial restrictions, the blockade and the limited access to international credits under favorable terms are still in force.

Consequently, a deficit amounting to 745,0 million pesos has been projected following the fiscal policy laid for the last four years. This figure represents 2.8% of the GDP calculated at current prices and it meets the principles of stability and sustainability that have made possible the stability of finances during this stage.

An amount of 9.166 million pesos have been allotted to budgeted business. This figure is higher than estimates by 607 million pesos out of which 176, 0 million pesos were used for rises in salaries in different sectors in 1999; 275,0 million pesos are used for maintenance and renovation in housing and road and social/cultural facilities. More than 90,0 million come from the rise in prices and almost 54,0 million to back the natural growth of the amount of professionals joining the fields of health and education. The entire expenditures represent 34.8% of the GDP.

An amount of 2.601 million pesos are disposed for transfers to the business sector and from this figure, 608.0 are allotted to subsidies for losses in state business. It should be stressed that all the institutions reduce the amount of loses scheduled as compared to 1999.

Resources appointed for subsidies due to the difference of prices are growing (subsidies to consumer families). The reason is the rise in prices of state collection centers of agricultural products without changing retail prices, considering that these are products of the basket of good sold to the population on the ration card. An amount of 560,0 million pesos are allotted for this end.

As a whole, transfers to the state business sector are lower by 9.8% as compared to the budget for 1999 and this means 292, 0 million pesos less than in that year.

Economic assistance to basic units for cooperative production (not involved in sugar cane plantations) is reduced due to the positive effects provoked by the rise in the prices of milk and meat and due to the increased management efficiency.

A Central Reserve of 190.0 million pesos has been considered for this year and it exceeds the figure budgeted for 1999 by 90.0 million pesos. The objective of this is to face new decisions including the continuation of a wage reform in the sectors that were not benefited in 1999.

An amount of 1.700 million pesos is appointed to finance investments and other capital expenditures (6.5 % of the GDP). This figure is below the budget of 1999 by 50,0 million pesos but it is in line with the forecasts for the end of the year according to the results of calculations showing that 100.0 million pesos would not be expended. So, when you compare with estimates it is foreseen that a growth of 3.0% would be attained.

So as to meet these needs of resources it has been envisaged to obtain incomes by an amount of more than 13.525 million pesos that exceed the plan for 1999 by 8.5%.

It should be stressed that the amount planned exceeds the estimates for 1999 only by 0.8% because non-repetitive incomes have been purged from the year 2000 mostly by reductions of tax rates that reduce the collection of such taxes.

Notwithstanding, these reductions are balanced by the prediction of higher collection of direct taxes linked to the profit of businesses and the Contributions by Yield according to the growth projected by the economy, the increase in business efficiency and the fiscal discipline of tax payers.

From the total amount of resources to collect via budget, 78% is made up by taxes and 22% comes from non-tax incomes.

THE POLICY OF PRICES

The price determination is fitted to the current conditions of the Cuban economy and generally, there is advance in establishing them centrally. Wholesale prices are based on our foreign trade prices or the domestic prices in hard currency.

Mechanisms are being introduced to make prices formation flexible and provide business with the possibility to negotiate them; this without renouncing to the central establishment of the policy of prices. So, wholesale trade in the local hard currency market develops under prices generally determined by business depending on the market.

It is under these conditions that a new complementary system of financial relations has been born. It sets the actions of the Cuban state as an owner, defining the procedures for the contribution by the yield of state investment in state businesses as part of the distribution of profits obtained once fiscal obligations are met.

This system conceives a closer link of business with the results of its economic management because it grants autonomy on the issue of financial management and stimulates the capacity and initiative of managers and strengthens their role to account for the efficiency of their actions.

In this sense, the system allows the creation of reserves and provisions from gross earnings so as to cover future loses and other eventualities as well as provisions for voluntary expenditures aimed at general repairs.

On the other hand, it allows for the partial allotment of retained profit to finance investments, regardless of the existence of other sources of finance such as decentralized resources from accumulated depreciation and the sale of idle capital assets or the bank credits. In this way, business progressively separate from the Budget on the issue of finance for investments, increase of working capital, stimulation of workers and other plans for development.

INSURANCE SUPERINTENDENCE

The Superintendency of Insurance of Cuba was created under Law-Decree No. 177, "On the arrangement of insurance and its agencies", dated on September 2nd, 1997. It is assigned to the Ministry of Finances and Prices and its role is to control and superintend institutions dealing with insurance and reinsurance procedures, support services for insurance and brokerage and insurance agencies. The protection of the insured is its mission.

Its scope is not limited to agencies operating in the national territory. It also deals with Cuban agencies or with Cuban interests based abroad that work in the field of insurance.

Currently, there are three national companies of direct insurance operating in Cuba: International Insurance of Cuba S.A., (ESICUBA), National Insurance Co. (ESEN) and Tourism Insurer, La Isla S.A. There are other institutions related to insurance such as Intermar S.A., a tallying and inspection agency and others; Asistur, providing assistance to tourism; Rado and Associates, consultant and lawyers; Conavana S.A., consultants of valuation.

There are branches of foreign life insurance companies liquidating contracts signed up to 1962 represented in Cuba and the Offices of the Lloyd's Register of Shipping and the Veritas Bureau. There is also a Center of Accounting, Financial and Insurance Studies.

INDUSTRY

The management, implementation and control of how State and Governmental policy is applied, in relation to industrial development there are seven specialised industrial ministries which are responsible:

Ministry of Basic Industry.

Ministry of Iron and Steel Mechanics Industry

Ministry of the Fishing Industry

Ministry of the Food Industry (Only available in spanish).

Ministry of Light Industry.

Ministry of Sugar.

The Ministry of Steel – Mechanical Industry (SIME) is the Cuban entity committed in the leading, execution and control of the State and Government policy regarding the activities of the Steel and Mechanical Industry and Recycling.

It was founded in 1974 as a result of the strengthening of investor process in the industrial sphere, a visionary conception of Major Ernesto Che Guevara in the dawn of the Revolution, when he was heading the Ministry of Industries.

Mechanical industry is undoubtedly a creation of Cuban revolution, one of its products. Before the Revolution this industry did not exist in Cuba, everything was imported, we depended entirely on American industry. In this primary stage, the creation of SIME meant the consolidation of a whole series of productions prioritized by the country, which were essentially necessary for the economic development of our nation.

Since its creation, SIME has had a vertical development line thanks to a properly structured and well thought investment plan aimed to the production of automotive and railroad equipment, agricultural machinery, iron & steel industry, construction equipment, machine tools, medical equipment and clinical furniture, supplies for hotel industry, etc.

This investor process started as early as years 1963-64, when such industries still belonged to the Ministry of Industries, which was created by Major Guevara and it was carried out in cooperation with the socialist countries, commissioning productive complexes in the central and eastern regions of the country.

Its creation was an important step that allowed the agglutination of human resources that were being significantly oriented from the beginning of the Revolution toward sectors of vital importance for our socialist development.

So can we see in statistics that soon after its creation, in 1976 it produces 246 millions of dollars, in 1977, 278 millions; in 1978, 304 millions; in 1979, 360 millions, till reaching in 1985 the quantity of 760 millions. This situation starts a sudden downward trend in 1989, because of the diminishing trade with the USSR and former socialist countries, and gets to its climax in 1992.

From 1993 on, the organism enters a recovery process, re-ordering its capacities toward new products lines, related to *the needs of the emerging sector of the economy* in this stage of special period, and *exports*. Other activities were incorporated in 1994, such as electronics, information science, recycling and the import – export possibilities in its competent activities, as a consequence of a re-ordain in the state apparatus whose objective was to transfer, on a mid term, the management of economy to enterprises in an important proportion and diminish the leading role of the central organism in an important quantity of decisions that should actually be taken by enterprises themselves.

These years have served to SIME for consolidating and make grow excellent workers' groups, who know their profession, are skilled and able to make our factories work in hard conditions, and will also be capable of making them evolve and develop.

These years have seen incorporating to SIME a large quantity of technicians and professionals, massive entering of university graduates who have enriched the possibilities and potential of its enterprises.

At the moment, the Ministry relies on:

12 Industrial Groups;
178 Enterprises;
6 Research and Development Centers;
4 Associations;
9 Commercial Firms
1 Formation Centers
6 Joint Ventures
4 Economic Associations in Cuba

Total quantity of SIME workers is 62642, 15% of which are professionals.

ACINOX Industrial Group

ALCUBA Industrial Group

CICLEX Industrial Group

DIVEP Industrial Group

GIMAC Industrial Group

Caribbean Ironworks

Raw Material Recovery

Refrigeration and Boilers

BK-CETI Industrial Group

General Machinery

FERROTAINO Industrial Group

UNECAMOTO Industrial Group

MAJOR GOVERNMENT AGENCIES

- Ministry of Sugar (MINAZ)
- Ministry of Agriculture (MINAGRI)
- Ministry of Science, Technology and Environment (CITMA)
- Ministry of Foreign Trade (MINCEX)
- Ministry of Domestic Trade (MINCIN)
- Ministry of Communications (MINCOM)
- Ministry of Construction (MICONS)
- Ministry of Culture (MINCULT)
- Ministry of Economics and Planning (MEP)
- Ministry of Justice (MINJUS)
- Ministry of Labor and Social Security (MTSS)
- Ministry of Education (MINED)
- Ministry of Higher Education (MES)
- Ministry of Finances and Prices (MFP)
- Ministry of the Food Industry (MINAL)
- Ministry of the Basic Industry (MINBAS)
- Ministry of the Light Industry (MINIL)
- Ministry of the Industry of Construction Materials (MIMC)
- Ministry of the Fishing Industry (MIP)
- Ministry of the Iron, Steel, Mechanical and Electronical Industry (SIME)
- Ministry of Foreign Affairs (MINREX)
- Ministry of Public Health (MINSAP)
- Ministry of Transportation (MITRANS)
- Ministry of Tourism (MINTUR)
- Ministry for Foreign Investment and Economic Cooperation (MINVEC)
- Institute of Civil Aeronautics of Cuba (IACC)
- National Institute of Hydraulic Resources (INRH)

- National Institute of State Reserves (INRE)
- National Institute of Sports, Physical Education and Recreation (INDER)
- Cuban Institute of Radio and Television (ICRT)
- Central Bank of Cuba (BCC)

GOVERNMENT AGENCIES SUPERVISING FOREIGN TRADE ACTIVITY

The Cuban State rules and controls foreign trade through the Ministry of Foreign Trade, guiding, controlling and supervising the country's foreign trade activities and those of entities empowered to perform them.

To such ends and with the authorization of the competent organ, it disposes the creation, merger, modification and extinction of foreign trade enterprises, with an independent juridical character and patrimony of its own, granting them faculties to perform export and import operations.

The following institutions participate directly or indirectly in Cuban foreign trade::

- Ministry of Foreign Trade, leading organ of foreign trade activity.
- Central Bank of Cuba, leading institution of the national banking system, which acts as central State bank.
- Ministry for Foreign Investment and Economic Cooperation, in charge of directing and controlling those negotiations related with the investment process.
- Ministry of Finances and Prices, in charge of leading and controlling the State and Government's financial policy.
- General Customhouse of the Republic, entity empowered to enforce the country's customs policy.
- Ministry of Economy and Planning, organ in charge of directing the State and Government's economic policy.
- Ministry of Foreign Affairs, organ in charge of international political relations.
- Chamber of Commerce of the Republic of Cuba, independent agency promoting and cooperating in the development of Cuban external relations.

There are other banking and financial institutions linked to the commercial activity and wich are detailed in the chapter of Banking System.

REGULATIONS

In accordance with the new changes happening in the Cuban economy, in its international economic relations, the experience gathered and the international practice, the Cuban legislation offers by means of the decree No.206 from April 1996 and the resolutions No. 24,25 and 26 from 1997 as a complement to that decree and that were stated by the Minister of Foreign Trade and by means of which possibilities are established that permit a better development of its foreign trade.

To such purposes, the branch offices of foreign mercantile societies and individual entrepreneurs interested in performing trade activities in the Cuban territory may establish themselves in it or be represented by previously authorized national entities, which will act as intermediaries.

Branch offices and agents authorized to act in the national territory must previously obtain the license issued by the National Registry of Branch Offices and Agents at the Chamber of Commerce of the Republic of Cuba, and be entered in the Registry of that organization.

Cuba's great concern for human health and the prevention of animal and plant disease has become evident by the enactment of a number of laws, decrees and regulations for the issuance of the corresponding export or import permit.

Public health regulations for the registration of foodstuffs, cosmetics, as well as personal and household articles The Ministry of Public Health through Instituto Nacional de Nutrici6n e Higiene de los Alimentos establishes the regulations for the registration of foodstuffs, cosmetics and articles for personal and household use consistent with the Cuban standards NC 38-03-06'87 for the import and export of foodstuffs and NC 95-37'87 for perfumes and cosmetics.

The Registry is designed to protect consumers' and users' health and is independent from the Veterinary

Registry for Goods of Animal Origin and the Phitosanitary Registry for Goods of Plant Origin established by the Ministry of Agriculture.

ANIMAL-HEALTH REGULATIONS

Decree-Law No. 137 of April 16, 1993 rules the veterinary activity and establishes the requirements for the export and import of animals and their products. Decree No. 181 of April 17 of the same year provides for transgressions of the law and corrective measures. The National Veterinarian Medicine Institute, under the Ministry of Agriculture, enforces such a legislation.

Animal species, either alive or preserved in any manner; animal-based products for consumption, industrial,decoration, experimental or research purposes; germ or parasitic agents; serum, vaccines, hormones or fermentations of animal origin; culture and diagnostic means using animal-based ingredients, and any item, product or packaging material of any origin that may carry animal diseases are all subject to veterinary control.

Animals and animal-based goods and raw materials destined for export must comply with the registrations established by the veterinary regulations in force as well as those demanded by the competent authorities from the importing country or the international treaties of which Cuba is a party.

In order to guarantee the veterinary conditions of the animals and animal-based goods and raw materials destined for export, the Ministry of Agriculture, through the National Veterinarian Medicine Institute, will issue the corresponding Veterinary Export Certificate.

PLANT HEALTH REGULATIONS

The National Plant Health Center, under the Ministry of Agriculture, is responsible for plant health control. The import and export of plants and related components are regulated by Resolution No. 366 of May 29, 1990, as amended by Resolution No. 45 of October 28, 1994.

Live plant species and related parts, crop and wild-plant seeds, food products of plant origin, both in their natural or semiprocessed form; feed and fodder; forest products; packages and containers that may carry pests; earth, soil or organic fertilizers; raw materials of plant origin; tobacco; organisms or microorganisms hazardous to agriculture and any agent that may act as a disease or pest carrier are all subject to plant-health controls.

Cuba does not apply any import or export license regime, regulations, quotas, etc. which may be obstacles to foreign trade.

All Cuban entities or international associations created under law 77 which have given authority to export or to import by Resolution of the Ministry of Foreign Trade could do operations of foreign trade, for the nomenclature of products listed in said Resolution.

Other regulations in force are those related to the preservation of the national patrimony and drug prohibitions, as well as health regulations and others relative to the preservation of the environment, protection of endangered species and movement of refuse and other dangerous materials beyond the frontier.

INTERNATIONAL ORGANIZATIONS

Cuba is a member state of the World Trade Organization, which became valid on January 1st 1995, as a successor body on the General Agreement on Custom's taxes and Trade.

Among the most important compromises to be fulfilled by Cuba we have the anti-dumping measures, the safeguard to commerce technical obstacles and the implementation of tax reductions.

Cuba's participation in the WHO has generated new obligations, but at the same time permits the defense of the country's commercial interests, and the denunciation of illegal measurements and opposite to the principles and objectives of free trading.

Cuban is also a member of many international agencies among them:

- United Nations Organization (UNO)
- United Nations Conference on Trade and Development (UNCTAD)
- Economic Commission for Latin America
- International Sugar Organization (ISO)
- International Coffee Organization (ICO)
- Wheat International Council (WTC)
- Permanent Court of Arbitration
- Group of Latin American and Caribbean Sugar Exporting Countries
- Universal Postal Union (UPU)
- Non-Aligned Countries Movement
- International Civil Aviation Organization
- World Organization of Industrial Property
- International Standardization Organization (ISO)
- Association of Caribbean States (ACS)
- UNICEF (UN Children´s Fund)
- International Labor Organization (ILO)
- United Nations Economic and Social Council (ECOSOC)
- Latin American Economic System
- International Air Transportation Association (IATA)
- United Nations Food and Agriculture Organization (FAO)
- United Nations Industrial Development Organization (UNIDO)
- United Nations Development Program (UNDP)
- Latin American Energy Organization

- World Health Organization (WHO)
- Pan American Health Organization (PAHO)
- United Nations Educational, Scientific and Cultural Organization (UNESCO)
- International Olympic Committee (IOC)
- International Court of Justice

ECONOMY

After the dissolution of the external economic relations with the socialist block, especially the Soviet Union, as a result of the political changes in those countries, and the tightening of the U.S. embargo on the island, the Cuban economy has gone through a process of transformation in the 90's which has enabled its reentrance in the international economy.

This transformation of the Cuban economy covers all spheres prone to changes.

Great transformations have happened in the spheres of foreign capital, the state no longer runs the monopoly of foreign trade. There are different organizations and types of property; there is now a possibility for the creation of joint ventures with foreign currency and more possibilities for entrepreneurial and territorial management.

The institutional changes carried out include the improvement of organization, direction and planning of the economy, where financial bases prevail.

As a result of these measures in 1994 the Cuban economy stopped its deterioration, and in 1995 the recovery process started, reaffirmed in 1996.

Last year a growth of a 2,5% in the Gross National Product was observed. These figures show comparable results with many Latin American and Caribbean countries.

The projection of The Gross National Product for that year was of a 4%, it was not achieved because of certain factors, such as the low production of the sugar economy, the deterioration of exchange relations as a result of a decrease in the production of that product and a decrease in the international prices for nickel, which are major exports of the economy. On top of that there was a fracture in the external financing due to the Helms Burton Act, damaging the economy. The negative effects of Lili Hurricane were felt, affecting the agriculture, and there appeared a number of plagues in different crops.

Incomes generated by tourism in 1997 increased over a 12% when the number of 1.18 millions of tourists was reached.
For 1998 a GNP increase of 2.5-3.5 is expected, taking into account the foreseen financial unbalance.

Foreign Trade and the economy were seriously affected in the decade of the 90's. One of these factors was the disappearance of commercial relations with the Soviet Union and CAME, what provoked the loss of preferential markets and investment projects, import and export preferential prices, elimination of collaboration agreements, and interruption of essential supplies for the development of the national economy.

On top of this we had the strengthening of the embargo on our island and the approval of the Torricelly and Helms-Burton Acts. As a result of them the access of financial credits to Cuba was limited, as well as commercial operations and foreign investment was being threatened.

The high banking interest rates in an international scale, fluctuations in the currency markets' quotations and the unfavorable alterations of exchange terms internationally were also factors that exerted a negative influence over the economy and its foreign trade.

This group of factors provoked a decrease in our commercial exchange, so the application of measures aimed at the reinsertion of Cuba in the international economy and the reorganization of its external markets was necessary.

The State's monopoly over foreign trade was eliminated with the aim of speeding external commercial activity and foreign investment was promoted because of its capital, technology and market's meaning.

This decentralization process of the Cuban foreign trade allowed for the appearance of state, private and joint enterprises, authorized to perform operations in this sphere, and other foreign enterprises and entrepreneurs were given opportunities to open a branch or to be represented in the country by an agent as well as the establishment of warehouses in free zones and industrial parks in custom's deposits.

An special emphasis has been placed in the strengthening of relations with Latin America and the Caribbean, thus reaching partial agreements with member states of the Latin American Integration Association (ALADI). Other talks have begun with MERCOSUR and is member of the Caribbean State's Association and CARIFORUM. Cuba is working on an agreement with the European Union which enables the development of commercial ties with that organization.

The trend towards recovery in commercial exchange has kept steady since 1995 and in 1997 despite the harsh national financial situation this orientation remained firm.

(Valor en pesos cubanos)

Años	Exportaciones	Importaciones	Intercambio Total	Saldo Comercial
1988	5518.3	7579.8	13098.1	-2071.5
1989	5399.2	8139.7	13538.9	-2740.5
1990	5415.0	7416.6	12831.6	-2001.6
1991	2961.5	4149.0	7110.5	-1187.5
1992	1784.0	2315.0	4099.0	- 537.0
1993	1156.7	2008.2	3164.9	- 851.5
1994	1330.8	2016.8	3347.6	- 538.3
1995	1491.6	2882.5	4374.1	-1390.9
1996(1)	1848.9	3480.6	5329.5	-1631.7
1997(2)	1860.0	4173.2	6033.2	-2313.2
1998(3)	2094.4	4584.3	6678.7	-2489.9

The Cuban economic policy has substantially evolved towards a process of adjustment according to the new circumstances under which its relations develop, the bank system playing a new and important role.

Bearing in mind this reality, the Cuban banking system has entered into an unavoidable process of reforms and decentralization, with the separation of the functions of central and commercial bank which Banco Nacional de Cuba had been conducting and the creation of Banco Central de Cuba as central bank.

In an autonomous form and with independent organization and juridical character, Banco Central de Cuba exerts the ruling, regulating and supervising authority of the financial institutions and of the representative offices established in the country, including the extra-territorial banking center, duty-free zones and industrial parks.

It performs other functions related to those of other countries' central banks.

In the process of reorganization of the national banking system have been conceded new licenses authorizing to different banks to do functions of national banking.

The new banking system is formed by:

- **Banco Central de Cuba (BCC)**, whose functions have already been explained.
- **Cuban National Bank BNC**. It gets and gives credits in national and hard currencies, accepts discounts negotiates and validates in any form exchange letters, checks and other negotiable documents. It keeps the record, control service and attention of the foreign debt contracted with foreign creditors, up to the date of validation of the decree No. 172 from 1997 from the Central Bank of Cuba.
- **International Financing Bank BFI.** It receives and gives deposits in cash at sight or by terms, loans or other forms of financing credits and funds transfer to and from abroad.
- **Commerce and Credit Bank BANDEC.** It performs typical functions of the commercial bank and thus all kinds of operations and businesses of financial mediation.
- **Popular Savings Bank BPA.** It attracts, keeps and receives cash in deposits at sight or by terms in the convenient modalities. It also lends money, credit and financing lines of all types, short medium and long-term, as well as invoices, financial leasing and other financing modalities.
- **Commerce International Bank S.A. (BICSA).** Exchange of hard currency; transfers, common accounts and deposits, deposits by terms and all kinds of document operations.

Within the reorganization process of the Cuban bank, it has also been created the New Bank Group which is made up of the following entities:

- National Financing (FINSA). It performs operations for export financing, imports and investment, leasing factoring and collecting management; forfaiting, financial engineering service and business management.
- Investment Bank S.A. (BI). It performs all kinds of banking businesses, especially those of investment financing and administration; it gets funds and gives credits on its own, or as a trustee agent.
- Exchange Offices (CADECA). It offers services of hard currency or Cuban convertible peso buying or sailing.
- Metropolitan Bank S.A. (BM). It offers normal account services in national currency and in hard currency. Accounts in deposits at a fixed term in hard currency; tax collections, payments sales of traveler's checks and credit cards.

- Trusteeship Companies (TC). Accepts and performs requests of all types given to the company by any person, corporation or judiciary authority, could also be a fiscal agent, testament executor, Judicial Administrator Trustee and other fiduciary activities recognized internationally; inter-enterprises money collections.

Other financial non-banking institutions and not belonging to the Nueva Banca group are:

- Rafin S.A. It finances export operations, imports and investments. Leasing, factoring and forfeiting.
- Finalse S.A. It finances export operations, imports and investment; it performs operations of leasing and invoices, it participates in operations of refinancing debts and it also brings engineering services and business management.
- Fimel S.A. It finances export and import operations, it gives services of financial engineering, business management, it promotes export projects, it serves as a consultant firm in economic financing and statistic matters.
- Panamerican Finance Society S.A.PANAFIN SA. It finances fuel import operations, food and chemicals with incomes coming from export pre-financing. Deals with the contracts necessary to clearly establish its rights and obligations and to guarantee the support of its records. According to the generally accepted principles.

Under the existing legislation there are 12 representative offices of foreign banks in the country, which constitute a relevant promotion and coordination link in the relations with their respective head offices. These banks are:

- The Netherlands Caribbean Bank
- The ING Bank (International Nederlanden Group)
- Havana International Bank Ltd.
- Banco Exterior de España
- National Bank of Canada
- Banco Sabadell
- Fransabank Sal
- Banco Bilbao Vizcaya
- Banco Nacional de Comercio Exterior de Mexico
- INKOMBANK
- Stolichny Bank of Savings

The national currency is the Cuban peso. Since 1993, the US dollar is also in circulation.

The official exchange rate fixed by BCC is 1 Cuban peso = 1 USD.

QUALITY CONTROL

To guarantee the quality of the products that enter or leave the country and the fulfillment of their standards, foreign trade enterprises include in their contracts, supervision of their goods in origin and destination in function of the technical parameters and others requirements to check.

CUBACONTROL's services are offered to more than 144 countries, with permanent offices in Russia and Mexico and itinerant inspectors in other countries, at the request of clients. In 1961, CUBACONTROL signed an agreement with the Societe Generale de Surveillance (SGS) from Switzerland, the leading multinational company in the world for merchandise certification.

Services that offer this enterprise are of inspection, customhouse and transitaries and posses a laboratory duly equipped with trail methods recognized for the executions of analysis to chemical products, fresh and canned goods, alcohol and beverages. Other enterprises offer similar services are ADESA S.A and AISA.

FOREING TRADE.

The Cuban economy and foreign trade were severely affected by a number of events that took place in the nineties. As a result, Cuba lost access to preferential markets and investment projects, to preferential prices for import and export, collaboration agreements were cancelled and supply of essential products for the development of our economy was discontinued.

All that was compounded by the strengthening of the United States embargo against Cuba and the adoption of Torricelli and Helms-Burton acts, which limit Cuba's access to financial credits in international institutions, hinder business transactions and put pressure on potential foreign investors.

Other factors also had serious damaging effects on Cuba's economy and its foreign trade during the nineties, namely, high bank interest rates at the international level, fluctuations in money market quotations as well as an unfavorable change in worldwide exchange terms.

All those factors as a whole caused a decrease in our business exchange. Therefore, it was necessary to take a number of measures intended to reinvigorate our economy with a view to inserting it into the global economy and reorganize our external markets.

For the purpose of facilitating our external trade activity, foreign trade stopped being a State-only function and foreign investment began to be given great support due to its significant contribution to bringing capital, technology and market into the country.

The role played by the Ministry of Foreign Trade of Cuba was reinforced as a leading, executing and monitoring institution for implementing State and Government foreign trade policies. In that respect, the Ministry is intended to guide, control and supervise the country's foreign trade activities and those carried out by authorized entities.

Such a decentralizing process in foreign trade operational management allowed for the establishment of State enterprises and joint ventures, as well as international economic associations having direct access to the overseas market. Foreign companies and businessmen were allowed to open branch offices or have representative agents in Cuba. Furthermore, consignment stocks and bonded warehouses were established and free zones and industrial parks were opened.

Special emphasis has been placed on the strengthening of Cuba's relations with Latin America and the Caribbean. In that respect, Cuba has signed Partial Scope Agreements with most member States of the Latin-American Association of Integration (ALADI), except for Paraguay: Argentina, Bolivia, Brazil, Colombia, Chile, Ecuador, Mexico, Peru, Uruguay and Venezuela.

Once Cuba enters into that Association, our country will have to renegotiate or adapt those agreements to the rules governing for those instruments established among member States, which would imply that concessions would only be granted to signatory countries. Thus, a "4+1" agreement would then be negotiated with MERCOSUR participants.

Cuba has an observer status in the Group of countries associated to the Lomé Convention, an association made up by African, Caribbean and Pacific countries and the European Union, with which we are working in order to sign an agreement that will allow for the development of closer commercial links.

Preliminary figures of our foreign trade activity in 1998 show a decrease in exports estimated at 11%, along with a 6% increase in imports. Those results were given by a number of internal and external factors, namely:

- Growing external financial tension influenced by: a more acute crisis caused by worldwide credit contraction and a price fall in the main Cuban exports;
- Problems relating to the economic embargo and aggression affecting the country;
- Serious damages to agricultural and sugar production due to excess rain, followed by a severe drought. All that was compounded by the damage caused by Hurricane George, which struck the country in September 1998.

Nevertheless, progress has been made in the commercial exchange with other countries. The geographical distribution of trade has radically changed with an increase in the proportional participation of countries. Europe has a 47% share in total commercial exchange, where Spain, Russia, France, Italy and Germany score most highly, followed by America with 37%, where Canada, Venezuela, Mexico and the Netherlands Antilles stand out as our most active business partners in the Hemisphere. Asia follows next with a 14% share.

Export goods have been improved and diversified mainly due to a decrease in sugar production and international prices, but also to an increase in other export items.

The best performing export items in 1998 over 1997 were raw sugar, rolled tobacco, rum, coffee, bottled genuine honey, citrus juice, electric wires and cables, scrap, houses, frozen fish, textiles, some biotechnology pharmaceuticals, medical equipment, cocoa products and bagasse boards.

Non traditional export items have a significant potential, taking into account existing and potential productive capacities. Some progress has been achieved in this area and the country is still working to this end.

Imports in 1998 showed an increase of 6%, as a result of a rise in the price of food, fuels and other raw materials, as well as in those inputs necessary to maintain an economic recovery. That increase in import expenses widened the country's commercial gap, having a negative effect on our foreign debt, along with additional prices that Cuba has to pay to its suppliers and the necessary expenses to reinvigorate our economy.

The decentralization process in foreign trade has continued with a rise in the number of entities separately involved in related activities. Consequently, production has been increasingly linked to international market conditions and new ways of business management have been established.

These changes have brought about a higher share of responsibility of enterprises in the stewardship of resources and closer links to the overseas market.

IMPORT AND EXPORT REGIME.

Cuba does not apply any import or export license regime, regulations or quotas that may hinder foreign trade.

All Cuban entities or international associations established under Act 77 as well as those granted an import and/or export permit under resolution by the Ministry of Foreign Trade for nomenclature of goods listed in said resolution will be able to do foreign trade transactions.

Other regulations in force are those relating to preservation of our national heritage, restraints on drugs, environmental preservation, protection of endangered species, across-the-border movements of waste and other dangerous materials and sanitary regulations.

REGULATIONS FOR THE ESTABLISHMENT OF BRANCH OFFICES AND AGENTS.

The Cuban legislation authorizes, under Decree 206 of April 1996, the establishment of offices by foreign business corporations or individual investors interested in having a branch office in the country for direct management of their business relations with Cuban enterprises and agencies. The above is based on the changes undergone by the Cuban economy in its international economic relations and the experience acquired in international practice.

Those foreign entities or individual businessmen who prefer to have a representative in the country rather than setting an office will need to apply for an agency contract, in order to be represented by a Cuban national entity legally entitled to act as an agent in our country.

Enrollment in the National Registry of Foreign Branch Offices and Business Corporation Agents is indispensable for the establishment of an office in the Republic of Cuba. The document accrediting such enrollment is the license issued by said Registry.

Note: The figures about increase and decrease of exports and its causes were taken from the Statement by José Luis Rodríguez during the second National Assembly Session, Granma newspaper, 23 December 1998.

DUTY FREE ZONES

The development of duty-free zones and industrial parks through foreign investment is an attractive option given Cuba's international communications facilities both by sea and air, geographical location, political and social stability and availability of skilled labor, among other advantages.

According to Decree-Law No. 165 of 1996, any individual or body corporate based abroad or any local body corporate may apply for a concession in respect to a duty-free zone, being committed to start up, operate, develop, maintain, manage and administer this concession.

The National Office of Free Zones of the Ministry for Foreign Investment and Economic Cooperation (MINVEC) is in charge of regulating and controlling the activities of the Duty-Free Zones. Facilities in the duty-free zones will be managed by the operators; i.e. individuals or body corporate based abroad or local individuals or body corporate duly authorized by MINVEC at the proposal of the concessionary. Any individual or body corporate that holds a may also act as an operator.

The duty-free zone operator may obtain approval for the following activities: production, manufacture, finished or semifinished product processing; trading, operations, banking, financial and insurance services; general and technological services, scientific research services, agricultural activities or others to be determined.

The operator may reserve up to 25 percent of productive, manufacturing, processing, trade and agricultural activities to the domestic market. Any higher proportion will require MINVEC approval.

The applicable preferential conditions on customs and taxes are similar to those existing in Latin America and the Caribbean.

Duty-free zones have the advantage that productions from those territories compete with imported ones since they are exempt from taxes, both for the purchase of raw materials and for their exports.

Duty-free zones have the advantage that domestic clients pay no customs tariffs if the product has a national aggregated component exceeding 50percent of its value, where by the cost of salaries, water and energy supply and other services may be calculated within that sum.

Presently there are in operations three industrial parks of the four authorized, one in the Wajay zone and other in Berroa Valley, both in the capital of the island and the third in the Mariel Port of Havana province.

The industrial park of Ciudad de La Habana is managed by Havana in Bond S.A., belonging to CIMEX Corporation, and is located in Berroa Valley, east of Ciudad de La Habana, with an easy access to Havana's port and airport.

TRADEMARKS

The protection of rights on inventions, scientifical discoveries, industrial models, trademarks and trade names, advertising of establishments, commercial slogans as well as the indication of origin and source is regulated by Decree Law No. 68 of May 14, 1983, as amended by Decree Law No. 160 on the application for patents of chemical and pharmaceutical products for agriculture.

Cuba is a member state of the World Organization for Intellectual Property (1975) and it is part of the treaties and agreements which protects these rights which are: The Paris Convention for the Protection of Industrial Property (1904), the Madrid Agreement Concerning the Repression of False Origin Indications in the Products (1905) The Madrid Agreement Concerning the International Register for Trademarks (1989) and the Protocol Concerning The Madrid Agreement on the Trademark International Agreement (1995), the Cooperation Treaty on Patents (1996), and the Lisbon Agreement concerning the protection of original denominations and their International Register (1958), and the Treaty on Trademarks Rights (1997).

PACKAGING

As a member of the World Trade Organization, Cuba is represented in its Committee of Trade Technical Obstacles by the National Standardization Office as competent national entity. This Office also acts as Information Point of the National Information Service on standards, technical regulations and procedures for the evaluation of acceptance (certification, inspection, trials, verification, quality control, among others).

The National Standardization Office represents Cuba in the International Standardization Office, the International Organization of Legal Metrology, the Codex Alimentarius Commission, the Pan American Commission of Technical Standards, the Inter-American Metrology System and the Inter-American Crediting Cooperation.

The implementation of the ISO 9000 standards started in Cuba in 1991. Many of the country's goods and service enterprises are involved in this process.

The ONC is the national certification organ, acknowledged by the Ministry of Economy and Planning.

The National Metrology Service, whose organization and control are conducted by the Office, is based on internationally acknowledged principles and particularly follows the recommendations of the International Organization of Legal Metrology(OIML).

The technical services of standardization, metrology and quality rendered by the Office are commercialized through the Cuban enterprise MACNOR S.A.

LABELING AND PACKAGING

The Cuban standards comply with the international praxis and basic principles on labeling, packing and marking with regard to the required information related to production and expiration dates, composition, marking, etc., with due regard to the ISO standards. The National Packing and Packaging Center is the Cuban entity overseeing this matter within the country on a central basis.

INVESTMENT REGULATIONS

Law No. 77 of September 5, 1995, rules foreign investment in Cuba and therefore has the purpose of promoting and incentivating foreign investment in the national territory, to perform profitable activities contributing to the strengthening of its economic capacity and sustainable development of the country, on the basis of respect to the national sovereignty and independence, and of the protection and rational utilization of natural resources.

Ministry for the Foreign Investment and Economic Collaboration (MINVEC) is charge of controlling negotiations to make the different types of economic associations with foreign participation.

It is possible to invest in all sectors except those of health and education services to the population, and in the armed forces except its entrepreneurial system.

Investments may take the form of mixed enterprises by nominative shares, contract of international association which does not imply the creation of a juridical person other than that of both contracting parties, and enterprises with a totally foreign capital.

Regarding payment of taxes and customs duties, a special regime has been created establishing payment of taxes by mixed enterprises, foreign investors and nationals who are part of international economic association contracts, on income and the use of labor force, as well as the contribution to social security, customs duties and remaining collectable rights in customs, land transportation and documents.

The law authorizes to export the production and import directly everything required for its purposes.

Concerning guarantees, these may include from compensation in case of expropriation to the assurance to the foreign investor of the free transfer of his income abroad.

Likewise, the - having received governmental authorization - may sell or transfer his total or partial participation to the State or to a third party, receiving the corresponding price in convertible currency.

The Cuban State also guarantees the foreign investor the free transfer in convertible currency, without payment of taxes or any other contribution related with that transfer; in the cases of:

- net profits, dividends or payments for expropriation
- his share of the liquidation, upon expiration of the authorization granted for his operations, in any of the investment forms he may be engaged in
- the sale or transfer to a third party of his total or partial participation in the investment.

Cuba has signed 19 promotional bilateral agreements and agreements of reciprocal investment's protection with Italy, Spain, Russia, Colombia, England, China, Ukraine, Bolivia, Viet Nam, Argentina, Lebanon, South Africa, Chile, Rumania, Barbados, Brazil, Federal Rep. of Germany, Greece, Switzerland, Venezuela, Eslovaquia, France, Lao, Ecuador, Cape Green, Jamaica, Namibia, Indonesia, Malaysia, Turkey and Belize.

Also approved and working are 317 associations with foreign capital mainly from Spain, Canada, Italy, France, Mexico, the Netherlands, Venezuela, Argentina, England and Chile in many sectors.

Cuba is a party to multilateral treaties that provide for significant trade rules on certain categories of sensitive products. These treaties include the following:

- Ozone Layer Protection Agreement, its protocol and amendments
- International Agreement on Trade of Endangered Species from the Flora and the Fauna (CITES)
- Basel Convention on Across-the-Border Movement and Disposal of Hazardous Wastes
- United Nations Convention on Illicit Traffic of Narcotics and Psychotropic Substances

AIR SERVICES

42 foreign lines from 3 continents and 26 countries participate in the Cuban market.

Europe: Spain Germany, Switzerland, Italy, Austria, The Netherlands, France, England, Russia, Ukraine, Sweden, Belgium, Denmark, Portugal and Finland.

North America: Canada.

Center and South America: Colombia, Panama, Costa Rica, Guatemala, Ecuador, Mexico, Brazil, Jamaica, West Indies

Africa: Angola

CUBANA AIRLINES. With almost 70 years of operations, it covers a range of 40 international destinies from Europe, America and the Caribbean, together with 15 local points.

AEROCARIBBEAN. This Cuban Regional Airline has over 15 years of experience in the Caribbean, Central America and the North of South America, with charter flights. It transports all kinds of loads with a fleet of Antonov-26 of up to 55 tons and IL-18 of up to 135 tons.

AEROGAVIOTA. Operates routes from Central America and the Caribbean, it takes loads to any destination, in executive-type planes, with a capacity of 40 metric tons in AN-26 and IL-76, 30.

AEROCARIBE. Airline Caribe S.A. C.V., it is the Mexican regional airline, their services are in DC-9. The destination to Cuba reaches a frequency of 4 weekly flights.

IBERIA. 6 weekly frequencies to Havana in Boeig-747, this enterprise offers connections from Madrid to all European capitals and countries from Asia and Africa. It does 312 flights a month non-stop from Spain to America.

AOM. This French airline partenaire de Swissair does 4 weekly flights to Cuba in planes DC-10-30.

Cubana de Aviacion and its cargo division, Cubana Cargo, provide their services all around the world and have established flight connection arrangements with other airlines.

Cubana Cargo has regular flights to Spain, Portugal, France, Italy, Germany, the United Kingdom, Russia, Canada, Mexico, Jamaica, the Dominican Republic, Martinique, Guadeloupe, St. Martin, Panama, Costa Rica, Venezuela, Ecuador, Colombia, Perú, Argentina, Brazil and Chile.

Other air transportation enterprises operating in Cuba appear among the service enterprises in this Directory.

SEA TRANSPORT

In Cuba there is a wide number of entities that are devoted to the international maritime service, which covers all necessary aspects to carry out import and export commercial operations, including insurance.

These companies transport dry and liquid cargoes, refrigerated, loose loads and by containers. They operate with services of regular lines, direct or combined, as well as TRAMP services.

Such firms are:

- Coral Container Lines SA
- Poseidon
- Mar America
- Friomar
- Nexus Reefer
- Melbridge Container Lines
- Nirint Shipping BV
- Acinox Shipping
- Petrocost
- Expedimar SA
- Melfi Marine Corporation SA

- Norstrand Maritime and Trading CO. LTD
- Transcargo International
- Cuflet Chartering
- Naviera Cubalse
- Navegacion Caribe
- Naviera Caribena

There are also entities which act as cargo agents, ship chartering, custom agent, supervisors inspections etc.

- International Supervision Services (Cubacontrol)
- Expedimar SA
- Transcargo Internacional
- Cuflet Chatering
- Transitorios Coral
- Intermar
- Adesa S.A.
- Arandia
- Perez SA
- Marinter SA
- Schenker International
- Servitally

The entities that work as ship consignors and as protector agents are:

- Consignataria Mambisa

- Servimar
- Destino
- Perez SA
- Marinter SA
- Maritima Caribeña

The principals ports of the country are:

- Havana
- Mariel
- Matanzas
- Cienfuegos
- Isabela
- Nuevitas
- Santiago de Cuba
- Antilla
- Felton
- Manzanillo
- Nueva Gerona

In Havana, Cienfuegos, Santiago de Cuba and Antillas there are facilities specialized for the unloading of cereals. There are also facilities specialized for sugar shipping in the ports of Mariel, Matanzas, Cienfuegos, Palo Alto, Guayabal, Carupano, Ceiba Hueca and Boqueron.

Details on the services offered by a group of enterprises:

- **EXPEDIMAR SA.** It gives services of cargo international expedition, ship chartering and cargo agencies to any country. Conventional cargo as wells, in containers or refrigerated. It has a transportation service regular to the Caribbean.
  Teleph. 242440/241881 Fax 240080/ 249472
- **TRANSCARGO.** It performs operations of cargo international maritime transportation according to destination out of regular lines, with trips to the north of Europe and the Mediterranean and it also has a line of containers.
  Teleph. 622425/ 622450 Fax. 338626
- **NEXUS REEFER.** It operates a service of refrigerated cargo with a frequency of two weekly trips to Progreso (Mexico) and another weekly from Santiago de Cuba to Dominican Republic (Boca Chica or Rio Haina). It also offers maritime transportation service between Cuba the Caribbean and Canada.
  Telephone: 629000/ 338448 Fax. 338446/ 338708
- **CORAL CONTAINER LINES SA.** It offers regular lines for Canada, Central America Barcelona, Genoa, where it uses containers with a 600TEUS capacity of 20 and 40 feet. It also offers transferring service by means of subcontracting.
  Telephone: 621071/ 622120 Fax.621867
- **MELFI MARINE CORP SA.** It has regular lines to Panama every 15 days, to Tampico and Veracruz (Mexico) every 10 days, to Progreso right in Mexico every 7 days and to The Dominican Republic every 15 days.
  Telephone: 334263/64 Fax 334265
- **COMPAÑIA TADAY MARINE SA.** Has its own container terminals for dry cargo and refrigerated in Havana and Santiago de Cuba provinces, offering their services to the Mediterranean and American geographical zone.
- **MARAMERICA.** It possesses a regular line Mariel (Cuban western part)-Tampico (Mexico) and it has general cargo ships for chartering operations. It has cement transporters of among 2500 and 5512 t of TDW.
  Telephone: 292076/298077 Fax. 248889
- **NAVEGACION CARIBE.** It offers cargo service to the Caribbean basin, on the basis of time chartering. It has to towed 800t rafts, with a 29-containers capacity (20-40 feet or 1300m3) and two Roll On-Roll Off cement containers.
  Telephone 615611 Fax. 338564
- **PETROCOST.** It operates tankers for liquid cargoes.
  Telephone 616528// 669498
- **NAVIERA POSEIDON.** It operates general cargo ships and performs chartering contracts.
  Telephone: 248887 Fax. 248627
- **NIRINT SHIPPING BV.** It operates ship in the European zone.
  Telephone: 243643/ 802784 Fax. 243332/ 240153
- **FRIOMAR.** It operates refrigerated ships.
  Telephone: 639580 Fax. 335185
- **ACINOX.** It performs trips to Colombia on a monthly basis, Nicaragua, Honduras, Dominica, Haiti and Trinidad and Tobago to Ecuador from time to time, Peru and Chile. It has 5 ships for the services.
  Telephone: 331643-47 Fax. 331648

ENTERPRISE FOR MARITIME WORKS

It possesses 5 ships that operate under the chartering system, three of general cargo and two of 499t asphalt-carrying tanker, dead weight each, though not given to transport for foreign trade, it could be contacted in the case of suing, and negotiable possibilities for the service.

Foreign Shipping enterprises represented in Cuba:

- **MELBRIDGE.** It trasnports merchandise for the north of Europe, being able to widen its service by means of transferring. It has a regular service every 14 days.
  Telephone. 244728 Fax. 244729
- **PEREZ NV.** Maritime transportation service to several destinations.
  Tel. 338224 Fax. 338225
- **MARINTER.** Maritime transportation service to several destinations.
  Tel. 338342 Fax. 338343

PORT SERVICES AND CUSTOMS HANDLING

Port services are offered by the state enterprise Consignataria Mambisa, which in turn subcontracts them from independent suppliers and operators. The service include harbor pilot, loading and unloading, hoisting means, water and fuel supply, health control inspectors, inmigration and others.

Importers are not allowed to conduct customs formalities directly, being obliged to employ a specialized agency or a representative of the importing enterprise, duly trained and registered with the Cuban Customs. There is a minimum tariff for these services.

The list of authorized agencies operating in the country appears in the service enterprises section.(Custom Services)

CUSTOMS

The Customs Tariff of the Republic of Cuba, promulgated by Decree-Law No. 124 of October 15, 1990, has undergone changes which have allowed a substantial reduction of its tariffs and their adequation to the changes occurred in the country's economic policy and reordering of its foreign trade, which include the gradual transfer of that activity to the productive entities.

The Customs Tariff has two columns:

a) the General Tariff (the highest), which is applied to non-member countries of the World Trade Organization, or countries which have not signed bilateral trade agreements with Cuba

b) the Most Favored Nation tariff, which is applied to member countries of the World Trade Organization which have signed bilateral trade agreements with Cuba.

This has brought about changes in the customs tariff structure, contained in the Joint Resolution of the Ministries of Finances and Prices and Foreign Trade, No. 5 of May 17, 1996, which became in force on January 1, 1997.

The changes in the simple tariff averages of the Customs Tariff show the following behavior:

General Column
51.5%
34.0%
23.8%
16.9%
Most Favored Nation

17.0%
14.0%
11.9%
10.7%

In addition, the Cuban customs regime has the following preferential systems:

> *a group of goods from countries making up the Global System of Trade Preferences (SGPC) among developing countries are granted lower customs tariffs than those corresponding to most-favored nation*
>
> *likewise, lower customs tariffs than those corresponding to most-favored nation are granted to products negotiated in the framework of the Agreements of Partial Reach with the member countries of the Latin American Integration Association (ALADI).*

Cuba has signed these agreements with Argentina, Brazil, Colombia, Mexico, Uruguay, Bolivia, Venezuela, Peru and Ecuador. As well as with Chile, waiting to be ratified by that country.

Besides, Cuba is part of the agreements on seeds and cultural goods signed by ALADI member countries, which derogate customs tariffs for these products.

The highest customs tariff in the General Column is 40 percent, and 30 percent in the Most Favored Nation column, which places Cuba at the same level of the Latin American country averages.

With regard to antidumping and compensatory duties and the adoption of safeguarding measures, Cuba abides by the provisions of the World Trade Organization on the subject.

GENERALIZED SYSTEM OF PREFERENCES

Cuba benefits from the Generalized System of Preferences (GSP) in the following countries:

- European Union
- Switzerland
- Hungary
- Norway
- Poland
- Czech Republic
- Bulgary
- Canada
- Japan
- New Zealand
- Australia

From CEI countries preferences are given to Russia, Belarus, Georgia, Ukraine and Kazajastan.

GSP gives Cuban exporters the opportunity to enjoy a preferential customs treatment for the goods covered by this scheme exported to the above markets. The Chamber of Commerce of the Republic of Cuba issues the corresponding certificates of origin (Form A) upon request of Cuban exporters.

From the 15 preferential schemes favoring goods, the most widely used by Cuba is that of the European Union, since this market is a recipient of most of the Cuban exports under this regime.

EXPORT-PODUCTS

Other food products

HARMONIZED SYSTEM CODE	DESCRIPTION
0208.90.	Cocodrile meat
0301.99.	Peces vivos para la alimentación
0302.66.	Anguiles, chilled
0302.69.	Tilapias,and carps, fresh or chilled
0303.76.	Anguiles, frozen
0303.79.	Tilapias and carps, frozen
0304.10/20	Tilapia and carp fillets and other meat, fresh, chilled or frozen.
0306.21.	Lobster, alive, fresh or chilled
0306.23.	Shrimps, fresh or chilled (including culture shrimps)
0409.00.	Natural honey
0504.00.	Guts and other edible offal
0901.21.	Coffee, toasted and grounded
1701.91.	Flavoring blends for beverages (instant soft-drinks)
1806.10.	Chocolate powder
1806...	Chocolate bars and tablets
2007.99.	Fruit pulp
2009...	Juice and concentrate of natural fruits
2201.10.	Bottled mineral water
	Purified and carbonated water
210390	Mayonnaise sauce
2202.10.	Soft-drinks
2203.00.	Beer
220421/29	Wines
	Ham, bacon

LIVE ANIMALS

HARMONIZED	DESCRIPTION

SYSTEM CODE	
0101.11/19	Horses - purebred breeding animals
0102.10.	Bovines - purebred breeding animals (for milk, meat, etc)
0105.91.	Fighting roosters
0106.90.	Fantasy birds (guacamayoes, cockatoos, flamingoes, buzzards)
0106.30.	Laboratory animals
0301.10.	Ornamental fishes

AGRICULTURE AND CATTLE INDUSTRIES

HARMONIZED SYSTEM CODE	DESCRIPTION
0511.10.	Bovine semen
0511.99.	Bovine embryo
0602.20.	Plantain, malanga and other "in vitro" plants
0602.00	Citrus fruit cuttings for graphting
1209.91.	Horticultural seeds (tomatoes, pimentos and others)
1209.99.	Papaya seeds
1209.99.	Citrus fruit seeds
1209.99.	Tropical forest tree seeds
3105.90.	Biofertilizers and organic fertilizers
3402.90.	Detergent citrus fruits washing
3404.00.	Wax for citrus fruits coating
3808.10.	Biological insecticide for mosquitoes
3808.20.	Insecticide against citrus fruit ants
3808.90.	Biological rodenticide and anti-parasites
130190	Natural pine resin
4201.00.	Leather saddles
0505.10	Goose and duck feathers
	Crop protectors and hothouses

	Orange and citron capsular cells

MEDICAL INSTRUMENTS AND EQUIPMENT

HARMONIZED SYSTEM CODE	DESCRIPTION
9018.11	Electrocardiograph (computerized)
9018.19	Ultrasonic system with Elisa techniques
9018.19	Dynamic system for ultrarapid antibiogram
9018.19	Digital electroencephalograph system
9018.19	Digital multimodal avoked potential system
9018.19	Register and processing system for biomedical signals
9018.19	Other laser and ultrasonic medical equipment .
9018.19	External bone fixer (plastic)
9018.90.	Diagnostic equipment and instruments (pipettes, washing pit, etc)

ART AND COLLECTION ARTICLES

HARMONIZED SYSTEM CODE	DESCRIPTION
3706.00.	Cinematographic films
4202.00.	Stamping on fine leather
4303.10.	Leather clothing
4901.10.	Text and children books
4904.00.	Written music
4905.00.	Maps and nautical charts
7118.00.	Collection coins of no legal tender
8524.32.	Compact discs, records and cassettes recorded by cuban artists and musical groups of all genre
8524.32.	Recorded radio programmes
9701/2/3	Works of modern Cuban art and decorative art
9704	Postage stamps for philatelic use, new or canceled from Cuba or abroad
9601	Handicraft of worked bones, tortoise shells and other materials(including miniatures)

FRUITS AND VEGETABLES

HARMONIZED SYSTEM CODE	DESCRIPTION

0701.90.	Potatoes
0709.60.	Pimento
0702 - 09	Other fresh or refrigerated vegetables
0801.11.	Dry coconut
0804.40.	Avocado
0804.50.	Mangoes
0805...	Citrus fruits
0807.20.	Papaya
091010	Ginger

MACHINES AND EQUIPMENT

HARMONIZED SYSTEM CODE	DESCRIPTION
8201...	Agricultural hand tools
8421.22/3	Vacuum rotary filter
8432...	Agricultural machinery- founded and Forged iron And steel products
8438.30	Machinery and equipment for the sugar industry-rolls, spindels cushions, bearings, couplings, transports, condensers etc. Rough machined roller shells Grooved roller shells without shaft and complete with shaft Machine finished roller shafts Rough and machine finished cast iron scrapers Rough and machine finished cast iron trash plate Machine finished mill brass bearings Cast iron mill couplings Pumps for various industrial uses Cane carrier chain Bagasse carrier chain Steam boilers and parts for the same Vacuum pans Evaporators Juice clarifiers Grain crystallisers Seed pans Large vessels Cane carriers, bagasse carriers, sugar belt and grasshopper conveyors Hoppers for sugar, filter cake, etc Sugar cane cutter KTP-3S
8479.10.	Machinery and equipment for the sugar industry-Winches, evaporators, elevators, machinery for the production of dovetail blocks, compacting machine, ceramic and wood saw, etc

ELECTRIC AND ELECTRONIC PRODUCTS

HARMONIZED SYSTEM CODE	DESCRIPTION
8504.10.	Ballast for fluorescent lamps
8544.20.	Electrical and telephone cables and wires
9028.30.	Electricity single-phase meter

INTERMEDIATE PRODUCTS

HARMONIZED SYSTEM CODE	DESCRIPTION
7408.11.	Copper wire 8 mm.
	Aluminum framework (doors, windows, etc)

OTHER INDUSTRIAL PRODUCTS

HARMONIZED SYSTEM CODE	DESCRIPTION
3304.00	Medicinal mud and water beauty products for care of the skin
3401.11/19	Toilet and washing soap
340220	Detergents
3922/23/24	Plastic products (multipurpose containers, buckets, brooms and brushes, absorbents, PVC and polyethylene pipes, etc)
3925/26	Plastic water tanks and boothes, with all the components, like electricity and water installations etc.
3925/26	Velum leather for musical instruments
4520..	Humidity control cases for cigar storing
4819.50.	Egg trays
6403.59.	All leather shoes
6406.99.	Leather soles
6908.10.	Bricks and paving tiles of acid resistant ceramic
6909.19/90	Ceramic products for technical use (rasching, leasing rings, etc)
6912.00.	Ceramic plates and other table service pieces
6913.90.	Ornamental ceramic
7017.00.	Laboratory glass ware
7615.00.	Kitchen and other household or hotel articles of aluminum (including pressure cooker), teflon pans.
8303.00.	Safe and strong-boxes, individual and wall fitting.
8480.00.	Molds and headers or shapers
9017.20.	Drawing and designing instruments
9306.00.	Cartridges caliber 5.6 and 12/16 for hunting
9403.20.	Stainless steel equipment for gastronomy, tourism and hospitals
9403.50/60	Wooden style furniture
94.03.30/40/50	Wooden furniture for all uses
94.03.70.	Plastic furniture reinforced with fiberglass

9403.80.	Rattan Furniture
9405.10/20	Decorative lamps
9502.10.	Dolls
9503...	Didactic toys
9506.99.	Sport articles for boxing, softball and baseball

MEDICAL PRODUCTS

HARMONIZED SYSTEM CODE	DESCRIPTION
3001.90	Natural pulmonary surfactant
3002.10	Blood products:Human Albumin Inmunoglobulin, etc.
3002.20	Human vaccines: Diphteria-Tetanus Leptospirosis Becterian polivalent
	Anti-hepatitis B recombinant
3002.20	Antimeningococcicus
3002.20	Other common monovalent and polivalent vaccines
3002.30	Veterinary vaccines, Anti PVC (anti parvovirus canine)
3002.30	Viral encephalomiocarditis (for pigs)
3002.30	Anti coccidiosis (for poultry)
3002.30	Other veterinary vaccines: (tetanus toxoid, Inactivated Aujeszky, Brucela, Symptomatic carbunco, pig cholera, contagious ectyme, equine encephalomielitis, canine hepatitis, leptospirosis, etc.
3002.90	Hiperimmune Gamma anti PVC (Parvovirus Canino)
3004.90	Streptokinase (recombinant)
3004.90	Epidermal growth factor
3004.90	Human trasfer factor
3004.90	Interferons
3004.90	Therapeutical Monoclonal antibodies (specially for kidney transplant)
3004.90	Citostatics, cephalosporines, antiarthritics, antiulcersand others
3004.90	Other therapeutic medicaments and dietetical supplements
3004.90	Hipocholesterolemic (PPG)
3004.90	Antivitilige
3004.90	Natural antiseptic healing for veterinary use
3004.90	Anti-mastitis (veterinary use)

3004.90	Natural antidiaharrea bulbs (for new born pigs)
3005.90	Plaster of Paris
3006.60	Oral contraceptives
3821.00	Culture means
3822.00	Monoclonals antibodies for diagnosis, purification, cell identification and lab investigation.
3822.00	Diagnostic kit for vaginal Candisiass, Trichomoniasis y Gerdnerella vaginales
3822.00	Diagnostic for VIH 1 y 2
3822.00	Other kits of diagnosis means
3822.00	Diagnostic kits for veterinary and agricultural desease detection

CONSTRUCTION INDUSTRY PRODUCTS

HARMONIZED SYSTEM CODE	DESCRIPTION
2522.00.	Calcium carbonate
5984.81/82	Sanitary hardware and fittings
6810.19.	Tiles, flagstone, bricks and similar cement or concrete articles
6810.91.	Rail concrete ties
6810.91.	Prefabricated structural components made from wood for houses
6905.10.00	Roofing tiles
6908.10.00	Glazed ceramic tiles or mosaics
6910.10.00	Sanitary furniture and accessories
7207.19/20	Corrugated steel bars and others
7214.20.	Corrugated steel bars and others
7218.99	Carbon stainless billet
9406.90.	Prefabricated structural components of concrete for houses
9406.90.	Low-cost building-material made from ecomaterial

TEXTILE PRODUCTS

HARMONIZED SYSTEM CODE	DESCRIPTION
5208/09	Unbleached woven fabrics of 100% cotton (including those for tablecloth, curtains, sheets, etc)
6114.20/90	Pullovers and other products with serigraphy images
6301.40.00	Linen clothes, docker trousers, pyjamas, socks

OTHER SERVICES

HARMONIZED SYSTEM CODE	DESCRIPTION
	Minting any kind of coins
	Postage stamp printing
	Medical services in specialized clinics and hospitals Ophthalmic Surgery Centre for Pigmentary Retinosis Neurological Restoration Centre Placental Histotherapy Centre Orthopedic, Pediatric and Gynecobstetric Specialized Centres
	Spare parts recuperation service for rail and shipping transport
	Recuperation and automatization service for machinery tool
	Aircraft reparation and maintenance service
	Naval reparation and maintenance service
	Designs for vessels' construction, reconstruction and repair
	Design development for construction and repairing of shipyards
	Marines construction
	Construction of fishing centres
	Designs and development of equipment and systems for the fish-processing industry
	Port dredging service
	Yacht building according to orders
	Designs of coast works
	Reproduction of publicity images in posters, serigraphy and other types of promotional articles.
	Serigraphy service
	Tampography service
	Musical shows (soloists and groups of all genre)
	Sport training service
	Low-cost appartment construction made from ecomaterial
	Freighter frozen cargo service to all the world
	Fishing agreements
	Frozen cargo storing capacity for handling and distribution
	Designs in health and sport branches: Hospitals, rehabilitation centres, sports and physical culture centres.

TRANSPORT

HARMONIZED	DESCRIPTION

SYSTEM CODE	
8409/8708	Cars and spare parts
8609.00.	Containers 20' y de 40' new and recuperated
8711.00.	Motorcycles
8712.00.	Bicycles
8902.00.	Fishing boats of small and medium sized
8903.00.	Sport boats

AGRICULTURAL TECHNOLOGIES

HARMONIZED SYSTEM CODE	DESCRIPTION
	Feasibility studies of soil, agroindustry diagnosis, equipment assembly and installing, post sale services, automation and reparation in all that concerns sugar industry
	Micropropagation of plants "in vitro"
	Technology to avoid deterioration of sugar cane
	Technology to obtain biofertilizer and fodder from sugar industry wastes
	Production and conservation of animal feeding products
	Machanization of green sugar cane harvest
	Forest consulting programmes
	Technology for poultry and birds viral sickness diagnosis
	Technology for the use of germoplasma of different species
	Application of biotechnology to vegetables and fruits improvement
	Non conventional pork feeding
	System for the genetic improvement of porks
	System for pork residue treatment
	Earthworm breeding for animal feeding
	Projects for citrus fruit plantation founding
	Citric packing industry project
	Technical assistance in the administration and exploitation of citrus fruit plantation and agricultural plantations in general.
	Training programmes in citrus fruits techniques
	Disease diagnosis and phytosanitary measures handling
	Whole plants and equipment installation services in citrus industry

INDUSTRIAL TECHNOLOGIES

HARMONIZED SYSTEM CODE	DESCRIPTION
	Social interest construction technologies
	Production technologies for glucose-fructose, tensoactives, inverted syrups enzimatique means, anticorrosives, printing paper and pulp.
	Other sugar industries technologies- bagasse drying, rum's rapid aging, residues treatment.

OTHER NATURAL PRODUCTS

HARMONIZED SYSTEM CODE	DESCRIPTION
0510.00.	Propoleo tincture
0510.00.	Apicultural diet supplements
0510.00.	Shark cartilage for diet supplement in form of dry powder or pills
0510.00	Bee poison
1211.90	Spirulina extracted from algae as a diet supplement
	Diet supplement (Estimulante PV-2)
	Diet supplement (Bioestimulín)
	Diet supplement (Ferrical)

OTHER PRODUCTS NOT CLASSIFIED

HARMONIZED SYSTEM CODE	DESCRIPTION
	Lactoperoxidasa system activator for the conservation of milk
	Braille module and other means for teaching blinds
	Diverse softwares and multimedia products
	Veterinarian biotechnological modules (bioterium, vivarium, etc)
	Educational programmes for technical and professional specialization in different branches of the agriculture and animal raising techniques
	Post-graduate and specialization programmes for medical science
	Post-graduate and summer school programmes on all university specialties, scientific, consultancy, projects and services, international events, guided scientific tours, etc.

CUBA EXPORT PRODUCTS

HARMONIZED SYSTEM CODE	DESCRIPTION

0208.90.	Cocodrile meat
0301.99.	Peces vivos para la alimentación
0302.66.	Anguiles, chilled
0302.69.	Tilapias,and carps, fresh or chilled
0303.76.	Anguiles, frozen
0303.79.	Tilapias and carps, frozen
0304.10/20	Tilapia and carp fillets and other meat, fresh, chilled or frozen.
0306.21.	Lobster, alive, fresh or chilled
0306.23.	Shrimps, fresh or chilled (including culture shrimps)
0409.00.	Natural honey
0504.00.	Guts and other edible offal
0901.21.	Coffee, toasted and grounded
1701.91.	Flavoring blends for beverages (instant soft-drinks)
1806.10.	Chocolate powder
1806...	Chocolate bars and tablets
2007.99.	Fruit pulp
2009...	Juice and concentrate of natural fruits
2201.10.	Bottled mineral water
	Purified and carbonated water
210390	Mayonnaise sauce
2202.10.	Soft-drinks
2203.00.	Beer
220421/29	Wines
	Ham, bacon

CENTER FOR EXPORT PROMOTION OF CUBA (CEPEC)

CEPEC offers specialized services to exporters of goods and services, particularly to small and medium enterprises, in order to create a space for them in the international market which contributes to the promotion, development and diversification of the Cuban export offer.

With that purpose, it carries out activities such as the spreading of information on the export offer, market research, consultant services to Cuban enterprises for the development of new items, creation of promotion programs, organization of trade missions and search of trade information.

CEPEC also participates in both domestic and international fairs, offering trade information services and professional assistance in market and promotion techniques to the Cuban enterprises, as well as promoting trade contacts with foreign firms.

Special emphasis has been placed on the Caribbean Fairs, which should be the most important trading partner for Cuba, participating there not just as a promoter of Cuban trade but also representing small enterprises, helping to identify potential clients and presenting their promotional materials. The results of these contacts are transmitted to the interested enterprises in order to give answers to the offer and information requests.

CEPEC has developed direct relations with the enterprises, allowing a wide spreading of their offers, according to their commercialization policy and target markets, based on their relations with trade promotion organs in developing or underdeveloped countries, by inserting the offer in specialized publications and using importer data bases.

The Center has been fostering international relations with similar entities and with imports promotional centers from European countries, Canada and Japan. These ties favor the acquisition of valuable information, on exportable offer among the foreign importing firms as well as the necessary information for trade development.

The canalization of trade opportunities detected in the provinces of the country allow to expand the possibilities of Cuban trade, specially of the new export products whose insertion to the exportable offer constitutes an essential element in the economic development of the country.

CEPEC' direct work with the export goods manufacturers allows the detection of their export potential and production obstacles, advising ways and forms to solve them in order to make their products comply with the requirements of the international markets.

Though recently created (1995), CEPEC carries out market research and is in charge of trade information since 1976, when was create. A considerable number of product and country market studies contain recommendations which have proven very useful when placing Cuban products in the market, since they have enabled the identification of trade opportunities as well as the regulations to be complied with and the intrinsical and apparent characteristics required of products to win a space in those markets.

Although the Center does not work with imports, it may render services to foreign enterprises wishing to sell their products in the Cuban market or invest in the country, since it has importer databases. Any Cuban exporting or importing enterprise may address CEPEC to identify trade opportunities.

PRACTICAL INFORMATION FOR BUSINESS AND INVESTMENT ACTIVITY

STARTING BUSINESS

To do business with the country, you should:

Identify the sector or sectors of interest (goods or services).
Exchange interests with those authorized to engage in foreign trade and foreign investment entities:
Importers and / or exporters belonging to many of these industry groups.
Joint ventures authorized to directly import or export their inputs and outputs.
Producing and service companies with interests in association with foreign capital.
Foreign branches facilitate contacts, but do not sign contracts.
Order a business visa at the Cuban consulate of the country of origin. Do not use a tourist visa in business.

INVESTING AND TRADING: POLICY AND LEGAL FRAMEWORK

In 1982, Decree Law 50 was enacted as Cuba's first foreign investment act in order to promote investment in Cuba. However, Law 50 was very vague and did little to facilitate investment. After the fall of the Soviet Union the Cuban government worked toward increasing investment and in 1995 the National Assembly approved Law 77, or "Ley de la Inversion Extranjera" (The Foreign Investment Act). Under this law three kinds of foreign investments are allowed: international association contracts, joint ventures(which can be entirely foreign-owned), and totally foreign-owned companies. Foreign investments must be approved by a government commission of the Council of Ministers. Certain investments must be approved by the Council of Ministers' Executive Committee, including Investments larger than $10 million US dollars, investments entirely under foreign ownership, investments that involve a foreign country, investments that use natural resources, and investments that involve government property or are in special sectors. Decisions for approval of foreign investments are given within 90 days.

Law 77 maintains that investors are guaranteed the ability to transfer profits to foreign countries, the right to transfer or sell shares, and no expropriation unless under extreme circumstances in which case compensation would be given. Additionally, it provides protection against third party claims under Cuban law. Moreover, Law 77 approves the creation of duty-free zones and industrial parks open to foreign investment. Though law 77 set up a special system covering each aspect, Law 165, enacted in 1996, created more flexible investment rules for free trade zones and industrial parks. Finally, it enables foreigners to gain ownership and property rights over real estate in Cuba. However, the real estate investments are limited to the development of the tourism sector, foreign company housing or offices, and other living structures dedicated to private residences or private tourism activity for temporary residents.

Other relevant Cuban laws include Decree Law 124, which define Cuba's tariff system by outlining the conditions for import permits, by establishing import tariffs and by creating the procedures for custom clearance as well as Decree Law 162, which discusses the functions of the customs system.

In order to legally export products to Cuba you must first obtain authorization from the Commerce Deptartment's Bureau of Export Administration. The applications are submitted electronically. Once approved, commerce export licenses are valid for 24 months. Exporters may bundle a few transactions under one license and all transactions must be paid in advance of export and in U.S. dollars.

For further information refer to the Export Administration Regulations or for guidance on specific license applications you may contact the US Commerce Department's Office of Strategic Trade & Foreign Policy Controls, Bureau of Export Administration. You can also contact the US State Department's Office of Cuban Affairs, Bureau of Inter-American Affairs as well as contact the US Treasury Department's Office of Foreign Assets Control.

In 1988 a new stage opened when the first joint venture was created between a Cuban enterprise and a Spanish company with the purpose of building a hotel in the tourist resort of Varadero on the basis of Decree-Law No. 50 of 1982.

From 1991 to 1994, foreign investment was accelerated as one of the important steps taken by the Cuban authorities to recover from the serious impact to the Cuban economy caused by the disappearance of the Soviet Union and the economic links with other Socialist countries in the framework of the Council of Mutual Economic Aid (COMECON). This impact resulted in the loss of 35% of Cuba's GDP in the first three years of the nineties with strong economic and social effects. From 1997 on, foreign investment further expanded and more complex deals were agreed with important partners in newly opened sectors.

At the present time, this activity is promoted by Law 77, the Foreign Investment Act, approved by the National Assembly on September 5, 1995. It stipulates that foreign investment should contribute to strengthening the country's economic capacity and sustained development, on the basis of respect for national sovereignty and independence, and the protection and rational use of natural resources.

This new legislation offers more guarantees, greater security and new benefits for the investor, as well as providing a more significant opening in various economic sectors, where associations with foreign capital can be constituted.

The opening is oriented toward meeting specific needs within the Cuban economy, among them: export diversification, in terms of quality and quantity; the acquisition of raw materials; the need for new capital; insertion into new markets; the acquisition of advanced technologies; and the introduction of more modern economic management practices.

Foreign investment, which rose from less than $100 million USD in 1990 to more than $2.1 billion in 1995, now plays an important role in the search for the markets, technology and financing that disappeared simultaneously with the collapse of the socialist bloc.

In addition to the benefits previously mentioned, the process of opening up to foreign investment in Cuba has played a complementary role to national efforts to maintain capitalization in those economic branches that offer the largest rate of return. Even in sectors such as tourism, where foreign capital has been present since its current stage of development began, it is calculated that only 20 % of the investments in new capacities has been financed by foreign partners.

Neither can it be said that in Cuba the foreign investment opening is part of an ongoing privatization process. Certainly economic association with foreign capital supposes that certain assets are no longer state property, at least for as long as the agreement is in effect, which is generally long-term. But, as Minister of the Economy and Planning José Luis Rodríguez recently stated, national policy is aimed at defending the prevalence of state property in all forms of joint ventures and only accepting a majority investment or 100 % foreign control in justified cases.

Foreign capital represents barely 3 % of the gross domestic product, and the work force employed in this sector is approximately 5 % of the country's total.

Cuba has signed bilateral investment promotion and reciprocal protection agreements with 18 countries: Italy (1993); Argentina (1995); Russia (1993); Lebanon (1995); Spain (1994); South Africa (1995); Colombia (1994); Romania (1995); United Kingdom (1995); Chile (1996); China (1995); Barbados (1996); Ukraine (1995); Greece (1996); Bolivia (1995); Germany (1996); Viet Nam (1995); Switzerland (1996).

The evolution of economic associations with the foreign capital has had several phases. The first one went from the emergence of the first association up until September 1991, when there were still very few associations and they consisted of small and medium-sized companies, aimed at braking the drop of global indicators.

Between that date and 1993 there were no significant variations, although more than 60 entities of that kind were constituted. Starting in September 1994, a new wave of joint ventures emerged, mainly in services, housing construction, real estate and telecommunications, and at that point associations were allowed in all the productive branches of the country. At that time, companies with great prestige and international ranking, mainly European, began to do business on the island.

In this process, ever increasing interest has been expressed by entrepreneurs from United States. Consultancies such as the U.S.-Cuba Trade and Economic Council, Inc., with headquarters in New York, have experienced significant growth in their membership since that Cuban legislation went into effect.

In recent years several Cuba-United States business encounters have taken place, with the participation of executives and representatives of major international companies such as Mobil Oil Corporation, Texaco Inc., Bristol Myers Squibb Co., Pharmacia and Upjohn Co., Continental Grain Co., Wyeth Ayerst International Inc., Caterpillar Inc. and Lincoln Property Co.

Economic associations with foreign capital have grown steadily, going from 20 in 1990 to 260 in 1996 and 317 in 1997. At the present time, there are a total of 332. Since the beginning, only 63 have been dissolved, for various reasons. In 1998, 74 % of the associations with foreign capital were concentrated in six sectors: basic industry, tourism, light industry, the food industry, construction and agriculture.

The most far-reaching agreements are those established in telecommunications, the nickel industry, tourism and petroleum exploration and extraction. Prospects in tourism are very positive and Cuban authorities plan to continue creating new capacities and remodeling existing facilities. The most recent additions to the regulations promoting foreign investment were the Duty-Free Zones and Industrial Parks Act and the new tariff system, which went into effect on July 1, 1996.

Furthermore, there are three duty-free zones functioning in the country: Berroa and Wajay, in City of Havana, and Mariel, in La Habana province. By late 1997, a total of 190 operators had been authorized to do business in the duty-free zones, 140 of them commercial

Today, investors from 46 countries operate in almost 400 ventures in 32 sectors of the Cuban economy; 52 % of those investors are from European Union countries: 24% from Spain, almost 15% from Italy, 4% from France, 3.5% from the United Kingdom. Tourism, Oil and Gas, Mining,Energy and Telecoms are the main sectors of investment. Thus, foreign direct investment, focused on the search for new external markets, competitive technologies and financing (mainly long term) has played an important role in the country's economic recovery.

Cuba is located in a region whose share in world investment flows is rapidly growing. This, together with the country's potential and prospects for attachment to the Latin American integration process, makes hundreds of business people contact the Economic Office of the Cuban Embassy in London in search for information about investment opportunities.

Foreign investment is not associated to a privatisation process in Cuba; it is rather focused on specific objectives that complement national development efforts. Hence it is important to note what those objectives are and and the space they offer for foreign capital involvement.

In 1992, the National Assembly of the People's Power (Cuba's Parliament) approved a number of ammendments to the Constitution of the Republic with a view to recognising forms of ownership other than the State ownership.Joint ventures were legalised and FDI-associated aspects defined. The latter include: the recognition by the Cuban State of the assets of legally constituted joint ventures and economic partnerships, and their use, enjoyment and disposal shall be governed by the provisions of the law and treaties, as well as by their own by-laws and rules.

A new Foreign Investment Legislation (Law No.77) was passed in 1995. This legislation is in line with international practice. Some of the regulations thereof are:

Ø Foreign investment in Cuba may adopt the form of: a Joint Company, an Economic Association Contract or a Wholly-owned Foreign Company -where the investor is acknowledged full conduction of the company and enjoyment of all rights, as well as the responsibility for all the obligations stipulated in the authorisation

Ø The authorisation of investments in Cuba is a faculty of the State. There are two organs empowered to grant authorisations: the Executive Committee of the Council of Ministers and a Government Commission appointed by that Council, according to the case.

The procedure to obtain the authorization results from a previous negotiation between the national investor and the foreign investor, in the case of a joint venture of a contract of international economic association, or between the foreign investor and the ministry in charge of the corresponding branch, sub-branch or economic activity in which the investment is to be carried out, which is the case of a company totally of foreign capital. Both parties, the national and the foreign investor, will submit the corresponding application to the Ministry for Foreign Investment and Economic Cooperation (MINVEC) to examine and channel the proposal for final approval. Once the required economic and legal documentation on the proposed business has been prepared and submitted to MINVEC, the decision denying or approving such foreign investment is handed down within a period of 90 calendar days.

Ø Some of the guarantees granted to investors, as provided for in the Law include:full protection and security; their asset cannot be expropriated, save cases of extreme social interest, in which case prior compensation to be paid; tax-free freely transfer of their dividends; right to sell or transfer, subject to prior authorisation by the Government, their shares.

Ø Foreign investors can directly export and import whatever is necessary for their purposes.

Ø A special taxation regime provides for:

. the application of a 30% net profit tax and,

. the application of a 11% payroll tax and 14% as a employer's contribution to social security which apply to the total wages and other income that may be received by workers of the entity except those granted as economic stimulation.

Ø Authorisation for the establishment of duty free zones and industrial parks in properly delimited regions within the Cuban territory.

Ø Foreign investment in Cuba has increased.Today almost 400 joint ventures are operating in the country , with a strong presence in sectors such as mining, oil prospecting and extraction, tourism, industries and telecommunication. Lately other ventures and negotiations have expanded in new sectors, such as power generation by natural gas, expansion of the cities domestic gas supplies, etc.

Ø Investors from more than 40 countries have placed their capital in Cuba. Outstanding among them are: Spain, Canada, Italy, France and the United Kingdom.

The Economic Office of the Cuban Embassy in London can help with the general and specific information that may be necessary to participate in the Cuban foreign investment procedure: including the organisation of contacts, meetings or other arrangements with Cuban officials or possible counterparts which could facilitate British investment.

CUBA'S COMPARATIVE ADVANTAGES FOR FOREIGN INVESTMENT
Cuba's comparative advantages for foreign investment include the following:

Ø A highly skilled labor capable of assimilating, in a short period of time, any new technology;

Adequate infrastructure; 95% of the national territory is electrified; additionally, the country's basic infrastructure in terms of power generation and distribution, oil extraction, prospection and refining, and communications, has remained and even developed supported by foreign investment.

Ø Social stability and safety climate for foreign investors;

Ø Bilateral agreements on promotion and reciprocal protection of investments entered into with more than 50 countries, and 5 agreements for the avoidance of double taxation, while others are being negotiated.

FREE ZONES AND INDUSTRIAL PARKS
After approval of Law No.77 of Foreign Investment, Decree Law No. 165 on Free Zones and Industrial Parks was issued on June 22, 1996. This legislation defines Free Zones as areas within the national territory, duly limited, without a resident population , of free import and export of goods, not linked to the customs boundaries. Industrial, trade, agriculture, technological and services activities will be allowed in this area under application of a special regime.

This special regime is concerned with regulations relative to the customs, banking, tax, labour, migratory and public order systems, less burdensome and strict than the ordinary regulations, as shown below:

Customs regime:

- It rules the total exception of custom duties and other duties to be collected by customs for the introduction of goods destined to the development of the authorized activities;

Tax regime:

- For concessionaires and operators of productive activities there is total exemption of income taxes and taxes for the use of labor force, for a period of 12 years, and a bonus of 50% for another 5 years.

- In the case of operators of trade and service activities, the total exemption of the above mentioned taxes will be for 5 years, and the 50% bonus for another 3 years.

- More favorable exemptions may be granted after particular analysis of each case, and the terms may be extended.

Concessionary:

Promotes and develops with his own resources the necessary infrastructure for the operation of the duty free zone and assumes or delegates its management.

Operator:

Is authorized to establish himself in the duty free zone in order to carry out production, trade or service activity.

Banking and financial regime:

- The possibility exists of establishing banking and financial services if the license is previously obtained from Banco Central de Cuba;

- The capital obtained from operations may be freely transferred abroad; and

Labor regime:

- The Ministry of Labor and Social Security will determine the minimum salaries.

- The concessionary of mixed capital may act as employing entity to engage his workers and those required by the operator. The concessionary of wholly foreign capital will engage the workers through an entity proposed by the Ministry for Foreign Investment and approved by the Ministry of Labor and Social Security.

Other incentives of the Cuban legislation are the following:

- It creates a system that allows the investor to perform any application or handling before state entities or institutions through a sole point or Central Office at the Free Zone.

- It allows the operator to allocate up to 25% of the goods resulting from his activities in the domestic market.

- For reasons of availability of labor force, transportation or handling of raw materials, the operator may be authorized to perform specific activities outside the duty free zone area.

- Both concessionaires and operators may purchase goods and services offered by the country's enterprises outside the area where they are established. In this regard, a program of cooperation between the industries located in the duty free zone and the national industry is being drawn up.

These regulations are applicable to concessionaries and operators of free zones as incentives for investment.

There are 3 zones operating: Berroa and Wajay, both in the City of Havana, and Mariel in the Province of Havana, with 365 authorised operators.

THE MINISTRY FOR FOREIGN INVESTMENT AND ECONOMIC COOPERATION

The Ministry for Foreign Investment and Economic Cooperation (MINVEC) is the Central Administration Agency of the Cuban Estate responsible for governing and controlling the foreign investment process and the development of Free Zones and Industrial Parks. It is also in charge of preparing the relevant legislation in this field.

Its main functions include:

Ø Promotion of inward and outward foreign investment;

Ø Guiding the negotiation process for the establishment of economic associations or any other forms of foreign investment;

Ø Assestment of compliance with the bases and principles set forth for economic associations between Cuban and foreign entities;

Ø Implementation of the economic cooperation policy; governing and controlling the development of the technical assistence provided to and by the country;

Ø Preparation, negotiation and signing of agreements and conventions entered into with official foreign institutions dealing with foreign investment.

THE INVESTMENT PROMOTION CENTRE

The Ministry for Foreign Investment has, since 1994, its own Investment Promotion Centre (CPI) which is responsible for promoting the existing business opportunities for foreign capital involvement in Cuba, as well as overseas investment by Cuban companies.

Main services provided by CPI include:

Ø Provision of up-to-date information on the country, foreign investment regulations, and opportunities for foreign investment involvement in the domestic economy;

Ø To arrange meetings with would-be Cuban partners for foreign investors interested in investing in Cuba;

Ø To prepare for business delegations the required program of meetings with Cuban agencies and entities, as well as to organise tours to places of business interest;

Ø Provision of information on investment-aid programmes that may favor investment flows into Cuba;

Ø Organising investment seminars, lectures, meetings, events and fora, both in Cuba and abroad;

Ø Making consultations within Cuba or from abroad in connection with the feasibility of any investment project in particular;

Ø Provision of up-to-date information to the business press and international institutions that contribute to promote investment;

Ø Overseas promotion of investment by Cuban companies with comparative advantages.

To render such services, CPI relies on a highly qualified staff composed of updated experts with broad knowledge and skills on business promotion techniques used at international level and for the carrying out of opportunity-prefeasibility studies. This group of experts works jointly with national organisations and entities in defining projects for foreign capital involvement.

CPI is a member of the Geneva-based World Association of Investment Promotion Agencies (WAIPA), under the auspices of UN

EXPORTS AND REEXPORTS TO CUBA, IRAN, LIBYA, AND SUDAN UNDER THE TRADE SANCTIONS REFORM AND EXPORT ENHANCEMENT ACT

Summary: On July 12, 2001, the Bureau of Export Administration (BXA) and the Department of the Treasury's Office of Foreign Assets Control (OFAC) published regulations implementing certain provisions of the Trade Sanctions Reform and Export Enhancements Act of 2000 (TSRA) (Title IX of Public Law 106-387). The regulations went into effect on July 26, 2001 and both agencies have instituted procedures that will allow U.S. exporters and reexporters in other countries to engage in certain transactions that are subject to TSRA. BXA implemented the requirements of TSRA for exports and reexports of agricultural commodities to Cuba. BXA created License Exception Agricultural Commodities (AGR) to permit such exports and reexports to Cuba. Exports and reexports of medicines and medical devices to Cuba are not eligible for AGR, but are eligible for existing BXA license application procedures. OFAC regulates exports of agricultural commodities, medicines, and medical devices to Iran, Libya, and Sudan.

Explanation of

License Exception Agricultural Commodities (AGR)

TSRA Eligible Agricultural Commodities

TSRA Eligible Medicines and Medical Devices

BXA's Prior Notification Procedures under License Exception AGR

Commodity Classification Requirements

Summary of BXA Requirements for Treasury Department authorized Exports to Iran, Libya, and Sudan

Frequently asked Questions

LICENSE EXCEPTION AGRICULTURAL COMMODITIES (AGR):

The Bureau has created a new License Exception Agricultural Commodities (AGR) in section 740.18 of the Export Administration Regulations (EAR) .

License Exception AGR authorizes exports and certain reexports of eligible agricultural commodities that are classified as EAR99 (i.e., not listed on the Commerce Control List) to Cuba, subject to certain criteria and restrictions.

License Exception AGR does not authorize exports or reexports of medicines or medical devices to Cuba.

Exporters must notify BXA and obtain confirmation from BXA that no agency of the U.S. Government that reviews these notifications objects to use of License Exception AGR prior to any export or reexport under authority of License Exception AGR. The proposed export must meet all of the criteria and restrictions listed below.

Exports and reexports must be made pursuant to a written contract and must take place within 12 months of the signing of the contract, unless the shipment is a commercial sample or a donation, in which case the contract requirement does not apply.

No exports may be made to a terrorist entity, including a Specially Designated Terrorist (SDT) or Foreign Terrorist Organization (FTO), a person denied export privileges by the Department of Commerce if the export would violate the terms of the denial order, or for use in weapons of mass destruction (WMD) programs (i.e., biological, chemical, nuclear warfare or missile proliferations activities). The Treasury Department's Office of Foreign Assets Control lists of SDTs and FTOs as part of the list of Specially Designated Nationals and Blocked Persons

No U.S. owned or controlled foreign firm may export or reexport from a third country to Cuba a foreign produced agricultural commodity.

TSRA ELIGIBLE AGRICULTURAL COMMODITIES

Agricultural commodities are defined in Section 102 of the Agricultural Trade Act of 1978 (7 U.S.C. 02).

For purposes of License Exception AGR, agricultural commodities include, but are not limited to, food, feed, fish, shellfish and fish products; beer, wine and spirits; soft drinks; livestock; fiber, including cotton, wool and other fibers; tobacco and tobacco products; wood and wood products, including lumber and utility poles; seeds; and reproductive materials such as fertilized eggs, embryos, and semen.

A list of eligible agricultural commodities is available for review at the U.S. Department of Agriculture Web site[1]. If you have questions regarding whether an item is eligible, you should consult Ms. Emiko Purdy at the Department of Agriculture, Foreign Agricultural Service, phone: 202-720-0762, fax: 202-720-0069.

Vitamins, minerals, food additives and dietary supplements, and bottled water are also considered to be agricultural commodities for the purposes of License Exception AGR.

Some organic and inorganic fertilizers are eligible and some are not. The distinction is as follows:

Dry fertilizers containing 15% or less ammonium nitrate are eligible for License Exception AGR.

Dry fertilizers containing more than 15% ammonium nitrate are classified as Export Commodity Classification Number (ECCN) 1C997 and are not eligible for License Exception AGR.

Liquid fertilizers are eligible for License Exception AGR regardless of the concentration of ammonium nitrate they contain.

Some agricultural commodities are not eligible, such as:

items on the Commerce Control List (CCL), including western red cedar and live horses;

items on the U.S. Munitions List;

items for use in weapons of mass destruction (WMD).

Agricultural commodities do not include furniture even if made from wood; clothing; agricultural equipment (whether hand tools or motorized equipment); pesticides, insecticides, or herbicides; or cosmetics (unless derived entirely from plant materials).

TSRA ELIGIBLE MEDICINES AND MEDICAL DEVICES

Medicines are drugs as defined in Section 201 of the Federal Food, Drug and Cosmetic Act (21 U.S.C. 321).

Medicines include prescription medicines and over the counter medicines for humans and animals.

Medical devices include medical supplies, instruments, equipment, equipped ambulances, institutional washing machines capable of sterilizing hospital clothing and bedding, and vehicles with installed medical testing equipment.

If you have questions regarding whether an item meets the definition of medicine or medical device under the Food, Drug and Cosmetic Act, you should consult the Food and Drug Administration (FDA). For medicines, contact the FDA's Office of Drug Information at 301-827-4570 (telephone); 301-827-4577 (fax); For medical devices, contact the FDA's Division of Small Manufacturers' Assistance at 800-638-2041 (telephone); 301-443-8818 (fax);

Medicines on the Commerce Control List are not eligible.

---

[1] See Supplements

INELIGIBLE MEDICINES:

The following vaccines, immunotoxins, medical products, diagnostic and food testing kits are controlled on the Commerce Control List in Export Control Classification Number (ECCN) 1C991 and are not eligible for export under the expedited procedures authorized by the Trade Sanctions Reform and Export Enhancement Act of 2000.

- Controlled vaccines are those which contain items listed in Category 1 on the Commerce Control List in ECCNs 1C351, 1C352, 1C353 and 1C354. To view a description of these items, go to the Export Administration Regulations on the Access GPO web site, scroll down to "Category 1" and select the format in which you wish to view the document.

- Controlled immunotoxins are antibody-toxin conjugates intended to destroy specific target cells (e.g., tumor cells) that bear antigens homologous to the antibody, where the toxin portion is listed in 1C351.d.

- Controlled medical products are pharmaceutical formulations designed for human administration in the treatment of medical conditions, prepackaged for distribution as medical products and approved by the Food and Drug Administration to be marketed as medical products, which contain toxins listed in 1C351.d.

- Controlled diagnostic and food testing kits are specifically developed, packaged and marketed for diagnostic or public health purposes, which contain toxins listed in 1C351.d.

Medical devices do not include general purpose furniture such as desks, tables, or lamps used in hospital offices and waiting rooms.

For Cuba, medicines and medical items are not eligible for License Exception AGR. These may be authorized for export to Cuba according to the provisions of the Cuban Democracy Act under an export license issued by BXA. A BXA export license is valid for two years.

BXA'S PRIOR NOTIFICATION PROCEDURES UNDER LICENSE EXCEPTION AGR:

Before making any shipment under License Exception AGR, exporters must submit a notification to BXA and obtain confirmation that no agency has raised an objection to the use of License Exception AGR for the transaction described in the notification. BXA informs exporters within 12 business days from the date the notice is registered in BXA's electronic database whether such objections have been raised. BXA's confirmation that no objections have been raised does not relieve parties to the transaction from the obligation to assure that they meet all of the requirements of License Exception AGR, other requirements of the Export Administration Regulations (EAR), and any other applicable law. The procedures for using this license exception are:

-Exporters must notify BXA prior to any export or reexport.

-Exporters provide this prior notification by submitting a completed BXA Multi-purpose Application Form (BXA-748P) or electronically through BXA's Simplified Network Application Process (SNAP).

Within two business days of the notification's registration in BXA's electronic database system, BXA will refer the notification electronically to the Departments of State, Defense, and other agencies, as appropriate, for review.

Any reviewing agency that objects to the use of License Exception AGR must provide notice of such objection to BXA within nine business days of the referral.

-An agency may object for one or more of the following reasons:

the commodity is not an agricultural commodity;

the items are not EAR99;

the export would violate the terms of a denial order;

the recipient may promote international terrorism; or

the transaction raises nonproliferation concerns.

If any agency objects, BXA will convert the notification into a license application and process it under standard export license application procedures.

An exporter may ship the goods after 12 days if no agency has raised an objection. Applicants may check the status of their notification or application via BXA's System for Tracking Export License Applications (STELA) at 202-482-2752 using the "Z" number on the 748-P form or provided by SNAP. Applicants may not make the export without confirming via STELA that no agency has raised an objection.

BXA also will notify the applicant in writing of the outcome of the interagency review.

COMMODITY CLASSIFICATION REQUIREMENTS:

Exporters must be sure that they are not attempting to use AGR as authority to export any item that is on the Commerce Control List (CCL). Only items classified as EAR99 are eligible for BXA's License Exception AGR or OFAC's expedited review procedures. EAR99 items are items that are subject to the Export Administration Regulations, but they are not specifically listed on the CCL.

Exporters may need to include, with their notification or application, an official BXA commodity classification to confirm the classification of an item as EAR99, as specified in greater detail below.

BXA is responsible for providing commodity classifications. Exporters may obtain a commodity classification by submitting a completed BXA's Multipurpose Application Form (BXA-748P) or electronically through BXA's Simplified Network Application Process (SNAP) indicating that they wish a commodity classification. See Section 748.3 of the Export Administration Regulations for more information.

BXA has already determined that most items that meet the definition of agricultural commodity are classified as EAR99. This includes most of the items on the Department of Agriculture's Eligible Commodities List (pdf) available from its Economic and Trade Sanctions Web page. This means that items on this list do not require a commodity classification with three exceptions: live horses; western red cedar; and fertilizers.

For these three types of agricultural commodities, BXA and OFAC require a BXA commodity classification for fertilizers, live horses or western red cedar prior to submission of a notification to BXA or a license application to OFAC, as these agricultural commodities may be on the Commerce Control List.

Medicines do not require a BXA commodity classification prior to OFAC review, unless you are unsure whether your item is a medicine (e.g., vaccines and immunotoxins) that BXA has identified on the Commerce Control List and thus on BXA's list of ineligible medicines.

Medical supplies (e.g., syringes, bandages and gauze) and devices require a BXA commodity classification prior to OFAC review, unless BXA has listed the item on the list of EAR99 medical supplies found on BXA's Web site.

EXPORTS AND REEXPORTS TO IRAN, LIBYA, AND SUDAN:

OFAC is responsible for authorizing exports of agricultural commodities, medicines, and medical devices to Iran, Libya, and Sudan. It is also responsible for authorizing reexport of these items by U.S. persons to Iran, Libya and Sudan.

BXA has licensing responsibility for reexports to Libya by U.S. or foreign persons of items requiring a license to Libya under the EAR, e.g., foreign produced medical equipment containing U.S. controlled content, reexports of U.S. origin medical equipment (see section 746.4 of the EAR).

If OFAC authorization is needed, exporters must submit an application in writing to OFAC identifying the item they would like to export and the purchaser, any intermediaries, and the end-user involved in the proposed transaction.

OFAC also has expedited procedures for reviewing such applications.

Exporters should check OFAC's Web site for additional information on OFAC's requirements.

Exporters can check the status of their OFAC applications by calling the OFAC Licensing Division at (202) 622-2480 between 9:00 AM and 5:30 PM Eastern time.

As described in the Commodity Classification Requirements summary above, to comply with OFAC regulations, exporters may need a BXA commodity classification.

FAQ ON CONDUCTING BUSINESS AND VISITING CUBA

U.S.-Cuba Trade and Economic Council, Inc.
30 Rockefeller Plaza New York, New York 10112-0002
Telephone (212) 246-1444 Facsimile (212) 246-2345
Internet: http://www.cubatrade.org

Can I export to Cuba?

The legislation liberalizes U.S. sanctions on exports to Cuba of agricultural commodities. However, strict laws remain in place on using U.S. dollars in Cuba, financing transactions, traveling to Cuba, and limiting U.S. Government assistance. Some Federal regulations and instructions will need to be developed regarding these issues. The principal agencies involved and where to turn for more information about regulations are USDA, U.S. Department of State, U.S. Department of the Treasury's Office of Foreign Assets Control, and the U.S. Department of Commerce's Bureau of Export Administration.

Until all these new regulations are in place, what can I do in Cuba?

Representatives of U.S. industry associations, state governments, and private companies may travel to Cuba provided they apply for and receive a specific license from the Treasury Departments Office of Foreign Assets Control. Under current regulations, travel transactions related to marketing, sales negotiation, and accompanied delivery of agricultural products are possible. Exporters are required to apply to the Treasury Department's Office of Foreign Assets Control for a license to engage in such transactions and to spend funds in Cuba. For information you may visit OFAC's website www.treas.gov/ofac or call (202)622-2520. Exporters should also check with the State Department for the most recent regulations for travel of U.S. citizens. Monitor the ***Federal Register*** to see proposed regulations on Cuba as they emerge and offer comments on how those regulations should be structured.

How do I find potential buyers?

U.S. exporters must vie for Cuba's trade with other, more established competitors such as Canada, France, and Mexico that already export agricultural commodities to Cuba. U.S. proximity to Cuba, the high quality of U.S. agricultural products, and the marketing expertise of the U.S. industry will slowly grow the Cuban marketplace for U.S. products, but only after considerable energy and effort has been made. For general information on Cuba, the U.S. Government operates a U.S. Interests Section in Havana located at Calzada between L & M Streets, Vedado, Havana, tel: (53-7) 33-3551 thru 3559, fax: (53-7) 33-3700. Also, the U.S. Department of Agriculture has a trade office in Miami , tel: (305) 536-5300 or fax: (305) 536-7577 that can help U.S. exporters search for markets throughout the Caribbean Basin, including Cuba. To do business in Cuba and find importers, an exporter should do in-depth market research and develop payment strategies that will conform to U.S. law.

Can representatives of U.S. agricultural cooperatives, trade associations, or state governments visit Cuba and perform market development activities?

Yes, but they must obtain a license and follow Federal law and regulations. The use of Federal funds to support export promotions is specifically prohibited by Congress. Private companies, cooperatives, trade associations, or state governments may use their own funds for market development purposes, but the use of funds in Cuba is tightly controlled. U.S. agricultural industry trade associations, such as FAS Foreign Market Development Cooperators or Market Access Program participants, are allowed to undertake market development activities in Cuba provided they obtain a license, but not with Federal funds. U.S. industry can use its own resources to explore the Cuban market, but prior to using any funds in Cuba, U.S. industry and associations must apply to the Office of Foreign Assets Control for a license.

How will I get paid?

The new law prohibits any U.S. person or company from providing payment or financing credit terms to anyone in Cuba. The law specifically rules out open account transactions, requiring cash in advance arrangements. Foreign banks may, however, finance transactions and U.S. banks may confirm or advise such foreign bank letters of credit or similar arrangements. Exporters should be alert to these provisions in law and how payment strategies will be affected by U.S. regulations. The U.S. Treasury Department's Office of Foreign Assets Control is the regulatory authority on currencies and payments with sanctioned countries and consulted regarding payment issues. For information you may visit OFAC's website www.treas.gov/ofac or call (202)622-2520.

What is the current level of Cuba's agricultural trade? What products?

Cuba imports about $600 million worth annually, primarily grain, pulses, meat, soybeans, vegetable oil, and dairy products. This amount has trended downward in recent years due to Cuba's current economic hardship. Cuba's 11 million inhabitants have an estimated per capita income of $1,500, equal to Guatemala. Adjusted to account for purchasing power parity this per capita income estimate rises to $3,500. This figure adjusts income for the relatively low cost of many items in the Cuban economy including subsidized rents and indicates that Cubans have greater purchasing power than indicated by that low nominal GDP figure. Growth in tourism and some reform of Cuba's centralized economy have the potential to turn around this picture and raise demand for imported foods. Tourism earns Cuba substantial foreign currency and is its No. 1 economic sector for growth. The United States might find new markets in Cuba for consumer-ready foods for the hotel and restaurant industry as tourism grows and as the United States begins to compete with other suppliers for bulk and intermediate commodity sales. Other agricultural products that hold promise for future U.S. sales are wood products and cotton.

VISITING THE REPUBLIC OF CUBA AND TRANSACTIONS WITH THE REPUBLIC OF CUBA

The following information is provided as a general overview of the regulations administered by the United States Department of the Treasury and the United States Department of Commerce. For specific information, including legal opinion, requests should be made directly to the appropriate representative of the United States government. Relevant information is contained within the Code of Federal Regulations (CFR)- 31 CFR Part 515.

Who is an Individual Subject To United States Law?
An individual subject to United States law includes: 1) Any individual, wherever located, who is a citizen or resident of the United States 2) Any person who is within the United States [a non-United States citizen in transit at an airport, for example] 3) Any corporation organized under the laws of the United States or of any State, territory possession, or district of the United States 4) Any corporation, partnership, or association, wherever organized or doing business, that is owned or controlled by persons specified in 1 and 3. Non-United States citizens who have visas are considered to be subject to United States law.

The Office of Foreign Assets Control (OFAC) of the United States Department of the Treasury in Washington, D.C., administers the regulations governing ***travel and financial transactions*** with respect to the Republic of Cuba by individuals subject to United States law.

Mr. R. Richard Newcomb
Director
Office of Foreign Assets Control
United States Department of the Treasury
Washington, D.C. 20220
Telephone: (202) 622-2480
Facsimile: (202) 622-1657
Internet: http://www.treas.gov/ofac

The Bureau of Export Administration (BXA) of the United States Department of Commerce in Washington, D.C., administers regulations governing the ***export of products*** (including donations and general aviation aircraft temporary sojourn licenses) to the Republic of Cuba by individuals subject to United States law and by businesses subject to United States law. However, Non-United States-based subsidiaries of United States-based companies must apply to the OFAC for licenses to export products to the Republic of Cuba. Applicants seeking to export products (including temporary sojourn licenses) to the Republic of Cuba (other than informational materials, which are exempt from licensing requirements) are required to use the Multipurpose Application Form BXA-748P which can be obtained by contacting the Office of Exporter Services at telephone (202) 482-4811 press 0.

Mr. John Bolsteins
Office of Strategic Trade and Foreign Policy Controls
Bureau of Export Administration
United States Department of Commerce
Washington, D.C. 20230
Telephone: (202) 482-3283
Facsimile: (202) 482-6088
Internet: http://www.bxa.doc.gov/

The Office of Cuban Affairs (OCA) United States Department of State in Washington, D.C., ***establishes the policies*** by which the OFAC and the BXA ***interpret the regulations by which laws are enforced***.

Mr. Charles Shapiro
Coordinator
Office of Cuban Affairs
United States Department of State
Washington, D.C. 20520
Telephone: (202) 647-9273
Facsimile: (202) 736-4476

Internet: http://www.state.gov/

Individuals subject to United States law can travel to the Republic of Cuba if they do so under the auspices of either an OFAC General License or an OFAC Specific License.

Individuals subject to United States law traveling to the Republic of Cuba (with the exception of individuals subject to United States law traveling to the Republic of Cuba on a "fully hosted" basis) under the auspice of an OFAC General License or OFAC Specific License are authorized to spend up to US$195.00 per day for hotels, meals, ground transportation, etc. Not included in the US$195.00 per day spending limit are expenses for telephone calls. Individuals who are full-time journalists traveling to the Republic of Cuba under a general license from the OFAC may also spend above the US$195.00 for expenses "incidental to journalist activities."

Exemptions to the US$195.00 per day authorization can be requested from the OFAC. "Fully hosted" travelers are not subject to spending limits while within the Republic of Cuba.

In August 1999, the OFAC increased the Per Diem allowance for employees of the United States government visiting the Republic of Cuba to US$195.00 (US$113.00 for lodging and US$82.00 for meals) from US$183.00 (US$102.00 for lodging and US$81.00 for meals), representing an increase of US$12.00 per day, or 6.16% from the Per Diem rate in effect from 1 December 1996. An increase in the Per Diem reflects an evaluation by the United States Department of State that prices within the Republic of Cuba have increased. Per Diem rates within the Republic of Cuba are based upon the Per Diem Rate For Foreign Areas issued by the Office of Allowances (202-663-1121) within the Office of Operations of the Bureau of Administration of the Under Secretary of Management of the United States Department of State in Washington, D.C. Per Diem values for travel to the city of Havana from 1995 through August 1999:

Effective Date	Lodging	Meals & Incidentals	Total Per Diem	% Increase From Previous Year
1 June 1999 to Present	US$113.00	US$82.00	US$195.00	6.16%
1 June 1999 to 1 December 1996	US$102.00	US$81.00	US$183.00	15.85%
1 December 1996 to 1 November 1995	US$90.00	US$64.00	US$154.00	-0-

Individuals (non-employees of the United States government) subject to United States law traveling to the Republic of Cuba under a general license from the OFAC or a specific license from the OFAC were permitted to spend US$100.00 per day (no distinction with respect to lodging and meals) from 1985 through May 1999. Since May 1999, individuals subject to United States law traveling to the Republic of Cuba under a general license from the OFAC or a specific license from the OFAC have been permitted to spend at parity with representatives of the United States government traveling to the Republic of Cuba on official business.

Individuals subject to United States law traveling to the Republic of Cuba under the auspices of either an OFAC General License (excluding "fully hosted" travelers subject to United States law) or an OFAC Specific License may return from the Republic of Cuba to the United States with up to US$100.00 worth of Republic of Cuba-origin products (such as cigars, rum, tee-shirts, crafts, etc.) for their personal use. For cigars, the United States Customs Service permits up to 100 cigars, but the total value must not exceed US$100.00. For example, if a traveler returns with 100 cigars which cost US$1.00 each, the traveler would not be permitted to bring any other Republic of Cuba-origin products (such as rum) because the total value of imported Republic of Cuba-origin products would then exceed US$100.00. If a traveler purchased 100 cigars for US$50.00, then the traveler would have an additional US$50.00 to spend on other Republic of Cuba origin products such as rum, tee-shirts, crafts, etc. Travelers subject to United States law should retain a receipt showing the amount paid for all Republic of Cuba-origin products.

OFAC General License:

An individual subject to United States law traveling to the Republic of Cuba under the auspice of an OFAC General License is neither required to inform the OFAC in advance of their visit to the Republic of Cuba nor obtain a written license from the OFAC.

1) Representatives of the United States government on official business, representatives of non-United States governments on official business, representatives of international organizations of which the United States government is a member on official business.

2) Individuals subject to United States law who are regularly (full-time) employed by a news gathering organization (television network, television station, television production company, radio station, newspaper, newsletter, magazine, video production company, etc.). Travelers are advised to have company identification (with photograph), business card, and/or a letter from the company confirming full-time employment of the traveler. United States Customs Service inspectors may request this information at the point of entry into the United States.

3) Individuals subject to United States law traveling once in a twelve (12) month period to visit close relatives in circumstances of self-defined humanitarian need.

4) Individuals subject to United States law who are professional researchers. This includes individuals who are acting on behalf of an organization with an established interest in international relations.

5) Individuals subject to United States law who are graduate students, under graduate students, or secondary school students under the auspice of a specific license issued to a school, college, university, etc.

6) Individuals subject to United States law traveling on a "fully hosted" basis. "Fully hosted" travel requires that the individual subject to United States law who is traveling to the Republic of Cuba does not spend any funds of their own while within the Republic of Cuba. Funds used to make payments for hotels, meals, ground transportation, sundries, etc., must originate from a) an entity within the Republic of Cuba b) an entity within another country or c) an individual within another country. The use of indirect transfers is not permitted. For example, the individual subject to United States law sends funds to another country within which a relative, friend, or business associate resides. The relative, friend, or business associate then makes payments within the Republic of Cuba on behalf of the individual subject to United States law. "Fully hosted" individuals subject to United States law traveling to the Republic of Cuba and departing from the Republic of Cuba are not permitted to use their own funds for the purchase of an airline ticket or a cruise ship ticket for such travel if the airline or cruise ship is controlled by an entity within the Republic of Cuba. For example, a "fully hosted" traveler subject to United States law is not permitted to use their own funds to purchase an airline ticket on Cubana Airlines to travel to the Republic of Cuba, but the traveler could use their own funds to purchase an airline ticket on Mexicana, Air Jamaica, Lacsa, Iberia, etc. A "Fully hosted" traveler subject to United States law may return from the Republic of Cuba to the United States with an unlimited value of artwork and informational materials (books, magazines, music tapes, CD ROM's, photographs, films, posters, phonograph records, microfilm, microfiche, compact disks, and newswire feed, etc.) A "Fully hosted" traveler subject to United States law may not return from the Republic of Cuba to the United States with Republic of Cuba-origin products such as those authorized for individuals subject to United States law who travel to the Republic of Cuba under an OFAC General License or an OFAC Specific License such as cigars, rum, tee-shirts, crafts, etc. A "Fully hosted" traveler subject to United States law may return from the Republic of Cuba to the United States with any gift received from a Republic of Cuba national. However, the gift must remain with the United States Customs Service at the point of entry into the United States. The "fully hosted" traveler subject to United States law may then request a license from the OFAC to take possession of the gift.

"FULLY HOSTED" TRAVELERS WARNING

Officials at the United States Department of State, officials at the Office of Foreign Assets Control (OFAC) of the United States Department of the Treasury, officers of the United States Customs Service, and officers of the Immigration and Naturalization Service, have re-confirmed that any individual subject to United States law returning to the United States after visiting the Republic of Cuba on a "fully hosted basis" will be subjected to increased scrutiny. This is especially true for high profile groups. Extreme caution should be taken as there is no longer a presumption of innocence, there is now a presumption of guilt and fines will be assessed. The term "fully hosted" means that all expenses within the Republic of Cuba (including travel to and from the Republic of Cuba if using a Republic of Cuba government-operated air carrier, such as Cubana Airlines, or other means of transportation) on behalf of the individual subject to United States law are paid for by an individual or entity not subject to United States law. No direct or indirect payments are permitted. A "fully hosted" traveler may return to the United States with an unlimited amount of informational materials (books, magazines, newspapers, music tapes, etc.) and an unlimited amount of artwork. A "fully hosted" traveler may not return to the United States with any other Republic of Cuba-produced products (such as cigars, rum, coffee, tee-shirts, etc.). The OFAC and the United States Customs Service confirm that "fully hosted" travelers should now expect the following: ***A)*** *A letter from an individual or entity not subject to United States law (or a letter from a United States-based law firm) confirming that the individual subject to United States law was "fully hosted" will not be accepted as "proof" that a visit was "fully hosted."* ***B)*** *The individual subject to United States law will be required to produce receipts for all daily expenses within the Republic of Cuba which demonstrate that all of the expenses were paid by an individual or entity not subject to United States law.* ***C)*** *At the entry point to the United States, the United States Customs Service may make a photocopy of the passport of the individual subject to United States law. The passport number may be entered in a permanent data base.* ***D)*** *The individual subject to United States law will be required to submit a signed letter confirming, under penalty of perjury, that all daily expenses incurred within the Republic of Cuba on behalf of the individual subject to United States law were paid for by an individual or entity not subject to United States law.* ***E)*** *The OFAC may send a letter to the individual subject to United States law requiring additional proof that the visit to the Republic of Cuba was "fully hosted."*

OFAC Specific License:

An individual subject to United States law traveling to the Republic of Cuba under the auspice of an OFAC Specific License is required to obtain a written license from the OFAC. An individual(s) subject to United States law who wishes to travel to the Republic of Cuba under the auspice of an OFAC Specific License should write a letter to the OFAC and include the following information: a) the date of the planned visit and the length of stay b) the specific purpose(s) of the visit c) name(s), title(s) of individual(s), and background(s) of the traveler.

1) Individuals subject to United States law who wish to identify commercial opportunities in the fields of agricultural products, air charter services, artwork, communications, entertainment, farm supplies, food sales, informational materials, medical equipment, medical instruments, medical supplies, medicated products, medicines, money transfer services, package delivery services, pharmaceuticals, telecommunications; travel services; register trademarks and patents; and organize and participate in trade shows;

2) Individuals subject to United States law more than once in a twelve (12) month period to visit close relatives in circumstances of self-defined humanitarian need.

3) Individuals subject to United States law who are employed as freelance journalists.

4) Individuals subject to United States law accompanying licensed (from the BXA) humanitarian donations.

5) Individuals subject to United States law traveling in conjunction with activities of recognized human rights organizations investigating human rights violations.

6) Individuals subject to United States law who are professional researchers. This includes individuals who are acting on behalf of an organization with an established interest in international relations.

7) Individuals subject to United States law who are graduate students or secondary school students.

8) Individuals subject to United States law who are athletes competing in an event(s).

9) Individuals subject to United States law who are members of a religious organization.

10) Individuals subject to United States law who wish to lecture at educational institutions.

11) Individuals subject to United States law who wish to engage in a public exhibition, such as a concert, trade show, etc.

Travel Visas From The Republic Of Cuba:

Individuals subject to United States law can travel to the Republic of Cuba using either an a) official visa or b) a tourist visa. Official visas are obtained from the Cuban Interests Section in Washington, D.C. A tourist visa can be obtained from: **1)** a travel agent licensed by the Office of Foreign Assets Control (OFAC) of the United States Department of the Treasury **2)** a non-United States-based travel agent **3)** at the ticket counter of the non-United States-based airline providing travel to the Republic of Cuba from a country other than from the United States or **4)** in some cases, upon arrival at an airport within the Republic of Cuba, although this is unadvisable.

The official visa is used for individuals subject to United States law who are traveling to the Republic of Cuba for any purpose other than tourism. Generally, if an individual subject to United States law travels to the Republic of Cuba using a tourist visa and then, while within the country, wishes to change his or her visa status, the change can be completed by contacting the United States Department of the Ministry of Foreign Affairs of the Republic of Cuba.

His Excellency

Dr. Fernando Remirez
Cuban Interests Section
2630 16th Street, Northwest
Washington, D.C. 20009
Telephone: (202) 797-8518 or (202) 797-8522
Facsimile: (202) 797-8521
Mr. Jose Barrios
Director- United States Department
Ministry of Foreign Affairs
Calle Calzada No. 360 e/ G y H, Vedado
Havana, Republic of Cuba
Telephone: 011 53 7 32 9190 or 011 53 7 30 50 31
Facsimile: 011 53 7 31 23 14 or 011 53 7 33 3085

Travel Arrangements To/From/Within The Republic Of Cuba:

Individuals subject to United States law traveling to the Republic of Cuba should only use travel agents which have been licensed by the Office of Foreign Assets Control (OFAC) of the United States Department of the Treasury:

Tico Travel
161 East Commercial Boulevard
Fort Lauderdale, Florida 33334
Telephone: (954) 493-5335 or (800) 493-8426
Facsimile: (954) 493-8466
E-mail: tico@gate.net
Internet: http://www.destinationcuba.com/
Mr. Joel Sanz
United States and Puerto Rico Division
Havanatur
Corporation Cimex S.A.
Edificio Sierra Maestra, Calle 1ra y O, Mirara, Playa
Havana, Republic of Cuba
Telephone: 011 53 7 23 97 16
011 53 7 23 97 90
011 53 7 23 97 91
011 53 7 24 24 24 (emergencies)
Facsimile: 011 53 7 24 2912 or 011 53 7 24 29 12
E-mail: joels@cimex.com.cu or georgina@cimex.com.cu

IS IT LEGAL TO GO TO CUBA? US LAW AND TRAVEL TO CUBA

"Fully hosted" Travelers

Individuals subject to US law traveling on a "fully hosted" basis can travel without a specific license so long as they do not spend any funds of their own while in Cuba. This includes travel on a prepaid, all-inclusive tour package with companies such as Last Frontier Expeditions (see Organized Tours in the Transportation chapter). Funds used to make payments for hotels, meals, ground transportation, sundries, etc., must originate from a) an entity within Cuba b) an entity within another country (Last Frontier Expeditions is an Aruba and Mexican based company) or c) an individual within another country. The use of indirect transfers is not permitted. A "fully hosted" traveler may pay for transportation only if aboard a non-Cuban carrier such as Mexicana, Air Jamaica, Lacsa, Iberia, etc. Travelers whose expenses are covered by a person not subject to US jurisdiction may not bring back any Cuban origin goods, except for informational materials (books, magazines, posters, etc.) and an unlimited amount of artwork. Gifts from Cuba nationals may be brought into the USA, but the gift must remain with the US Customs Service at the point of entry; the traveler subject must then request a license.

Qualified Travel Service Providers Referring to travel agencies and tour operators, "It is possible to provide travel services to US persons legally able to travel to Cuba for family visits, professional research, or news gathering," says Michael Krinsky, a partner in the law firm of Rabinowitz, Boudin, Standard, Krinsky and Lieberman, which represents the Cuban government in the United States. US travel agencies can also provide services to third countries, from where a traveler makes his or her own arrangements for travel to and within Cuba. They may also be able to provide services, such as travel arrangements to Jamaica, where a component includes an excursion to Cuba. Treasury Department regulations do not "show a clear penalty against travel agents who book travel this way."

Contrary to popular belief, US law does not prohibit US citizens from visiting Cuba. However, to visit Cuba legally you must either spend no money there, or qualify for a license issued by the US Treasury Dept. in order to buy goods (a meal at a hotel, for example) or services (an airline ticket, tour package, or hotel room). In order to apply, you need a good reason. Except as specifically licensed by the Office of Foreign Assets Control, payments in connection with any other travel to Cuba are prohibited, whether travelers go directly or via a third country such as Mexico, Canada, or another Caribbean Island. US citizens and any person in the USA is subject to these restrictions, regardless of citizenship. Under these restrictions, spending money relating to Cuban travel is prohibited unless the traveler is licensed. The regulations change frequently and are open to interpretation by the understaffed office (interpretation often shifts with the political breeze). For example, in May 1999 the Clinton administration announced new regulations that will expand travel opportunities. US universities and non-governmental organizations may now apply for two-year travel permits to Cuba that will permit any of its members to travel to Cuba without requiring individual certification. And the amount that U.S. citizens can spend in Cuba was raised from US$100 to US$185 per day.

To determine if you or your organization qualify for a general license (which does not require prior government authorization) or a specific license (which does require prior government authorization), contact:

Licensing Division, Office of Foreign Asset Control (OFAC)
US Department of the Treasury
1500 Pennsylvania Ave.
NW, Washington, D.C. 20200
tel. 202-622-2520 or 202-622-2480
fax 202-622-1657
- Request the ***Cuban Assets Control Regulations***.

The Office of Cuban Affairs (OCA)
Department of State
Washington, D.C. 20520
tel. 202- 647-9273
fax 202-736-4476
web site: **www.state.gov**
-establishes the policies by which the OFAC interpret the regulations by which laws are enforced. The following regulations

applied at press time:

Who is an "Individual Subject To United States Law"

An individual subject to US law includes: any individual, wherever located, who is a citizen or resident of the USA; any person who is within the US (a non-US citizen in transit at an airport, for example); any corporation organized under the laws of the USA or of any State, territory possession, or district of the USA; any corporation, partnership, or association, wherever organized or doing business, that is owned or controlled by persons an individual or individuals subject to US law. (Non-US citizens who have H-1 visas are generally considered to be subject to US law.)

GENERAL LICENSES?

The following categories of travelers are permitted to spend money for Cuban travel without the need to obtain special permission from OFAC, nor are they required to inform OFAC in advance of their visit to Cuba:

Official Government Travelers: US and foreign government officials, including representatives of international organizations of which the United States is a member, who are traveling on official business.

Journalists: Individuals who are regularly (full-time) employed by a news gathering organization (television network, television station, television production company, radio station, newspaper, newsletter, magazine, video production company, etc.). Travelers are advised to have company identification (with photograph), business card, and/or a letter from the company confirming full-time employment.

Persons who are visiting close relatives: People with close relatives in Cuba may visit them in circumstances of humanitarian need. This authorization is valid only once every 12 months.

SPECIAL LICENSES?

A specific license requires written government approval. Applicants should write a letter to the OFAC stating the date of the planned visit and the length of stay; the specific purpose(s) of the visit; plus the name(s), title(s), and background(s) of the traveler. OFAC has been understaffed and is notoriously slow: allow two or three months. Special licenses are issued by OFAC on a case by case basis authorizing travel transactions by persons in connection with the following travel categories:

Humanitarian Travel: Persons traveling to Cuba to visit close relatives in cases involving hardship more than once in a 12 month period; persons traveling to Cuba to accompany licensed humanitarian donations (other than gift parcels); or persons traveling in connection with activities of recognized human rights organizations investigating human rights violations.

Educational Research: Travel in connection with professional research or similar activities, for clearly defined educational or religious activities, including academics intending to lecture at educational institutions or attend a meeting or conference, and activities related to study for an undergraduate or graduate degree sponsored by a college or university located in the United States.

Commercial "Opportunists": Individuals wishing to identify commercial opportunities in the fields of artwork, communications, entertainment, informational materials, medical equipment, medical instruments, medical supplies, medicated products, medicines, pharmaceuticals, and telecommunications; register trademarks and patents; organize and participate in trade shows; authorize consumer credit cards to be valid for use; and provide travel services and provide air transportation services.

Others: Freelance journalists; athletes competing in an event; and individuals wishing to engage in a public exhibition, such as a concert, trade show, etc. Many travelers have successfully been approved as "freelancers." If you want to go it alone and try the "journalist" or "researcher" angle, write to the OFAC, which requires a written statement of why your proposed trip falls within the rules for permissible travel.

WHAT YOU MAY SPEND?

Licensed travelers are authorized to spend up to US$185 per day. Exemptions to the US$185 per day authorization can be requested from the OFAC. "Fully hosted" travelers are not subject to spending limits while within the Republic of Cuba.

Money may be spent only for purchases of items directly related to travel such as hotel accommodations, meals, and goods personally used by the traveler in Cuba, or for the purchase of $100 worth of Cuban merchandise to be brought into the United States as accompanied baggage. Purchases of services related to travel, such as nonemergency medical services, are prohibited. The purchase of publications and other informational material is not restricted in any way. Licensed travelers may return from Cuba with up to US$100 worth of Cuban products (such as cigars, rum, tee-shirts, crafts, etc.) for their personal use. For cigars, the US Customs Service permits up to 100 cigars, but the total value must not exceed US$100. For example, if a traveler returns with 100 cigars which cost US$1 each, the traveler would not be permitted to bring any other Cuban products (such as rum). Travelers should retain a receipt showing the amount paid for all Republic of Cuba-origin products.

VISAS FOR LICENSED TRAVELERS?

All licensed travelers to Cuba must have a visa from the Cuban government prior to reserving your flight. Tico Travel and Marazul (see above) can assist you in acquiring your visa. (Tico Travel charges US$120 for the visa and preparing the documents.) There are two different forms: one for those born in Cuba and one for those born outside Cuba. Allow thirty days for processing.

* See the Immigration and Customs section in the Information chapter for information on tourist visas.

Cubans and Cuban-Americans: Anyone who permanently left Cuba after December 31, 1970 must have a valid Cuban passport (people born in Cuba who left Cuba permanently before that date don't need a Cuban passport). If you don't have a Cuban passport and you left Cuba after December 31, 1970 you must contact the Cuban Interests Section in Washington D.C., tel. 202-797-8609, 797-8610. to get the required paperwork. Cubans who left Cuba permanently prior to 1959 can acquire a slightly less expensive 359 Visa, acquired directly with the Cuban Interests Section.

ILLEGAL TRAVEL?

About 103,000 US citizens visited Cuba in 1998. The majority did so legally (most went with organized groups), while the rest slipped in through third countries and spent freely without a license. The US government has recently sought to tighten control of unsanctioned travel. Since May 1998, persons subject to US jurisdiction who travel to Cuba without a license bear a "presumption of guilt" and may be required to show documentation that all expenses incurred were paid by a third party not subject to US law.

IS IT SAFE IN CUBA?

The oftentimes negative statements from our government and the media about Cuba has left many of us with the false impression that Cuba is unsafe. Few places in the world are as safe for visitors as Cuba. Most visitors are far less likely to run into problems in Cuba than they are in their own cities and towns. Cubans are very honest and friendly towards foreign guests and each other.

CAN US CITIZENS USE CREDIT CARDS OR TRAVELERS CHECKS IN CUBA?

Cash is King in Cuba! US citizens can only use US dollars in Cuba as is the policy with all other foreign countries. Only credit cards issued from a foreign bank may be used by US citizens.

Please do not confuse the new "convertible pesos" that you may receive in change with the real Cuban peso. The convertible peso is only for tourist and is in reality just a much more colorful US dollar. And, there is really no need to have any Cuban pesos since they are not accepted in any of the government run tourist establishments.

American Express and Thomas Cook travelers checks can be redeemed at Cuban banks and many of the larger hotels. But, please be advised not to say that you are taking them to Cuba when you are ordering them from your bank or travel agency. Recently the agency for Thomas Cook checks has refused to issue them to US citizens traveling to Cuba.

DO WE NEED A US PASSPORT TO GO TO CUBA?

Yes: Unlike Mexico, a birth certificate will not gain you entry into the Republic of Cuba.

HOW DO YOU GET TO CUBA?

The most popular points of demarcation for US citizens going to Cuba are Cancun, Mexico; Nassau, Bahamas and Toronto, Canada. Beware that in both Nassau and Toronto US Customs pre-clears incoming passengers who are returning to the USA.

Last Frontier Expeditions has been utilizing Cancun, Mexico for entry into Cuba for many reason.

1. It is accessible from the USA via many air charter companies.
2. We maintain an office and staff in Cancun and personally make sure you get your visa, airline tickets and get on the plane. In fact, our representatives personally meet you upon arrival in Cancun, Mexico.
3. Cancun offers flights to Cuba on Aerocaribe Airlines (Mexicana) so we do not have to take the additional risk of violating US law by using the Cuban government airlines (Cubana).

4. With departures from Cancun we are able to offer our clients airport VIP service in Havana. This needs to be requested ($20 fee) in advance. The good part? While the others are waiting in Customs lines you are in the VIP lounge with a cool drink and/or a cigar!
5. Whether on an organized tour, traveling in small groups or alone, you will always be personally be met in Havana by one of our representatives.

MEDICAL INSURANCE

For a $5.00 USD per day you will be covered for a maximum of $25,000.00 USD in medical benefits at Havana's International Hospital. Arrangements to be made in advance

PROVINCIAL CHAMNERS OF COMMERCE

Sección Provincial de Matanzas.
Fué creada el 20 de julio de 1999.
Nombre: Lourdes M. Rodríguez Rodríguez y Oreste Bello García.
Dirección: Calle Jovellanos No. 5, entre Medio y Río, Matanzas, Cuba.
Teléfonos: (052) 24 2483
E-mail: propind@atenas.inf.cu
Sección Provincial de Villa Clara.
Fué creada el 21 de julio de 1999.
Nombre: Osmel Aroche Pérez (Abogado), Aleyda Hernández y Carmen Elisa Roché.
Dirección: Cuba No. 364, entre Carretera Central y Serafín Sánchez, Santa Clara, Villa Clara, Cuba. C. Postal 50100
Teléfonos: (422) 7 3567
E-mail: ocpivc@civc.inf.cu

Sección Provincial de Camagüey.
Fué creada el 16 de noviembre de 1999.
Nombre: Boris Rodríguez Porrata y Aldo Alonso Muñoz (Abogado).
Dirección: General Gómez No. 325, entre San Miguel y Perro, Apartado 384,Camagüey, Cuba.
Teléfonos: (322) 9 7901
E-mail: boris@caonao.cmw.inf.cu

Sección Provincial de Holguín.
Fué creada el 17 de noviembre de 1999.
Nombre: Martha Morejón Borjas.
Dirección: Calle 18, entre 1ra y Maceo, Reparto "El Llano", Holguín, Cuba.
Teléfonos: (24) 42 2203, 46 8306
E-mail: mar@holguin.inf.cu, ciget@holguin.inf.cu

Sección Provincial de Santiago de Cuba.
Fué creada el 18 de noviembre de 1999.
Nombre: Yordanka Masó Dominicico (Abogada), Ma. Angeles Alpizar Terrero, Isabel Rodríguez Moreno, Blancet García Querol.
Dirección: Calle Carnicería No. 459, entre Enramada y San Gerónimo, Santiago de Cuba, Cuba. C. Postal 90100
Teléfonos: (226) 2 7402, 2 8291, 2 6909
E-mail: yordanka@megacen.ciges.inf.cu, mangeles@megacen.ciges.inf.cu

SELECTED LAWS AND REGULATIONS AFFECTING BUSINESS

LEGAL AND BUSINESS CLIMATE

The Republic of Cuba has many tourist attractions, including extensive areas of magnificent beaches and virgin cays with varied vegetation. In addition, there is a considerable agriculture structure and a wide range of available industrial capacity. These aspects, plus other, socially positive factors, such as the nationwide health-care system, the country's cultural richness, the high level of education, social stability and the people's characteristic hospitality, made Cuba an excellent tourist destination with attractive offers for businessmen.

Complementing its investment efforts in top-priority sectors of the economy, the Cuban Government is promoting foreign investments in those areas and branches in which capital, technology and markets are most needed, employing various forms of economic association for this purpose: joint ventures, cooperative production efforts, marketing agreements, joint accounts and others, in accord with the regulations established by the laws in force.

Article 23 of the Constitutional Reform Law approved by the National Assembly of People's Power in July 1992 states that the Government will respect the property of the joint ventures and other economic associations that are set up under the law.

Legislative Decree sn, of February 15, 1982, establishes the legal conditions under which economic associations involving Cuban and foreign entities may be created and developed.

The Cuban Government has entrusted a negotiating group of the State Committee for Economic Cooperation with the job of handling and promoting all aspects of the establishment of economic associations and coordinating specific actions with the various Cuban entities to facilitate rapid decision-making except for those related to tourism, which are handled directly by the agencies in that sector. In turn, the Executive Committee of the Council of Ministers appointed a governmental commission to authorize Cuban governmental entities to join in economic associations with foreign interests in profitable activities of reciprocal benefit.

After approval has been obtained for the creation of a joint venture and the legal procedures for setting it up have been complied with, the joint ventures acquires legal status and becomes completely independent of the Government. It will have absolute freedom in appointing its Board of Directors and managers, defining its production program, setting prices and drawing up sales plans, directly exporting and importing, deciding how many staff members it will have and selecting them, signing contracts with Cuban and foreign entities, deciding on which accounting system it feels is best and drawing up its financial policy. All joint ventures will take the fond of corporations with nominal shares.

The legislative decree referred to above states that the conditions which the joint venture shouid abide by and those of the leases and contributions in temporary usufruct to it will be established when authorization is granted for the establishment of the economic association. Its duration will be set forth in the approval contract, keeping in mind that the capital invested should be recovered and profits attained to make the investment attractive to both parties.

The parties in the economic avssociations are represented internationally by the foreign partner, which may be an enterprise or other economic entity based abroad which engages in industrial or commercial activities, no matter what its form. The Cuban party may be an enterprise, state union or other national organization, such as the public enterprises which function as private entities or entities owned either entirely or mainly by the Cuban Government.

The other forms of economic association which, unlike the joint ventures, do not have, independent legal status are legalized by means of partnership contracts that may be issued by a notary public, or the partners may dispense with this prerequisite. Contracts of economic association become legally binding as soon as they are recorded in the Registry of Economic Associations of the Chamber of Commerce of the Republic of Cuba.

The content of partnership contracts will be that agreed to by the parties interested in forming the partnership.

Any economic association, whether or not it is a joint venture, may be modified and/or liquidated in conformity with the provisions agreed to by the partners. Such modifications and dissolutions will be recorded in the Chamber of Commerce Registry referred to above.

Any disputes that may arise between the partners will be settled in accordance with the procedures set forth in the memorandum of association and articles of association, if it is a joint venture, or partnership contract if it is some other form of economic association. The partners will abide by the decisions of the International Court of Arbitration attached to the Chamber of Commerce, unless they have agreed upon another way to settle disputes.

All of the forms of economic association should involve contributions; in the case of corporations, these contributions will be of capital, which may be in the form of cash or other assets, such as land and other grants, buildings, raw and other materials, tools and machinery, whose value will be measured in convertible currency The same will be done with the contributions of the partners in other forms of association, which will not constitute capital stock.

Original foreign participation in the capital of a joint enterprise may be as much as 49 percent, but, after its legal status is created, foreign participation may be accepted without any limits. In practice. however, none has been authorized for more that 50 percent.

All economic associations should open convertible currency accounts in banks pertaining to the national banking system, through which they will make collections and payments. Usually, this is the National Bank of Cuba, but it may be another one, such as the International Bank of Finance. When estimating the convertible currency value of the economic associations' services, wages, taxes and other expenditures in national territory, the of financial exchange rates set by the National Bank of Cuba will be applied.

Every economic association must set aside a part of its profi ts to create a reserve for meeting any contingency that may arise, in ao cord with the norms set by the State Committee for Finances.

The Cuban Government guarantees the foreign partner that he may freely transfer abroad his dividends, or net profits, the payment by the Cuban party in case they agree to transfer to the Cuban party all or part of the foreign partner's contribution, and the foreign partners's fair share in case the economic association is liquidated. In any of these cases, the foreign partner may remit such sums in convertible currency through the National Bank of Cuba.

The joint ventures and the parties to the other forms of economic association are exempt from payment of taxes on gross income, personal income, and transfers of real estate and commercial establishments. Al I will remain subject to the 30-percent tax on profiles and the 25-percent tax on payments to workers and other work-related income. In addition, they are subject to other, smaller taxes, such as tariffs, and other customs duties, assessments on the ownership of vehicles and document fees. The State Committee for licenses is empowered to grant total or partial exemption for some of those taxes.

The joint enterprises and the parties to the other forms of economic association must provide the State Committee for Finances with periodic financial statements.

The commercial regulations governing these economic associations state that they have the right to export their products directly, but this does not mean that they may not, if they wish, get a Cuban foreign trade enterprise to handle those exports for them which is recommended when the volume of production is not very great, when the creation of an export apparatus is not justified.

Cuban state enterprises will have first option on supplying fuel, raw materials, tools, equipment, spare parts, accessories and consumer goods; purchasing the finished products or services provided by the economic association; and shi pping and providing marine insurance for the products, as long as they offer internationally competitive prices and other conditions.

The Cuban state enterprises will guarantee the joint enterprises and the parties to the other forms of economic association the supplies and services agreed upon; supplies of electric power, gas and water; telephone, fax and teletype services; transportation services; and other services, as contracted.

The labor regulations governing the joint enterprises and other forms of economic association establish that, in general, except for those filling managerial or technical posts, the workers employed by these associations should be Cubans, who will maintain their labor relations with the Cuban entity which contracts the work force for the associations and pays their wages, in accord with the rates set by the State Committee for Labor and Social Security in this case, the Contracting Agency for Commercial Representatives (ACOREC S.A.) Foreign employees of the joint venture or other form of international economic association may remit abroad in convertible currency that percentage of their salaries determined by the National Bank of Cuba.

Specialized services may also be contracted in Cuba, including legal counselling; services provided by a notary public; audils: lechnical, market and feasibility studies; managelllelll overall plans; architectural and enginecring projects; and the design and exploitation of computer systems.

Joint ventures are expected to establish economic incentive fund for the Cuban workers. The amount of the contributions to this fund will be determined on a case-by-case basis and will not be subjeot to the workers' payroll tax; they will be considered a deductible expense in determining the profits tax.

In certain areas of tourist development, special fiscal, labor and migratory regulations and regulations concerni ng the ma i ntenance of public order may be established that are more favorable than those governing other economic associations. Economic associations in tourism are governed by other complementary laws, as well.

The provisions of international agreements that Cuba has signed, such as those concerning shipping and trade marks and patents, are applicable.

Cuba is willing to create additional investment projects with preferential treatment for Latin American and Caribbean partners as a step toward regional economic integration.

Below, we list the fees charged by the Chamber of Commerce, in accord with the official exchange rates of the National Bank of Cuba.

Entry of presentation $50.00
Inscription of joint enterprise $500.00
Inscription of partnership contracts that formalize
other forms of economic association $400.00
Other annotations or inscriptions $100.OO
Cancellations, modifications, substitutions or annulment $100.00
Exact certification of an inscription entry $1OO.00
Summarized certification with certain particulars
of an inscription $50.00
Negative certification $50.00

CUBAN FOREIGN INVESTMENT LEGISLATION

Decree Law 50 of 1982 ("Decree Law 50") was Cuba's first foreign investment act authorizing the formation of international joint-ventures with foreign investors. In general, Decree Law 50 authorized the creation of joint venture companies and the execution of other international economic association contracts, both permitted under the present Foreign Investment Act, but did not authorize the creation of full foreign ownership companies. When the new Foreign Investment Act was adopted in 1995, existing foreign investment vehicles created under the authority of Decree Law 50 were brought under the application of the new Act, although the latter provides an express grandfathering provision in respect of all benefits granted to such foreign investment vehicles under the earlier legislation.

FOREIGN INVESTMENT ACT OF 1995

At present, the primary legal framework governing foreign investments in Cuba is set out in the Foreign Investment Act (Law 77 of 1995 on Foreign Investment). Detailed rules applicable to the operations of foreign investment vehicles are contained in generally applicable legislation dealing with matters such as tax, banking, environment, construction, labour, insurance and others, as well as in the Cuban Commercial Code and the Civil Code.

The Foreign Investment Act provides basic investment protection and other general rules relevant to foreign investors and sets out the principal legal structures for the implementation of investment projects in Cuba. In general, the Foreign Investment Act classifies foreign investments as *direct investments* or *indirect investments*. In the case of a direct investment, the foreign investor participates in the equity structure of the entity developing the project in question and actively participates in the management of operations. Conversely, in the case of indirect investments, the role of the foreign investor is generally limited to the provision of finance for a given investment project, without any participation in the management of the project. Under the Foreign Investment Act, all sectors of the Cuban economy are open to foreign investment, with the exception of health, education and the sector of the armed forces. The acquisition of ownership and other property rights over real estate (in accordance with current legislation) is expressly allowed by the Foreign Investment Act for residential, tourism and commercial projects.

The Foreign Investment Act provides the following main vehicles for foreign investment in Cuba:

- joint venture company;
- international economic association contract; and
- full foreign ownership company.

Joint venture companies and international economic association contracts are referred to in the Foreign Investment Act as "international economic associations".

Investment Protection Provisions

The Foreign Investment Act provides that foreign investments in Cuba enjoy full protection and security and may not be expropriated, except for reasons of public utility or national interest, as declared by the Cuban Government in accordance with the Cuban constitution, current legislation and international mutual investment protection treaties executed by Cuba. In the event of expropriation, prior compensation based on the agreed commercial value of the assets and payable in a freely convertible currency must be paid. SwissCubanCham is not aware of any expropriation of foreign assets since 1982, the year of enactment of Decree Law 50, the predecessor of the Foreign Investment Act.

At any time, a foreign investor may sell or transfer to the Cuban Government or a third party, in whole or in part, its interest in a Cuban joint venture company or other international economic association, subject to agreement between the parties and prior approval of the Cuban Government. The proceeds of such sale or transfer must be paid in a freely convertible currency. The purchase price will be set, in the case of a joint venture company or an international economic association contract, by agreement between the parties, or, in the event that no agreement can be reached, by an organization with internationally recognized expertise and prestige in business valuations authorized by the Ministry of Finance and Prices to operate in Cuba. It is generally possible to establish in the corporate documents creating Cuban foreign investment vehicles rights of first refusal and similar rights regarding the sale or transfer of interests therein.

The Foreign Investment Act guarantees that net profits, dividends and the proceeds resulting from the expropriation, liquidation or sale of shares in a Cuban joint venture or full foreign ownership company or of investment assets may be freely repatriated abroad (free from taxes, withholdings and deductions) in a freely convertible currency. In the event of dispute over the amount payable to the foreign investor following any expropriation, sale, transfer or liquidation of investment assets, such dispute will be settled by an organization having internationally recognized expertise and prestige in business valuations that is authorized by the Ministry of Finance and Prices to operate in Cuba. To the best knowledge of SwissCubanCham, no such organization has been so authorized to date.

In addition, the Foreign Investment Act provides that foreign investments are protected against third party claims made in accordance with Cuban law and rulings of national courts. It should be noted that claims of US nationals resulting from expropriations that took place after 1959 and made pursuant to US law do not fall under this category.

Cuba has executed bilateral investment protection treaties with a number of countries. These treaties provide additional protections to investors of signatory countries.

Taxation

The Foreign Investment Act contains special tax rules and rates for foreign investment vehicles (see Part V entitled "Taxation"). The Ministry of Finance and Prices may generally grant exemptions in respect of all applicable taxes and customs duties. The granting of such exemptions will generally depend on the perceived benefits and size of the investment, the rate of recovery of capital, instructions given by the Executive Committee of the Council of Ministers regarding the priority sectors of the economy and the benefits that may result for the national economy.

Approval Procedures

Following the selection of an investment project and the conclusion of preliminary agreements (usually a letter of intent or a memorandum of understanding) with the Cuban counterpart and/or the relevant Cuban Ministry or Ministries responsible for the investment sector, the procedure for the establishment of a foreign investment vehicle will consist in 5 different stages:

- feasibility study and negotiation of main corporate documents;
- investment proposal to Ministry responsible for project sector;
- joint presentation of investment proposal to Ministry of Foreign Investment and Economic Collaboration by foreign investor and Ministry responsible for project sector;
- consultation with all relevant Government bodies;
- presentation of final investment proposal to Executive Committee of Council of Ministers for approval.

Under the Foreign Investment Act, the decision approving or denying the foreign investment must be rendered within 60 days counted from the date on which the investment proposal is accepted by the Ministry of Foreign Investment and Economic Collaboration. The approval of the Executive Committee of the Council of Ministers is given in the form of a resolution setting out, amongst others, the terms and conditions that will be applicable to the investment. In accordance with article 48 of the Foreign Investment Act, all entities incorporated under the Foreign Investment Act must, within 30 days following the decision mentioned above, be registered on the appropriate commercial register maintained by the Cuban Ministry of Justice.

Resolution of Disputes

The Foreign Investment Act gives to the parties complete freedom to designate in the corporate documents of the foreign investment vehicle any forum for the resolution of disputes arising within the context of their joint activities. In practice, most joint venture agreements and international economic association's contracts contain international arbitration clauses, including International Chamber of Commerce (ICC) and United Nations Commission on International Trade Law (UNCITRAL) arbitration. Cuba is a party to the New York Convention of 1958 on the Recognition and Enforcement of Foreign Arbitral Awards.

Other Provisions

Cuban foreign investment vehicles must generally denominate and carry out their operations entirely in a freely convertible foreign currency, although local payments are now largely made in Cuban Convertible Pesos (CUC). Only in highly exceptional circumstances will a foreign investment vehicle be permitted to make any payment in non-convertible Cuban Pesos (CUP). Foreign investment vehicles may open bank accounts in the Cuban banking system denominated in freely convertible foreign currencies and, with prior approval of the BCC, in Convertible Cuban Pesos (CUC). Such vehicles may only open bank accounts abroad with the prior approval of the BCC. Joint venture companies, full foreign ownership companies and foreign parties to international economic association contracts have the right, in accordance with applicable legislation, to import and export directly all goods necessary to carry out their approved activities.

Foreign investment vehicles must generally comply with applicable labour and social security legislation and must hire Cuban employees in preference to foreign nationals, with the exception of certain top supervisory, administrative and technical positions that may be filled by foreign temporary residents. Temporary residents employed by foreign investment vehicles are not subject to Cuban labour and social security legislation. In general, Cuban employees must be hired through a Cuban employment agency, with the result that foreign investment vehicles pay for employees in freely convertible foreign currency or Cuban Convertible Pesos (CUC) but such employees receive their salary in non-convertible Cuban Pesos (CUP). In certain circumstances, hard currency incentive funds may be established for the benefit of Cuban employees.

Although no maximum term is established in the Foreign Investment Act, joint venture companies are generally established for a term of 25 years. International economic association contracts generally are established for a term of 10 years or less. In all cases, the term of the foreign investment vehicle may be extended by agreement of the parties and with the approval of the Cuban Government for an additional period equal to the original term.

Cuban foreign investment vehicles must establish contingency reserves, charged to profits. Insurance must generally be contracted with insurance providers authorized by the Ministry of Finance and Prices to operate in the country, provided their coverage and premiums are competitive internationally. It should be noted that, to date, no foreign insurer has be so authorized and in practice, insurance coverage must be contracted with Cuban insurance providers.

Foreign investment vehicles may freely determine the accounting system that shall govern their activities, provided that Cuban financial reporting standards are complied with.

Commercial Code and other Legislation

To the extent that foreign investment vehicles take the form of an anonymous share company (S.A.), such vehicles are subject to the application of certain provisions of the Cuban Commercial Code. It should be noted that significant parts of the Commercial Code have been repealed by subsequent legislation. Other generally applicable legislation, such as the Cuban Civil Code, the Banking Act, the Environmental Protection Act, the Tax Act, the Procedures Act and others will also be applicable to the operations of foreign investment vehicles.

INTELLECTUAL PROPERTY

Cuba is a party to a number of international treaties and agreements dealing with the protection of intellectual property, including

- Agreement on Trade-Related Aspects of Intellectual Property Rights;

• World Intellectual Property Organization;

• Paris Convention;

• Lisbon Agreement; and

• Madrid Protocol.

The Cuban Office of Industrial Property is the organization responsible for the protection of intellectual property rights in Cuba.

TAXATION IN CUBA

The general Cuban tax rules are set out in Law no.73 of 1994 on the Taxation System (the "Tax Act"), as well as in various tax resolutions issued by the Ministry of Finance and Prices (the "Ministry of Finance") and other complementary legislation. The tax rules applicable to corporate income tax are set out mainly in the Tax Act and in Resolution 379 of 2003 on Corporate Tax issued by the Ministry of Finance (the "Corporate Tax Regulation"). In addition, the Foreign Investment Act contains particular tax rules applicable to the Cuban operations and activities of foreign investors.

The principal rules relating to personal income tax are laid out in the Tax Act and in Resolution 24 of 1995 on Personal Income Tax issued by the Ministry of Finance.

Decree-Law 169 of 1997 on Tax Norms and Procedures and the Cuban Criminal Code contain additional procedural and penal provisions.

In general, the Ministry of Finance is empowered to grant exemptions (total or partial) to foreign investors in respect of the payment of tax, including exemptions on the payment of corporate tax and personal income tax.

Corporate Tax

Cuban and foreign legal persons, whatever their form of organization or property regime, are subject to the payment of corporate tax (called a "profit tax – *impuesto sobre utilidades*") in connection with their commercial, industrial, construction, financial, agricultural, fishing, service, mining or extraction or other business activities carried out in Cuba. In the case of Cuban legal persons (including Cuban joint venture companies and full foreign ownership companies); corporate tax is payable in respect of world-wide income. In the case of foreign legal persons that are party to an international economic association contract or that have a permanent establishment in Cuba, corporate tax is payable only in respect of Cuban source income attributable to such contract or permanent establishment.

A foreign legal person is normally subject to the payment of corporate tax in Cuba when it has a permanent establishment, a fixed place of business or some form of representation for the purpose of contracting on its behalf in the Republic of Cuba. The term "permanent establishment" is defined in the Tax Act as "any place of business where corporate, commercial, industrial or exploration/extraction of mineral resource activities are carried out, including branches and offices". The Corporate Tax Regulation confirms further that a foreign legal person will be deemed to be carrying out business activities in Cuba at a permanent establishment when any place of business or work area of any nature is at that person's disposal in a continuous manner.

A permanent establishment is also constituted by branches, offices, manufacturing and other facilities, warehouses, shops or other establishments, work sites, agencies or representatives authorized to contract on behalf of the foreign person, mines, oil and gas wells, agricultural/fishing/forestry or other natural resource installations, as well as the provision of corporate consulting or management services (for a continual period of at least 6 months within a single 12 month period).

In the case of the foreign investment vehicles provided under the Foreign Investment Act, corporate tax is payable on net taxable income at a rate of 30%. The Executive Committee of the Council of Ministers may determine that, in the case of renewable or non-renewable natural resources, the tax rate may be increased up to a maximum of 50%.

Net taxable income is calculated as the sum of all income earned during the fiscal year, minus deductible expenses, losses carried forward from previous periods and allowable reserves and provisions. For the purposes of calculating net taxable income, all receipts that increase the patrimony of the person in question, whether in cash, in kind, of valuable title or other, shall be counted as income. Where, as a result of the corporate form or other characteristics of a legal person, it is impossible to determine in an efficient manner satisfactory to the Ministry of Finance the net taxable income of such person, that person may be required to pay corporate tax on the basis of its gross income in accordance with rates established by the Ministry of Finance rather than on net income.

Corporate expenses are deductible if they are (i) necessary (a necessary expense is an expense that is proper to the activity or business in question, actually incurred, current, and that does not arise as a result of a fine or penalty), (ii) properly accounted for in accordance with Cuban Financial Reporting Standards established by the Ministry of Finance and by regulation, and (iii) duly justified by required documentation.

Assets may be depreciated and deducted in accordance with the rates fixed in the Corporate Tax Regulation. If it can be demonstrated that the depreciation of a particular asset should be carried out at a different rate, a request may be made to the Ministry of Finance for this purpose. In addition, in a section dealing with "other authorized adjustments", the Corporate Tax Regulation provides that, in the mining sector, persons subject to the payment of corporate tax may, if so authorized by the Executive Committee of the Council of Ministers, allocate a portion of profits, prior to the application of corporate tax, to the amortization of exploration and development costs characterized as recoverable expenses.

Proper accounting books and records must be maintained in accordance with Cuban Financial Reporting Standards, which [have been adopted from the International Financial Reporting Standards (IFRS) issued by the International Accounting Standards Board (IASB)] are set out in Resolution no.235 issued by the Ministry of Finance in 2005. The financial statements of any entity subject to taxation in Cuba must be audited annually by an auditor that is duly authorized by the Ministry of Finance.

DECREE-LAW ON FREE ZONES AND INDUSTRIAL PARKS.

CHAPTER I PROVISIONS

ARTICLE 1.1. This decree-law aims to promulgate rules concerning the establishment and operation of free zones and industrial parks.

2. The provisions of this decree-law relating to free zones apply to industrial parks accordingly.

3. Export processing zones and industrial parks aid in the economic and social development, international trade and stimulating addition to attracting foreign capital, pursue the following specific purposes:

a) the generation of new jobs and raising the qualification of workers;

b) inclusion of more national industrial added value, using the resources of the country and

c) development of new domestic industries through the assimilation of advanced technologies and export of domestic products.

4. This decree-law also includes rules of a special regime in respect of customs, banking, tax, labor, immigration and law enforcement involving facilities and incentives for foreign investment.

CHAPTER II DEFINITIONS

ARTICLE 2.1. This decree-law are used for brevity, the following terms:
Zone by zone and industrial park.
Executive Committee, Executive Committee of the Council of Ministers.
Commission, Commission of Free Zones.

2. In the text are used with the meaning that in each case indicated, the following terms:
Free Trade Zone: a space in the country, properly defined, no resident population of free import and export of goods, customs disconnected from the river, which made industrial, commercial, agricultural, technological and service, with application special arrangements.

Industrial Park: an area within the national territory, with characteristics similar to the free zone, but in which the activities are predominantly in developing industrial and services that support these.

Special Conditions: rules relating to customs systems, banking, tax, labor, immigration and public order, less expensive and rigid than the common or ordinary, applicable to contractors and operators of free zones as incentives for investment.

Concession: unilateral act of the Government of the Republic of Cuba, which is given to a natural or legal person the power to promote and operate a free zone, subject to fulfillment of certain conditions.

Dealership: the natural person or legal entity residing abroad and foreign capital or domestic legal entity, in exercise of the corresponding grant equity and encourages and develops the infrastructure necessary and sufficient for the installation and operation of the free zone , and then assumed the management and administration thereof.

Operator: The person or entity, residing abroad and foreign capital or domestic legal entity, which the Ministry for Foreign Investment and Economic Cooperation, proposed by the licensee, authorized to settle in the zone for there one or more of the activities within the legal framework for this occupation.

Official Record: books, booklets or magnetic media established and organized by the Ministry for Foreign Investment and Economic Cooperation for the registration of dealers and traders.

CHAPTER III THE CREATION AND CONTROL OF EPZS.

Section One

From the creation of free zones

ARTICLE 3. The Executive Committee of the Council of Ministers, on its own initiative or proposal of the Ministry for Foreign Investment and Economic Cooperation, provides for the establishment of free zones.

Section Two Control of free zones

ARTICLE 4.1. The Ministry for Foreign Investment and Economic Cooperation is the organization of the central state administration in charge of regulating and controlling the activities taking place in the EPZs.

2. For this purpose, it is incumbent:

a) Executive Committee proposes to base the creation of free zones and the granting of concessions;

b) propose to the Executive Committee's policy to follow in regard to free zones and the development of such programs;

c) make rules of each proposed free trade zone for the respective dealer or failing that, at his discretion;

d) organize and coordinate relations with other entities whose activities are related to those performed in export processing zones;

e) establish, in conjunction with the Ministries of Finance and Prices, Foreign Trade, Economy and Planning, Labor and Social Security, and Interior and the National Bank of Cuba, the General Customs of the Republic and other State agencies, a system by which the steps or procedures to be carried out or to meet dealers and operators of free zones before them, are made from a single point or central office, in your own zone;

f) create, organize and regulate the Official Register for entry in the same dealers and operators;

g) receive applications for approval of zone operator, entertain them and make necessary decisions;

h) determining the amounts and determine the manner in which dealers must make security deposits to ensure compliance with conditions of grant;

i) perform such other duties legally imposed upon it in relation to the zones.

ARTICLE 5.1. The Ministry for Foreign Investment and Economic Cooperation, in order to ensure continuity and effective operation of free zones, also serves as the regulator of these, and as such, and for ensuring compliance with the conditions imposed on the respective licensees and operators, and respond appropriately to any violation.

2. Licensees and operators must provide the information and perform the acts that the Ministry for Foreign Investment and Economic Collaboration, within its powers, requiring them to improve the performance of its obligations of supervision.

CHAPTER IV OF THE COMMISSION ON FREE ZONES

ARTICLE 6.1. Establishing a Free Trade Zone Commission, advised the Ministry for Foreign Investment and Economic Collaboration with the competence and functions are listed below.

2. The Free Trade Zone Commission consists of the Minister for Foreign Investment and Economic Cooperation, as president, and a representative from each of the following organizations as members:

- Ministry of Economy and Planning
- Ministry of Finance and Prices
- Ministry of Foreign Trade
- Ministry of Labor and Social Security
- Ministry of the Revolutionary Armed Forces
- Ministry of Interior
- Ministry of Science, Technology and Environment
- Ministry of Transport
- Banco Nacional de Cuba
- General Customs of the Republic

3. In cases where, by the nature of the issue in question is considered helpful to have the opinion of any body or agency not included among those listed in the preceding paragraph of this article, the President shall request the address thereof, to appoint a representative who, to this effect, act as a voice over the Commission.

4. The functions of the Commission:

a) collaboration with the Ministry for Foreign Investment and Economic Cooperation in drafting the Comprehensive Development Program of Free Zones;

b) give opinion on the proposed creation of free zones and concessions, and

c) recommend, among other measures and enforcement actions it deems necessary for the development of free zones.

5. The Commission itself, with the subsequent approval of the Ministry for Foreign Investment and Economic Cooperation, will draft the regulation to be guided, which decide the frequency with which they hold their meetings, the number of votes required to adopt agreements and how to record these and other provisions deemed appropriate.

CHAPTER V DEALERS FOR FREE TRADE ZONE

Section One The authority granting the concession

ARTICLE 7. The Executive Committee may grant administrative concessions on certain zones.

Section Two In the application for authorization and processing.

ARTICLE 8.1. They can apply for the grant of an administrative concession for a particular zone, natural or juridical persons, residing abroad and foreign capital or domestic legal persons.

2. The application is submitted to the Ministry for Foreign Investment and Economic Collaboration, and together with it, a statement which contains the following information:

a) name and address of the applicant;

b) description of the objectives, activities, structures, organization and planned services, consistent with the master plan for development of the territory concerned;

c) surface area and location of the zone;

d) technical feasibility study, financial and economic market of the project and predictable;

e) indication of the composition of capital;

f) Project implementation schedule, including the initial investment and future investment scheme;

g) documentation proving your identity and your financial situation, and be a legal person, domestic or foreign, copies of the documents constituting the entity and to justify the powers of the respondent as the legitimate representative of the same, duly authenticated and

h) other data and information required in individual cases by the Ministry for Foreign Investment and Economic Collaboration.

ARTICLE 9. The Ministry for Foreign Investment and Economic Collaboration, once it has reviewed the documentation submitted and consulted where appropriate with other agencies or organizations, send the proceedings to the Commission, these elements offer your opinion, and finally move the conformed to the effect file to the Executive Committee to resolve as appropriate.

Section Three The granting of the concession

ARTICLE 10. The award will be granted or denied within sixty (60) calendar days from the date of filing, and the government's agreement to be delivered must be notified to the concerned through the Ministry for Foreign Investment and Economic Cooperation.

ARTICLE 11.1 The granting the concession agreement must contain the following information:

a) the identity and legal status of the concessionaire;
b) geographic location of the zone that is permitted;
c) conditions imposed on the concessionaire;
d) investment program;
e) project characteristics;
f) activities to develop;
g) special scheme;
h) term on the franchises and
i) Any other deemed necessary or desirable to include.

2. The term for which the grant is awarded, shall not exceed fifty (50) years and may be extended for successive periods to match the original set.

3. Expiration of the term of the lease and the extension or extensions, if any, original dealer will have preference for granting a new concession on equal terms with other stakeholders.

Section Four The powers and duties of the concessionaire

Article 12.1. The development, installation and operation of free zones is carried out by dealers, who for this purpose perform the activities described in the agreement of the Executive Committee granting the concession, within the following framework:

a) develop land and build on them office buildings, factories, warehouses, depots, service and other activities, and any necessary and appropriate infrastructure for the development of those, both for their own use and for lease to third parties to be established in them;

b) give land on lease or surface rights for conduct of activities authorized;

c) provide boot services and partial or full operation of plants to support or carry out the activities of operators;

d) build, promote and develop training centers and technical training, health care and sports and recreational facilities and public services, including transport, for the use of operators and their employees;

e) perform the necessary facilities for the provision of electricity, gas and water, local and international communications, safety, sewerage, sewage treatment and waste, as well as others that are required to enable compliance with the purposes free zones;

f) develop outside the zones, and areas that are selected in a timely manner, housing, hotels and other lodging facilities, hospitals, schools and the more they can contribute to the smooth functioning of the free zone;

g) operate airports, ports, docks, loading or unloading places, railway stations or railway lines or ground loading and unloading, according to the respective legal regulations in force, and

h) any other that the Executive Committee has included in the award.

2. The dealer to hold the leases and the granting of surface rights shall be governed by provisions in effect in the Civil Code of the Republic of Cuba.

3. The rest of the above activities will also be conducted in compliance with regulatory standards, with respect thereto may exist.

ARTICLE 13. The dealer, after carrying out the award, must;

a) invest in developing the free zone in an amount not less than that proposed in the application and ratified by the provision that granted the lease, and within the scheduled period;

b) initiating a period not exceeding one hundred eighty (180) days after the investment referred to in the preceding paragraph has elapsed from its entry in the Official Register of Licensees and Operators;

c) ensuring the existence and maintenance of infrastructure, consistent with the terms of the concession, which allows adequate working conditions and provision of basic and essential services, including green and recreation areas in accordance with international practices;

d) promote and develop training programs that result in technical-vocational training for workers when this is required;

e) ensuring the efficiency of the facilities of the zone, so that operators have the necessary conditions for the development of its activities;

f) implement and enforce existing standards or those enacted relating to environmental protection, elimination of pollution, soil conservation, parks and marine flora and fauna as well as veterinary control and Plant;

g) comply with legal provisions on hygiene and safety at work.

h) prepare the draft rules of the free zone for subsequent approval by the Ministry for Foreign Investment and Economic Cooperation;

i) make the security deposit if such obligations are among the conditions for granting and

j) provide the Ministry for Foreign Investment and Economic Cooperation's annual report and any other activities that the body requires.

ARTICLE 14. The dealer can freely set the price to meet the operator for the transmission of goods, lease of facilities and transfer of rights to make in his favor, and the services it agrees to lend.

ARTICLE 15. The dealer, after approval of the Ministry for Foreign Investment and Economic Collaboration, can perform its functions through an agent or attorney, which always act on behalf and under the responsibility of the former.

ARTICLE 16. The dealer, for the start of its operations and activities must be registered in the Official Register of Licensees and Operators within thirty (30) days from the date of grant of the concession.

CHAPTER VI OPERATORS ZONE

Section One The authority to authorize the operator

ARTICLE 17. The Ministry for Foreign Investment and Economic Cooperation, proposed by the licensee, authorize the establishment of facility operators in the free zone.

Section Two

In the application for authorization and processing operator

ARTICLE 18. Can be operated zone natural persons or legal entities residing abroad and foreign capital or domestic legal persons interested in conducting as such.

Article 19.1. To manage the authorization of the operator, interested parties must submit a formal request to the dealer accompanied by a statement containing the following information:

a) For natural persons: name, nationality, passport details and address.

b) For legal persons: name of company, company or partnership name, country under whose laws it is incorporated, indicating data entry in the relevant public register and names of its representative legal. A copy of the certificate attesting the incorporation and legal representative character raised by the respondent, who shall be duly authenticated, as established by Cuban law;

2. With the application, shall, also, information, properly documented on the following points:

a) applicant's financial solvency;
b) intends to develop activities;
c) list of the main machinery, equipment and accessories and raw materials and other media to be used;
d) estimated number of jobs generated by the project, according to economic studies, financial and market made;
e) initial investment and future investments, including project implementation schedule and
f) other information and data required in each case by the concessionaire.

3. The formalities provided for in the preceding paragraphs, the concessionaire shall transmit the file formed the Ministry for Foreign Investment and Economic Collaboration, and its impact.

Section Three Operator Authorization

SECTION 20. The Ministry for Foreign Investment and Economic Collaboration, once you have reviewed and assessed all submissions and held consultations with relevant bodies of the central state administration will resolve it from within a period not exceeding forty - five (45) days from the date of filing.

ARTICLE 21. The operator authorization must contain information regarding the identity of the latter, the free trade zone will develop its role, immediate and future planned investments, their business activities, minutely described, special arrangements and any others deemed necessary or desirable.

ARTICLE 22. The operator, for the start of its operations, must enroll in the Official Register of Licensees and Operators within thirty (30) days from the date you receive the authorization.

Section Four The powers and duties of operator

ARTICLE 23. The zone operator can perform the activities described in the permit within the following framework:

a) Production and manufacturing, or processing of raw materials or intermediate products;

b) assembly, or manufacture of finished products or semi-processed through the system installation and adjustment of parts, components or accessories;
c) processing or semi-finished products, or finished or semi-finished products, parts, components, accessories or parts, to be subjected to any process that is necessary in order to make possible the commercialization of the product in question;
d) trade, ie, handling, packaging and repackaging, storage, storage and sale of products;
e) operational, ie, use of ports, airports, docks, loading and unloading sites, stations and railway sidings, loading and unloading land or other similar activities;
f) banking, finance and insurance, or provision of these services into a free zone that is established in other zones or outside.
g) general services, or provide services to free zones and operators and their employees, such as restaurants, laundries, pharmacies, beauty salons, gyms, health care and other similar nature;

h) other services, or marketing services, auditing, administration, information technology, consulting and similar to established traders in the same zone or in other of the country or for export;
i) technological and scientific research, or research to improve the technological level of industrial

and agribusiness;
j) agricultural, or farming and raising livestock, and

k) other activities previously identified by the Ministry for Foreign Investment and Economic Collaboration.

ARTICLE 24. Any application or process that is required to submit or make operators with state institutions and authorities must do so through a single point or central office of the zone.

ARTICLE 25. For reasons of availability of labor, transportation, handling of raw materials and other relevant reasons and express prior approval of the Ministry for Foreign Investment and Economic Cooperation, the operator can make the area outside the zone in which it is established activities as specified in the relevant decision of that body, although these cases may be missing from customs controls, appropriate fiscal and labor.

Article 26.1. The zone operator to conduct the business of manufacturing, manufacturing, assembling, processing or semi-finished products, trade and agriculture, the market can allocate up to twenty-five percent (25%) of the goods from their production activities.

2. Where the operator asks you in the market a greater percentage of twenty five percent (25%) of the property subject to its activities, the question shall be decided by the Ministry for Foreign Investment and Economic Cooperation and the Ministry Foreign Trade.

3. Imports from free zones into national customs territory are subject to the same regulations and to pay the same tariffs as those applicable to imports from other countries are carried out, excluding the payment of the same percentage of domestic value added incorporated.

4. Not pay customs duties introduced in the domestic market, duly authorized, in assets that have undergone a transformation or processing (value added costs) that will bring them at least fifty percent (50%) of its value end.

ARTICLE 27. Operators should have the following obligations:

a) keep track of their production activities, facilities, according to the universally accepted principles;
b) invest in their projects in an amount not less than the amount stated in the application and any terms specified in the authorization;
c) promote and develop training programs that allow technical-vocational training and retraining of workers, when necessary;
d) report annually to the Ministry for Foreign Investment and Economic Cooperation, through the dealer, a report containing the following information: jobs created, investment, volume, amount, type and destination of exports (goods or services), actual production , inputs used (amount, source and type) and any others that indicate that body;
e) submit annual fiscal reports to the Ministry of Finance and Prices, with the data reported by the authority;
f) take necessary measures for the efficiency and effectiveness of inspections and investigations available to the competent authorities for the proper control of the conditions of the permit;
g) make deposits in the cases proceed, and

h) develop their activities in the terms and conditions set forth in the authorization issued.

CHAPTER VII OTHER PROVISIONS CONCERNING DEALERS AND TRADERS

ARTICLE 28. The licensee may exercise concurrently with the activities that are specific to the operator, being applicable in such circumstances, correspondingly, the regulations pertaining to both occupations.

ARTICLE 29. The concessionaire and the operator held a contract that includes, among other stipulations, those in which the first transferred to the latter, for sale, lease or other possessory, a certain portion of the facilities of the zone, the rights he relents and agrees to the services provided to make feasible its mission, as well as setting the level, form and terms of price to pay.

ARTICLE 30. The concessionaire and operator can acquire in the country, outside the geographical area where they are established, goods or services offered by companies based in the country.

CHAPTER VIII THE SPECIAL REGIME

Section One Scope of the special arrangements

Article 31.1. The special provisions referred to earlier in this decree law and defined in Article 2.2 thereof applicable to licensees and operators of free zones as incentives for investment, is made up of customs regulations, banking, tax, labor and also special order, or more attractive and less rigid and onerous than the common or ordinary. As for immigration, these are entered in issue resolution to be the lead agency in the space of 90 days from the effective date of this decree-law.

2. Dealers and traders enjoy the special regime provided for by this decree-law, provided that in no case be altered to their disadvantage.

Section Two Of special customs regulations

Article 32.1. Licensees and operators are exempt from tariffs and other duties collected by customs, by the introduction in the area of the zone of developing products for authorized activities.

2. The goods to be exported from the zone are not taxed by tariffs and other duties collected by customs.

ARTICLE 33. It can be introduced into the free zone weapons, explosives or products of export or import is prohibited, suspended or restricted by law.

ARTICLE 34. The General Customs of the Republic shall establish the necessary mechanisms and attenuated controls regarding the import and export activities undertaken by concessionaires and operators of free zones.

Section three Of special tax regulations

Article 35.1. Licensees and operators of free zones, benefiting from the special scheme, are exempted from payment of tax liabilities as follows:

a) tax on profits, and
b) imposed by the use of the workforce.

2. These exemptions are granted as follows

With respect to licensees and operators engaged in production, manufacturing, assembly, processing or semi-finished products and agricultural,

a) total exemption for the first twelve (12) years and
b) bonus of fifty percent (50%) over the next five (5) years.

For operators conducting commercial activities and services,
a) total exemption for the first five (5) years and
b) bonus of fifty percent (50%) during the following three (3) years.

ARTICLE 36. By granting concessions and authorizations approved operator can grant exemptions from taxes are more favorable than those contained in the initial article of this section or other incentives to agree, taking into account the benefits that the specific activity in question would contribute to the development country's economic characteristics of the proposed investment and regulations applicable to different sectors of the economy.

ARTICLE 37.1 The terms of tax exemptions provided for in the preceding paragraphs, may be extended by the same terms as the original.

2. Once the deadlines have passed exemptions in place and throughout the remainder of its activities, dealers and operators of free zones have received benefits paid the aforesaid special tax as regulated in the Law about No.77 / 95, Law on Foreign Investment.

Section four Of special banking regulations

Article 38.1. The dealer and the zone operator can transfer abroad, in freely convertible currency, without payment of taxes or other charges in connection with such transfer, the net profits or dividends to obtain, from their activities.

2. Foreign citizens serving in a free zone, provided they are not permanent residents in Cuba, they can transfer assets abroad to receive, in proportion and according to other rules specified for it by the National Bank of Cuba;

ARTICLE 39. The operators authorized to provide banking and financial services in free zones, may conduct their activities only within the limits of the zone in which they are established in other zones of the country and abroad, and regulated in accordance with this regard by the National Bank of Cuba.

ARTICLE 40. Transactions within the limits of free zones and those referred to in Articles 25 and 30 of this decree-law, made dealers and traders in freely convertible currency.

ARTICLE 41. There may be denominated in local currency or executed acts of measurement values and price formation or the payments made in providing services, under contracts entered into by concessionaires and operators within the territory free zones, except those expressly authorized.

ARTICLE 42. Notwithstanding the provisions of the preceding articles, the National Bank of Cuba will issue additional special regulations required for the development of the activities of operators allowed to provide banking services in the EPZs.

Section five Special regulations of labor

Article 43.1. Workers who provide services to licensees and operators of free zones will, as a rule, Cubans or foreigners residing permanently in Cuba.

2. For the performance of certain technical occupations or top administrative positions, dealers and operators of free zones may contract directly with individuals not permanently resident in the country, and in such cases, the regime applicable labor and rights and obligations of migrant workers, previously managing the relevant work permit.

ARTICLE 44. The Ministry of Labor and Social Security set minimum wages by occupation to be paid to Cuban workers and foreigners with permanent residence in the country, providing services to dealers or operators of free zones.

Article 45.1. The dealer Cuban or mixed capital contracts directly with Cuban workers and permanent resident aliens in the country, and serves also as employing entity regarding the workers required by operators.

2. The employing entity referred to in the previous section hires individual workers concerned, pays its assets and maintains working relationship with them.

3. The Ministry of Labor and Social Security sets the standards the licensee must comply, in its capacity as employer.

4. Cuban workers and permanent resident aliens in the country provide services to licensees and operators of free zones, which are wholly foreign capital, under a contract which they celebrated with one employing entity proposed by the Ministry for Foreign Investment and Collaboration Economic and approved by the Ministry of Labor and Social Security.

ARTICLE 46. Notwithstanding the foregoing Articles of this Chapter, the Executive Committee, the agreement that provides for the establishment of a free zone, you can determine that with respect to it and so unique, special labor regulations are established.

Section Six Special regulations for public order.

Article 47.1. Public order in the free zones shall be in accordance with the regulations to this effect issued by the Ministry of Interior.

2. The cost of the surveillance and protection shall be determined in accordance with international practice, and will be borne by the dealers and operators in the proportions that they agree.

CHAPTER IX ON VIOLATIONS COMMITTED BY DEALERS ZONES AND OPERATORS

ARTICLE 48. Failure by dealers to the obligations relating to amounts and timing of investment to be made, may be sufficient cause for revocation of the concession.

ARTICLE 49. Administrative violation is the failure of licensees and operators of the conditions imposed by their titles and also the transgression of the rules of this decree-law or Regulation of the Zona Franca, in regard to them.

Article 50 1. Violations of dealers and traders referred to previous articles may determine the withdrawal of a diploma by the state agency that granted it, unless it is established that the failure was due to unforeseeable circumstances or force majeure.

2. The revocation of the title consist of total or permanent cancellation of the concession or approval of operator and loss, to the State, property and rights of the offender related to the free zone.

CHAPTER X OF CONFLICT RESOLUTION

Article 51.1. The conflicts that arise in their internal relations between dealers and operators of free zones are resolved in the manner provided in the contracts signed by them.

2. The same rule applies when a conflict arises between operators.

ARTICLE 52. Disputes concerning the implementation of economic contracts arising between the licensees and operators with state enterprises or other entities, are the responsibility of the instances of the Economic Chambers of the People's Courts established by the Governing Council of the Court Supreme People.

SPECIAL PROVISIONS

FIRST: The provisions for the better implementation of this Decree-Law shall be ordered by the competent bodies of the Central State Administration no later than ninety (90) days after its entry into force.

SECOND: The bodies of the central state administration and other government institutions, take appropriate action, so that permit applications, consultation and other services related to export processing zones are resolved within a period not exceeding forty (40) days in all cases, counted from the date of acceptance of that application.

DISPOSAL
few laws are repealed and lower rank equally oppose the provisions of this Decree-Law, which will take effect after its publication in the Official Gazette of the Republic.

SUPPLEMENTS

IMPORTANT CONTACTS FOR TRADE AND INVESTMENTS

U.S..- Cuba Trade and Economic Council, Inc.

30 Rockefeller Plaza New York, New York 10112-0002

Telephone (212) 246-1444 Facsimile (212) 246-2345
e-mail:council@cubatrade.org
Internet: http://www.cubatrade.org

Alamar Associates
Mailing Address:
8305 Whitman Dr
Bethesda, MD 20817
Phone:301-520-4297
Fax: 202-478-0839
Email: AlaCuba@aol.com

CONTACT INFORMATION FOR FOOD AND AGRICULTURAL PRODUCT

Exports To The Republic Of Cuba

Mr. Pedro Alvarez Borrego
Chairman and Chief Executive Officer
Alimport
Infanta No. 16, 3rd Piso
Vedado, Plaza
La Habana, Republica de Cuba
Telephone: 011 53 7 855 0573 or 011 53 7 873 2014
Facsimile: 011 53 7 873 3151
E-mail: alimport@alimport.com.cu

Mr. Igor Montero Brito
President and Chief Operating Officer
Alimport
Infanta No. 16, 3rd Piso
Vedado, Plaza
La Habana, Republica de Cuba
Telephone: 011 53 7 873 0026 or 011 53 7 873 2014
Facsimile: 011 53 7 873 3151
E-mail: montero@alimport.com.cu

Mr. Alexander Perez Cartaya

Commercial Department
Alimport
Infanta No. 16, 3rd Piso
Vedado, Plaza
La Habana, Republica de Cuba
Telephone: 011 53 7 873 2014
Facsimile: 011 53 7 873 3151
E-mail: alexander@alimport.com.cu

Ms. Yaili Escobar Rodriguez
Commercial Department
Alimport
Infanta No. 16, 3rd Piso
Vedado, Plaza
La Habana, Republica de Cuba
Telephone: 011 53 7 873 2014
Facsimile: 011 53 7 873 3151
E-mail: yaili@alimport.com.cu

Ms. Ana Vivian Alvarez Rodriguez
Director- Meat Division
Alimport
Infanta No. 16, 3rd Piso
Vedado, Plaza
La Habana, Republica de Cuba
Telephone: 011 53 7 873 2014 or 011 53 7 855 0582
Facsimile: 011 53 7 873 3151
E-mail: combi@alimport.com.cu

Mr. Emerio Izquierdo Gonzalez
Deputy Director
Union de Empresas Combinado Avicola Nacional
Ave. Independencia y Conill
Edificio de MINAG, 5th Piso
Plaza, La Habana
Republica de Cuba
Telephone: 011 53 7 884 5478
Facsimile: 011 53 7 881 8931
E-mail: emerio@uecan.com.cu

Mr. Agustin E. Gonzalez Rivero
Manager- Food Buying
Distribuidora Cimex S.A.
Edificio Sierra Maestra
Calle 1st e/O y 2, Miramar, Playa
La Habana, Republica de Cuba
Telephone: 011 53 7 23 9250/9673
Facsimile: 011 53 7 24 2163/2098
E-mail: agustin@cimex.com.cu

STRATEGIC GOVERNMENT AND BUSINESS CONTACTS

"Jose Martí" International Airport
Rancho Boyeros, Cuba
Telf. : 45-3133, 33-5666,33-5777, 33-5753
Telex : 51-1304
Fax : 33-5169

General Customhouse of the Republic of Cuba
Calle 39 esq. 6, Nuevo Vedado Ciudad de La Habana, Cuba
Telf. : 55-5466 AL 71
Fax : 33-5222

Havana Subcontracting Exchange
Calle 17 No. 55 Apto. 1-B Edif. FOCSA, Vedado, Plaza Ciudad de La Habana, Cuba
Telf. : 30-9556
Telex : 51-1555
Fax : 30-9556

Chamber of Commerce of the Republic of Cuba
Calle 21 No. 661, esq. A, Vedado, Ciudad de La Habana, Cuba
Telf. : 30-3356 al 58
Telex : 51-1754 CAMAR CU
Fax : 33-3042

National Packing and Packaging Center (CNEE)
Ave. Del Bosque No. 121, Nuevo Vedado, Ciudad de La Habana, Cuba
Telf. : 81-0197 / 81-2100 / 81-3422
Fax : 33-3150

National Plant Health Center
Ayuntamiento No.231 e/ San Pedro y Lombillo, Siboney, Ciudad de La Habana, Cuba
Telf. : 79-1339 / 78-4976 al 79
Fax : 70-3277 / 79-6654

Center for Export Promotion of Cuba (CEPEC)
Infanta No. 16 esq. 23, Vedado, Ciudad de La Habana, Cuba
Telf. : 55-0428 / 54-2185 / 54-2194 /55-0405 / 55-0425
Telex : 51-1174 / 1175 y 1176 MCEX CU
Fax : 66-2220 / 55-0376
E-Mail: cepecdir@infocex.cu
cepecsic@infocex.cu
cepecmer@infocex.cu

Cuban Radio and Television Institute
Calle 23 No. 258, Vedado, Ciudad de La Habana, Cuba
Telf. : 32-1568 / 32-4775 / 33-4256
Fax : 33-3107

Cuban Civil Aviation Institute
Calle 23 No. 64 esq. Infanta, Vedado, Ciudad de La Habana, Cuba

Telf. : 33-4412
Fax : 30-4618

Hydraulic Resources National Institute
Virtudes No.680 esq. a Belascoaín, Centro Habana
Telf. : 70-5571

Institute of Veterinary Medicine
Calle 12 No. 355 e/15 y 17, Vedado, Ciudad de La Habana, Cuba
Telf. : 3-7330 / 3-7077 / 30-6615
Fax : 30-3537

National Institute of Sports, Physical Education and Recreation
Ave. Independencia y Vía Blanca, Ciudad de La Habana, Cuba
Telf. : 40-3390 / 81-5176 / 41-1415
Fax : 33-5310

Ministry of Science, Technology and the Environment
Industria y Barcelona, Capitolio Nacional, Ciudad de La Habana, Cuba
Telf. : 62-0420 / 60-3411
Telex : 51-1290
Fax : 33-8654

Ministry of Labor and Social Security
23 y P, Vedado, Ciudad de La Habana, Cuba
Telf. : 70-4571 / 70-9311

Ministry of Culture
Calle 2 No. 258 e/ 11 y 13, Vedado, Ciudad de La Habana, Cuba
Telf. : 55-2236 / 55-2239-40 / 55-2256
Fax : 33-3013 / 66-2284

Ministry of Economy and Planning
20 de Mayo y Ayestarán, Plaza, Ciudad de La Habana, Cuba
Telf. : 51-5371 / 81-3798
Telex : 51-1421 / 51-1806

Ministry of Education
Obispo No. 160, Habana Vieja, Ciudad de La Habana, Cuba
Telf. : 61-4534 / 62-8011
Fax : 62-2547

Ministry of Finances and Prices
Calle Obispo No.211 esq. a Cuba, Habana Vieja, Ciudad de La Habana
Telf. : 57-3000
Fax : 33-8050

Ministry of Construction
Ave. Carlos Manuel de Céspedes y Calle 35, Plaza, Ciudad de La Habana, Cuba
Telf. : 82-0244 / 81-6978
Telex : 51-1275
Fax : 81-5376

Ministry of the Construction Materials Industry
Calle 17 esq. O, Plaza, Ciudad de La Habana, Cuba
Telf. : 32-2541 al 49 / 32-9494
Telex : 51-1517 / 51-1329 / 51-1205
Fax : 33-3004

Ministry of Agriculture
Ave. Independencia e/Conill y Santa Ana, Ciudad de La Habana
Telf. : 81-2875 / 84-5770
Telex : 51-1966 / 51-1968
Fax : 33-5086

Ministry of the Food Industry
Calle 41 No. 4455 esq. 50, Playa, Ciudad de La Habana
Telf. : 23-6801 al 09 / 23-4671
Telex : 51-1123
Fax : 29-6089 / 24-0517

Ministry of the Sugar Industry
Calle 23 No. 171 e/ N y O, Vedado, Ciudad de La Habana, Cuba
Telf. : 55-3194
Telex : 51-1292
Fax : 33-3193

Ministry of the Basic Industry
Salvador Allende No. 666 e/ Oquendo y Soledad, Ciudad de La Habana, Cuba
Telf. : 57-5031 al 37
Telex : 51-1325
Fax : 33-5345

Ministry of Foreign Trade
Infanta No. 16 esq. 23, Vedado, Ciudad de La Habana, Cuba
Telf. : 54-3237 / 54-2265
Telex : 51-1174, 1175 MCEX CU
Fax : 550356

Ministry of Domestic Trade
Obispo No.302, Habana Vieja, Ciudad de La Habana, Cuba
Tlf. : 60-3311

Ministry of Communications
Ave. Independencia y 19 de Mayo, Plaza, Ciudad de La Habana, Cuba
Telf. : 82-0088
Telex : 51-1713, 51-1915
Fax : 33-5253

Ministry of the Light Industry
Empedrado No. 302 esq. Aguiar, Ciudad de La Habana, Cuba
Telf. : 57-0387
Fax : 62-5575

Ministry of Justice
Calle O No. 216 e/23 y Humboldt, Vedado, Ciudad de La Habana, Cuba
Telf. : 55-3451 al 59
Fax : 33-3038

Ministry of Foreign Affairs
Calzada No. 360 esq. G, Vedado, Ciudad de La Habana, Cuba
Telf. : 31-2206 / 30-5031 / 55-3260
Telex : 51-1122
Fax : 33-3460 / 32-5178

Ministry of Public Health
Calle 23 No. 201 esq. N, Vedado, Ciudad de La Habana, Cuba
Telf. : 55-3332 al 41 / 55-3345 al 48
Telex : 51-1149
Fax : 66-2537

Ministry of Tourism
Calle 19 e/ A y Paseo, Vedado, Ciudad de La Habana, Cuba
Telf. : 33-4319 / 33-4323
Fax : 33-4325

Ministry for Foreign Investment and Economic Cooperation
Calle Primera 18 y 20, Miramar, Ciudad de la Habana, Cuba
Telf. : 29-2828 / 22-5196
Telex : 51-1445 / 51-1341
Fax : 24-6951 / 24-3183

Ministry of the Fishing Industry
5ta. Ave. y Calle 248, Barlovento, Santa Fé, Ciudad de La Habana, Cuba
Telf. : 24-1189 / 29-7930 / 29-7942
Telex : 51-1206
Fax : 24-9167/68

Ministry of Transportation
Ave. Independencia y Tulipán, Plaza, Ciudad de La Habana, Cuba
Telf. : 81-1782 / 55-5031 al 39
Telex : 51-1181
Fax : 33-5118

Ministry of the Iron, Steel, Mechanical and Electronic Industry
Ave. Rancho Boyeros y Calle 100, Altahabana, Ciudad de La Habana
Telf. : 45-3911 / 45-3978
Telex : 51-1179 / 51-1473
Fax : 27-1163

Ministry of Justice (Special Notary's Office)
Calle O entre 23 y 25, Vedado, Ciudad de La Habana, Cuba
Telf. : 55-3451 al 59
Fax : 33-3038

Cuban Office of Industrial Property
Picota No.15 e/ Luz y Acosta, Habana Vieja, Ciudad de La Habana, Cuba
Telf. : 61-0185 / 61-3602
Fax : 33-5610

National Standardization Office
Calle 13 esq. E, Vedado, Ciudad de La Habana, Cuba
Telf. : 30-0022

National Office of Free Zones
Calle 22 No.318 e/ 3ra y 5ta, Miramar, Ciudad de La Habana, Cuba
Telf. : 29-0686 / 24-7636 / 29-0685 al 89
Fax : 24-7637

Food Nutrition and Health National Institute
Calzada de Infanta No.1158 e/ Llinaz y Clavel, Centro Habana, Ciudad de La Habana Cuba
Telf. : 70-3104 / 78-5919 / 78-1429

City Havana Free Zone
Carretera de Berroa Km 1, Habana del Este, Ciudad de La Habana, Cuba
Telf. : 33-8137 al 39 / 33-8923
Fax : 33-8140 / 66-9898
E-Mail: victor p.@cimex.com.cu

Mariel Free Zone
Carretera de Quiebra Hacha Km 8 ½, Vista del Mar.
Península de Angosta, Mariel, Ciudad de La Habana
Telf. : 33-5924
Fax : 33-5925

Wajay Free Zone
Carretera Aerocaribbean, Km 1 ½, Wajay, Ciudad de La Habana, Cuba
Telf. : 33-5884
Fax : 33-5885

MINCEX Territorial Delegation
Santiago de Cuba-Granma-Guantánamo
Santo Tomás No.565, 3er piso e/ Aguilera y Enramada, Santiago de Cuba
Telf. : (0-226)2-9144 / 2-6725
Fax : (0-226)8-6290

MINCEX Territorial Delegation
Holguín-Las Tunas
Calle 10 de Octubre No.3 e/ Luz y Mario Pozo, Rpto.Luz, Holguín
Telf. : (0-244) 6-2379 / 6-2865
Fax : (0-244) 6-2379

MINCEX Territorial Delegation
Camaguey-Ciego de Avila
Calle 6ta. E/ 1ra y B, Rpto. Julio A. Mella, Camaguey
Fax : 7-1725

MINCEX Territorial Delegation
Cienfuegos
Ave.37 (Prado)No.4406 e/ 44 y 46, Cienfuegos
Telf. : (0-432) 3321 y 8591
Fax : (0-432) 8951

National Code(537)

BASIC TITLES ON CUBA

IMPORTANT!

All publications are updated annually!

Please contact IBP, Inc. at ibpusa3@gmail.com for the latest ISBNs and additional information

Title
Cuba A "Spy" Guide - Strategic Information and Developments
Cuba A "Spy" Guide - Strategic Information and Developments
Cuba Air Force Handbook
Cuba Air Force Handbook
Cuba Army Defense Policy and National Security Handbook
Cuba Army Defense Policy and National Security Handbook
Cuba Army Weapon Systems Handbook
Cuba Army Weapon Systems Handbook
Cuba Army Weapon Systems Handbook
Cuba Banking & Financial Market Handbook
Cuba Banking & Financial Market Handbook
Cuba Business and Investment Opportunities Yearbook
Cuba Business and Investment Opportunities Yearbook
Cuba Business and Investment Opportunities Yearbook Volume 1 Strategic Information and Opportunities
Cuba Business Intelligence Report - Practical Information, Opportunities, Contacts
Cuba Business Intelligence Report - Practical Information, Opportunities, Contacts
Cuba Business Law Handbook - Strategic Information and Basic Laws
Cuba Business Law Handbook - Strategic Information and Basic Laws
Cuba Business Law Handbook - Strategic Information and Basic Laws
Cuba Business Law Handbook - Strategic Information and Basic Laws
Cuba Clothing & Textile Industry Handbook
Cuba Clothing & Textile Industry Handbook
Cuba Company Laws and Regulations Handbook
Cuba Constitution and Citizenship Laws Handbook - Strategic Information and Basic Laws
Cuba Country Study Guide - Strategic Information and Developments
Cuba Country Study Guide - Strategic Information and Developments Volume 1 Strategic Information and Developments
Cuba Customs, Trade Regulations and Procedures Handbook
Cuba Customs, Trade Regulations and Procedures Handbook
Cuba Diplomatic Handbook - Strategic Information and Developments
Cuba Diplomatic Handbook - Strategic Information and Developments
Cuba Ecology & Nature Protection Handbook
Cuba Ecology & Nature Protection Handbook
Cuba Ecology & Nature Protection Laws and Regulation Handbook
Cuba Economic & Development Strategy Handbook
Cuba Economic & Development Strategy Handbook
Cuba Education System and Policy Handbook
Cuba Energy Policy, Laws and Regulation Handbook
Cuba Export-Import and Business Directory

Title
Cuba Export-Import and Business Directory
Cuba Export-Import Trade and Business Directory
Cuba Export-Import Trade and Business Directory
Cuba Foreign Policy and Government Guide
Cuba Foreign Policy and Government Guide
Cuba Healthcare Sector Organization, Management and Payment Systems Handbook - Strategic Information, Programs and Regulations
Cuba Immigration Laws and Regulations Handbook - Strategic Information and Basic Laws
Cuba Industrial and Business Directory
Cuba Industrial and Business Directory
Cuba Internet and E-Commerce Investment and Business Guide - Strategic and Practical Information: Regulations and Opportunities
Cuba Internet and E-Commerce Investment and Business Guide - Strategic and Practical Information: Regulations and Opportunities
Cuba Investment and Business Guide - Strategic and Practical Information
Cuba Investment and Business Guide - Strategic and Practical Information
Cuba Investment and Business Guide - Strategic and Practical Information
Cuba Investment and Business Guide - Strategic and Practical Information
Cuba Investment and Trade Laws and Regulations Handbook
Cuba Justice System and National Police Handbook
Cuba Justice System and National Police Handbook
Cuba Labor Laws and Regulations Handbook - Strategic Information and Basic Laws
Cuba Land Ownership and Agriculture Laws Handbook
Cuba Medical & Pharmaceutical Industry Handbook
Cuba Medical & Pharmaceutical Industry Handbook
Cuba Medical and Healthcare System and Regulations Directory
Cuba Mineral & Mining Sector Investment and Business Guide - Strategic and Practical Information
Cuba Mineral & Mining Sector Investment and Business Guide - Strategic and Practical Information
Cuba Mining Laws and Regulations Handbook
Cuba President Fidel Castro Handbook
Cuba President Fidel Castro Handbook
Cuba Recent Economic and Political Developments Yearbook
Cuba Recent Economic and Political Developments Yearbook
Cuba Recent Economic and Political Developments Yearbook
Cuba Research & Development Policy Handbook
Cuba Research & Development Policy Handbook
Cuba Research & Development Policy Handbook
Cuba Starting Business (Incorporating) in....Guide
Cuba Taxation Laws and Regulations Handbook
Cuba Telecom Laws and Regulations Handbook
Cuba Telecommunication Industry Business Opportunities Handbook
Cuba Telecommunication Industry Business Opportunities Handbook
Cuba: How to Invest, Start and Run Profitable Business in Cuba Guide - Practical Information,

Title
Opportunities, Contacts

BASIC LAWS AND REGULATIONS AFFECTING BUSINESS[2]

COUTRY	LAW TITLE
Cuba	1312 Act Migration Act
Cuba	1313 Aliens Act
Cuba	229 Decree Law on Collective Labor Agreement
Cuba	Act 1312 Immigration Act
Cuba	Act 1313 Foreign Resident
Cuba	Act 14-1977 Copyright
Cuba	Act 73 of the Tax System Law
Cuba	Act 76 Mining Act
Cuba	Act 77, In foreign investment
Cuba	Act Cultural Heritage Protection
Cuba	Act foreign investment. 09/05/1995
Cuba	Act national and local monuments. 08/04/1977
Cuba	Act National Archives of the Republic of Cuba
Cuba	Act No. 24-1979 Social Security
Cuba	Act No. 24-79 On the Social Security Act
Cuba	Act No. 49 - Labor Code
Cuba	Act No.93 Law Against Acts Of Terrorism
Cuba	CITMA-MINCEX Joint Resolution No. 1/1998
Cuba	Civil Code Law No. 59 of 16.07.1987
Cuba	Code childhood youth
Cuba	Code of Civil Procedure, Administrative and Labor
Cuba	Constitution of the Republic of Cuba, 1992
Cuba	Copyright Act 14-1977
Cuba	Copyright Law
Cuba	Copyright Law
Cuba	Courts Act Popular
Cuba	Criminal Code. 29/12/1987
Cuba	Criminal Procedure Law
Cuba	Customs Law
Cuba	Decree Law 165: In the free zones and industrial parks
Cuba	Decree Law 173 on Banks and Non banking Financial Institutions
Cuba	Decree Law 234 of Motherhood Women Workers
Cuba	Decree Law no 156
Cuba	Decree Law No 172 Central Bank of Cuba
Cuba	Decree Law No. 176 Justice System Labor
Cuba	Decree Law No. 203 of the Minister of Science, Technology and Environment, May 22, 2000.
Cuba	Decree Law No. 221 From The Files Of The Republic Of Cuba
Cuba	Decree No. 91 / 81sobre facilities studies workers
Cuba	Decree-Law No. 176-97 Approves Labor Justice System
Cuba	Decree-Law No. 177 of the Planning and Insurance Entities

[2] For ordering texts of specific laws in English, Spanish or French, Please contact Global Investment Center USA at ibpusa3@gmail.com

Cuba	Decree-Law No. 229-02 establishes the collective labor agreements.
Cuba	Decree-Law No. 234-03 From Maternity Worker.
Cuba	Decree-Law number 183/1998 De La Metrology
Cuba	Decree-Law on Free Zones and Industrial Parks
Cuba	Electoral Law of the Republic of Cuba (Law No. 72)
Cuba	Environmental Law No 81
Cuba	Family Code - Law 1289 of 14/02/1975
Cuba	Forest Act. 07/21/1998
Cuba	Geographical Indications as objects of industrial property rights Decree Law No. 228
Cuba	Inventions, Scientific Discoveries, Industrial Models, Trademarks Decree Law No. 68
Cuba	Labor Code - Law 49 of 28/12/1984
Cuba	Law 72 Electoral Act
Cuba	Law 85 of Forestry Law
Cuba	Law 88 for the Protection of National Independence and the Economy of Cuba
Cuba	Law against acts of terrorism
Cuba	Law No . 13 protection and work hygiene
Cuba	Law No. 13-77 on the Law of Health and Safety at Work
Cuba	Law No. 41 on public health
Cuba	Law No. 49-84 establishes the Labor Code (zip)
Cuba	Law No. 65 - General Housing Act
Cuba	LAW No. 73 Taxation System
Cuba	Law No.95 Production Unions Law Of Agricultural And Credits And Services
Cuba	Law of Municipal Museums
Cuba	Law of the tax system. 04-08-1994
Cuba	Law on Foreign Investment
Cuba	Mining Act. 21-12-1994
Cuba	Modification of patent applications for pharmaceutical and agricultural inventions Decree Law No. 160
Cuba	Of National Monuments Act and Local
Cuba	Penal Code - Law No. 62 of 12.29.1987
Cuba	President of the Academy of Sciences, Resolution No. 1100/83
Cuba	Procedures concerning mechanisms of inventions and industrial designs Resolution number 2416/2003
Cuba	Public Health Act. 07/13/1983
Cuba	Representatives of Industrial Property Agents Resolution No. 659 / 2002
Cuba	Resolution No. 2620/2000 of the Director General OCPI
Cuba	Resolution No. 999, the President of the Academy of Sciences of Cuba, from June 13, 1983.
Cuba	Resolution number 980/2001, the General Director of the OCPI of May 28, 2001.
Cuba	Science, Technology and Environment Resolution number 72/02
Cuba	Tariffs for the activity of trade marks, trade names, logos, signs and slogans * Resolution No. 2496/2000
Cuba	Trademarks and Other Distinctive Signs Decree Law No. 203

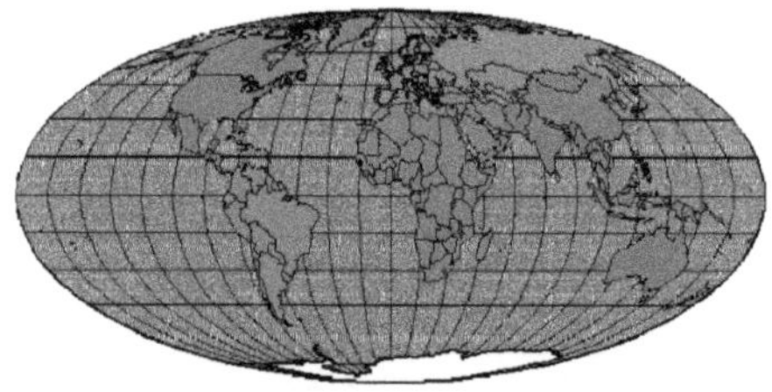

TITLE
Belgium Business and Investment Opportunities Yearbook Volume 1 Strategic, Practical Information and Opportunities
Belize Business and Investment Opportunities Yearbook Volume 1 Strategic, Practical Information and Opportunities
Benin Business and Investment Opportunities Yearbook Volume 1 Strategic, Practical Information and Opportunities
Bermuda Business and Investment Opportunities Yearbook Volume 1 Strategic, Practical Information and Opportunities
Bhutan Business and Investment Opportunities Yearbook Volume 1 Strategic, Practical Information and Opportunities
Bolivia Business and Investment Opportunities Yearbook Volume 1 Strategic, Practical Information and Opportunities
Bosnia and Herzegovina Business and Investment Opportunities Yearbook Volume 1 Strategic, Practical Information and Opportunities
Botswana Business and Investment Opportunities Yearbook Volume 1 Strategic, Practical Information and Opportunities
Brazil Business and Investment Opportunities Yearbook Volume 1 Strategic, Practical Information and Opportunities
Brunei Business and Investment Opportunities Yearbook Volume 1 Strategic, Practical Information and Opportunities
Bulgaria Business and Investment Opportunities Yearbook Volume 1 Strategic, Practical Information and Opportunities
Burkina Faso Business and Investment Opportunities Yearbook Volume 1 Strategic, Practical Information and Opportunities
Burundi Business and Investment Opportunities Yearbook Volume 1 Strategic, Practical Information and Opportunities
Cambodia Business and Investment Opportunities Yearbook Volume 1 Strategic, Practical Information and Opportunities
Cameroon Business and Investment Opportunities Yearbook Volume 1 Strategic, Practical Information and Opportunities
Canada Business and Investment Opportunities Yearbook Volume 1 Strategic, Practical Information and Opportunities
Cape Verde Business and Investment Opportunities Yearbook Volume 1 Strategic, Practical Information and Opportunities
Cayman Islands Business and Investment Opportunities Yearbook Volume 1 Strategic, Practical Information and Opportunities
Central African Republic Business and Investment Opportunities Yearbook Volume 1 Strategic, Practical Information and Opportunities
Chad Business and Investment Opportunities Yearbook Volume 1 Strategic, Practical Information and Opportunities
Chile Business and Investment Opportunities Yearbook Volume 1 Strategic, Practical Information and Opportunities
China Business and Investment Opportunities Yearbook Volume 1 Strategic, Practical Information and Opportunities
Colombia Business and Investment Opportunities Yearbook Volume 1 Strategic, Practical Information and Opportunities
Comoros Business and Investment Opportunities Yearbook Volume 1 Strategic, Practical Information and Opportunities
Congo Business and Investment Opportunities Yearbook Volume 1 Strategic, Practical Information and Opportunities
Congo, Democratic Republic Business and Investment Opportunities Yearbook Volume 1 Strategic, Practical Information and Opportunities
Cook Islands Business and Investment Opportunities Yearbook Volume 1 Strategic, Practical Information and Opportunities
Costa Rica Business and Investment Opportunities Yearbook Volume 1 Strategic, Practical Information and Opportunities

TITLE
Cote d'Ivoire Business and Investment Opportunities Yearbook Volume 1 Strategic, Practical Information and Opportunities
Croatia Business and Investment Opportunities Yearbook Volume 1 Strategic, Practical Information and Opportunities
Cuba Business and Investment Opportunities Yearbook Volume 1 Strategic, Practical Information and Opportunities
Cyprus Business and Investment Opportunities Yearbook Volume 1 Strategic, Practical Information and Opportunities
Czech Republic Business and Investment Opportunities Yearbook Volume 1 Strategic, Practical Information and Opportunities
Denmark Business and Investment Opportunities Yearbook Volume 1 Strategic, Practical Information and Opportunities
Djibouti Business and Investment Opportunities Yearbook Volume 1 Strategic, Practical Information and Opportunities
Dominica Business and Investment Opportunities Yearbook Volume 1 Strategic, Practical Information and Opportunities
Dominican Republic Business and Investment Opportunities Yearbook Volume 1 Strategic, Practical Information and Opportunities
Ecuador Business and Investment Opportunities Yearbook Volume 1 Strategic, Practical Information and Opportunities
Egypt Business and Investment Opportunities Yearbook Volume 1 Strategic, Practical Information and Opportunities
El Salvador Business and Investment Opportunities Yearbook Volume 1 Strategic, Practical Information and Opportunities
Equatorial Guinea Business and Investment Opportunities Yearbook Volume 1 Strategic, Practical Information and Opportunities
Eritrea Business and Investment Opportunities Yearbook Volume 1 Strategic, Practical Information and Opportunities
Estonia Business and Investment Opportunities Yearbook Volume 1 Strategic, Practical Information and Opportunities
Ethiopia Business and Investment Opportunities Yearbook Volume 1 Strategic, Practical Information and Opportunities
Falkland Islands Business and Investment Opportunities Yearbook Volume 1 Strategic, Practical Information and Opportunities
Faroes Islands Business and Investment Opportunities Yearbook Volume 1 Strategic, Practical Information and Opportunities
Fiji Business and Investment Opportunities Yearbook Volume 1 Strategic, Practical Information and Opportunities
Finland Business and Investment Opportunities Yearbook Volume 1 Strategic, Practical Information and Opportunities
France Business and Investment Opportunities Yearbook Volume 1 Strategic, Practical Information and Opportunities
Gabon Business and Investment Opportunities Yearbook Volume 1 Strategic, Practical Information and Opportunities
Gambia Business and Investment Opportunities Yearbook Volume 1 Strategic, Practical Information and Opportunities
Georgia Business and Investment Opportunities Yearbook Volume 1 Strategic, Practical Information and Opportunities
Germany Business and Investment Opportunities Yearbook Volume 1 Strategic, Practical Information and Opportunities
Ghana Business and Investment Opportunities Yearbook Volume 1 Strategic, Practical Information and Opportunities
Gibraltar Business and Investment Opportunities Yearbook Volume 1 Strategic, Practical Information and Opportunities
Greece Business and Investment Opportunities Yearbook Volume 1 Strategic, Practical Information and Opportunities

TITLE
Greenland Business and Investment Opportunities Yearbook Volume 1 Strategic, Practical Information and Opportunities
Grenada Business and Investment Opportunities Yearbook Volume 1 Strategic, Practical Information and Opportunities
Guam Business and Investment Opportunities Yearbook Volume 1 Strategic, Practical Information and Opportunities
Guatemala Business and Investment Opportunities Yearbook Volume 1 Strategic, Practical Information and Opportunities
Guernsey Business and Investment Opportunities Yearbook Volume 1 Strategic, Practical Information and Opportunities
Guinea Business and Investment Opportunities Yearbook Volume 1 Strategic, Practical Information and Opportunities
Guinea-Bissau Business and Investment Opportunities Yearbook Volume 1 Strategic, Practical Information and Opportunities
Guyana Business and Investment Opportunities Yearbook Volume 1 Strategic, Practical Information and Opportunities
Haiti Business and Investment Opportunities Yearbook Volume 1 Strategic, Practical Information and Opportunities
Honduras Business and Investment Opportunities Yearbook Volume 1 Strategic, Practical Information and Opportunities
Hungary Business and Investment Opportunities Yearbook Volume 1 Strategic, Practical Information and Opportunities
Iceland Business and Investment Opportunities Yearbook Volume 1 Strategic, Practical Information and Opportunities
India Business and Investment Opportunities Yearbook Volume 1 Strategic, Practical Information and Opportunities
Indonesia Business and Investment Opportunities Yearbook Volume 1 Strategic, Practical Information and Opportunities
Iran Business and Investment Opportunities Yearbook Volume 1 Strategic, Practical Information and Opportunities
Iraq Business and Investment Opportunities Yearbook Volume 1 Strategic, Practical Information and Opportunities
Ireland Business and Investment Opportunities Yearbook Volume 1 Strategic, Practical Information and Opportunities
Israel Business and Investment Opportunities Yearbook Volume 1 Strategic, Practical Information and Opportunities
Italy Business and Investment Opportunities Yearbook Volume 1 Strategic, Practical Information and Opportunities
Jamaica Business and Investment Opportunities Yearbook Volume 1 Strategic, Practical Information and Opportunities
Japan Business and Investment Opportunities Yearbook Volume 1 Strategic, Practical Information and Opportunities
Jersey Business and Investment Opportunities Yearbook Volume 1 Strategic, Practical Information and Opportunities
Jordan Business and Investment Opportunities Yearbook Volume 1 Strategic, Practical Information and Opportunities
Kazakhstan Business and Investment Opportunities Yearbook Volume 1 Strategic, Practical Information and Opportunities
Kenya Business and Investment Opportunities Yearbook Volume 1 Strategic, Practical Information and Opportunities
Kiribati Business and Investment Opportunities Yearbook Volume 1 Strategic, Practical Information and Opportunities
Korea, North Business and Investment Opportunities Yearbook Volume 1 Strategic, Practical Information and Opportunities
Korea, South Business and Investment Opportunities Yearbook Volume 1 Strategic, Practical Information and Opportunities

TITLE
Kosovo Business and Investment Opportunities Yearbook Volume 1 Strategic, Practical Information and Opportunities
Kurdistan Business and Investment Opportunities Yearbook Volume 1 Strategic, Practical Information and Opportunities
Kuwait Business and Investment Opportunities Yearbook Volume 1 Strategic, Practical Information and Opportunities
Kyrgyzstan Business and Investment Opportunities Yearbook Volume 1 Strategic, Practical Information and Opportunities
Laos Business and Investment Opportunities Yearbook Volume 1 Strategic, Practical Information and Opportunities
Latvia Business and Investment Opportunities Yearbook Volume 1 Strategic, Practical Information and Opportunities
Lebanon Business and Investment Opportunities Yearbook Volume 1 Strategic, Practical Information and Opportunities
Lesotho Business and Investment Opportunities Yearbook Volume 1 Strategic, Practical Information and Opportunities
Liberia Business and Investment Opportunities Yearbook Volume 1 Strategic, Practical Information and Opportunities
Libya Business and Investment Opportunities Yearbook Volume 1 Strategic, Practical Information and Opportunities
Liechtenstein Business and Investment Opportunities Yearbook Volume 1 Strategic, Practical Information and Opportunities
Lithuania Business and Investment Opportunities Yearbook Volume 1 Strategic, Practical Information and Opportunities
Luxembourg Business and Investment Opportunities Yearbook Volume 1 Strategic, Practical Information and Opportunities
Macao Business and Investment Opportunities Yearbook Volume 1 Strategic, Practical Information and Opportunities
Macedonia Business and Investment Opportunities Yearbook Volume 1 Strategic, Practical Information and Opportunities
Madagascar Business and Investment Opportunities Yearbook Volume 1 Strategic, Practical Information and Opportunities
Madeira Business and Investment Opportunities Yearbook Volume 1 Strategic, Practical Information and Opportunities
Malawi Business and Investment Opportunities Yearbook Volume 1 Strategic, Practical Information and Opportunities
Malaysia Business and Investment Opportunities Yearbook Volume 1 Strategic, Practical Information and Opportunities
Maldives Business and Investment Opportunities Yearbook Volume 1 Strategic, Practical Information and Opportunities
Mali Business and Investment Opportunities Yearbook Volume 1 Strategic, Practical Information and Opportunities
Malta Business and Investment Opportunities Yearbook Volume 1 Strategic, Practical Information and Opportunities
Man Business and Investment Opportunities Yearbook Volume 1 Strategic, Practical Information and Opportunities
Marshall Islands Business and Investment Opportunities Yearbook Volume 1 Strategic, Practical Information and Opportunities
Mauritania Business and Investment Opportunities Yearbook Volume 1 Strategic, Practical Information and Opportunities
Mauritius Business and Investment Opportunities Yearbook Volume 1 Strategic, Practical Information and Opportunities
Mayotte Business and Investment Opportunities Yearbook Volume 1 Strategic, Practical Information and Opportunities
Mexico Business and Investment Opportunities Yearbook Volume 1 Strategic, Practical Information and Opportunities

TITLE
Micronesia Business and Investment Opportunities Yearbook Volume 1 Strategic, Practical Information and Opportunities
Moldova Business and Investment Opportunities Yearbook Volume 1 Strategic, Practical Information and Opportunities
Monaco Business and Investment Opportunities Yearbook Volume 1 Strategic, Practical Information and Opportunities
Mongolia Business and Investment Opportunities Yearbook Volume 1 Strategic, Practical Information and Opportunities
Montserrat Business and Investment Opportunities Yearbook Volume 1 Strategic, Practical Information and Opportunities
Montenegro Business and Investment Opportunities Yearbook Volume 1 Strategic, Practical Information and Opportunities
Morocco Business and Investment Opportunities Yearbook Volume 1 Strategic, Practical Information and Opportunities
Mozambique Business and Investment Opportunities Yearbook Volume 1 Strategic, Practical Information and Opportunities
Myanmar Business and Investment Opportunities Yearbook Volume 1 Strategic, Practical Information and Opportunities
Nagorno-Karabakh Republic Business and Investment Opportunities Yearbook Volume 1 Strategic, Practical Information and Opportunities
Namibia Business and Investment Opportunities Yearbook Volume 1 Strategic, Practical Information and Opportunities
Nauru Business and Investment Opportunities Yearbook Volume 1 Strategic, Practical Information and Opportunities
Nepal Business and Investment Opportunities Yearbook Volume 1 Strategic, Practical Information and Opportunities
Netherlands Business and Investment Opportunities Yearbook Volume 1 Strategic, Practical Information and Opportunities
New Caledonia Business and Investment Opportunities Yearbook Volume 1 Strategic, Practical Information and Opportunities
New Zealand Business and Investment Opportunities Yearbook Volume 1 Strategic, Practical Information and Opportunities
Nicaragua Business and Investment Opportunities Yearbook Volume 1 Strategic, Practical Information and Opportunities
Niger Business and Investment Opportunities Yearbook Volume 1 Strategic, Practical Information and Opportunities
Nigeria Business and Investment Opportunities Yearbook Volume 1 Strategic, Practical Information and Opportunities
Niue Business and Investment Opportunities Yearbook Volume 1 Strategic, Practical Information and Opportunities
Northern Cyprus (Turkish Republic of Northern Cyprus) Business and Investment Opportunities Yearbook Volume 1 Strategic, Practical Information and Opportunities
Northern Mariana Islands Business and Investment Opportunities Yearbook Volume 1 Strategic, Practical Information and Opportunities
Norway Business and Investment Opportunities Yearbook Volume 1 Strategic, Practical Information and Opportunities
Oman Business and Investment Opportunities Yearbook Volume 1 Strategic, Practical Information and Opportunities
Pakistan Business and Investment Opportunities Yearbook Volume 1 Strategic, Practical Information and Opportunities
Palau Business and Investment Opportunities Yearbook Volume 1 Strategic, Practical Information and Opportunities
Palestine (West Bank & Gaza) Business and Investment Opportunities Yearbook Volume 1 Strategic, Practical Information and Opportunities
Panama Business and Investment Opportunities Yearbook Volume 1 Strategic, Practical Information and Opportunities

TITLE
Papua New Guinea Business and Investment Opportunities Yearbook Volume 1 Strategic, Practical Information and Opportunities
Paraguay Business and Investment Opportunities Yearbook Volume 1 Strategic, Practical Information and Opportunities
Peru Business and Investment Opportunities Yearbook Volume 1 Strategic, Practical Information and Opportunities
Philippines Business and Investment Opportunities Yearbook Volume 1 Strategic, Practical Information and Opportunities
Pitcairn Islands Business and Investment Opportunities Yearbook Volume 1 Strategic, Practical Information and Opportunities
Poland Business and Investment Opportunities Yearbook Volume 1 Strategic, Practical Information and Opportunities
Polynesia French Business and Investment Opportunities Yearbook Volume 1 Strategic, Practical Information and Opportunities
Portugal Business and Investment Opportunities Yearbook Volume 1 Strategic, Practical Information and Opportunities
Qatar Business and Investment Opportunities Yearbook Volume 1 Strategic, Practical Information and Opportunities
Romania Business and Investment Opportunities Yearbook Volume 1 Strategic, Practical Information and Opportunities
Russia Business and Investment Opportunities Yearbook Volume 1 Strategic, Practical Information and Opportunities
Rwanda Business and Investment Opportunities Yearbook Volume 1 Strategic, Practical Information and Opportunities
Sahrawi Arab Democratic Republic Volume 1 Strategic Information and Developments
Saint Kitts and Nevis Business and Investment Opportunities Yearbook Volume 1 Strategic, Practical Information and Opportunities
Saint Lucia Business and Investment Opportunities Yearbook Volume 1 Strategic, Practical Information and Opportunities
Saint Vincent and The Grenadines Business and Investment Opportunities Yearbook Volume 1 Strategic, Practical Information and Opportunities
Samoa (American) A Business and Investment Opportunities Yearbook Volume 1 Strategic, Practical Information and Opportunities
Samoa (Western) Business and Investment Opportunities Yearbook Volume 1 Strategic, Practical Information and Opportunities
San Marino Business and Investment Opportunities Yearbook Volume 1 Strategic, Practical Information and Opportunities
Sao Tome and Principe Business and Investment Opportunities Yearbook Volume 1 Strategic, Practical Information and Opportunities
Saudi Arabia Business and Investment Opportunities Yearbook Volume 1 Strategic, Practical Information and Opportunities
Scotland Business and Investment Opportunities Yearbook Volume 1 Strategic, Practical Information and Opportunities
Senegal Business and Investment Opportunities Yearbook Volume 1 Strategic, Practical Information and Opportunities
Serbia Business and Investment Opportunities Yearbook Volume 1 Strategic, Practical Information and Opportunities
Seychelles Business and Investment Opportunities Yearbook Volume 1 Strategic, Practical Information and Opportunities
Sierra Leone Business and Investment Opportunities Yearbook Volume 1 Strategic, Practical Information and Opportunities
Singapore Business and Investment Opportunities Yearbook Volume 1 Strategic, Practical Information and Opportunities
Slovakia Business and Investment Opportunities Yearbook Volume 1 Strategic, Practical Information and Opportunities

TITLE
Slovenia Business and Investment Opportunities Yearbook Volume 1 Strategic, Practical Information and Opportunities
Solomon Islands Business and Investment Opportunities Yearbook Volume 1 Strategic, Practical Information and Opportunities
Somalia Business and Investment Opportunities Yearbook Volume 1 Strategic, Practical Information and Opportunities
South Africa Business and Investment Opportunities Yearbook Volume 1 Strategic, Practical Information and Opportunities
Spain Business and Investment Opportunities Yearbook Volume 1 Strategic, Practical Information and Opportunities
Sri Lanka Business and Investment Opportunities Yearbook Volume 1 Strategic, Practical Information and Opportunities
St. Helena Business and Investment Opportunities Yearbook Volume 1 Strategic, Practical Information and Opportunities
St. Pierre & Miquelon Business and Investment Opportunities Yearbook Volume 1 Strategic, Practical Information and Opportunities
Sudan (Republic of the Sudan) Business and Investment Opportunities Yearbook Volume 1 Strategic, Practical Information and Opportunities
Sudan South Business and Investment Opportunities Yearbook Volume 1 Strategic, Practical Information and Opportunities
Suriname Business and Investment Opportunities Yearbook Volume 1 Strategic, Practical Information and Opportunities
Swaziland Business and Investment Opportunities Yearbook Volume 1 Strategic, Practical Information and Opportunities
Sweden Business and Investment Opportunities Yearbook Volume 1 Strategic, Practical Information and Opportunities
Switzerland Business and Investment Opportunities Yearbook Volume 1 Strategic, Practical Information and Opportunities
Syria Business and Investment Opportunities Yearbook Volume 1 Strategic, Practical Information and Opportunities
Taiwan Business and Investment Opportunities Yearbook Volume 1 Strategic, Practical Information and Opportunities
Tajikistan Business and Investment Opportunities Yearbook Volume 1 Strategic, Practical Information and Opportunities
Tanzania Business and Investment Opportunities Yearbook Volume 1 Strategic, Practical Information and Opportunities
Thailand Business and Investment Opportunities Yearbook Volume 1 Strategic, Practical Information and Opportunities
Timor Leste (Democratic Republic of Timor-Leste) Business and Investment Opportunities Yearbook Volume 1 Strategic, Practical Information and Opportunities
Togo Business and Investment Opportunities Yearbook Volume 1 Strategic, Practical Information and Opportunities
Tonga Business and Investment Opportunities Yearbook Volume 1 Strategic, Practical Information and Opportunities
Trinidad and Tobago Business and Investment Opportunities Yearbook Volume 1 Strategic, Practical Information and Opportunities
Tunisia Business and Investment Opportunities Yearbook Volume 1 Strategic, Practical Information and Opportunities
Turkey Business and Investment Opportunities Yearbook Volume 1 Strategic, Practical Information and Opportunities
Turkmenistan Business and Investment Opportunities Yearbook Volume 1 Strategic, Practical Information and Opportunities
Turks & Caicos Business and Investment Opportunities Yearbook Volume 1 Strategic, Practical Information and Opportunities
Tuvalu Business and Investment Opportunities Yearbook Volume 1 Strategic, Practical Information and Opportunities

TITLE
Uganda Business and Investment Opportunities Yearbook Volume 1 Strategic, Practical Information and Opportunities
Ukraine Business and Investment Opportunities Yearbook Volume 1 Strategic, Practical Information and Opportunities
United Arab Emirates Business and Investment Opportunities Yearbook Volume 1 Strategic, Practical Information and Opportunities
United Kingdom Business and Investment Opportunities Yearbook Volume 1 Strategic, Practical Information and Opportunities
United States Business and Investment Opportunities Yearbook Volume 1 Strategic, Practical Information and Opportunities
Uruguay Business and Investment Opportunities Yearbook Volume 1 Strategic, Practical Information and Opportunities
Uzbekistan Business and Investment Opportunities Yearbook Volume 1 Strategic, Practical Information and Opportunities
Vanuatu Business and Investment Opportunities Yearbook Volume 1 Strategic, Practical Information and Opportunities
Vatican City (Holy See) Business and Investment Opportunities Yearbook Volume 1 Strategic, Practical Information and Opportunities
Venezuela Business and Investment Opportunities Yearbook Volume 1 Strategic, Practical Information and Opportunities
Vietnam Business and Investment Opportunities Yearbook Volume 1 Strategic, Practical Information and Opportunities
Virgin Islands, British Business and Investment Opportunities Yearbook Volume 1 Strategic, Practical Information and Opportunities
Wake Atoll Business and Investment Opportunities Yearbook Volume 1 Strategic, Practical Information and Opportunities
Wallis & Futuna Business and Investment Opportunities Yearbook Volume 1 Strategic, Practical Information and Opportunities
Western Sahara Business and Investment Opportunities Yearbook Volume 1 Strategic, Practical Information and Opportunities
Yemen Business and Investment Opportunities Yearbook Volume 1 Strategic, Practical Information and Opportunities
Zambia Business and Investment Opportunities Yearbook Volume 1 Strategic, Practical Information and Opportunities
Zimbabwe Business and Investment Opportunities Yearbook Volume 1 Strategic, Practical Information and Opportunities

www.ingramcontent.com/pod-product-compliance
Ingram Content Group UK Ltd.
Pitfield, Milton Keynes, MK11 3LW, UK
UKHW051458290926
15471UKWH00008B/1274

9 781438 776552